The Peasant in Nineteenth-Century Russia

The Peasant in Nineteenth-Century Russia

Edited by Wayne S. Vucinich

Contributors

John S. Curtiss
Terence Emmons
Donald Fanger
Mary Matossian
Michael B. Petrovich
Nicholas V. Riasanovsky
Donald W. Treadgold
Francis M. Watters
Reginald E. Zelnik

Stanford University Press Stanford, California

To the Memory of Robert J. Kerner
Sather Professor of History at the University of California at Berkeley
and Pioneer in Slavic Studies in the United States

Stanford University Press
Stanford, California
© 1968 by the Board of Trustees of the
Leland Stanford Junior University
Printed in the United States of America
Cloth SBN 8047–0637–9
Paper SBN 8047–0638–7
Last figure below indicates year of this printing:
79 78 77 76 75 74 73 72 71 70

Preface

The history and culture of the Russian peasant have received relatively little attention from Western scholarship in general and American scholarship in particular in comparison with such fields of study as Russian intellectual history and the closely related history of the revolutionary movement. It is the aim of the present volume to rectify this situation in small measure by presenting to the interested student of Russian history a collection of papers that deal in some depth with important aspects of Russian peasant life and the role of the peasant in nineteenth-century Russian culture. The papers have emerged from a conference on "The Russian Peasant in the Nineteenth Century," sponsored by the Faculty Seminar on East European Studies at Stanford University and held on December 2–3, 1966. The contributions are based on printed Russian and foreign materials, and some, like those by Professors Emmons and Zelnik, make extensive use of archival material that the authors collected during their recent studies in the Soviet Union.

The editor wishes to express his profound thanks to Stanford's Committee on International Studies for the encouragement and financial assistance that made it possible to organize the conference and to prepare the manuscript for publication. He is especially indebted to Professors Terence Emmons and Ivo Lederer for generous help and advice in connection with the conference and the publication of the symposium. Heartfelt thanks are also due to John Ackerman for invaluable editorial assistance. The greatest debt of gratitude is of course to the contributors, whose participation made the conference a success.

W. S. V.

Contents

Contributors

JOHN S. CURTISS, who studied at Princeton and Columbia Universities, is the James B. Duke Professor of History at Duke University. He is the author of *Church and State in Russia* (1940), *An Appraisal of the Protocols of Zion* (1941), *The Russian Church and the Soviet State* (1953), and *The Russian Army under Nicholas I, 1825–1855* (1965).

TERENCE EMMONS is Assistant Professor of History at Stanford University. His book *The Russian Landed Gentry and the Peasant Emancipation of 1861* will be published this year.

DONALD FANGER taught at Brown University from 1960 to 1965, was Visiting Lecturer in Slavic and Comparative Literature at Harvard in 1965–66, and is now Director of the Slavic Division of the Department of Modern European Languages at Stanford. He founded the Brown Slavic Reprint Series, for which he edited the first four volumes, and he is the author of *Dostoevsky and Romantic Realism*.

MARY KILBOURNE MATOSSIAN, a lecturer in history at the University of Maryland, has written *The Impact of Soviet Policies in Armenia* (1962), and several articles on the ethnography and problems of developing areas.

MICHAEL B. PETROVICH, a graduate of the Russian Institute of Columbia University, is Professor of History at the University of Wisconsin. He is the author of *The Emergence of Russian Panslavism 1856–1870* (1956), and has also written several shorter studies on Russian and Balkan historiography.

NICHOLAS V. RIASANOVSKY teaches Russian history at the University of California at Berkeley. His published works include *Russia and the West in the Teaching of the Slavophiles* (1952), *Nicholas I and Official Nationality, 1825–1855* (1959), and *A History of Russia* (1963).

DONALD W. TREADGOLD studied at the University of Oregon, Harvard, and, as a Rhodes Scholar, at Oxford. He is Professor of Russian History at the

University of Washington, and is the author of *Lenin and His Rivals*
(1955), *The Great Siberian Migration* (1957), and *Twentieth Century
Russia* (2nd ed., 1959). From 1961 to 1965 he was the editor of *Slavic
Review*.

FRANCIS M. WATTERS studied at the University of Washington and did his
graduate work at the University of California at Berkeley. He is Chairman of the Department of Economics at Chico State College, Chico,
California.

REGINALD E. ZELNIK, who is Assistant Professor of Russian History at the
University of California at Berkeley, studied at Princeton, Stanford, and
the University of Vienna, where he was a Fulbright scholar. He has published several articles on Russian social history and is currently preparing
a two-volume study of the labor question in St. Petersburg during the
reign of Alexander II.

Introduction

In 1903 Lenin published his pamphlet "To the Rural Poor," a clear sign of his growing recognition that the peasant masses would be an important element in any revolutionary struggle. Acknowledging that the peasants had received something less than complete freedom in 1861, the man who had called himself "the child of the landlords" now sought to introduce his young political party to the peasants and to assure them that the Social Democrats intended to win for them the political freedom that men in other European nations had acquired.[1] Less than fifteen years later Lenin suddenly found himself in control of a state in which every problem, with the possible exception of the continuing war, was subordinate to the desperate situation of the peasants, whose critical political role he had gradually come to realize. The revolutionary leader was confronted with the problem that had consumed the energies of the tsars who had preceded him; yet Marxism provided no solution to this problem, and it was necessary for Lenin and his aides, through the vicissitudes of civil war and economic chaos, to forge and implement a workable peasant program. But Lenin had had little direct contact with the peasantry; he had experienced very little of Russian village life. "I know Russia very little, Simbirsk, Kazan, Petersburg, exile—and that's about all," was his significant admission to his friend Maxim Gorky.[2]

Lenin's situation illustrates both the remarkable persistence of the peasant question as a central issue in Russian history and the surprising lack of attention given this important problem. It is hardly an exaggeration to state that most of Russia's internal problems were at that time in some way linked to the problem of the peasantry, which constituted the vast majority of Russian society.

Despite the overwhelming amount of scholarly material that has attempted to explain the nature of the Russian peasant, he still remains in large part a mystery, a man of contradictions. Renowned for his piety, for his closeness to the earth and his devotion to Holy Mother Russia, the peasant could at times exhibit behavior motivated by a materialism that stood in direct contradiction to any religious beliefs. Kindness often alternated with outbursts of cruel fury; sentimentality was balanced with a strong-willed stubbornness. A remarkably long tolerance of despotism, squalor, and exploitation was broken by sudden and violent rebellions, but even in the midst of revolt the agelong pattern of command and obedience would assert itself when the peasant sought a master to tell him how to fight.[3]

The peasant's earthy humor is storied, his pagan superstitions make many doubt that he was ever really Christianized, his credulity is phenomenal. Sir Donald Mackenzie Wallace observed that what the peasant wanted was "a house to live in, food to eat, and raiment wherewithal to be clothed, and to gain these first necessaries of life with as little labor as possible."[4] The peasants' basic social unit was not the individual but the family, "developed to save the individual by suppressing him."[5] The family structure was patriarchal. All authority was vested in the head of the family, and without his knowledge and permission nothing could take place in the tiny peasant house (*izba*), whose size precluded any possibility of individual privacy. Wallace stated that discipline in the Russian peasant family was nearly perfect, but added that this could be disturbed by "the chatter of female tongues, which do not readily submit to the authority even of their owners."[6] This comment reassures us of the peasant's enduring, often endearing, humanity; and it helps to offset the stark picture that Vakar has drawn of the peasant family as a "totalitarian society in miniature."[7]

Traditionally suspicious of the city and its inhabitants, the peasant had little tolerance for the various urban officials who visited him. The educated person, also often an urbanite, had a difficult time penetrating the peasant mind, a mind with neither the time nor the inclination to attempt understanding political causes and ideologies. Thus when M. V. Petrashevsky built a model phalanstery for the peasants of his estate, they responded by burning it down.[8] And the Populist students who rushed to the people during the "mad summer" of 1874 were greeted by the peasants, whom they had idealized so fervently, with a mixture of surprise, consternation, suspicion, and some outright hostility.

But none of these observations on the peasant can completely explain his nature, for there remains some quality that eludes our analysis. Slavophiles and Populists have tried to explain the peasant on the basis of this very enigma, and have talked in vague terms about the unfathomable Slavic soul and the peasant's mystic closeness to earth. Such talk will bring us no closer to understanding the peasant's nature, but we cannot deny the quality in the Russian peasant that has evoked such explanations. It is certainly this quality that caused Dostoevsky's rational, Euclidean Ivan to confess to his brother Alyosha that "the stupider one is, the clearer one sees," and to express a desire to revert to the form of a simple Russian peasant woman "setting candles before the icons." Perhaps this is simply a naive and nostalgic fascination with a world and a way of life that is lost and that therefore seems somehow simpler and more desirable than ours. But even granting full awareness of the terrible hardships and unromantic complexities of the peasant's daily life, there remains something in his cosmos that continues to fascinate men living in a world now barren of ritual.

Nineteenth-century Russia was the first great example of a peasant-dominated society being confronted head-on by those forces of change collectively subsumed under the term modernization. It was a society seriously out of joint, a tradition-bound society desperately attempting to cope with the forces that were steadily undermining that tradition: industrialization, urbanization, and secularization. In every case the changes produced by these broader trends had their most profound influence upon the peasantry. The peasants' reactions—the ways in which they submitted, resisted, or initiated changes of their own— are central to the studies in this volume.

Russia was the last European country in which serfdom was abolished. The onerous dues and services that the serf owed both his lord and the state, his inability to appeal to any law for protection, the terrible and demoralizing poverty—all these characteristics of the Russian serf's life need not be elaborated upon here. The result of such

conditions had been a retrogression in the Russian social order starting in the early eighteenth century, a paradoxical development given
the considerable advances made in commerce and industry beginning
around that time.

Educated "Europeanized" Russians were hardly blind to the fact
that the existence of this huge enserfed and impoverished mass at the
core of the state placed critical obstacles of a social, political, and economic nature in the path of Russia's modernization. Beginning with
Radishchev, in his *Journey from St. Petersburg to Moscow,* people
from every social stratum criticized the "hundred-headed monster of
serfdom" and drafted their own programs to ensure the most effective elimination of its evils. By the late 1820's, in the aftermath of the
abortive Decembrist Revolt, there was a growing realization even in
official governmental circles that something had to be done to alleviate
the sufferings of the serfs and to remove this check on Russia's economic and social progress. Although Nicholas I was perennially preoccupied with the problem, a fear of change seems to have prevented
him from expressing his concern in concrete action. He tried to buy
time with a policy expressed by Count Uvarov's formula of Official
Nationality, but it was by this time too late for Russia to turn back
the clock on the peasant question. The tension within a preindustrial,
traditional society subjected to the onrushing forces of modernization
had become too great. The voices of criticism were not to be stilled.

It was late in Nicholas I's reign when the Russian intellectuals
finally began to come to terms with the full implications of the peasant problem.[9] It would be difficult to find two more differing social
forces than the Russian peasantry and the intelligentsia. The most
obvious difference between the two was in the matter of sheer numbers, for the intelligentsia always constituted a group less than one
one-hundredth the size of the peasantry. Its members also tended to
come from the more prosperous segments of Russian society, a situation made unavoidable by the nature of the economy and the tsarist
educational system. But despite the chasm that separated the two
groups, it was this small minority, the intelligentsia, that from the
1840's onward challenged tsardom in the name of the people and
attempted to enroll additional forces in that struggle. Influenced by
currents of thought then prevalent in Western Europe, most Russian

intellectuals chose socialism as the best alternative to their hated system. Liberalism and conservatism were, for various reasons, found quite unequal to the job the intellectuals felt called upon to perform, a job in which the highest priority was given to the satisfaction of the peasantry's material needs. The various theories of Western socialism with which the Russians came in contact were gradually transformed into a uniquely Russian form, Populism, with an emphasis on the potential of the *obshchina,* the peasant village commune. This was the institution which the German Baron Haxthausen had analyzed in such detail following his 1843 trip through Russia. The Populists were influenced by his writings to believe that the *obshchina* constituted a potential model for free productive associations of the type advocated by the French utopian socialists, and they hoped that it would facilitate Russia's direct conversion to a socialist society without making it necessary for the country to suffer through a capitalist period such as that which Western Europe was then enduring.

Never a unified political ideology, Russian Populism was a loose, nonhierarchical movement that permitted varying interpretations by the remarkable array of strong-minded individualists who placed themselves under its banner. The attempt to realize often varying objectives as part of a vaster program of social change led to a number of controversies within the Populist intelligentsia, especially ones concerning the nature of the organizational framework best able to support the movement's energies in its struggle against the autocracy. The appeal of secret, conspiratorial, ruthless, and hierarchical revolutionary organizations, such as those espoused by Tkachev and practiced by Nechaev, was always quite limited. It was instead the written word that the intelligentsia used (superbly) as its primary weapon. Herzen and Ogarev's *Kolokol* and Chernyshevsky's *Sovremennik,* which were the most brilliant representatives of the radical press, made numerous important contributions to the debate over peasant emancipation.

Such articles were part of the increased clamor for thoroughgoing reform that had followed Russia's Crimean War debacle of 1856. The Russian state now saw that it must take measures to ensure economic growth and social and political stability. It believed that foremost among these measures was a radical reform of the peasant situation.

After a protracted period of complicated deliberation and formulation set against a background of increased peasant disturbances, student unrest, and continuing demands from the radical press, Alexander II promulgated the Manifesto of Emancipation on February 19, 1861. With the publication of this famous document, Russian serfdom was abolished with one stroke and the era of the Great Reforms was ushered in. But despite this act, the peasant question remained the great politico-economic issue of Russian history. Alexander II had seen in emancipation the revolution from above that alone could prevent some future mass uprising, but the introduction of this promising reform was unable to keep the regime from following the increasing crisis-ridden path that ended in peasant revolt.

The tragic shortcomings of the emancipation itself partly explain the fact that a crisis in peasant society continued to confront the tsarist government. Although the peasant was finally liberated, he did not receive all the land he had so long hoped for. The landowning nobility retained more than half of the best land, and the peasants often were left with smaller, less fertile holdings than they had tilled for their own needs as serfs. Another shortcoming was the heavy redemption price the peasant was forced to pay for his land. This, coupled with high taxes, created a fiscal burden that was a prime cause of increasing rural poverty. The fact that land ownership was commonly vested in the *obshchina* and not held as private property had particularly unfortunate consequences, as detailed in Professor Watters's article. The result was what I. M. Strakhovsky called "a peasant nation consistently segregated from the general life of the community,"[10] a situation exacerbated by the growing lag in development between the urban centers and the rural villages. Modernization continued to leave the great mass of the Russian populace behind; the emancipation had not successfully altered the essential nature of the peasantry or of the nation's predominantly agrarian economy.

If the emancipation was inadequate, events from 1861–1917 hardly compensated for its shortcomings. In the nineties, which began with the disastrous famine of 1891–92, it became clear that attempts to bring Russia's agrarian sector peacefully into the modern, industrial world were failing. This was the era of intense capital industry formation directed by Finance Minister Sergei Witte. State and economy were linked in Witte's rush to industrialize, but the peasant sector, forced to pay most of the cost of his program, was ignored. It was not until the 1899 depression that the stresses produced by the Witte system began to be obvious. The boom was broken, foreign credit had evaporated, and the increasingly miserable masses now suffered an even more obvious cultural lag vis-à-vis the rest of Russian society.

In 1905, military defeat intervened once more to focus attention on the drastic failures of tsarist rule. This time the peasantry's response was both widespread and violent. They wanted more land, and in the course of the 1905 Revolution demonstrated that, if necessary, they were now determined to take illegal means to secure it. The state's investment in the *obshchina* as a conservative social institution had obviously failed. Reform followed, mainly in the form of Stolypin's legislation to break up the *obshchina* and individualize peasant land tenure. Redemption payments ceased in 1907, and the government at last began to consider ways of improving the low technological level of peasant agriculture. One may debate the motivation of Stolypin's policies and whether or not they did or could contribute to agricultural progress and social peace, but the fact remains that by 1917 less than half of the peasant households with communal tenure had switched to the individual, hereditary form. In the end this was all too little and too late. By August 1914, time had finally run out on the Russian Empire. The Great War was the final blow, and by the time near military collapse and revolution came in the spring of 1917, the strain that the war had imposed upon both natural and human resources had further exacerbated the crisis of the Russian peasantry.

This then was the legacy to which Lenin so suddenly found himself heir. In the first days of his fledgling revolution he read to the Soviet Congress the hurriedly drafted "Decree on Land": "The point is that the peasants should be firmly assured that there are no more landowners in the countryside, that they themselves must decide all questions, and that they themselves must arrange their own lives."[11] The new Soviet regime had taken over the attempt to solve the great question which had plagued tsarist Russia for so long.

Lenin's Bolsheviks had never had any significant following among the peasantry, but they did accede to peasant demands in order to win political control in Russia. Those demands were bluntly obvious in 1917: the peasants wanted peace and they wanted land. Once in power, the Bolsheviks demonstrated that they were not going to

continue the series of reforms that, since 1861, had been slowly transforming Russian society. But the peasants were still a definite center
of power in that they controlled the state's food supply. Now they
refused to submit to the authority of their erstwhile supporters. The
Bolsheviks accordingly conceived a solution that would be both final
and total: they attempted to accelerate history as they forced the peasants into collectives "in order to make them the main basis and victims of the socialist version of primary capitalist accumulation."[12]

In a sense the Bolsheviks have achieved their objectives; the peasantry can no longer be considered a distinctly separate economic nucleus,
and a workable method of supplying agricultural products to the
cities and to industry has been evolved. At the same time, collectivi-
zation, a social revolution from above whose magnitude is without
precedent in human history, has produced many changes in the peasant's existence. The more superficial changes are perhaps indicative of unmeasurable substantive transformations. Thus literacy rates
among the rural population approach 100 per cent, compared with
approximately 20 per cent at the end of the nineteenth century. The
izba is generally better constructed, and over half are lit by electricity.
Families have grown smaller, and the rural population in general is
older. The youth have been drawn away to the cities where they can
find better educational opportunities and get secure jobs in industry.
Technical progress is gradually altering the age-old peasant culture.
The geneticist, the soil chemist, and the laboratory researcher are
replacing the traditional reliance on intuition, superstition, or just
plain luck. In short, agriculture is becoming more professionalized,
with all the profound implications that such a development has for
the relationships between country and city.[13]

And yet, despite the upheavals of fifty years, the peasantry is still
a population apart from the rest of Soviet society. The imposition of
ideology has failed to totally solve Russia's most perplexing question.
The peasant seems somehow alienated from the Soviet state; the
odyssey upon which the Soviet regime embarked in November 1917
is not yet completed.

Soviet scholars have of course been greatly interested in the long
history of the peasant problem and in the continuing presence of a
peasantry that both baffles and frustrates the State. The result has been

an unusually large amount of material dealing with the peasant problem, material that not only assesses the problem's contemporary aspects but also delves into its origins.

An exceptionally rewarding volume of Soviet scholarship on the peasantry has been produced on the period with which the present volume is concerned. This includes a large number of articles and monographs, based largely on previously unpublished sources, devoted to the economic conditions of the serfs during the first half of the nineteenth century.[14] N. M. Druzhinin's monumental study, *The State Peasants and the Reform of P. D. Kiselev,* is still perhaps the most remarkable piece of Soviet scholarship on the nineteenth-century peasantry.[15] P. A. Zaionchkovsky's outstanding study *The Realization of the Peasant Reform of 1861* deals with the economic outcome of the emancipation.[16] The *Yearbooks on the Agrarian History of Eastern Europe* that have been published since 1958 indicate that interest in the peasant question among Soviet scholars continues unabated.[17] These yearbooks consist of papers read by historians at annual conferences sponsored by the Academy of Sciences of the USSR.

Recent Soviet scholarship on the peasant reveals an important new trend toward a more ethnographic and anthropological approach. Ethnographers and anthropologists have been busy gathering data on the life and culture of Russian peasants in contemporary society as well as in the past. They intend to observe the transformation that has taken place as a result of the Communist Revolution and the introduction of Soviet rule.[18] The Soviet planner is interested in what values and habits the peasant has retained and what he has rejected. The information revealed by such important studies will enrich our knowledge of peasant psychology and social change.

Similarly, the studies of foreign scholars and observers have created many useful perspectives on the Russian peasant. Outstanding early examples include A. Leroy-Beaulieu's masterful portrait of Russian society in the late nineteenth century, *The Empire of the Tsars and the Russians,*[19] and Sir Donald Mackenzie Wallace's *Russia.*[20] Among the major studies in more recent scholarship are Geroid T. Robinson's valuable analysis of the social and economic history of peasant Russia before the revolution, *Rural Russia under the Old Regime,*[21] and Sir John Maynard's book *The Russian Peasant and Other Studies.*[22] The enduring interest of American scholars in the history of the Russian peasant is illustrated by several contributions to the symposium *The Transformation of Russian Society*[23] and by Jerome Blum's impressive history of rural Russia, *Lord and Peasant in Russia from the Ninth to the Nineteenth Century*.[24]

The present volume is part of this continuing expansion of scholarship on the peasantry. The eight papers it contains are important not only as timely assessments of the present state of scholarship on the Russian peasantry, but also as original contributions that add significantly to the record of that scholarship. Each study deals with a single, often long-neglected, aspect of the peasant's life, and all are concerned with the effects of modernization on a traditional, agrarian society. Professor Riasanovsky's sensitive and judicious "Afterword" deals with the theme of modernization in more general terms, and directs the reader toward some tentative conclusions.

A student of social change has observed that it is no longer possible "to take seriously the view that the peasant is an 'object of history,' a form of social life over which historical changes pass but which contributes nothing to the impetus of these changes."[25] It is hoped that the present volume will cast new light on the active role played by the peasant in a time of great historical change, and that we will be brought to a better understanding of the peasant's nature, and, in particular, of those qualities that have allowed him to persevere in a time of cataclysmic change and against incredible odds. Thus we shall see how he was able to preserve his unique cultural identity.

The Peasant in Nineteenth-Century Russia

1. The Peasant Way of Life

Mary Matossian

Introduction

What follows is not a "realistic" picture of the Russian peasant way of life in the nineteenth century: it has little to say about the brutality and violence of the peasant world. Neither is it an "idealized" picture, in that the things described were rare or uncommon in peasant experience. Rather, this study is intended to provide a description of the peasant way of life under normal conditions around 1860, on the eve of emancipation. It is a time of neither unusual prosperity nor unusual deprivation. The village and family presented are neither unusually rich nor unusually poor, neither "backward" nor "progressive."

The Russian peasant way of life was full and abundant in its own way. Although the peasants were materially poor by our standards, their life was rich in symbols and rituals and in the drama of everyday life. It was a life of sweat and heartbreak, but it had its moments of peace and joy as well.

Settlement Patterns and Housing

In the nineteenth century, before extensive railroad building, the villages of Russia were generally located near a good natural source of water: at the edge of a lake or river, or—in the south—along a ravine where spring water was available. The Great Russian villages varied in size from a few households in the far north to four hundred or more households in the south. The buildings were almost all built of weathered, unpainted logs, and the narrow, unpaved streets were often rivers of mud and filth in spring, summer, and fall. Trees and gardens around the houses were exceptional. And yet to its inhabitants, for whom it was the center of the universe, the village might be a beautiful place.[1]

> I love my country, but that love is odd:
> My reason has no part in it at all! ...
> A well-stocked barn, a hut with a thatched roof,
> Carved shutters on a village window: these
> Are simple things in truth,
> But few can see them as my fond eye sees.
>   *Mikhail Lermontov* (1841)

The layout of the Russian village might be one of several different types. The most ancient types, but relatively rare in the nineteenth century, were the cluster (*gneszovyi, kuchevyi*), free-form (*bezporiadochnyi*), and hollow-form (*krugovoi, zamknutyi*) types of settlement. The cluster type consisted of scattered nuclei, each of which was probably at one time inhabited by a kin group. Free-form villages developed in locations remote from space-defining rivers or roads, such as on the open steppe of the southern Ukraine. The hollow-form village was built around three or four sides of a hollow square or rectangle, in the center of which was a lake, a field, a common pasture, a church, or a marketplace.

The most typical village layout, as ancient as the first millennium A.D., was the linear type, its houses set in one or more lines along the bank of a lake, a river, or (rarely) a road. As the population of the village increased, new structures were added on lines running parallel or perpendicular to the original line.

The gridiron-type layout, with streets between rows of houses and sidestreets between clusters of houses, first appeared in the eighteenth century and became widespread only in the nineteenth. Most such villages were the result of government decrees from 1722 on intended to reduce the danger of devastating fires by the wider spacing of buildings. Frequently a village was reconstructed in this manner after having once burned down.

A Russian farm family normally lived in its own dwelling on a farmstead. The farmstead was usually rectangular in shape, with the living quarters of the family near the street. In the north Great Russian village it was characteristic for the shorter side of the house to run parallel to the street; in the south, the longer side. Besides family living quarters, a farmstead would ordinarily include a barn, a hayshed, and a kitchen garden. The northern and central Great Russian farmstead also had an *ovin* for drying sheaves before threshing, a *riga* (threshing barn), and a *gumno* (threshing floor). In the southern regions, grain was dried in the open air in sheaves and was more likely to be threshed in the open air. The northern Great Russian farmstead usually included a *bania* (steam bath house), but in the south the peasants did their bathing outdoors or on the family stove. Sometimes all the barns and sheds of the peasants were located on the edge of the village for greater fire protection, and the bathhouses were built as a separate group near the river. In villages where the population engaged in a great deal of handicraft work, special workshops would be found among the farmstead buildings.

Most peasant farmsteads had their own wells, but wells were communal in those villages with deep-lying subsoil water. Such commune wells became centers of village gòssip: according to the Russian proverb, "Had wells but ears and tongues, not all the water they contain would put out the fire." In the streets of the village there were small ponds, and on the edge of the village large ponds for watering cattle, washing clothes, and bathing. In warm weather the peasants could bathe in rivers and lakes, but frequent cases of drowning made them cautious.

Apart from wells and ponds, the size and complexity of communal facilities varied a great deal in peasant settlements. A *derevnia* (small village or hamlet) had few such facilities; it was not administratively, economically, or sacramentally self-sufficient. The inhabitants of the *derevnia* went to a *selo* (large village or market town) to obtain the goods and services not available at home. Each *selo* had a number of satellite *derevni*. A *derevnia* did not have a church with resident clergy. A *selo* usually did, and the clergy periodically made a circuit of the satellite *derevni* to perform rituals.* The communal buildings of a *selo* might include a windmill or watermill, a tavern, a grain supply store, various shops, a dairy, a firehouse, a school, a workshop for extracting resin from coniferous trees, and a *volost'* government office building.[2]

---

* However, a large old village in southern Russia without a church would sometimes be called a *selo*.

There were three basic types of peasant houses in nineteenth-century Russia: the north Great Russian *izba,* the south Great Russian *izba,* and the Ukrainian *khata.*

The north Great Russian *izba* was made of hewn logs as long as the serviceable part of tree trunks available in the area. In northern Russia the dwelling tended to be relatively large, since timber was plentiful and extended-type families were common there longer than in the south. Because of the severe winter climate the house was built high off the ground, its timber floor raised above ground level over a cellar (*podklet'*) one-and-one-half to three meters deep. The yard, barn, hayshed, *ovin, riga,* and other outbuildings were all covered by a single roof. Sometimes a small unheated frame of logs, the *klet,* was built in the yard. In winter it was used for storage; in warm weather a young married couple without an *izba* of their own could sleep there in privacy. The northern *izba* had a saddleback roof (pitched, with two slopes, to shed snow) and was covered with planks or shingles. The peasants cut windows in the facade of the *izba* and often added a balcony encircling the house at the level of the higher windows. They liked to decorate their window frames, shutters, and roofs with animal, bird, and geometric designs. Especially characteristic of this house was a pair of carved horses' heads (*parnye kon'ki*), facing in opposite directions, sticking up at the end of the roof ridge. These horses were probably an ancient symbol of paired contrasting forces (light and dark, life and death) bound together in an ultimate unity. The horse symbol was also found inside the Great Russian peasant house, carved on the sleeping bench (*konik*) of the male head of the house. Since the care of horses, plowing with horses, and fighting on horseback were characteristic male functions in Russian culture, the horse appears to have been a symbol of masculine vitality. Thus if a Russian peasant was suffering a long death agony, someone in the family might go to the roof of the *izba* and break its ridge (*konëk*) to bring death.[3]

The south Great Russian *izba* was also built of hewn logs, but did not rise as high off the ground. It was usually built over a shallow cellar (*podpol'e*), for in this part of Russia there was little danger from floods and deep snows. Some houses had only a floor of beaten earth and no cellar, however. The southern *izba* usually had a hip roof (four slopes) for protection against strong winds. It was less richly decorated than the northern *izba,* and was more apt to be painted than carved. There was no massive roof covering the courtyard and outbuildings. All but the poorest peasants had a *klet* (for storage or summer sleeping) and a *seni* (an anteroom, used for storage or summer sleeping) attached to their *izba.*[4]

The third type of peasant house was the Ukrainian *khata.* It usually had a *seni* and less frequently a *komora,* equivalent to the *klet.* The walls of the *khata* were plastered and whitewashed, but underneath the plaster there were different kinds of construction. In the northern Ukraine the main construction material was wood, but in the southern Ukraine wood was used only for roof supports, and the walls were constructed of clay, stone, or chalk blocks. The *khata* was built without a cellar and had an earthen floor. Its roof had four slopes and was usually covered with straw thatching (less commonly with reeds, tile, or iron). The peasants often painted brightly colored designs on both the inner and outer whitewashed walls of the *khata.*[5]

The allocation of space in the main room of the Russian peasant home was strictly traditional. There were four regional patterns. In all four there were (1) a cooking corner, where the *pech'* (*pechka*: stove, oven) was located; (2) a *perednyi* (*sviati, krasnyi*) corner, where the icons were hung, guests were entertained, and the family dined on a whitewashed table; and (3) a sleeping corner.

The *pech'* occupied one-fourth to one-fifth of the space in the room. It was usually built of clay, but in the latter part of the nineteenth century many prosperous peasants built them of burnt brick. In the more primitive "black" *izba* of the poor, which survived here and there to the end of the nineteenth century, the *pech'* had no chimney: smoke was supposed to escape through the door or through a special opening in the wall, but since it often failed to do so, the interior became blackened. The *pech'* had many functions: not only did it heat the house and cook the food, but it was used for washing, for drying clothes and agricultural products, and for sleeping in cold weather. The placing of the stove determined the placing of the other elements in the room. The icon corner was always on a diagonal line from the stove.

The north and central Great Russian arrangement is shown in

BASIC PLANS OF PEASANT HOUSES IN
NINETEENTH-CENTURY RUSSIA

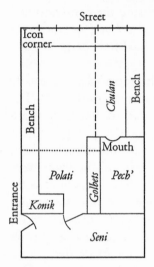

Fig. 1. North and Central
Great Russian *izba.*

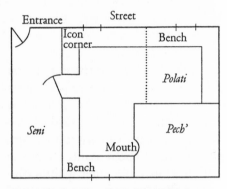

Fig. 2. Southeastern Great Russian *izba.*

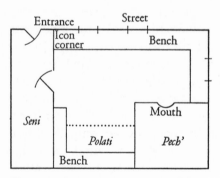

Fig. 3. Southwestern Great Russian *izba.*

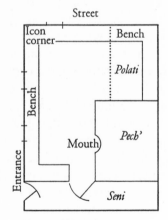

Fig. 4. *Khata* of Western
Great Russia, Belorussia
and the Ukraine.

Figure 1. This layout was characteristic of the *izba* of the non-black-soil *gubernias* of European Russia and of Siberia. The *chulan*, an area to the right of the broken line next to the *pech'*, was considered the women's side of the house and was sometimes separated from the rest of the house by a curtain or wooden partition. (Names used in other regions for the *chulan* include *upech, sereda, kut', sholnush*, and *shomnusha.*) Here women prepared meals and kept their cooking supplies. A long cupboard, the *golbets* (*kazenka, karshina*), was built along the left side of the *pech'*. Under the *golbets* a stairway led down to the cellar.

From the left of the entrance to the side wall was a wide bench, fastened to the wall, on which the master of the house, and sometimes other men of the house, slept. It was often decorated with a carved horse's head and was known as the *konik*. Along the other three walls there were also benches, tightly fastened to the walls. Overhanging the benches, higher up the walls, were shelves (*polavoshniki*) on which small articles were kept.

In the rear of the house (where the stove and entrance were located) there extended a sleeping loft, or *polati,* from the stove to the side wall. The area under the *polati* was regarded as an "anteroom." Livestock were sometimes kept there in the coldest part of the winter. It was considered unmannerly for a stranger to pass beyond the *polati* without an invitation. If invited, he would be entertained in the front left of the house, near the icon corner, which was the "clean" quarter. Between the icon corner and the *polati* there were usually a loom and a spinning wheel facing the long bench on the left side wall. There the women passed the tedious winter days spinning, weaving, knitting, and sewing.[6]

The southeastern Great Russian variant of the interior arrangement is shown in Figure 2. The southwestern Great Russian variant is shown in Figure 3. The peasants illuminated all three types of *izba* by suspending from the ceiling beam a *svetets* (*luchnik, komin*), in which they could put a burning splinter (*luchina*).* Kerosene lamps were not ordinarily found in peasant homes until the late nineteenth century. The baby's cradle or *liulka* (*zybka, kolushka*) also hung from a ceiling beam.

---

* Or they might use an earthen saucer (*kazanets, zhirnik*) filled with animal fat and a wick inserted.

The *izba* was usually equipped with a water barrel and dipper. The peasant washed not by plunging and rinsing, but by getting another person to pour water on his head and hands. More thorough bathing could be done in the bathhouse (*bania*), a log structure included in most north Russian farmsteads. In one corner of the *bania* was a *pech'kamenka,* a flueless dome made of stone masonry, sealed with clay, under which a fire was built. When the stones were hot, the peasants poured water over them until the *bania* was full of steam. At the sides of the *bania* were tiers of benches for the bathers to lie on. To remove dirt and stimulate circulation they beat each other with birch twigs. When it got too hot inside they ran out into the snow to cool off.

Russian ethnographic sources are discreetly silent about peasant excretory arrangements. Human waste was probably either collected in a bucket in the *izba* or deposited in a hole in the *seni.* Some peasants must have had outhouses. (Incidentally, cockroaches, lice, and bedbugs were standard equipment in an *izba.*)[7]

The fourth variant arrangement—the *khata*—was typical of western Great Russia (e.g. Smolensk *gubernia*), Belorussia, the Ukraine, and the Don and Kuban cossack areas. It was also typical of Poland and much of the eastern Baltic shore. It is shown in Figure 4. In the *khata* important dates in family life (birth, marriage, death) were often written or carved in a special roof beam, the *svolok,* and the icon corner was decorated with vigil lights, eggs, dried flowers, or doves made of dough.[8]

The Economic Base

In the nineteenth century the Russian peasant family grew crops with tools and techniques little changed since the Kiev period. The basic technique was plowing with animal power. For milling grain there was wind and water power. In order to survive, the peasant family had to produce each year a minimum of food for its own use, seed for the next year's crop, livestock feed, and a replacement fund for equipment necessary for production and consumption. The surplus production of the family had to cover ceremonial expenses (e.g. weddings, Christmas), its obligations to a landlord, and taxes. In order to meet all these demands the peasant family might resort to any of four supplementary activities: (1) animal husbandry and bee-keeping, (2) handicrafting for direct sale, (3) "cottage industry" on a "putting-out" basis, and (4) seasonal labor outside the village. The more fortunate and/or able peasants might be able to hire poor peasants to help with the work; they might obtain additional land to cultivate; they might even invest in improved seed, stock, or tools. But most peasant families felt fortunate if they could simply get enough to eat without falling into debt.

All arable land allotted to peasant families was divided into strips subject to obligatory rotation among families. The peasant commune usually distributed this land among its constituent households according to the number of taxable persons in each household (i.e., all men from seventeen to fifty-five years and all married women up to fifty years of age). Common pastures and meadows were used jointly by peasants and landlords. Forests usually belonged to landlords, who tried to keep peasants from poaching game.[9]

In the first part of the nineteenth century about two-thirds of the Russian peasants cultivated their arable land with the three-field (*parovaia*) system. A given field was alternately left fallow, sown with winter grain (rye, winter wheat), or sown with a spring grain (oats, barley, millet, spring rye, spring wheat). Two other systems were also used. In the *zalezhnaia* system a given piece of land was sown continuously for several years and then served as a pasture or hayfield until it again became fertile. This system was most often found around Ufa, Orenburg, Stavropol, Samara, and Astrakhan. One might find a third system, the slash-and-burn (*lesopolnaia, podsechnoognevaia*), in the northern forest region (Archangel, Olonets, and Vologod regions). Families using this system cleared land of standing trees one spring by cutting them down and leaving them where they fell. Then the following spring they burned the fallen wood, spread the ash around, and at once sowed the soil with barley or turnips in the far north, with rye or wheat a bit farther south. But after 1861 the peasants tended to switch from the latter two systems to the three-field system.[10]

Many of the principal crops cultivated in Russia in the nineteenth century had been cultivated since ancient times. These crops included cereals: rye, wheat, barley, oats, millet, and buckwheat; vegetables:

turnips, cabbage, peas, beans, lentils, onions, and cucumbers; fodder: vetch and clover; hops, flax, and hemp. Crops introduced relatively late—between the seventeenth and nineteenth centuries—included corn (maize), tomatoes, potatoes, sugar beets, sunflowers (latter part of nineteenth century), tobacco, and *makhorka* (shag tobacco).[11]

Rye was the basic crop in northern and central Russia; indeed, in the nineteenth century Russia led the world in rye production. Wheat was basic in the south. Oats were the most common spring crop. Barley was used for brewing beer and for fodder. Buckwheat was valued by beekeepers as a nectariferous crop, and cooked buckwheat groats (*kasha*) was a daily dish in the Russian army.

Thread from Russian flax, grown in the northern region, was exported by Novgorod and Pskov between the thirteenth and sixteenth centuries. The Russian peasants made their undergarments of homespun linen until the development of the cotton textile industry in the nineteenth century. They processed hemp fiber into rope and canvas and hemp seeds into cooking oil and cattle fodder.[12]

The basic plowing tool of the north Russian peasant was the *sokha,* a light wheelless wooden plow, usually with an iron share. It was adapted to the stony, shallow topsoil of the forested non-black-soil belt and the north and northeast black-soil belt. The *plug* (*sabany*) was a wheeled wooden plow with iron share that had to be pulled by up to three pairs of horses or six pairs of oxen. It was used in the steppe and forest-steppe areas of the south for turning up fallow fields and virgin soil. The *ralo* was a heavy plow with many teeth, pulled by one to five pairs of oxen, and used for small-scale plowing in the south. For breaking up clods, the peasants used a harrow (*barona*) pulled by animals. Their other principal tools were hand tools: the scythe (*kosa*) for mowing hay (and, from the eighteenth century on, also for reaping), the sickle (*serp*) for reaping, and the flail (*tsep*) for threshing. They used hand tools in their kitchen gardens, except in the cultivation of potatoes, where the *sokha* was used.[13]

Prior to 1861 the Russian peasant family kept animals mainly for family use, not for the market. These animals were usually horses, cattle, sheep, goats, chickens, and geese. Ducks and pigs were relatively uncommon on peasant farmsteads before the end of the nineteenth century. The peasants usually overworked their horses and

fed and maintained them poorly. In winter the horses got straw, with
hay and oats if they were doing heavy work (like hauling firewood).
In summer they were fed hay, oats, and rye mash when doing heavy
plowing; the rest of the time they grazed in pastures. In the north,
horses grazed unguarded in meadows and forests; in the central and
southern regions, when not working, they were kept in a fenced-in
area near the village and guarded at night by the peasants in turn.
In cold weather the peasants kept them in stables that were hung
with icons representing Floris and Lauris, the patron saints of horses,
or with stones of unusual shape with a hole in the center called "horse
gods."

The peasants kept cattle mainly as work animals or for milking.
They used oxen (bullocks) to pull the heavy plows. The care of cattle
was similar to that of horses except that in the south herders tended
them in warm weather. The care of horses and bulls was considered a
man's job, and only men and boys (usually from poor families) served
as herders. Women cared for the remaining domestic livestock: cows,
sheep, goats, and poultry. In the fall the peasants might market some
of their animals or slaughter them for ceremonial use. Only the richest
peasants ate meat regularly.

To guard their domestic animals from harm, the peasants hung
their sheds with many kinds of charms: stones with holes in them,
multicolored scraps of fabric, sheep's wool, tinsel, crusts of bread, and
ancient coins with representations of horses. These offerings were
directed to the *domovoi* (family spirit), whom they considered "master" of the family animals. In time of epizootic outbreaks, the Russian
peasants resorted to a ritual similar to one practiced by the ancient
Greeks and Romans. At night the cattle were shut inside the village,
and the men hid. The women of the village, naked or wearing only
shifts, and with their hair flowing loose, gathered in a field outside
the village. They yoked the oldest woman to a plow, and at midnight
plowed a furrow three times around the village, making as much
noise as they could with frying pans, iron pots, etc., singing and
shouting obscenities. Sometimes they carried an icon of St. Vlasia
(*Yegoria*), the patron saint of domestic animals. Thus they tried
to drive "death" from the village.[14]

Peasant handicraft work was of four types: (1) for family use, (2) to order for a customer(*remeslo*), (3) for the market directly (*promysel*), and (4) on an order from a capitalist ("putting out"). Women made things mostly for household use, especially textiles of linen, wool, and hemp. They did their spinning on spindles until the end of the eighteenth century, when the spinning wheel was introduced. They used horizonal looms except in the Ukraine, where vertical looms were used in rugmaking.

Men usually made commodities for the market, especially articles of wood and other materials from the forest. Such activity was most common in northern Russia. The men extracted resin, burned charcoal, and constructed barrels, wooden bowls, spoons, toys, bast matting, bast shoes (*lapti*), baskets, wickerwork, and birchbark dishes. Ceramic production was widespread in Russia. Peasant potters shaped dishes on a potter's wheel and fired them in a common kiln. At the river they tanned leather and worked maple and aspen wood into art objects with a simple lathe powered by the river current.[15]

In order to move their firewood from the forest, their crops from the field, and their fishing catch from lake or stream to their homes, the peasants devised carts (two- and four-wheeled), sledges, sleighs, and simple boats (either dugouts or boats made of wooden planks). In the second half of the nineteenth century the richer peasants traveled in carriages of various types. Such carriages usually had springs and a collapsible top, and were pulled by one to three horses.[16]

Food

The peasant toiled in order to eat, but what did he eat? He ate bread, mainly. He treated a loaf of bread reverently, standing it upright on the table and breaking it instead of cutting it. It was bread made by his wife from sourdough leavened with yeast, *kvas,* or beer lees. In hard times she had to adulterate the dough with bran and pigweed.[17] She baked it in the *pech',* usually on a clean hearthstone. The peasant woman prepared many other dishes based on dough for special occasions (and in richer peasant families, on ordinary days). The most famous were *pirogi*—tarts stuffed with fish, cottage cheese, berries, cabbage, etc., *blini*—thin pancakes, and *knyshi*—puff pastries layered with *kaimak* (cream taken from boiled milk). Another important cereal food in the daily fare of peasants was groats (*krupa*)* prepared from oats, wheat, or buckwheat, and known as *kasha* after simmering.

Vegetables were next in importance in the peasant diet. First came the hardy cabbage, eaten fresh in summer and in the form of sauerkraut in winter. In times of fasting, bread, sauerkraut, and *kvas* were the only food of the poor peasants. Cabbage was the basis of a popular north and central Russian soup—*shchi*.† In south Great Russia and the Ukraine the favorite soup was *borshch,* made ideally with meat stock and beets, cabbage, onions, and sometimes tomatoes. In the course of the nineteenth century potatoes became part of the daily diet of even the poor peasants. Other staple vegetables were cucumbers, salted in barrels for winter use, and onions for seasoning. Vegetable oils, from hemp, flax, and sunflower seeds, added vital calories to the diet. For variety there might be peas, horseradish, melons, berries, and other produce from the family garden, as well as mushrooms, nuts, and berries gathered from nearby woods and salted and dried for winter use.

The average peasant associated meat with special celebrations. Late in the fall he killed the livestock and poultry intended for consumption during the winter. (It is interesting that Russian peasants observed a taboo on eating the meat of the bear, the horse, and the hare.) Of greater importance than meat in the peasant diet were fish, especially in villages near lakes and streams, milk and milk products such as cottage cheese (*tvorog*), and eggs.

The most widespread peasant drink around 1861 was probably *kvas,* a near beer made from bran, malt, dried crusts of bread, flour, and water. Another type of home brew was *braga,* usually made from oats, with malt and hops. In some villages it was traditional for the peasants to take a holiday to prepare beer together. Tea was first introduced into Russia from China in the seventeenth century, but it was not a common drink in the villages until the 1880's, when many vil-

---

* Groats are hulled grain broken into fragments larger than grits. They can be prepared for eating in about fifteen minutes by simmering.

† In the far north where cabbage did not grow, *shchi* referred to a thick soup of potatoes and groats.

lage homes had samovars. However, these samovars were often used to prepare home-grown "teas" of herbs, carrots, berries, or fruits.

Peasant cooking and eating utensils were of wood, pottery, or metal, with earthenware pots often being used for cooking. Some of the most interesting utensils, from an artistic point of view, were wooden scoops (*kovshi*) and wooden dishes in the shape of a hollowed-out duck.[18]

Dress

The male peasant had his hair parted in the middle and trimmed in the shape of an inverted bowl. His beard, especially before 1861, usually was not trimmed if he was a Great Russian. (Ukrainian males shaved for ceremonial occasions.) In warm weather he wore a cylindrical hat felted from sheepswool* and in winter a fur or lambskin cap, sometimes with earflaps. During the nineteenth century the visor cap (*kartuz*) came into fashion as well.

The basic male garment was the *rubakha,* a long tunic-like shirt with sleeves and a stand-up collar made from homespun linen or a commercial fabric. All peasant garments were fastened by placing the right side of the garment over the left, as American female garments are fastened now. Such a style was typical of peasants in Eastern European valleys as far east as the Volga, and distinguished the peasants from the steppe nomads, who fastened their garments left over right.

There were distinctive regional variations in the decor of the peasant shirt. The more ancient Ukrainian type was fastened in the middle front of the body, had a stand-up collar and was often embroidered. The Great Russian type, which probably diffused from Moscow not earlier than the fifteenth century, fastened at the left side of the neck. It was often decorated with *poliki*—embroidered insets—placed on each shoulder. In north Great Russia, Belorussia, and the Ukraine these insets were "square," and in south Great Russia, "slanted" or trapezoidal.

A peasant's trousers in Great Russia, Belorussia, and right-bank

---

* At the time of Haxthausen's visit (1843), and in early photographs, this felt hat had a brim, and the cylinder was encircled by a ribbon fastened with a buckle, reminiscent of the English and American Puritan hats of the seventeenth century.

Ukraine were tight-fitting, but in left-bank Ukraine, under Cossack and ultimately nomad influence, men wore loose, full, baggy trousers (*sharovary*). Great Russian and Belorussian men wore their shirts hanging out over their trousers, in the ancient peasant style. Ukrainian peasants, under nomad influence, tucked their shirts in.

The peasant's outer dress was usually the *kaftan,* a long tunic girdled at the waist and fastened on the left side. It was made of coarse brown or grey homespun wool or of some heavy commercial fabric. In severe weather he wore a sheepskin coat, often wool side in, either long and wide (*tulup*) or short (*polushubki*). His legs were wrapped with linen or cotton rags, inside of which he might deposit small precious items, such as coins. These leg wrappings were held in place by ties attached to *lapti*—woven bast shoes—usually of linden (limewood) bark. Sometimes he wore birchbark clogs on his bare feet or (especially in the Ukraine) crude leather moccasins. But what he preferred to wear, if he could afford them, was a pair of high-top boots (*sapogi*). They were expensive and had to be bought in town, so he often wore them only on holidays. In very cold weather he kept his feet warm in high-top all-felt boots (*valenki*), first produced in Russia in the early nineteenth century.[19]

A Russian peasant girl did not cut her hair, but braided it in a single plait, sometimes with ribbons and other decorations entwined on festive occasions. Only on her wedding day did her hair flow loose in public. In warm weather she sometimes wore a circlet with an open crown. In cold weather she might wear a kerchief (*platok*), but this custom was relatively new in the nineteenth century. A married woman always covered her hair, especially in the presence of strange men and older men of her husband's family. When a girl assumed the headdress of a married woman it was an important moment in the wedding ceremonies. Tokarev thinks that these customs are rooted in a primitive belief in the magic power of hair, especially long head hair. An unmarried girl's hair was not considered dangerous to her own family, but a married woman was an "alien" to her husband's family, and her hair was therefore "dangerous" to them. The married woman's headdress in northern Great Russia was usually based on the *kokoshnik,* which resembled a tiara covered with brocade or other valuable material and embroidered with pearls and precious stones (real or imitation). In southern Great Russia the headdress base was the *kichka,* which resembled a pair of horns. The married woman parted her hair in the middle and braided it in two braids that were fastened to the head under the headdress.

The basic female garment, the *rubakha,* was like the male's. In the summer unmarried girls might wear this "shift" without any overgarment, but a married woman always wore an overgarment. The most primitive of these was the south Great Russian *ponëva* (Ukrainian *plakhta*), ritually placed on the bride during the wedding ceremony. It was made of three widths of woolen fabric that were not sewn together, but hung as flaps from the waistband. During the nineteenth century the *ponëva* was gradually replaced by either a true skirt, borrowed by Ukrainian and Belorussian women from the West several centuries earlier, or the north Great Russian *sarafan,* which was given the name *shubka.* The *sarafan,* typical overdress of the north Great Russian woman, resembled a jumper with narrow shoulder supports, or a pinafore without ruffles. It came to Russia from the West in the fifteenth and sixteenth centuries.* The other overgarments and footgear of the peasant women resembled those of the men.

In her holiday attire the peasant woman was colorful: red predominated, followed by yellow and blue. She decorated herself with embroidery, woven strips, ribbons, glass beads, spangles, drake and peacock feathers, and goose down. She especially treasured river pearls. Haxthausen reports that all the women he saw in the Nizhi-Novgorod area had at least three or four strings of pearls.[20]

The Peasant Family

We know relatively little about the Russian peasant family of the nineteenth century, but its general characteristics can be described. The Russian peasant family in the nineteenth century might be a

---

* The most ancient type of *sarafan* had false sleeves hanging down behind called *shushun* (*sushpan, sukman*). In the nineteenth century these were worn in the Pskov, Novgorod, and Olonets regions, chiefly by old women. Similar false sleeves, vestiges of the medieval gown, were worn in the West from the sixteenth to eighteenth centuries. (See Philippe Aries, *Centuries of Childhood* [New York, 1965], p. 56.)

"small family," which included parents, children, and possibly grand-parents, or a "large extended family," which included two or more married brothers with their offspring and possibly their parents, the essential characteristic being the presence of collateral lines in a single household. At the beginning of the century the large extended family was the more common of the two types, but families tended to split up after 1861, and the average family had only five to six members in 1897. Small families were most typical in the north Great Russian non-black-soil region and in the Ukraine. The large extended family was most likely to be found (1) in the south Great Russian black-soil zone, (2) among middle peasants who engaged in seasonal work out-side the village, (3) in border areas where land allotments were rela-tively large, such as Cossack areas and Siberia, (4) in the far northern forest district of Tver *gubernia* and in the Belozersk district of Nov-gorod *gubernia,* and (5) among rich peasants generally in north Russia.[21]

The figure of central authority in the family was usually the patri-arch (*bol'shak, batiushka, nabol'shii khoziain*; Ukrainian: *starshii*; Belorussian: *bats'ka, dziadz'ka*). He managed the collective family property, making the ultimate decisions on the timing of field work and the buying and selling of alienable property. Normally he was the oldest male member in full possession of his faculties; however, a more competent junior male or senior female might be more influen-tial in actual practice.

Much of the traditional work of the man in the family had sym-bolic significance. A man plowed and sowed the fields: these actions were regarded as symbolic of the male role in sexual intercourse. A man cared for his horse: the horse was a masculine symbol. A man cut firewood and constructed wooden buildings using an axe, another masculine symbol. A man also harrowed the fields, mowed hay, threshed grain, and carted tools and produce. In the crowded *izba* he kept order through the long winters, which often forced a peasant family to live in a single room, perhaps ten feet by fifteen feet, for seven months of the year.

The strongest member of the family in practice, however, might be *matushka*—mama—a symbol in Russian culture of endurance and healing love. She was often the great binding force in the family.[22] All year long she cooked, cared for children, spun, wove, sewed, washed, milked cows, and cared for domestic cattle and poultry. In summer she would, in addition, rake hay, reap grain, weed, pull flax, and care for the kitchen garden. Although she had no right to inherit a share in the real estate of the family of her birth, she could dispose of her dowry (which might include land and livestock) and the fruits of her *babskoe khoziaistvo* (handicrafts and products of livestock and poultry in her charge). Then her daughters might inherit from her.

The children of the family were expected to assume responsibilities in the work of the family at an early age.[23] They were trained to respect the authority of elders, and were taught the importance of harmonious teamwork and of restraining their aggressive tendencies. They learned to perform routine tasks reliably, since such routine performances might make the difference between survival or catastrophe. As adolescents they did not suffer from the strain of deferring marriage long past puberty, nor did they take on the responsibilities of running an independent household immediately after marriage.

There were two especially difficult roles in the peasant family. One was that of the daughter-in-law (*snokha*). In the early nineteenth century, according to some reports, an underage boy might be married to an older girl for economic reasons, and she would become mistress of her father-in-law (who was then called a *snokhach*).[24] After the abolition of serfdom such arrangements became uncommon. Even when they did not exist, however, there must have been frequent tension arising from the presence of an eighteen-year-old female and a forty-year-old male, no blood kin to each other, living in a tiny room together for many months. In the warm weather a young couple could retire to the *klet,* but in winter they might be forced to move in with the older couple to economize on fuel. Sexual rivalry was probably a factor in the notoriously hostile mother-in-law and daughter-in-law relationship. The daughter-in-law often felt overworked and unappreciated in her husband's family; the mother-in-law often considered her lazy and irresponsible. Sad indeed was the fate of a daughter-in-law whose husband was drafted—at least before the 1874 Reform. Any children they had were cared for by his fam-

ily, but he was lamented as if dead, and she might be treated as a
family hired hand or sent away to work in a factory.

The other difficult role was that of son-in-law (*ziat'*). A well-to-do
family with no sons of its own might "adopt" a son-in-law of humble
birth and take him into the household. According to a Russian proverb, "If you have no devil in the house, take in a son-in-law." One
can imagine his discomfort as a dependent of a woman's family.

The experience of family living was so influential in shaping the
Russian peasant's mentality that he tended to people Nature with
imaginary families. The *leshii* (wood spirit) and *vodianoi* (water
spirit) were sometimes said to have wives and children. When there
was a storm in the forest or the water churned in the river, it meant
that the spirit therein was "celebrating his marriage." Jack Frost in
Russia was "Grandfather Frost" (*Ded Moroz*). The earth itself was
sometimes personified as "Damp Mother Earth," to whom the peasants addressed prayers in ancient times.

The Russian peasant's home was a place of worship—the worship
of the family itself as an ongoing, living entity. This worship was
bifocal. One focus was at the *pech'*. When a family moved from one
house to another it carried embers from the fire of the old stove in a
jar to start a fire in the new stove. If the distance was too great, the
family merely took the fire shovel and other implements of the old
stove. In the Ukraine, a piece of clay from the stove (*pechyna*) was
wrapped in the swaddling clothes of a newborn infant when it was
taken for baptism. The stove was also involved in wedding rituals
(*see below*).

The Eastern Slavs believed that in each home resided an ancestral
spirit, or *domovoi* (*khoziain, dedushka, susedko, sam*; Ukrainian:
domovik, khovanets, vikhovanok, skarbnik). This family spirit was
usually in or behind the *pech'*. When the family pushed the embers
of the old stove into the new stove they repeated the formula "*Domovoi na tebe sani, poezzhai s nami*" (*Domovoi*, the sleigh is ready for
you, go with us). A *domovoi* was supposed to be warm and soft, like
a sheepskin coat. In general he was a protective spirit, but he might
engage in malicious teasing, such as making noises that kept the family awake at night. They propitiated him by putting offerings of food,

especially eggs, on the stove. In Belorussia the *domovoi* was called *tsmok* (snake), which suggests the ancient Greek association of housesnakes and ancestors. A Russian family in a new neighborhood hung in their stable another animal symbol, a bear's head, to protect them from the house spirits of their new neighbors.[25]

Diagonally across from the *pech'* was the other sacred place in the room: the icon corner (*perednii ugol, krasnyi ugol, sviati ugol*). When a stranger entered a Russian household he was supposed to take off his hat, cross himself facing the icon corner, and then greet the heads of the household. The jar that a family used to carry embers from an old stove to a new was broken and buried at night under the icon corner of the new house. In order to safeguard the family head or the first member of the family to enter a new home, they killed an animal, usually a rooster, and sprinkled the foundations of the new house with his blood. Then they buried his head, in private, in the spot where the icon corner was to be located. In the pre-Christian era the icon corner may have been the place where ancestral images were kept. Some Russian peasants believed that after a dead member of the family was buried his soul took up residence behind the family icons.[26]

A Russian family gave special thought to its dead on certain occasions during the year: the eve of *Maslenitsa* (Shrovetide), *Radonitsa* (Tuesday of the second week after Easter), St. Dimitri's Saturday (the eve of October 26), and *Semik* (Thursday before Trinity Sunday). The family celebrated such occasions by visiting the graves of the family dead. There at the cemetery they had a picnic that the dead might attend and "enjoy." They left offerings of food for the dead and asked them to help make the crops grow.[27]

The Life of a Typical Peasant Family

Let us try to imagine an ordinary day in January, 1860, in the life of the Ivanovs, a peasant family living in the *derevnia* of Beryozka just north of Moscow. At daybreak, Marya, the *matushka,* sits up on her pallet of straw on the sleeping bench, throws aside her sheepskin cover, and stirs up the fire in the stove. She has bread for breakfast on hand: dark sourdough rye loaves. All that is needed besides is to draw some *kvas* from the barrel in the cellar. While she is in the cellar she gets some sauerkraut, onions, and buckwheat groats to make into *shchi* and *kasha* for dinner. She does her cooking for the whole day now, and leaves the food in the *pech'* until needed. The rest of the family get up soon after and begin the morning chores. Marya's husband Ivan and her son Andrei cut firewood and care for the horses. Her daughter, Marfa, and Andrei's wife, Anya, fetch water for the water barrel from the family well, take out the straw pallets, care for the cow, sheep, and poultry, sweep the floor, and set the table in the icon corner. Then the family gathers for breakfast. Seated at the table under the icons is Ivan (the *bol'shak*), 45 years old; next to him is his eldest son, Andrei, who is 25; opposite the men are Marya (43), their unmarried daughter Marfa (16), and Andrei's wife Anya (23), who is feeding oatmeal porridge to their son Petka (4). One member of the family is missing, namely Sergei (20), who is away for the winter working in a textile factory in Ivanovo-Voznesensk. Sergei is unmarried and sends most of his earnings home. So far he has not been taken into the army, and Marya prays each day that the draft will pass him by.

Winter days are short in Beryozka, so the Ivanovs take advantage of the hours of light to make salable articles for the Moscow market. Marya embroiders a blouse, Anya weaves, and Marfa knits on a sweater. Ivan and Andrei carve wooden spoons and toys. In the early afternoon the family gathers for dinner, consisting of *shchi,* bread, and *kvas*. After Ivan says grace, each member of the family dips his wooden spoon in the common soup bowl in the middle of the table. In the afternoon they take their handwork to a neighbor's *izba* for socializing and storytelling. The neighbor offers them a snack of tea with fruit preserves on bread. Then they return home to finish the evening chores before dark. They must care for the animals, prepare firewood for the *pech',* and lay out straw to sleep on. The last meal of the day consists of buckwheat *kasha* with some flax seed oil and *kvas*. Then Ivan and Andrei go off to drink at the village tavern (*traktir;* Ukraine and Belorussia: *korchma*) and to hear the latest news. Meanwhile Marya sits near the stove and tells Petka the ancient tale (*skazka*) of Maria Morevna. When the light of the last *luchnik* flickers out in the *svetets,* everyone is stretched out asleep on a straw pallet under a sheepskin. They hope that the *domovoi* will not wake them by scratching around in the back of the stove.

Days such as the one described above melt one into the other, making little impression on the memory of the Ivanovs. But every Ivanov remembers, discusses, and is influenced by the vital events of family life, especially birth, marriage, and death.

The Ivanovs want to have a big family and do not practice birth control. Marya Ivanov has three children, but she gave birth to three others who died in infancy. Her daughter-in-law Anya lost a baby last summer. Petka, like most children in the village, was born in the family bathhouse. Anya lay upon a straw pallet with a smooth cover laid on one of the wide shelves usually used by bathers to enjoy the steam. The village midwife (*babka*) delivered Petka easily; in difficult cases she might resort to the magic of untying knots, unlocking locks, etc.—symbolic of the unbinding of vital forces.[28] The peasants believe that childbirth is easier if few are present; single girls are not allowed to attend. Petka's umbilical cord was cut with an axe, symbol of masculinity; a girl's cord would have been cut with a distaff.

About three days after his birth Petka was formally received into the Ivanov family and the Beryozka community. This was done by the Christian ceremony of baptism, at home or in church; not only Ivanov kin, but other villagers attended. During the ceremony Petka's godparents played the most active role, while his parents remained in the background. After the ceremony the Ivanovs entertained kin and friends, who provided refreshments and gifts for Petka. The special dishes served on this occasion were *krestil'naia kasha* (christening pudding) and *kisel'* (a starchy jelly leavened with yeast), which is also served at other major family celebrations. On the day of the christening, or thereabouts, there was an additional, purely family ceremony of purification of mother and midwife (*razmyvki;* Ukrainian: *zlivki;* Belorussian: *zhmurinki*). In the days between delivery and this ceremony Anya was separated from the rest of the family and considered "unclean."* She did no housework and could not

---

* A curious reverse interpretation of the actual biological situation, since Anya was in greater danger of contamination by the family than vice versa.

eat with the family, milk the cows, or touch an icon. At the *razmyvki*
the midwife and Anya mutually washed their hands. The Ivanovs
then paid the midwife with some coins, which they dipped in water.
Petka settled down in his curtained-around swinging cradle of bast
(*liulka, zybka*), and his mother resumed her housework. In a week
she might be performing all her normal duties.[29]

Petka was nursed at Anya's breast for fifteen months, but he was
given solid foods—thin oatmeal and scrambled eggs—much earlier.
When Anya was too busy to rock his cradle she gave him a pacifier
(*khlebnaia* or *kashnaia soska*) made of flour, bread, or cooked groats
tied in a rag. Anya has little time to entertain her boy, but she and all
members of the family treat him with great affection. He loves to
hear his grandmother tell stories in the evening. As he grows older
he will enjoy the outdoors more and more: in summer, finding birds'
nests, fishing, and exploring; in winter, playing in the snow. When
he is about seven years old he will begin to help his father with "man's
work": chopping firewood, caring for the horse, sowing, plowing,
etc. He is learning to be honest, obedient, and hardworking, and he
is learning early, for as the peasant proverb puts it: "If you don't
teach him when he lies across the width of the sleeping bench, then
you will not be able to teach him when he stretches out on the whole
length of the bench."

Marfa has been helping with housework since she was six, and has
learned most domestic skills. At harvest time this year she will no
longer baby-sit with Petka but will wield a sickle all day behind
Marya. She is looking forward to haymowing time when the whole
village will be out mowing together.

There is no school in Beryozka, and all the Ivanovs there are illiterate. But twenty miles away, in the *selo* of Staritsa, there is a three-
year parish school that one of their cousins, Alexander Vladimirov,
attends. At thirteen he can read a newspaper haltingly. Will the Ivanovs send Petka to school in Staritsa? That will depend upon how
much they need his help at home, how prosperous they are, his apti-
tudes, and the climate of opinion about the value of education. They
will probably not hire him out as a herdsboy or apprentice him to an
artisan in Staritsa, as poor families must do with their sons.[30]

There is no question of sending Marfa to school. But she doesn't miss it: right now she is having the time of her life. Almost every evening this winter she goes to a *posidelka* (Ukrainian: *bechornitsa*; Belorussian: *becherok*) at an *izba* that Marfa and her girlfriends (aged sixteen to twenty) have rented for the winter from an elderly couple without children. The *podrostki* (girls aged fourteen and fifteen) have their own *posidelki,* as do the *perestarkie* (girls over twenty). The girls work on their spinning, knitting, sewing, and embroidering under their mothers' supervision. At such sessions they often sing lyric songs about the life of women. Later in the evening the young men come: one bringing firewood, another his concertina, and the others refreshments—nuts, seeds, candy, cakes. The girls turn from work to play: games, singing, dancing. Then the boys may escort the girls home.* During the spring and early summer the same gang will sing, dance *khorovody,* and play games together outdoors. On the threshold of marriage the boys and girls of a village are well acquainted. But if they wish to seek a mate outside the village they

---

* According to one Soviet source, in some villages, especially in the Ukraine, the youths and girls might spend the night together after a *posidelka* (S. A. Tokarev, *Etnografiia narodov SSR* [Moscow, 1958], p. 82). D. S. Shimkin says that young men visited girls sleeping in haylofts in summer and that an illegitimate child might enhance a girl's chances of marriage, since it showed her to be highly fertile. (See his "Culture and World View: A Method of Analysis Applied to Rural Russia," *American Anthropologist,* 55 [1953], p. 331.) However, a recent Soviet ethnographic summary declared that if a girl lost her virginity before marriage the family gate might be tarred and the family might have a hard time finding her a husband (*Narody Mira* [Moscow, 1964], pp. 408–9). The demand for "proof" of virginity after the wedding night in peasant customs tends to support this view.

One may account for such differences in testimony on the grounds that different regions are involved. Also, peasants (and indeed human beings everywhere) have highly ambivalent feelings about the power of sexual attraction: they both fear it and worship it. It makes marriages and breaks them. According to a Russian proverb, "The devil pours a spoonful of honey into someone else's wife." It seems likely that the Russian peasants condoned some premarital sexual experimentation, especially between a couple who were good candidates for a match. There were surely many opportunities for this in warm weather in the countryside. On the other hand, girls were usually married before they developed a taste for a variety of sexual partners.

However, cases of adultery after marriage appear to have been fairly common. Although the village would gossip about such a case, peasants not directly involved would not intervene unless a married woman of the village paired off with a man from outside the village. Ordinarily it was the husband's duty to punish an errant wife. (See A. N. Engelgardt, *Iz derevni: 12 pisem 1872–1877* [Moscow, 1937], p. 36.)

will look the prospects over in Staritsa at the holiday fairs. Or they may find a mate on a pilgrimage to some chapel, miraculous spring, or other holy place.

When it is time for a Russian peasant girl to marry, her parents might either discreetly seek out a husband for her or sanction an already blooming romance. They will want the boy to be of a family at least as well-off as themselves, in good physical and mental health, and of good moral reputation. In case either his parents or her parents disapprove of the match, the couple may elope and get married secretly (marriage by *samokhodka, samokrupka, ubeg*). Then they will wait awhile, perhaps until the birth of their first child, after which they will apologize to the reluctant parents, asking their forgiveness.[31]

For over a year Marfa has been flirting with Vladimir Petrov (19) at the holiday fairs in Staritsa. In the fall of 1860 their engagement takes place in the following manner. One evening the Ivanovs have some "surprise" visitors—at least the Ivanovs act surprised. The visitors, dressed in their best clothes, include Anton Petrov, uncle of Vladimir Petrov (Vladimir's *svat*), and Dunia Stepanov, Vladimir's married aunt (the *svakha*). First the visitors chat casually with the Ivanovs, and then make complimentary references to both Marfa and Vladimir. In a little while, the Petrov contingent, sensing a warm response, makes a formal marriage proposal. The Ivanovs refuse gently at first, saying that Marfa is "too young to marry" or "too much needed at home." Both families refuse to commit themselves: since there is a business side to the deal, any undue eagerness on one side can be materially damaging. The only person who has a material interest in agreement per se is the *svakha,* and she pushes the negotiations forward.* The Ivanovs say they will think the matter over and give their answer in a few days. Since the answer is favorable, the Petrov party visits again to make the betrothal agreement. Ivan, speaking for the Ivanovs, bargains with Anton Petrov as to the size of Marfa's dowry (*pridanoe*), which may include bedding, livestock, and even land, as well as the customary linens prepared and embroi-

* Such proceedings are depicted in the Soviet film *And Quiet Flows the Don.*

dered by the bride. They also discuss the *kladka* (the groom's contribution for the bride's wedding apparel and for the wedding expenses). The matchmaker is successful: Ivan finally accepts the proposal, and both parties drink a toast to the union (ritual of the *malyi zapoi*). After this the Ivanovs pay a visit to the Petrov home in Dubrava to see if it is satisfactory. Satisfied, they invite the Petrovs back to their *izba* in Beryozka for the *rukobit'e* (*bol'shoi zapoi, zapivanie, propivan'e*) when, with ceremonial toasts, the two families strike the final bargain. After this, neither party can break the agreement without making some compensation to the other "to pay for the dishonor."

Once engaged, Marfa is freed from all housework. With the help of her girlfriends she finishes preparing her needlework dowry. She goes about in a special "sad" dress, covering her head, as she bids her relatives in the village farewell. It is befitting that she at least appear sad, for the Russian proverb declares: "Weeping bride, laughing wife; laughing bride, weeping wife." On the day before the wedding she and her girlfriends go to the bathhouse for a ritual bath. Then Vladimir visits the *izba* bringing her presents. That evening there are two parties. At the Petrov house is a bachelor party (*mal'chishnik, parnëvik*), with drinking, singing, joking. At the Ivanovs is the *devichnik* for Marfa and her girlfriends at which there is a dramatic ceremony of Marfa's farewell to maidenhood. Her maidenhood is symbolized by the *krasnaia krasota,* a wreath of ribbons, flowers, and ornaments Marfa has twined in her single braid of maiden hair. Singing ritual songs, the girls unbraid Marfa's hair and then rebraid it for the last time in a single braid.* One of the young married women of the bride's family or among her friends warns her in a song that she will be ill-treated by her in-laws. Marfa, she says, should go out in the open country and wash away her grief:

> Fall down on the damp earth,
> Upon the burning stones,
> For surely you know, dear sister,
> That our mother, the damp earth, will not betray you,

---

* If the Ivanovs had been richer, Marfa's hair would have been rebraided with strings of pearls and pieces of gold intertwined.

That the burning stones will not repeat it.
But you will go to strange people,
You will wipe off the burning tears.
Do not show your feelings to people.[32]

Meanwhile Marya and Anya Ivanov, with all their married female kin and friends, are busy making wedding refreshments. The married women of the Petrov household are doing the same thing.

The next day comes the main event—the church wedding—but there are also rituals of pre-Christian origin. In the morning Marfa's friends help her dress and adorn her with the bridal crown. Her parents and godparents bless her. Vladimir's parents bless him with the family icon in their *izba*. Then Vladimir sets out with his party to fetch Marfa. His suite includes all his available kin and friends, cast in various formal roles. The *druzkha*, or best man, who leads the suite and serves as master of ceremonies at the wedding feast later, has been chosen from among Vladimir's married male kin. The symbols of his office are a piece of linen thrown over his shoulders, a gun, and a lash. There are various companions of the groom (*podruzh'e, druzhki, tiasiatskii*), the *svat* and *svakha*, the groom's parents and godparents, and the groom himself. On the road they meet various obstacles placed by the bride's party, such as barricades and straw bonfires. The best man "buys off" the obstructionists with little gifts. At the Ivanov house the parties of bride and groom have an antiphonal choral contest. Vladimir's party goes into the Ivanov *izba* and there is a joking scene: Vladimir "buys" a seat next to Marfa; the best man "buys" Marfa from Petka (since she has no younger brother); and then one of Marfa's girlfriends steps forward pretending to be Marfa. Following this the two parties have some refreshments together. The bride and groom are led to the middle of the *izba* and placed on a fur coat (in this case a sheepskin) laid with the nap side up. Ivan and Marya Ivanov come forward and bless them. The *svakha*, Dunia Stepanov, unbraids Marfa's hair. Marfa touches the Ivanov *pech'*, pulling off a bit of clay, in a last farewell. Then they are ready to leave for the church in Staritsa.

As the couple departs, there are various magic rituals to ward off evil: the best man shoots his gun into the air and cracks his whip.

In Staritsa the wedding party circles the church three times, carrying an icon, and making as much noise as possible to ward off evil spirits. As the Orthodox Christian ceremony goes on, various doors and windows are closed to exclude evil spirits. Just after the church ceremony Marfa's loose flowing hair is braided into two braids, fastened to her head, and crowned with the headdress of the married woman. Then the wedding party sets out for the Petrov house. The bride's movable dowry is transferred there too.

When Vladimir and Marfa arrive, Vladimir's parents are there to meet them with ceremonial bread and salt. They bless the young couple and sprinkle them with hops and kernels of grain. Vladimir's father removes Marfa's bridal veil. Then the newlyweds sit down at the table in the icon corner and are welcomed by the whole family. The guests begin the wedding feast, but Vladimir and Marfa eat separately in the *klet* or in the *chulan* behind a partition. Then they are led to the general feast table. During the feast there is an orgy of singing, dancing, and drinking, led by the best man and the *svakha*. In the wedding songs the bride and groom are compared to a white swan (quail, duck) and a falcon, a duck and drake, a pair of doves, the moon and sun (dawn), a pearl and *iakhoni* (ruby, sapphire, or amethyst), a marten and hunter, a grape vine entwining a post or large tree, an oak (or *iavor,* sycamore) and a *kalina* (snowball tree, guelder rose).[33] Marfa gives her new relatives little sweets, and they give the young couple money (this is the "gilding"—*zolochenie*). Marfa, according to ancient custom, takes off Vladimir's boots as a sign of submission for all the company to see. During the feast she sits wrapped in a scarf, but does not participate in the merrymaking. At the end of the feast the best man and the *svakha* lead Vladimir and Marfa to bed in the Petrov *klet,* while the wedding guests sing bawdy songs.

The following morning Vladimir and Marfa are awakened by the best man and *svakha,* who collect Marfa's shift, now spotted with blood. Then they parade around this "proof" of her premarital virginity, beating earthen pots. Vladimir and Marfa get up and take a ritual steam bath together. Having gathered at the Petrovs, the guests now go back to the Ivanovs for the *chuloba* ritual. The first dish served is an omelette, which Vladimir tastes. Then he puts money in a glass of wine and gives it to Marya Ivanov to make it understood that he regards Marfa as "honorable." After this, the wedding guests return to the Petrovs for a second day of feasting. On the third day Marfa takes off her scarf, dances, and makes merry with the guests. The Petrovs playfully "test" her domestic skills by making her work hemp and then sweep. At first they throw litter under her broom, then money. After the third day of feasting there may be other parties given by relatives invited to the wedding in honor of the newly-weds. Marfa has now officially taken up residence with the Petrovs. But she and Vladimir will try to visit the Ivanovs on Sundays and holidays and especially during *Maslenitsa* (Shrovetide) week.[34] And so Vladimir and Marfa begin married life only after passing through elaborate rituals, richly loaded with symbols from the deep past. And however shabby the *izba* in which they live, their lives together will be symbolically rich.

After Marfa's wedding Ivan Ivanov feels increasingly unwell, and one morning Marya finds him lying in agony on his sleeping bench. She decides that he is dying, and summons Marfa and Sergei and a priest for the Orthodox last rites. In order to end Ivan's suffering they cut an opening in the wall of the *izba* (an old superstition).* When he finally dies, Andrei pulls his body over to the bench in the icon corner, pointing his head in the direction of the icons and his feet toward the outer door of the *izba*. Then he goes out to finish the coffin he had begun earlier. The Ivanovs dress Ivan's body in his best clothes and lay it in the coffin with his axe, a loaf of bread, and a lump of salt. Leaving the top of the coffin off, they carry it out of the *izba* through a window, taking care not to let it touch the house, so that no evil spirit might attach itself to the house or find its way back in through the front door. With Marya, Anya, and Marfa and a few close female relatives lamenting loudly all the way, they carry the

---

* In the Ukraine a dying man was laid on a straw pallet on the earthen floor so that he wouldn't "die hard." This suggests a belief in the soothing effect of Mother Earth. To prevent prolonged suffering the ridge (*konёk*) of the roof would be broken. The Ukrainians and Belorussians put a candle in the hands of a dying person, perhaps to light his way into the darkness of the beyond (Tokarev, p. 85, and W. R. S. Ralston, *Songs of the Russian People*, 2d. ed. [London, 1872], p. 314).

coffin to the cemetery, where it is buried with Orthodox rites. The priest performs these just before sunset; thus the sun can show Ivan's soul the way to his future abode in the dark beyond.

Back at home the Ivanovs set to work to purify the *izba*. They take the clothing in which Ivan died and his rag bedding to the henhouse. They burn the straw on which he lay, sweep the floor, and strew it with grain. They discard all the water that had been in the house at the time of his death. When the house is clean, the Ivanovs and a few close kin eat the funeral repast (*pominka*). Ivan's place at the table is left vacant, for the family believes his spirit to be still among them. The meal includes *blini, kisel'*, and *kut'ia* (a cereal dish with honey). The Ivanovs will pray for Ivan's soul on the ninth, twentieth, and fortieth days after his death, and again six months after his death. In addition they will remember him on the various days on the Church calendar set aside for the remembrance of the dead.[35] In these many ways the link between living and dead is strengthened and any negative feelings of the living toward the dead are discharged.

Thus the Russian peasant family endures through the cycle of birth, marriage, and death, each generation joining hands with the next. And though each knows he must die—Ivan, Marya, Andrei, Sergei, Marfa—each believes that the Ivanov family will endure, and he seeks to make it prosper.

Village Life

Beryozka, the village in which the Ivanovs live, is too small (eighty households) to have its own church, but large enough to constitute a commune (*mir, obshchina*). Andrei as head of household now represents the Ivanovs at the meeting (*skhod*) of the commune, usually held in the open air near the center of town. The village elder (*starosta*) and his assistants, chosen at the *skhod,* are part-time officials, not professional bureaucrats. Beryozka has its own smithy and tavern, but it is too small to support other commercial ventures. Thus the Ivanovs often make trips to the *selo* of Staritsa, a market town with a church, a resident clergy, parish school, *volost'* government center, fire station, general store, and marketplace, where the local fairs (*iarmarki*) are held.

The various households of Beryozka are largely self-sufficient, but they will cooperate on an ad hoc basis for particular projects and help households in unusual need. Such help (*pomochi*) is given gratis on Sundays or holidays to build a house for a family burned out of its *izba*, to gather crops for widows and orphans, to help families crippled by illness,* and to build a church. In the fall the women will process flax and hemp and mince cabbage cooperatively, and the men will brew beer together.

Another form of peasant cooperation is the *supriaga,* a union of two or more households for joint working of the land. This is particularly common in the south, where a heavy plow pulled by several pairs of work animals is needed: peasant households short of persons of working age or of the needed work animals are attracted to such an arrangement.[36]

Every vital event in the life of the Ivanov family, and every other family, is not only a matter of common knowledge but of common concern in Beryozka. In particular, a wedding is a big event for the village. If both bride and groom are from Beryozka the whole village might participate in the wedding.

When a young peasant is drafted, the whole village mourns him. He is expected to go on a drunken debauch until the date he is to report for duty. The village holds a *pechal'nyi pir* (sorrowful repast) for him, at which professional wailers bewail his loss in the name of his mother, wife, sisters, and other dear ones. After being blessed by his parents, the recruit is accompanied by a great crowd of peasants to the outskirts of the village.[37]

The people of Beryozka participate in a seasonal cycle of holidays and work common to Russian Orthodox peasants everywhere. One of the holidays is November 14—St. Philip's Day. The village is still discussing the wedding of the fall, but the splurge of celebrations is over: it is time for Philip's fast, which will end Christmas Eve. The men are threshing the last of the grain, hauling firewood, and mak-

---

* In time of illness the peasants might call a *koldun* (*koldun'ia*: scorerer, witch), whose "gift" is regarded as coming from an unclean source; or a *znakhar* (*znakharka*), whose "gift" is regarded as coming from God. These healers use some rational kinds of cure as well as the power of suggestion (*Narody Mira,* p. 411). (Modern medical care did not reach the villages until the *zemstvo* program late in the century.)

ing agricultural tools for the coming year. The women are finishing the processing of hemp.[38]

The Yuletide season is the first of two major winter holidays. In pre-Christian times it was probably a holiday celebrating the winter solstice, the time of rebirth of the sun. In the nineteenth century it lasted from *Rozhdestvenskii Sochel'nik* (December 24 evening) to *Kreshcheniia* (January 6). This holiday period was a time not only of merrymaking but of ritual activity to further the well-being of the family and insure an abundant harvest in the coming year.

On December 24 the Ivanovs go through their usual holiday preparations and make wax candles. The family will eat no regular meal during the day, but the women are working on a special Christmas Eve feast. Andrei clears away snow from the *izba* door, gets the sleigh ready, and goes to Staritsa to buy a fish for the family's Christmas dinner. Perhaps he will go to the woods and cut a little fir tree (*yolka*) to decorate.

The Christmas Eve meal is a rather serious family affair, joyous and peaceful. Under the tablecloth grains of all kinds of cereals are laid on the table in the shape of a cross. Andrei throws a handful of grain into the air saying, "Health for men, for cows, for sheep." The special dish of the evening is *kresty*—crosses of baked dough.[39]

The Yuletide season usually includes various parties, with characteristic games, caroling, and special dramatic presentations. The amount and complexity of celebration depends on the size and wealth of the community. One year when the harvest was good the well-to-do Vladimirov family, cousins of the Ivanovs in Staritsa, decided to give a big party on New Year's Eve, to which the Ivanovs and other cousins were invited. The Vladimirovs had a large, magnificently decorated *yolka*. The main dish of the evening was roast suckling pig, symbol of abundance and fertility. The other refreshments included fish jellied in aspic, jellied cold cuts, *pirogi,* slices of cold roast meat, *shchi* made with meat stock, chicken and noodles, milk, *kasha, kisel',* dumplings, and fruit compote with vodka, brandy, and beer.[40] The party games included Burial of the Gold. A gold ring was passed from hand to hand, and a girl in the center of the circle had to detect it. While passing the ring, the group sang that the ring had fallen among guelder roses, raspberrries, currants (symbols of a nubile girl), that it was hidden in dust, grown over with moss.[41] Fortune-telling was another feature of the party. The tail of the suckling pig was broken into pieces and distributed among the single people present. Then a dog was let into the room. It was foretold that the person whose piece was first devoured by the dog would be married within a year.[42]

In a gay mood the young people decided to go caroling to the homes of their friends. The carols (*koliadki*) included almost no Christian motifs: typically they invoked good harvest, wealth, luck. Singing such songs the carollers went from *izba* to *izba,* asking each master's permission to enter, honoring him with songs, and scattering grain on the listeners. Then they received previously prepared refreshments and sometimes a few coins.[43]

Yuletide ends on January 6. In Staritsa a cross-bearing procession from the church goes to an ice hole in the river, and the priest consecrates the waters. The more pious and hardy souls take a quick dip in the ice hole. During January the Ivanovs are forced to stay indoors much of the time to avoid the bitter sub-zero cold. Andrei finishes threshing grain and transporting hay from the meadow. Marya and Anya skim and store cream for use in the coming holiday cycle. In February the weather is still very severe. The family does handicraft work indoors.[44]

The second winter festival is *Maslenitsa* (Shrovetide, Carnival), which falls in late February or early March, the last week before the beginning of Lent. This celebration is dominated by symbols of the sun, and the festivities are probably pre-Christian ways to "help" the reanimating sun. The traditional dish is *blini*—round pancakes. At a safe distance from the village the peasants light bonfires and wheels of straw on poles. But the greatest diversion is sleighing, with special runs sometimes being constructed. The sleighs and horses (harnessed troika-style preferably) are decorated and driven in a circle around the village. Marfa and Vladimir come to Beryozka for a visit. The Ivanovs take fried eggs to the cemetery as offerings for Ivan and the other departed Ivanovs. The climax comes with the burning of a straw dummy representing "the spirit of Maslenitsa." First the peasants pull it on a sledge to the outskirts of the village, singing bawdy songs* and urging winter to depart. After setting the dummy afire they pull it apart with sticks, chasing each other with firebrands, tossing and scattering them.[45]

After Maslenitsa comes the Great Fast—Lent—which lasts the seven weeks preceding Easter. Lent is a time of preparation for spring work. Andrei repairs his tools and carts. In March the birds begin to come back from the south, and March 9 is the day of welcoming the birds and "calling" spring. Marya bakes some little birds made of dough, and Petka takes them to the field and tosses them into the air, crying "Fly to the field, bring health: first to the cows, second to the sheep, third to man!" The girls of the village form two choral groups and, imitating birds, ask spring to come. The women go out in the meadow, spread out a white linen cloth, place bread on it, and say, "This is for you, Mother Spring."[46]

As the snows thaw in March the ceiling of the Ivanov *izba* begins to leak badly. In April the ice on the rivers breaks up, and the upward roads become mud wallows. This is called the time of *rasputitsa* (roadlessness). The first greenery to be seen is the shoots of wheat or rye sown the previous autumn. Within ten days the scene may change from one of grey ice, snow, and slush, with yellow flattened grass, to one with tender green carpeting all around. The flowers blossom: lily-of-the-valley, cowslips, solomon's seal, the golden globe flower. The most beautiful of the flowering trees is the *cherëmukha* (black alder, bird cherry).[47]

Lent ends at midnight Easter Eve. The Ivanovs go to Staritsa for midnight mass, which culminates in joyous embracing among the people assembled. Christ is risen! Indeed he is risen! There are two distinctive Easter dishes served on Easter night and Easter day: *kulich,* a very rich bread, and *paskha,* a cylindrically shaped mixture of curds, eggs, and sweetening. And of course there are brightly colored Easter eggs, some of which the Ivanovs leave at the cemetery on Easter Sunday. Easter games include swinging on swings (an ancient rite thought to enhance fertility) and rolling the Easter eggs.

Following Easter are the seven most joyous weeks in the year, espe-

---

* Maslenitsa, like Shrovetide and Carnival, has overtones of a sexual orgy. See Y. M. Sokolov, *Russian Folklore* (New York, 1950), p. 187.

cially the seventh week (*Zelenie Sviatki, Russal'naia Nedel'ia*). The nubile boys and girls go outside the village to dance, sing *khorovody*, and play games, many of which are the same as the Yuletide games.[48]

But the Ivanovs are working, as well as celebrating the arrival of spring. In April they thresh the grain which will be used for sowing, and Andrei plows the field for spring crops. Andrei, who is now the *bol'shak,* does the sowing. To prevent the weeds from germinating he wears a clean garment. He carries the seed to the field in unfastened bast bags so that the soil will not "tie up" the seed. Sowing by hand, he puts in the spring wheat first. Then, when the ground is still very moist, he sows the oats. The women manure the kitchen garden and put in all their vegetable crops except garlic (sown in the fall). They sow cabbage in a special patch in a damp low place near the river, and put the potatoes in the spring crop area, as near to the village as possible.[49]

On April 23, the Day of Yegorii (Vlasia), who is the protector of domestic cattle, the Ivanovs join their neighbors for the blessing of the cattle. All the cattle are driven to the common pasture, where public prayers are conducted with consecration of water.[50] In May the women weed and thin the sprouts in the kitchen garden. Andrei sows the remaining oats, then hemp and flax. As soon as the spring floods are over, he works with his neighbors to repair the village bridge, badly damaged by the torrents. He also patches his roof and does other necessary repairs on the *izba*. In early June he sows buckwheat and barley. Then he takes manure to the fallow field and plows it in.[51]

Trinity Week (*Zelenie Sviatki*) is the climax of the spring holiday cycle. Instead of the Yuletide fir, the people of Beryozka honor the birch, symbol of reanimated nature. On Thursday or Saturday before Trinity Sunday the girls of Beryozka go into the woods to choose birch trees and garland each with flowers. They single out one birch and put fried eggs and beer under it. Joining hands in a circle, they sing and dance around it. Then they kiss each other through the garland on the trees, making oaths of friendship and adoption. On Trinity Sunday they will go back and look at the garlands. If a garland is withered, the girl who made it will marry in the coming year or die, they believe. If it is not wilted, the girl will stay a maiden. The garlands are then thrown into the river: if they don't sink, that means good luck.

During Trinity Week the peasants dig up a choice birch from the forest and plant it in the village. The young people of the village do a circle dance and play games around the tree. The peasants decorate their *izbas* and the church with birch, maple, and linden branches, flowers and fragrant herbs. They build bonfires and jump over them, and go bathing in the river.

Shortly after the summer solstice comes the Day of St. John Kupalo —June 24. The oldest person in Beryozka lights a bonfire by rubbing pieces of wood together, and the peasants go leaping over it. They drive their cattle over a bonfire of nettles to protect them from evil spirits, associated with the "waning" power of the sun. Some peasants go bathing in the river and sprinkle others with water. As during Trinity Week, the girls go through sister adoption rituals and throw garlands in the river to tell fortunes. The children play a game in which a woman called "Kostroma" plays dead, is mourned, and then suddenly jumps up and startles the children. The peasants make another straw dummy, which is buried with lamentations, torn to pieces, burned, or drowned. On the evening of June 24 the peasants look for a special fern in the forest which they think can help them find buried treasure. They also gather medicinal herbs, assuming the vegetation is now at its height and greatest medicinal potency.[52]

The Day of St. John Kupalo falls within the period of St. Peter's Fast, which lasts from Trinity Sunday (the seventh Sunday after Easter) until St. Peter's Day (June 29), three to six weeks in all. On the first Monday of Peter's Fast the peasants make a ceremonial farewell to spring. They construct a straw dummy, and after various rituals tear it apart and throw the straw to the wind.[53] St. Peter's Day, at the end of this period, is the last day of fun before the most grueling work of the year. The youths of Beryozka swing on swings in the woods, dance, and sing *khorovody*. As the sun sets they kneel or bow to it, saying, "Farewell, beautiful Spring, farewell! Come back quickly again." On this day the village presents its herders with oil, cottage cheese, eggs, and bread, as payment for services rendered.[54]

After St. Peter's Day the entire able-bodied population of Beryozka turns out to cut hay in the common meadow. The target for finishing the haymaking is July 8. The men do the cutting with scythes, the women rake the hay into heaps, and whole families work at putting it in shocks. The shocks are then placed on a platform to keep the hay from rotting. Once haymaking is done the men harrow the fallow fields and the women begin to reap cereals, starting with winter rye. Reaping is the hardest of women's work, and this period is called the time of *strada* (toil). Marya, as the senior able-bodied woman in the family, leads her daughter-in-law Anya to the field, bearing bread, salt, and a Christmas candle. As they reap the first sheaf they repeat, "*Stan' moi snop, na tysiachu kop*" ("Stand, my sheaf, for 60,000 sheaves"). The first sheaf, called the *imyaninnik,* they take home and place near the icons. They thresh it separately and either mix it with the seed corn for the next season or use it to fight cattle diseases.[55] The women leave the sheaves in the field to dry in the sun. When they are ready to harvest the hemp and the flax to be used for fiber the women do not cut them, but uproot them. They soak them a little to make them rot, and then crumple, swingle, and comb them.

The peasants take a rest from their toil on July 20, the Day of St. Ilya (Elijah), the protector of cattle. They gather at the church in Staritsa, where cattle are slaughtered and the meat is distributed to the poor and the parish clergy, as well as used for a common dinner of the people. The dinner meat is boiled in parish vats and laid out on long tables for all the adults of the parish. The priest blesses the beer (*kanunnoe pivo*) that the peasants have brewed especially for this day. Then they drink beer and eat *pirogi* at a picnic in the meadow.[56]

The women continue harvesting through August, taking in barley, wheat, oats, and buckwheat. Meanwhile the men thresh grain for family use and sow winter wheat and rye (which will sprout in early spring). On August 18, the day of Floris and Lauris, they drive the horses to an outdoor chapel to be blessed and sprinkled with holy water.[57] On the night of August 31 the people of Beryozka extinguish all their fires; on the morning of September 1, they relight them ritually.* The girls make small coffins of turnips and other vegetables, enclose flies and other insects in them, and bury them with laments.[58]

---

* These customs of August 31–September 1 are probably vestiges of the period 1348–1700, when the New Year was celebrated at this time of year.

In late August or early September Marya and Anya, with Andrei's
help, finish the reaping. As they approach the end they roll or somer-
sault over the field saying,

> Stubble of the summer grain,
> Give back my strength
> For the long winter.[59]

While this is being said, a pregnant woman or a priest in full vest-
ments is put in a cart and driven across the field. All work together
on the last strip of oats. A few stalks are left standing and Marya, the
oldest person in the family, twists them tight, saying *"Vot tebe Ilya,
boroda, a ty poi i kormy moego dobrogo konia"* ("This is for you,
Ilya, the beard, but the feed and mash of my dear horse"). The reference to the beard, possessed by the billy goat as well as men, is probably connected with the primitive Eurasian belief that the spirit of the
harvest is a billy goat, or a goat-like creature, that is pursued by the
reapers and hides in the last unreaped sheaf. When Marya twists or
knots the stalks of this sheaf she is "plaiting the beard of Ilya," and
thus protecting the harvest. She leaves bread and salt at the unreaped
patch, and it is taboo. Then the Ivanovs take the last sheaf of oats
home ceremoniously and put it under the icon of Floris and Lauris
until Pokrov Day, October 1, after which they feed it to the livestock.[60]

The grueling work continues in the month of September. The men
complete the sowing of winter wheat and rye and begin to thresh the
harvested grain. (If the weather has been dry the sheaves have dried
in the field and are ready for threshing. But if it has not, in October
and November the Ivanovs have to put them in the upper room of
their *ovin* [drying shed, or oven]. They start a fire in the lower room,
and the heat, rising through an opening, dries the damp sheaves during the night so they are ready for threshing in the morning.) The
Ivanovs have a covered threshing floor. Since they have only three
threshers in the family, they form a labor pool with their neighbors,
the Vasilievs. After threshing comes winnowing, which they do with
shovels, and cleaning of the grain by sifting. They then take the
threshed grain to the local watermill for processing into flour and
groats, after which they store it in their log granary (*zhitnitsa*).[61]

The women meanwhile are doing additional chores. Marya and

Anya are processing hemp and flax, harvesting the kitchen garden, shearing the sheep, and slaughtering some geese (September 15) and chickens (November 1). Many peasants brew beer in September and October; Andrei attends a beer bust for men only.[62] In October Andrei collects and chops firewood for the winter, while the women process hemp. The Ivanovs can now relax and celebrate. Food is abundant, and there are several weddings in Beryozka.

But soon the snows will be upon them. It is time to repair the chinking of the *izba* walls and straighten the shutters. As the roads turn to rivers of mud once again the Ivanovs feel ready for the long winter ahead: the firewood it cut, the granary is full, and there is flax, hemp, and wool fiber ready for spinning and weaving. The geese have left; it is time to climb up on the *pech'* and wait for spring.

Conclusion

The Russian peasant way of life represents a skillful adaptation to a harsh environment. The peasant family could survive the long, frigid winters of Russia only with great toil and careful management, given the backward technology of 1860. What the family dreaded most was infertility: crop failure, barrenness in livestock, lack of children. What it revered above all was fertility, which meant life and the continuation of the family. The individual Russian peasant sought immortality through the survival of his offspring.

The Russian peasants acted out the drama of life in a world whose central focus was the church in the *selo*. The church was the meeting place for heaven, earth, and the world underground. From heaven to the altar and down into the crypt: this was the peasant *axis mundi*. But there was a secondary axis for each peasant family, which passed through its own *izba*.

Within the village and in the surrounding fields the peasants felt secure. But as they moved out into the dark forest, the world became increasingly chaotic and menacing. "Out there" were the *leshii* and his companion, the bear, as well as wolves and other carnivores. But the forest also had treasures which could be gathered in summer: berries, nuts, mushrooms, medicinal herbs, flowers. In the forest there were also bark for *lapti* and fuel for the winter. Going into a forest, as well as sailing down a river, meant adventure.

The peasants tended to regard time as cyclical, passing through an

endless round of death and rebirth. The cyclical pattern was most evident in the recurrent seasons. They tried to hasten the end of an "old"
season and give birth to a new one by various ancient rituals: destroying or burying a dummy representing the spirit of the old season,
lighting "new" fires, leaping over bonfires, bathing ritually, staging
contests, caroling, and engaging in wild orgies of drinking.

The lifetime of the peasant contained critical moments celebrated
in ritual. One was birth, celebrated both by baptism and *razmyvka*.
Then there were complicated wedding rituals that were dedicated to
fertility. Finally there were funeral rituals that served to purify the
home from the "pollution" of death, and to stress the sacred union of
living and dead. Life was thus an endless round of birth, death, rebirth. And this round took place in a cosmos of concentric circles with
a symbolic sacred axis at the center. This center was the church in the
selo: Moscow and the tsar were far away.

2. The Peasant and the Emancipation

Terence Emmons

On March 30, 1856 (old style), a short while after the signing of the Treaty of Paris that had ended Russia's disastrous involvement in the Crimean War, Alexander II went to Moscow and pronounced before the assembled gentry* of that province the historic words:

You yourselves know that the existing order of ruling over living souls cannot remain unchanged. It is better to abolish serfdom from above than to await the day when it will begin to abolish itself from below.[1]

In thus expressing a thought that his father, Nicholas I, had long held but upon which he had, for a variety of reasons, failed to take definitive action, Alexander II set in motion the preparation of the emancipation legislation that was signed into law five years later. First, a "secret committee" of state dignitaries was formed to discuss reform; then, beginning in November 1857, the landed gentry of the Empire were invited to gather in provincial committees to draw up local emancipation projects; and in early 1859 the "editing commissions," a much larger body than the "secret committee" set about the task of drafting the legislation. The statutes, after review by the State Council, were signed into law by the Emperor on February 19, 1861, the anniversary of his coronation.

The emancipation removed some 23,000,000 peasants from servile bondage to the nearly 104,000 gentry landowners on whose estates they lived.† As a legal order, serfdom in Russia was not, on the eve

* In this paper, the term "gentry," or "landed gentry," is used to designate the noble land- and serf-owning class, as distinct from the general status of "noble" or "nobility" (*dvorianin/dvorianstvo*); it is also used interchangeably with the Russian term *pomeshchik* ("estate-owner").

† According to the "Tenth Revision" (1858–1859), the total serf population in Russia was about 22,700,000, or 30.7 per cent of the total population of the Empire at that time (74,000,000).

of its abolition, a decrepit survival of a once viable system. It was, rather, a rigid system of personal dependency that very nearly approached the "peculiar institution" so far as the legal status of the serf was concerned. Moreover, this system had become more, not less, rigid during the last century or so of its existence. Although the state had acted in the first half of the century to remove some of the more flagrant slavery-like practices, such as the advertised public sale of peasants taken from the land and the splitting up of peasant families at auction, the general result of the expansion of the bureaucratic administration over this period, especially at the provincial level (where gentry estates had been created and had been given general administrative functions), was to make gentry domination over the peasants ever more encompassing. Serfdom was, in fact, the "law of the land," and all state institutions—the courts, the schools, the army, the tax system—were organized in accordance with it. Such a system, as Tsagolov[2] and other scholars have pointed out, could be abolished only by an act of the state.

The same was true of serfdom as an economic system.* Russian land relations under serfdom resembled neither those of France before 1789, where most peasant obligations had been commuted to quitrent and there was little demesne land, nor those under the East Elbian Junkers, where an active and rapidly expanding gentry entrepreneurial economy was encroaching on peasant holdings. The situation in Russia was especially complicated.† There was demesne land, but in a real sense and with relatively few exceptions there was no such thing as "gentry farming" in Russia before 1861. There was only peasant farming. The situation that Michael Confino found prevalent at the end of the eighteenth century[3] still held true for the mass of gentry estates in the mid-nineteenth century: there was a peasant

---

* In Russian scholarship, a distinction is traditionally drawn between "serf law" (*krepostnoe pravo*) and "serf economy" (*krepostnoe khoziaistvo*).

† Alexander Gerschenkron has aptly remarked that in any case involving the gentry's retention of demesne lands that are cultivated by the peasants, the untying of the economic knot of serfdom must be a very complicated process, since the economies of the peasants and their lords are closely bound one with the other; problems of labor supply and capital must be resolved. "Agrarian Policies and Industrialization, Russia 1861–1917," in *Cambridge Economic History of Europe,* Vol. VI, part 2 (Cambridge, 1965), pp. 712–13.

economy, with all the land, both demesne and peasant allotments, parcelled and worked in traditional fashion by the peasants, who provided all the equipment and livestock. Most gentry estates, whether small or large, were worked in this way, so that there was no large-scale farming, only agglomerates of peasant operations.

There were, of course, regional variations in the serf economy and in the way in which peasants fulfilled their obligations. Demesne production and its accompanying labor obligations (*barshchina*) were extensive in the fertile black-soil provinces of central Russia, along the Volga, in the fertile southern-steppe provinces, in Belorussia, and especially in the Ukraine. Quitrent (*obrok*) either predominated or nearly equaled *barshchina* in the relatively infertile non-black-soil provinces of north central Russia, where the nonagricultural sector of the economy had expanded considerably since the eighteenth century. In addition, on many estates the peasants owed obligations in both *obrok* and *barshchina*. (For the Empire as a whole, *barshchina* predominated, but in many "Great Russian" provinces the balance between the two forms of obligations was nearly equal.)

The state took upon itself the dual task of sundering the bonds of servile dependence and untangling the extremely complicated economic situation. The one could be accomplished with fair rapidity; the other demanded a long-range plan for the gradual extinguishing of peasant obligations and for the division of property. There were two overriding considerations in the state's decision to bring about emancipation: a concern for economic development, and a desire to ensure social and political stability. Both considerations were accentuated by the Russian defeat in the Crimean War. It was clearly understood by Alexander II and by the "enlightened bureaucrats," who were the actual architects of the reform, that the Crimean defeat was a direct result of Russia's general economic and technological backwardness, and it was believed that the main obstacle to overcoming this backwardness was the existence of serfdom.

It has often been remarked that the government's attitude toward industrialization—in particular the creation of large factory centers—was at best ambiguous, because of the fear of creating a "landless proletariat," the danger of which had been demonstrated most recently in the European events of 1848.[4] In the government's view, however, it was not industrial development alone that presented the possibility of strengthening the material basis of state power. As always, the government was seeking new sources of state revenues, especially at this time, when the treasury had been depleted by the enormous expansion of the army and administration under Nicholas I and by the costs of the war. Thus, improvement of Russia's predominantly agrarian economy was a major concern, and in prevailing thought, which was heavily indebted to the doctrines of economic liberalism, such improvement was predicated on the abolition of serfdom.[5]

It was, however, concern for the maintenance of social and political stability, expressed partly in fear of peasant unrest, that was uppermost in the minds of the Emperor and his advisers. This fear had haunted Nicholas I throughout his reign, and serious peasant disorders during the Crimean War[6] had impressed the government with the debilitating effects of serfdom on the waging of military campaigns. From the beginning to the end of the reform's preparation, the official explanation for the emancipation was that it had been made necessary by the deterioration of relations between the peasants and their gentry masters.* In any event, it was surely this concern more than any

* This was mentioned in Alexander's speech to the Moscow gentry in 1856, which opened the preparation of the reform, and in the manifesto of emancipation, which closed it in 1861. In a recent study that came to my attention after this article had been written, Alfred J. Rieber argues that "military reform provided the decisive impetus for freeing the serfs," and, specifically, that it was the realization that a modern army with trained reserves could be developed only on the basis of a free population which led to the emancipation. Rieber produces persuasive evidence for the importance of this consideration, at least for Alexander II personally; but he overstates the case by essentially discounting the importance of broader social, political, and economic issues. Although, as he correctly observes, no one in the government at that time, least of all Alexander II, thought in terms of state-led economic development in the modern sense, the fact remains that the state had a very long experience in manipulating the social and economic structure of the country with an eye to increasing revenues for military expenditures. Moreover, although Rieber is certainly correct in criticizing the view that emancipation was provoked by frantic fear of imminent peasant rebellion, the fact also remains that, in educated Russian society as a whole, serfdom was looked upon as an (at least) potentially dangerous social anachronism separating Russia from the societies of Western Europe. Thus, although the shock of the Crimean defeat to the state's *amour propre* and the damage to its military stance in Europe were of primary importance as an impetus to reform, it seems doubtful that the reassessment called forth by the defeat was cast—even in Alexander II's mind—solely in terms of

other that shaped the character of the reform legislation. In this respect the emancipation was looked upon as a conservative measure above all.

The history of agrarian reform in Central Europe was well known in Russian governmental circles, and the main lesson drawn from this history was that the state must, at all cost, avoid the creation of a "landless proletariat" as a result of the emancipation.[7] The government therefore set about at the outset to provide the machinery that would, it was believed, allow an orderly and gradual untying of the economic relations of serfdom. The aim was to preserve social and political stability by making landowners of the peasants, while at the same time safeguarding the interests of the gentry, and maintaining the general economic and fiscal stability of the state.

According to the emancipation legislation, the peasants* were freed in their rural communities (sel'skie obshchestva). For two years after the emancipation proclamation they were to remain essentially under the old order so that land charters (ustavnye gramoty) could be drawn up on each estate according to established rules. Until nine years after the proclamation, the peasants were to be obliged to remain on their allotments, paying obrok or barshchina for their use. In theory, they were to be free to leave after that date, but in practice they could not even then, except in rare instances, leave the land. They were bound by their communities, which needed every peasant to share the responsibility of the obligations that fell to the community as a whole (krugovaia poruka). Departure required payments that were impossible for all but a few peasants. For most peasants, the only escape from the "temporary-obligatory" status of land-users (which was given no time limit) was through the concerted redemp-

---

providing a social fabric capable of supporting a system of universal, short-term military conscription. See Alfred J. Rieber, ed., *The Politics of Autocracy: Letters of Alexander II to Prince A. I. Bariatinskii, 1857–1864* (Paris and The Hague, 1966), pp. 15–58.

* Excluding the household serfs (dvorovye liudi), who numbered about a million and a half. They were freed by special arrangements, without land. (Only a very general description of the legislation as it affected the majority of the peasants is given here. For a more detailed description in English of the complex body of legislation, see P. Lyashchenko, *History of the National Economy of Russia to the 1917 Revolution* [New York, 1949], pp. 376–402.)

tion of allotments by whole communities. Redemption was voluntary for the estate owner (*pomeshchik*), but mandatory for the peasants if their former master chose this solution. Redemption was guaranteed by the state, which upon the conclusion of redemption agreements was to pay 80 per cent (in some cases 75 per cent) of the capital value of the redeemed allotments to the *pomeshchik,* partly in interest-bearing bonds, partly in immediately exchangeable credit paper. The remainder was to be paid directly by the peasant communities through private agreement with the estate owner, but only if redemption were agreed to by them. If not, the *pomeshchik* was left with the government certificates only. The peasants were to redeem their allotments by payments to the state extended over a period of 49 years.

With allowance for considerable regional variations, it can be said that the legislation provided that the peasants were to retain about the same *obrok* obligations as before the reform during the "temporary-obligatory" period, but that their allotments were to be generally reduced in size (about 16 per cent on the average for European Russia as a whole).* *Barshchina* obligations were standardized at 40 days of "male labor" and 30 days of "female labor" per household annually for the maximum allotment. Since it was actually peasant obligations, or annual gentry income, that were redeemed, and not simply the value of the land, the yearly redemption payment of the peasant remained the same as his *obrok* dues, the latter being capitalized at 6 per cent to arrive at the redemption figure.

For all practical purposes the *pomeshchik* was deprived of direct authority over his peasants, and the peasants were to be "self-governing" in their communities and in *volosti* (constituting several peasant communities), which were the basic administrative units of peasant self-government. Freed from the direct control of the *pomeshchiki,* the peasants were to be subjected to the authority of the peace mediators (*mirovye posredniki*) and other government officials who had wide powers of both formal and ad hoc nature over the organs of peasant administration. The elders of the communities and *volosti,*

---

* According to the first post-emancipation land survey (1877–78), the ex-landlords' peasants in 44 provinces held a total of 33,755,658 *desiatinas* of land. The total holdings of the gentry in the Empire were 73,163,774 *desiatinas.*

who exercised general administrative and police authority over their electors, were themselves to be directly responsible to the peace mediators and the district (*uezd*) authorities. The peace mediators were to be appointed by the government from lists of candidates drawn up by the local gentry.

Thus did the government attempt to have its proverbial cake and eat it too—to untie the bonds of personal servitude and set out on the path toward eventual creation of a landowning peasantry without overstraining state finances or disturbing social tranquillity, and at the same time to provide for the gentry. Its policies in fact kept the peasants bound to the land, so that the gentry would be assured a source of income and labor during the "temporary-obligatory" period and the state would be assured proper payment of taxes and obligations then and during redemption. Redemption was made voluntary for the *pomeshchik* rather than obligatory for all, in the belief that this would permit a gradual transition from the temporary status to the final solution without unduly straining the state finances.

In the rest of this paper particular attention will be given to an examination of the response to emancipation by the group most directly affected by it: the landlord's peasants. The focus will be primarily on the years 1861–62, the "waiting period" between the emancipation proclamation and the onset of the "temporary-obligatory" phase— the time during which the peasants were forced to accommodate their various expectations to the reality of the reform legislation. In view of the fact that an understanding of peasant response to the emancipation in these years is impossible without some knowledge of the character of these expectations, an effort will be made to describe their development in the years preceding 1861.

The "specter of Pugachev" loomed large over the reform deliberations in the first years of the reign of Alexander II. Both within the government and among the landed gentry the threat of a *Pugachevshchina* (peasant war) was invoked with almost tiresome frequency by abolitionists and conservatives alike.[8]

Most students of Russian history are familiar with the figures, gathered by Ignatovich from the files of the Ministry of Interior, that show the mounting frequency of peasant disturbances during the reign of Nicholas I.* Although most disturbances over this period resulted from peasant refusal to fulfill the traditional obligations (especially *barshchina* duties), the seriousness and occasionally violent nature of peasant action could not be ignored: according to government records, 144 *pomeshchiki* were murdered by their serfs between 1835 and 1854. Of great significance, from the government's point of view, was the fact that these disturbances involved, with mounting frequency, rumors of liberation. Such rumors had been connected with a rash of peasant disturbances in 1826, at the time of Nicholas's coronation. By 1841 the Chef de Gendarmes, Count Benkendorf, was warning Nicholas I: "The idea of the liberation of the peasants spreads among them [the peasants] without ceasing. These dark ideas of the *muzhiki* are becoming more and more widespread, and promise something bad."[9] Ignatovich found that although the specific cause of most disturbances over this period could be traced to concrete peasant complaints (increased obligations, transfer to poor land, etc.), an effort to gain liberation underlay nearly half of them.†

By the late 1840's, rumors about impending emancipation or particular ways of winning liberation were affecting the lives of thousands of peasants. In 1847, a year of drought and hunger in Vitebsk province, rumors that liberation could be achieved by volunteering for work on railroad construction or by resettlement elsewhere prompted thousands of peasants in that province to leave their estates

* I. Ignatovich, "Krest'ianskie volneniia," in *Velikaia reforma. Russkoe obshchestvo i krest'ianskii vopros v proshlom i v nastoiashchem,* III (Moscow, 1911), 41–65. Ignatovich found that disturbances of sufficient seriousness to be brought to the attention of the Ministry of Interior had occurred on 674 estates over the period 1826–1854, or on 23 per year on the average. She also found that the frequency of disturbances increased noticeably in the 1840's, then fell off in the first four years of the 1850's. Apparently, the heightened frequency in the 1840's, especially the late 1840's, involved the western provinces primarily, where Polish agitation, the influence of the Galician peasant uprising of 1846, and preparation of "inventories" (regulated peasant-gentry relations) contributed to unrest. Conversely, the relative decline in the frequency of disturbances in the early 1850's was attributable especially to the falling off of unrest in these areas that came with the amelioration of the peasants' lot after the introduction of the "inventories."

† As Ignatovich expresses it, many disturbances occurred "either on the basis of rumors about liberation or on the basis of false or real rights to liberation" ("Krest'-ianskie volneniia," p. 49).

without permission. The government intervened with troops and economic assistance, and eventually some six thousand peasants were returned.

In 1854–56, rumors about liberation connected with the Crimean War swept throughout the country. In 1854 and 1855, calls for volunteers for the navy and army resulted in rumors that these volunteers would be freed at the end of the war. Many thousands of peasants, from at least a dozen provinces, but especially in the south, responded to these rumors by quitting the land and seeking the opportunity to enlist. The government, hard-pressed as it was for men to carry on the war, had to use valuable troops to put down these movements and return the peasants to their villages. Although it is impossible to judge their extent or influence, stories also circulated among the peasants during the war that the English and the French wanted to emancipate them.[10] In 1856, after the termination of hostilities, a rumor began to circulate that peasants were being summoned to resettle the devastated Crimea as free men. In the southern provinces of Ekaterinoslav and Kherson, near the Crimea, this rumor resulted in a massive movement of some twelve thousand peasants out of their villages, a movement that had to be brought under control by military commands. Repercussions on a much smaller scale were felt in at least nine other provinces.[11]

Whether or not increasing peasant unrest in the decades before emancipation can be ascribed ultimately to worsening conditions, produced in part by population growth and in part by increased burdens placed on the peasants by their gentry masters, is a subject of complex controversy that cannot be dwelt on here.[12] However, most —but by no means all—scholars believe that peasant obligations (especially *obrok*) had been significantly increased, both absolutely and in relation to peasant income, since the end of the eighteenth century. One thing is clear: the peasants were becoming increasingly aroused by the prospect of emancipation, and the spread of rumors about liberation had become a force that caused the government ever-increasing concern. This became especially obvious in the 1854–56 disturbances. At the same time, there can be little doubt that, as some contemporary landowners claimed, growing peasant unrest and growing tension between the peasants and the gentry were at least in part attributable to the government's piecemeal moves toward emancipation during preceding decades. The "law on free cultivators" (1803),* the emancipation of the Baltic peasants (1816–19), the "law on obligated peasants" (1842),† the edict allowing peasants to purchase their freedom if the estates on which they lived were sold at auction (1847)—these and other measures, as well as a good deal of "secret" discussion of emancipation under Nicholas, modest as their results may have been, were the ultimate sources of the rumors of impending liberation.

According to the compilations of the Third Section, the number of peasant disturbances calling for the interference of "higher government authorities or the use of military commands" rose during the years of the reform's formal preparation from 86 in 1858, to 90 in 1859, and to 108 in 1860.[13] These figures were greater than for preceding years (not counting the extraordinary movements of 1854–56), being approached only by the year 1848, in which 70 disturbances were reported by roughly the same kind of count.[14] To some extent these statistical increases merely reflected the growing nervousness of government officials, but undoubtedly rumors about the promised emancipation contributed to peasant unrest. It was widely believed, for example, that the Tsar had already declared the peasants free, but that the *chinovniki,* or officials, and the *pomeshchiki* were not allowing the transmission of this news. The large majority of disturbances in any year continued to result from peasant refusal to fulfill obligations, especially *barshchina.*[15] Also, numerous attempts by the gentry to reduce peasant allotments, to transfer peasants to poorer lands, or to otherwise increase their demesne lands in anticipation of emancipation, must have had their effect on the rate of peasant disturbances.[16] (So frequent were such activities that the government found it necessary to issue an edict forbidding further transfers of peasants or reductions in their allotments.)

---

* The "law on free cultivators" provided for the voluntary emancipation of serfs with land by their owners.

† The "law on obligated peasants" provided for voluntary redemption, as in the 1803 legislation, but, instead of requiring the *pomeshchik* to part with land in the process, it provided for the regulated use of land by the peasants in a semi-indentured state.

As noted earlier, during the years of the reform's preparation Alexander II and his officials profoundly feared the possibility of a peasant rebellion. Experience with the force of rumors on the peasants in recent years had led them to believe that announcement of the November Rescript would produce massive disorders.[17] The relatively modest absolute increase in the rate of disturbances did not justify their fears. Government reports testified to a remarkable and unexpected passivity of the peasants throughout the period of reform preparations (November 1857 to February 1861). The official report of the Third Section for 1858 read in part as follows:

Not one disorder has taken on significant proportions or continued for long. Although the instances of disobedience were in sum rather many, in the vast Empire they are scarcely noticeable.... One can say that general calm has been preserved, and that incomparably fewer disorders have so far taken place than were expected and predicted.[18]

It would appear, then, that the government fears of peasant unrest were related less to the immediate state of peasant activities than to a number of other factors—the ever-present "specter of Pugachev"; recent impressions, such as the bloody peasant rebellion in neighboring Galicia in 1846;[19] the disorders among the peasants in the last years of the Crimean War; and, most of all, apprehension about the possible response of the peasantry to the emancipation.

Alexander II and the planners of the reform had good reason to be apprehensive about the way in which the peasants would greet the reform, for they knew well that the emancipation they were planning bore little resemblance to the aspirations of the peasants. The latter tended toward considerable and unrealistic extremes. Peasant speculation about emancipation inclined toward a belief that all the land would be theirs, free of charge or obligations, and that all responsibilities toward the *pomeshchiki*, and even toward the state, would come to an end. Even before the November Rescript, reports of the following kind (a conversation overheard on an estate) were coming into the central office of the Third Section:

First peasant: They say that we will soon be free.
Second peasant: Probably like the state peasants?
First peasant: No, that's just it—completely free: They won't demand

either recruits or taxes; and there won't be any kind of authorities. We will run things ourselves.[20]

By the end of 1858, the Chef de Gendarmes was reporting, in the same memorandum in which he had referred to the unexpected passivity of the peasants, that

Many understand freedom in the sense of freebooters,* others think that the land belongs to them as much as to the *pomeshchiki,* and are even more convinced that their houses and homesteads belong to them.[21]

Similar reports were contained in numerous communications from the provinces during this period. One of the basic arguments of liberal abolitionists of the day, whose platform was predicated on the necessity of emancipating the peasants with their plots, was that the peasants, whatever the law said, considered this land to be theirs.[22] Their description of peasant beliefs was probably too conservative: it was widely believed among the peasants that they would be given not only their allotments but all the estate-lands, and without any charge.[23]

On the basis of such reports, the Emperor and his advisers were not optimistic about how the peasants might react to the news of the terms of emancipation, and they grew increasingly uneasy as the day of the emancipation proclamation approached, despite the relative calm that prevailed in the countryside.† Under these circumstances, the military-bureaucratic mind turned naturally to the elaboration of plans for a military response to disorder. One of the first such plans was elaborated early in 1858 by General Rostovtsev, later head of the editing commissions, who was virtually obsessed by fear of a *Pugachevshchina.* He proposed the appointment of special military governors-general for the provinces, to be given extraordinary powers during the period of the reform's promulgation. Although provisionally approved by Alexander II, this plan was ultimately rejected because

---

* *Vol'nitsy:* Literally, the groups of runaway serfs who, like the cossacks, established themselves on the borderlands of the Russian state.

† Early in 1858, Alexander, commenting on the peasant mood, wrote: "Now, of course, the people are calm in anticipation, but when their expectations about freedom, in the sense that they understand it, are not realized, who can say what then will be?" (*Velikaia reforma,* V, 165).

of opposition from the Ministry of Interior, which jealously guarded its own authority.[24]

Rostovtsev's project was followed by numerous plans developed in the War Ministry for handling possible disturbances during promulgation of the reform. Military resources and forces were reviewed throughout the Empire, special instructions were sent out to army commanders in the field, and an elaborate plan for suppression of rebellion in the capitals was devised.[25] Although the Rostovtsev plan was not adopted, high-ranking officers were dispatched on the eve of emancipation, one to each province, for the purpose of ensuring the maintenance of order during the reform's proclamation and promulgation. To this end they were empowered to command all civil authorities and military forces in the provinces. They were also directed to report regularly and in detail directly to the Emperor on their actions and on general conditions in the provinces.[26]

In addition to these military precautions, the government sought to ensure the speedy assumption of their duties by those officials who were to be charged, after the proclamation, with the maintenance of social order and the preparation of the peasants for entrance into the "temporary-obligatory status," i.e., the peace mediators and the peasant officials (the *volost'* and communal leaders),* who would be subject to the mediators' authority. Plans for the speedy institution of the *uezd* and provincial offices, which would coordinate and supervise the work of the peace mediators, were also developed.[27]

Finally, the government took the trouble to release the emancipation proclamation† through the Church: the manifesto was written in pious and archaic language by the Metropolitan Filaret, and was read for the first time to the peasants by their parish priests. Although the legislation was signed into law on February 19, the anniversary

---

* The *volost'* institutions had to be created from scratch and their officials—elders, deputies, and judges—elected by the participating peasant communities. In many cases the elected officials at the communal level had to be newly elected also, since the new "village-community" did not always coincide with the traditional commune (*obshchina*). Even though peasant officials were elected by the peasants themselves, from the government's point of view—especially at this time—they were regarded primarily as instruments for controlling and disciplining the peasants. They were the links that connected peasant Russia with bureaucratic Russia.

† Not to be confused with the statutes of emancipation, which were also publicly released.

of the Emperor's coronation, the manifesto—laden with reminders to the peasants of their responsibilities and of the gentry's generosity and right to remuneration—was made public only at the beginning of the Lenten season when, it was assumed, the peasants would be in a properly submissive mood for clerical exhortation, and would also be abstaining from alcohol.*

The government's concern over how the peasants would respond to the emancipation proclamation was well-justified. The reports of the officers sent into the provinces, numerous other official communications,[28] and private memoirs reveal quite clearly the manner in which most peasants responded to the terms of emancipation. A typical description was given by V. A. Artsimovich, then governor of Kaluga province:

The first impression made by the manifesto and the Statutes can be described in several words: a preliminary, involuntary, and short-lived joy, afterwards heavy incomprehension and sorrowful disenchantment.... The people took from the church the impression that their hopes had not been realized. They had expected full and unencumbered freedom, and, in the bargain, free allotment of land, which, in the words of the peasants, they had *earned* by long acquittal of obligations. The people took leave of this hope with such reluctance, that at first they were more inclined to think in terms of a deceit or forgery than to think of rejecting their beloved dream.[29]

Immediately following the proclamation of emancipation, peasant disorders on an unprecedented scale began to be reported from practically all the provinces. According to one count, more than 1,300 disturbances of one sort or another were reported throughout the Empire for the first five months of 1861 (primarily in March, April, and May), 718 of which led to armed intervention by government troops.† (According to the records of the General Staff, for the period of

---

* See P. A. Zaionchkovskii, *Provedenie v zhizn' Krest'ianskoi reformy 1861 g.* (Moscow, 1958), pp. 49–64, for a description of the mechanics of the reform's proclamation. The manifesto was first read in the provinces on March 7, the first day of Lent. (It was read in the two capitals on Sunday, March 5.) Several weeks passed before the manifesto and the statutes reached all the provinces.

† *Krest'ianskoe dvizhenie v Rossii v 1857–mae 1861 gg.* (Moscow, 1963), p. 736. The following were counted as "disturbances" (*volneniia*): "Refusal [of peasants] to fulfill *barshchina* obligations, and nonsubmission to *pomeshchiki*; resistance against the authorities and army commands; seizure of lands and property of the *pomeshchiki*,

March through May 1861, there were 47 battalions, 187 infantry companies, 38½ cavalry squadrons, and 3,000 cossacks participating directly in the suppression of peasant disturbances.)[30]

The nature of these peasant disturbances following the proclamation should not be misunderstood. They were provoked by general confusion and disappointment with the terms of emancipation. In no case, however, were they organized movements, nor did any of them involve the expression of revolutionary demands. Violence was rare, even when troops were called out. Rather, the disturbances consisted, in their overwhelming majority, of passive refusal to continue to carry out the traditional obligations to the *pomeshchiki*, as called for during the two-year preparatory period. For the peasants at large, without any doubt, "emancipation" meant first of all abolition of *barshchina*, and it was simply incomprehensible to them that it should continue after the emancipation was proclaimed.

The peasants were not at all ready to give up their optimistic expectations of what the emancipation would consist of; and what Governor Artsimovich, in the quotation cited above, said of the peasants in his province—that they were "more inclined to think in terms of a deceit or forgery than to think of rejecting their beloved dream" —was true of the peasantry throughout the country. Many peasants at first concluded that the manifesto and the statutes had not been explained to them adequately; later on they decided that the manifesto was false, and that the true one was being suppressed by the *pomeshchiki* and the *chinovniki*.

The peasants' first response—their belief that the manifesto and statutes needed only to be read correctly in order to reveal the "real freedom" that had been granted the peasants by the Emperor—was by far the more important of the two, especially during the troubled spring of 1861. The results of this belief were concisely summed up by the head of the Third Section in his report for 1861:

---

etc." Cases of murder, physical violence, and runaways were not included, but they constituted an insignificant minority of total reported difficulties. It is remarkable that in the period of most intense peasant activity—from March to the end of May in 1861—only one case of assault was reported, and no murders of *pomeshchiki* were committed, although (as will be seen below) the *pomeshchiki* were generally blamed for perverting or hiding the "real freedom" (*Ibid.,* pp. 418–21, 736).

The majority of peasants had hoped to receive complete freedom from obligatory obligations to the *pomeshchiki* and free allotment of land. Not understanding sufficiently the new measures, they turned for explanation to priests, sextons, retired soldiers, and various semiliterate persons. But of these, some, because of their lack of education..., could not give advice, and others, for personal gain, tried to accommodate themselves to the wish of the peasants, and interpreted the measures in an incorrect way. This gave the peasants occasion to shun their former obligations, to mistrust the *pomeshchiki* and local authorities and finally to give themselves up to willfulness.[31]

Descriptions of the various forms that peasant "willfulness" took can be found in the recently published "chronicles" that describe in their chronological order the peasant disturbances recorded by local government agents over the period extending from February 1861 to February 1863.[32] In March, April, and May of 1861, at least 49 cases either of collective refusals to continue fulfilling obligations or of other irregular behavior—some involving thousands of peasants, others single villages—were reported to have been connected explicitly with interpretations of the legislation "in the spirit of peasant demands," that is, with the refusal to accept the interpretations or summaries of the legislation initially read to the peasants by their village priests.[33]

Illustrative of this type of peasant disturbance was the tragic "Bezdna Affair," which occurred in April 1861, in a village of Kazan province. The outcome of this affair was a uniquely large amount of bloodshed; in all other respects it was typical. The peasants of this village had fully anticipated that the proclamation would give them the "real freedom" they desired. According to the report of the president of the investigating commission that was formed to study the Bezdna tragedy, the peasants reasoned in the following manner upon hearing the manifesto read:

They sent no books [i.e., proclamations] to our fathers and grandfathers, and they knew that they were serfs and had to work for the *pomeshchik*. But they have been saying about us for a long time that we will be free, and after all this talk have sent the books and ordered them to be read. We are at fault! We thought: Why then send the books, if there is no freedom in them?[34]

The Bezdna peasants, accordingly, not satisfied with what they heard
from the manifesto and articles of the statutes read to them, concluded that the absence of reference to "freedom" in what they heard was
to be explained either by the fact that the readers had been bribed by
the *pomeshchiki* (and had thus intentionally suppressed the "freedom"), or that they were unable to read properly.[35]
Acting on this assumption, the peasants proceeded to seek readers
of their own, and to pay them; they continued to do so until they
found someone who read to them what they wanted to hear. This
was Anton Petrov, a respected local peasant who was also a religious
sectarian of apparently mystical inclinations. At best semiliterate, Petrov was nevertheless invited to read the statutes and to explain them
to the people. He locked himself up, and for three days pored over
the texts that would have been bewildering for the best-educated of
men. Believing, as did all his neighbors, that the statutes contained
the desired freedom, Petrov had no trouble finding it with the aid
of simple confusion.*
Petrov emerged to announce his discovery and to tell the peasants
that they were free—indeed, had been free since 1858—and that they
"should not listen to the *pomeshchiki* and authorities." He told the
peasants "not to go on *barshchina,* not to pay *obrok,* not to fulfill
drayage duties." He also apparently said that the land belonged to the
peasants, with only a third remaining to the *pomeshchiki.*[36] The
news of Petrov's discovery spread rapidly, aided by his instructions
that word be sent around to various villages to come hear about the
freedom. Some four thousand peasants crowded into Bezdna, nearly
emptying the surrounding district.
Hearing that troops were to be sent on April 12, the peasants sur-
rounded the hut in which Petrov was staying in order to prevent his
arrest. Believing that they were in fact fulfilling the Tsar's will, they
refused to give him up to the soldiers, crying: "We do not wish it;
we will die for the Tsar."[37] (Petrov had told the peasants, among
other things, that it was their duty to the Tsar to take their freedom,
that Nicholas I had been killed by the *pomeshchiki* for his attempt

---

* In reading the statutes, Petrov mistook a figure meaning 10 per cent for the seal
of St. Anne, and he decided that this was the sign granting liberty. This was only one
of several misinterpretations he made.

to free the serfs, and that the life of Alexander II was also in danger!)[38]

Steadfastly refusing to surrender Petrov, the peasant crowd was at last fired upon by a large number of infantry. After several volleys, the crowd fled and Petrov was seized; the outcome was 61 peasants killed instantly and 112 wounded, of whom 41 later succumbed.[39] Petrov was condemned by field court-martial and shot.

Essentially the same process was repeated in the "Kandeevka Affair" in Penza province. Although it ended with less bloodshed than the Bezdna episode, the behavior of the peasants that led to their being fired on by government troops was in some respects more aggressive (at one point two soldiers, one a junior officer, were held hostage by the peasants), and their numbers were considerably greater—as many as ten thousand.

This particular "disturbance" got underway in early April, shortly after the proclamation was read in the area, and was accompanied by the same sort of "interpretations" of the statutes that Petrov was giving in Bezdna. According to an official report, the interpreters of the manifesto were declaring that:

The Sovereign Emperor ... has sent to all former serfs a paper proclaiming their complete freedom ..., in which the Sovereign has written that, in giving freedom to the peasants, he has forbidden them to go on *barshchina,* but the *pomeshchiki* have withheld this paper,* the Sovereign is suffering at the hands of the *pomeshchiki* for this, so that the Sovereign has ordered all peasants to gain their freedom from the *pomeshchiki* by force; if any of the peasants have not done so by Holy Easter, they will be anathematized, damned.[40]

As in Bezdna, the peasants of this region, upon hearing of the sending of troops, gathered *en masse* in the village of Kandeevka to await their arrival. The confrontation took place on April 18, and culminated in the troops' firing on the crowd after the commander had repeatedly asked the peasants to disperse and return to their duties.

---

* It was apparently believed by the peasants involved in these disorders that the manifesto had included a special ukase proclaiming the "real freedom," but that this had been torn out by the priests. Cf. *Krest'ianskoe dvizhenie v Rossii v 1857–mae 1861 gg.,* pp. 420–21.

The only answer he received was: "We will not obey. We want nothing. We will die for God and Tsar." After each of three volleys fired at them, the crowd repeated the same words,* but it was finally dispersed after a frontal attack following the third volley.[41] As a result of this incident, eight people were killed instantly, 27 were wounded (most of them subsequently died), and 410 persons were arrested.[42]

The notion that the manifesto and the statutes were actually false was less widespread among the peasantry than the belief that they were being misinterpreted, and on the whole it appears to have taken root somewhat later. Perhaps it began to develop only after it was fairly well understood what the official documents, as circulated, contained. In any case, it was but a short logical step from the ideas current in Bezdna and especially in Kandeevka to the idea that the official documents were forgeries. And the conclusion drawn by the peasants from this idea was obvious: the "real freedom" was contained in ukases or "golden charters" (*zolotye gramoty*) prepared by the Tsar, but suppressed by the *pomeshchiki* and *chinovniki*.

Appropriate documents—forgeries to be sure—obligingly began to appear. "Golden charters" proclaiming the "real freedom" were circulated in the lower Volga provinces during the spring of 1861.[43] Similar manifestos were being circulated in Tambov province as early as April. All such manifestos and charters evidently proclaimed the same sort of freedom that Petrov and many other "interpreters" had been reading into the official documents. One such charter, seized from a junior military officer who had been reading it to the peasants in a village of Kharkov province, was composed in the following manner:

Article 1: His Imperial Majesty explains: My beloved children, I send you happiness and abundance. Do not listen either to the *pany*† or to the priests, [for] they will deceive you, but find yourselves a man of good will.

---

* It appears that the peasants gathered in Kandeevka believed that they were being tested, and that if they withstood three volleys, "the authorities themselves [would] proclaim...real freedom" (*Krest'ianskoe dvizhenie v Rossii v 1857–mae 1861 gg.,* p. 433).

† A synonym of Polish origin for the Russian *barin* (master) used in the Ukraine.

He will read to you my favor correctly, and you pay him a silver kopeck each. Listen to what he will read, and do as it says. If they send *chinovniki* against you, beat them, stay in bunches, and do not surrender the one who will be doing the reading, and come to me however you can and you will be in the right.*

Article 2: Work on *barshchina,* men two days and women one day per household.† All the *pomeshchik's* land is given to the peasants, and for the *pomeshchiki* there remain the marsh grasses and the swamps, in order that they may have a place to nest, like the devils. The water will vanish and the land will remain—and that will be the people's. But two steps around the house of the *pomeshchik* will be left.

Article 3: At harvest time do not go to work for the *pomeshchik,* [but] let him gather grain with his family; what he gathers, that is his, but if there remains unharvested grain, then it shall be gathered by the commune and divided by the commune.

Article 4: Pay no kind of taxes or obligations for five years. The Sovereign pardons them.

Article 5: The *pomeshchik* must plow the land himself, ... and if he cannot steer the plow, then the peasant who may be there, if the *pan* asks him, must fix it, without laughing.

Article 6: The *pan* must live with the peasants as a good neighbor, but if a cow or a chicken wanders into his garden or his plot of land and he drives it out, then let his house and all his buildings be torn down, the place be cleared, and him be driven from the village.

Article 7: The *pan* must build a hut for each family of household servants, give them a horse, a cow, a plow, harrow, and all necessary equipment, and one hundred silver rubles each; if he does not do this, then let all his property and buildings be sold, and [the proceeds] divided among the commune.

Article 8: To the *pomeshchik* there remains a piece of field land for his family of the same size as for the *muzhik,* but nothing more.[44]

Apparently such documents were composed either by peasants or by persons closely associated with peasant interests; perhaps, as Ar-

---

* Apparently Petrov, in Bezdna, also believed that the first step toward attainment of the "real freedom" would be to make direct contact with the Tsar. Cf. Ignatovich, "Bezdna," p. 214.

† That is, per week. It is not clear what this means, since it appears that all obligations to the *pomeshchik* were to cease, according to Articles 3 and 5. Perhaps it should be understood simply as the product of confusion between ideals and anticipated real alleviations.

ticle 1 of this charter suggests, by persons who gave the peasants what they wanted in return for financial gain. There is no evidence that the forged charters and manifestos of this period were ever the work of the revolutionary intelligentsia, although they must have given inspiration for the later composition of "golden charters" by revolutionary groups, the first of which appeared in the famous "Kazan conspiracy" of 1863. This promised, in the name of the Emperor, "full liberty to all Our faithful subjects" and all the land without redemption.[45]

This first phase in the response of the peasants to the emancipation came to an end quite abruptly with the appearance in the countryside of the new peasant officials and the peace mediators. The chronicles of peasant disturbances make this clear: Only one disturbance arising from interpretations of the statutes and manifesto was reported in June 1861, and none was reported thereafter.[46] A few reports on the circulation of false manifestos and golden charters were made later in the year.[47] The product and expression of confusion and disappointment, the "deceit or forgery" thesis was heard throughout Russia, and it coincided in time with the period of greatest unrest, March through May of 1861.

A new period in the history of the peasant response to the emancipation began with the arrival of the peace mediators. By June 1861, the mediators were at work nearly everywhere in the provinces, and as they began to explain the terms of emancipation and to set up a system of authority in the organs of peasant self-administration, they succeeded almost overnight in disabusing the peasants of their hopes of finding the "real freedom" through interpretation of the manifesto or the discovery of "golden charters." Consequently, the rate of peasant disturbances steadily declined. As the governor of Simbirsk put it in a typical, but overly optimistic, report: "From the time of the opening of the *volosti* and village-communities, almost all the misunderstandings that had arisen on the part of the peasants in connection with the acquitting of obligations to their *pomeshchiki* were removed."[48] Only 519 "disturbances" occurred between June and December in 1861, according to calculations based on a definition of "disturbances" apparently more inclusive than that which produced a figure of over 1,300 for the earlier months.[49] There then followed a still fairly unstable situation during the period in which the charters defining peasant obligations and allotments for the "temporary-obligatory" phase were drawn up, that is, roughly until early 1863, when the two-year breathing space that had been planned for this purpose came to an end. After this time, the rate of disturbances declined markedly again, and continued to fall throughout the 1860's. According to the most recent and complete collection of statistics, the rate of reported peasant disturbances in the 1860's, beginning in 1861, was as follows:

Year	Total Number of Disturbances
1861	1,859 (1,340 from Jan. 1 to June 1)
1862	844
1863	509
1864	156
1865	135
1866	91
1867	68
1868	60
1869	65[50]

The difficulties that the peace mediators had to contend with during the two-year preparatory period continued to be the product of the peasants' persistent unwillingness to accept the proferred emancipation. Now, however, the peasants' resistance expressed itself in their refusal to accept the terms laid down in the charters that defined obligations and land settlement for the "temporary-obligatory" period. It was the task of the mediators to see to the composition of such charters for each estate.

Some indication of peasant attitudes toward the land charters is provided by the fact that of all the charters drawn up before January 1, 1863, only about 42 per cent were approved by the peasant communities involved.[51] (The charters could be put into effect without peasant approval.) It may be that an important cause of the peasants' refusal to approve or to abide by the terms of the charters was simply that they were considered unfair to the peasants within the context of the legislation.[52] In this regard, some historians have argued that most mediators, who were after all recruited from among local gentry landowners, grossly favored the gentry in composing the charters.[53] Others have emphasized the dispassionate behavior of the mediators, and have cited conflicts that flared up in several provinces between the local gentry and the mediators.[54] In the opinion of this writer, the limited evidence suggests that the first group of mediators (those who had the task of drawing up the mass of land charters) were selected with some care by the government, and that on the whole they appear to have been reasonably fair in handling their responsibilities. That is, they abided closely by the terms of the legislation.*

In any case, to attempt to explain peasant discontent in terms of the behavior of the peace mediators is to miss the point. It was not the character of their activities in implementing the legislation that led to most of the peasant discontent and disturbances. It was the legislation itself that the peasants were not prepared to accept.

Forced to dispense with the idea that the manifesto had been misinterpreted or forged, but still unwilling to accept the emancipation described there, the peasants in the new phase of their response seized upon a notion that was most frequently expressed in the term *slushnyi chas* ("the promised hour").†

This idea had its origin in the belief that the proclaimed terms (*malaia volia* as they were often called) were to endure only for the announced two-year waiting period, after which the "real freedom" (*bol'shaia volia*) would arrive. The crucial date was February 19, 1863, the date at which the "temporary-obligatory" period was to begin. Many peasants believed that the terms of the full freedom would be announced on that date, while others declared that these terms were already included in the 1861 legislation.[55]

The rumor of *slushnyi chas* was extremely widespread among the peasantry. In the weekly reports of the Minister of Interior to the

---

* Nikolai Miliutin, in the Ministry of Interior, had taken considerable pains to appoint mediators who he had reason to believe were favorably disposed toward the emancipation (A. N. Kulomzin, "Vospominaniia mirovogo posrednika," *Zapiski otdela rukopisei, Biblioteka im. Lenina, vypusk 10*, p. 10). The second group of mediators (appointments were for three years) was less impressive in this respect, partly because of the government's desire to mollify gentry feeling.

† This term was not of Russian origin, and apparently originated in the western lands of the Empire, either the Ukraine or Belorussia. The terms *srochnyi chas, sluchnyi chas,* and *bol'shaia volia* were frequently used too.

Emperor, it was said to exist in 25 out of 45 provinces where land charters were being drawn up. Many of the reports referred to it as a belief common to the peasantry at large.[56] It is remarkable that this rumor became current only after the peace mediators had arrived to dispel notions about the character of the manifesto and to confront the peasants with the hard reality of the land charters.* There is little doubt that it contributed to the frequent refusal of peasants to approve the land charters.[57] Here is the report of a local marshal of nobility to the governor of Kharkov on the subject:

The peasants have positively convinced themselves that according to the manifesto they are to work only two years until the promised hour, ... that whoever in the course of this time signs a land charter will enserf himself anew, but that he who withstands [the pressure to sign] for these two years will be free. Therefore no conditions whatever must be agreed upon with the *pomeshchik,* nor agreement made to any land charter.[58]

In addition, the idea of *slushnyi chas* resulted in nearly universal refusal of the peasants to be transferred from *barshchina* to *obrok* during the two-year period, a change in which the gentry was becoming ever more interested. Moreover, it encouraged the peasants to refuse to abide by the terms of the charters, signed or not, for fear that the acceptance of any new arrangements would become binding. Thus, in the period extending from June 1861 to February 19, 1863, according to the chronicle, there were at least 26 significant disturbances related to peasant anticipation of full freedom in 1863.[59] Troops had to be called out in 16 of these incidents.

On the whole, however, the myth of *slushnyi chas* had a pacifying effect on the peasantry, leading them to accept the necessity of continuing the fulfillment of obligations for the time being, that is, to "work as formerly, but only until *slushnyi chas,*"[60] even though this often meant a rigid refusal to accept any new conditions of labor or obligations. It was certainly not the *cause* for the decline of peasant disturbances after May 1861; it was, rather, a pathetic piece of "ideology," a justification for grudging acceptance of a situation the peasants did not want to accept but did not know how to combat.

---

* No reference to such a notion appears in the published documents before June 1861.

There was considerable tension in the air, both in the capital and in rural Russia, as the nineteenth of February, 1863, approached. In many villages the peasants filled the churches on that day, expecting to hear at last of their "real freedom."[61] But in spite of some predictions of a general rising in the spring or summer of 1863 and a widespread fear among the gentry that the peasants would try to seize all the land at the expiration of the two-year waiting period,[62] the frequency of peasant disturbances continued to decline throughout that year, with only a small relative resurgence in the weeks immediately following February 19.[63] After this date, the peasants' dissatisfaction was demonstrated primarily in their refusal to agree to the redemption of their allotments,* and also in frequent demands for the "gift" or "beggar's" allotment—usually one-fourth of the standard plot—whose recipients, according to the legislation, were to be absolved of any redemption obligations. It is noteworthy that peasant demands for this allotment, often significantly called "the Tsar's *desiatina*,"[64] had been very limited in the first two years after the proclamation of emancipation, but almost immediately thereafter these demands became a frequent element in incidences of peasant disorder.† By the time the land settlement was finally decided, some 500,000 or 5 to 6 per cent of the peasant "souls" had taken this way out, often with disastrous consequences.‡

---

* Cf. Zaionchkovskii, *Provedenie v zhizn'*, pp. 316, 363. By January 1865, about one-fourth of the 16,000 redemption arrangements concluded by that time in 32 provinces were unsigned by the peasants. Peasant willingness to agree to these charters of course varied greatly in accordance with the specific terms involved. Also, those peasants who were willing from the first to redeem their plots presumably did so in the early years of the operation, so that the percentage of one-sided contracts was lower in this period than later (Zaionchkovskii's figures confirm this). Also, *pomeshchiki* who could not get peasant agreement tended to hold out, since a one-sided contract meant a loss of 20 to 25 per cent to them.

† The "quarter-allotment" could be received only by mutual agreement according to the original legislation. By the law of June 27, 1862, the peasants could demand this solution if and when the *pomeshchik* opted for redemption. On the frequency of disturbances related to this issue, see *Krest'ianskoe dvizhenie v Rossii v 1861–1869 gg.,* "Khronika."

‡ Zaionchkovskii, *Provedenie v zhizn'*, p. 295. The percentage of peasants seeking this solution in a given area depended to some extent on local land conditions and prices. It was especially attractive where land was both fertile and plentiful, that is in the extreme south and southeast. Here peasants could avoid obligations and lease

The overall extent of the peasant "disturbances" of these first two years after emancipation should not be exaggerated: they probably never involved more than 4 per cent of the Russian villages, and for all the tendency of the peasants to lay the blame on the *pomeshchiki,* priests, and functionaries, the amount of violence perpetrated against these elements of the population was negligible. One way of measuring the material results of peasant discontent in this period is by considering the information available on the conduct of harvest and field work in 1861. The available evidence indicates that the situation of the rural economy was not grave. The crucial periods of spring planting, fall harvest, and preparation for winter seeding were weathered apparently without drastic decline in work or production.* The weekly reports from the Ministry of Interior did note some complaints coming in from the provinces about the progress of the harvest, but in most cases these were not serious problems, and the Ministry's assessment of the progress of the harvest and the fulfillment of peasant obligations was in general optimistic. The reports argued, in fact, that those instances in which planting and harvest were not proceeding as well or as rapidly as usual were to be explained less by peasant recalcitrance than by bad weather and by the fact that peasant labor obligations had been placed within strict limits by the legislation.[65] (In other words, the *pomeshchiki* had a smaller labor reservoir on which to draw.) The head of the Third Section was less optimistic in his report for 1861. While agreeing that "in general the granting of rights to the former serf population did not produce, with a few exceptions, such great disorders as many *pomeshchiki* feared," he claimed that many peasants had either shunned their obligations

---

land cheaply. (Thus in Orenburg province over 70 per cent of the peasants took this solution.) It is known, however, that the majority of peasants who took the gift allotments came out significantly worse off than they would have been had they accepted the normal allotment and obligations. The main factor here was the rapid rise in land prices and rents after emancipation. Cf. G. Pavlovsky, *Agricultural Russia on the Eve of Revolution* (London, 1932), p. 73.

* In Kaluga province, where in 1861 a great number of the gentry had predicted economic ruin, a senatorial investigation conducted at the end of the 1861 harvest season found the gentry agricultural economy to be in no serious danger (A. Kornilov, "Krest'ianskaia reforma v Kaluzhskoi gubernii pri V.A. Artsimoviche," in *V. A. Artsimovich. Vospominaniia. Kharakteristika* [St. Petersburg, 1904], pp. 366–69).

or worked carelessly; as a result some grain remained unharvested, and the planting for 1862 was reduced, "in some places by a third," and in Riazan and Samara provinces by half the customary quantity.[66] The more detailed weekly reports of the Minister of Interior for this period indicate, however, that these were exceptional cases.

Conclusion

The response of the peasants to the emancipation described here should be no surprise to the student of Russian history. The peasants' attitude expressed in the phrase "We are yours, but the land is ours" (*My vashi, a zemlia nasha*) is well known. And the central position of the *tsar-batiushka,* the father-tsar, in the political mythology of the Russian peasant is proverbial. Study of the peasants' response to the emancipation provides, however, a unique opportunity to test these sweeping generalizations about the peasant mind—so elusive of verification—against a pattern of well-documented events. They survive the test remarkably well. The uniformity throughout Russia of the peasants' expectations and of their response to the emancipation, especially the ideas and rumors it generated, is striking. The apparently simultaneous appearance of uniform elements in the peasants' response throughout a land of primitive communications provokes thoughts of something like Durkheim's *conscience collective,* reacting as a whole to a given set of stimuli. Even allowing for word-of-mouth circulation, as in the case of the rumor of *slushnyi chas,* the lightning rapidity of dissemination indicates an underlying uniformity of susceptibilities and traditions, parallel to the broad uniformity throughout the Empire in the social and economic conditions of the peasantry under serfdom.

A famous student of the Russian peasantry once remarked that it was the hold of the "tsarist myth" on the peasant mind that prevented the "revolutionary situation" of the reform period from growing into a true peasant revolution. In a broader context, it has become a commonplace to say that the hold of the "ruler myth" on the peasants was a fundamental factor in the maintenance of social and political stability under the old regime, and that this regime remained reasonably secure until that hold was broken—a development traditionally associated with Bloody Sunday, January 9, 1905. This may be

so, but it does not constitute sufficient explanation of the events of
1861–62. There was in Russia, after all, a long tradition of peasant
revolts "against the Tsar in the name of the tsar," from the Time of
Troubles to Pugachev. It appears, as one scholar has remarked, that
"the peasant ... demanded that all his actions be covered by higher
authority. Even in rebellion he sought out the familiar pattern of
command and submission."[67] (This was aptly demonstrated, on a
lower scale, in the spring of 1861, when the peasants proclaimed they
were fulfilling the Tsar's will in refusing to perform *barshchina* or pay
obrok.) Thus the "ruler myth" cannot simply be equated with indiscriminate submission to established authority. Peasant political psychology expressed itself in certain images and myths, but these did
not necessarily determine the character of the peasants' response to
any given situation.[68]

In 1861–62 the peasants remained unfailingly loyal to Emperor
Alexander II. That they did so is understandable, but not only in terms
of the general suasion of the "tsarist myth." The Emperor was, in a
more specific way, firmly identified in the peasant mind with the cause
of emancipation, in part through his own actions and in part through
a legacy inherited from his immediate predecessors. The peasants' belief that the tsars desired their liberation apparently went back to the
time of Pugachev, when the idea was current that Catherine and her
aristocratic cohorts had put aside Peter III because he had intended,
after "emancipating" the nobility in 1762, to do the same for the
serfs. This belief had become firmly entrenched during the reigns of
Alexander II's immediate predecessors, Alexander I and Nicholas I.
(Witness the rumors heard in 1861 that Nicholas I had been murdered by the *pomeshchiki* because he had intended to free the serfs.)
These two rulers had contributed to this belief by the measures taken
during their reigns, modest though they were, to encourage and prepare for emancipation. These actions had stimulated the peasants' desire for liberation, and had also contributed to the growth of peasant
disturbances. Alexander II, son and legitimate heir to Nicholas I, inherited this legacy, brought the issue before the public, and undertook to finish the job. There was little danger of his being dissociated
from the cause of liberation in the minds of the peasants.

The peasants' faith in the good intentions of the Emperor led, in time-honored fashion, to laying the blame for the disappointment of their hopes on the *pomeshchiki* and *chinovniki*, and even to calling for the "union of Tsar and people." It could be argued that in this respect the "tsarist illusions" of the peasantry contributed to political and social instability, but the nearly complete lack of violence against the *pomeshchiki* and *chinovniki* indicates that this was not a serious problem. On the contrary, the peasants' identification of the Emperor's aims with their own contributed on the whole to their passivity, by acting as a psychological "shock absorber" that facilitated a reasonably smooth descent from the height of their expectations to the reality of the emancipation settlement. In functional terms, the elaboration of the "deceit or forgery" thesis, the inclination to blame the *pomeshchiki* and *chinovniki,* and the idea of *slushnyi chas* were all parts of this process.

Such was the response of the peasants to the government's emancipation in the two years immediately following its publication. The peasants, unorganized, inarticulate, and "maximalist" in their desires, could express themselves only by refusing to fulfill the obligations demanded of them and, occasionally, by gathering in large, milling throngs, a situation that invariably brought the only response the authorities knew in dealing with peasants—calling out the troops. There was no dialogue between peasant Russia and official Russia, no ground and no machinery for a political give-and-take.

Perhaps, after all, the peasants' long habituation to servitude and submission to authority had rendered their expectations of freedom somehow unreal and thus unattainable, like the visions of heaven they may have received in church. In any case, the thought of active opposition seems never to have occurred to them in this crucial period, even when their state of excitement and their numbers were considerable, as in Bezdna or Kandeevka. It is conceivable, of course, that disturbances such as these could have grown, given enough time, to much larger and more serious movements. But they were always halted while still in the "passive" stage by the intervention of troops.

The story of the peasants' plight after emancipation needs no lengthy recounting here. The peasants were freed with allotments that were, in size and quality, insufficient for subsistence, or at least insufficient under existing agricultural practices to support them and allow them to cover redemption payments and general taxes. Agricultural improvements were made difficult, if not impossible, for most peasants because they remained tied to the communes and thus to the traditional communal practices. The results of this situation in the decades following 1861 were that many peasants defaulted on payments, and developed a compulsive land-hunger that was accelerated by booming population growth. (Peasant population was increasing at the rate of nearly one million per year by the 1890's.) Consequently, land prices shot upward at the same time grain prices were declining over most of the second half of the nineteenth century. And it was on this immensely unstable foundation that the government proceeded in the 1890's to undertake a policy of rapid industrialization financed by relentless tax pressure on the peasant population.

Nevertheless, the emancipation did succeed in effectively removing, for several decades at least, the threat of serious peasant disorders, and even the frequency of "ordinary" peasant disturbances was drastically reduced. The emancipation had broken the direct hold of the gentry on the peasants, and the volatile situation that was produced in the decades before 1861 by increasing exploitation at the same time that peasant expectations of liberation were growing was removed. The causal nexus of most pre-reform disturbances had been broken, despite the continuing difficult economic circumstances of the peasantry. Before 1861, most disturbances had arisen from peasant failure to acquit obligations to the *pomeshchik*. A typical "disturbance" had occurred when a landlord, faced with this situation, turned to the authorities to seek disciplinary action. After 1861, this ceased to be necessary: peasant failure to keep up on obligations no longer led automatically to a "disturbance." Even before redemption was undertaken on a given estate, there existed, after June 1861, a network of authorities and a variety of means that allowed an elastic response to the situation: the peasants could have fines levied against them, they could be charged interest for arrears, their allotments could be reduced temporarily, unfulfilled labor obligations could be translated into money debts, and so forth. And after redemption was arranged, the *pomeshchik* was removed from the scene altogether, the peasants were responsible to the state treasury, and failure to maintain redemption payments was responded to in even more elastic fashion.

Peasants could and did accumulate huge arrears without any definitive confrontation with the authorities. In a word, the circumstances that before 1861 had resulted in "disturbances" gave rise after that date to the accumulation of arrears. The state could afford what the individual *pomeshchik* could not, and the peasants, held in their communes by an elaborate system of coercion based on the "mutual responsibility" of all for obligations, became in a sense their own worst oppressors.

3. The Peasant and Religion

Donald W. Treadgold

Introduction

The Russian word for peasant—*krest'ianin*—is given the following meanings in the chief Old Russian dictionary: "Christian," "human being in general," and "taxpaying villager" or peasant. The illustrations given of the word's use in the sense of "Christian" range from Cyril of Turov, who lived in the mid-twelfth century, to a document of 1400; the last given for use as "human being in general" is 1392; the first given for "peasant" is 1391.[1] Thus near the beginning of the fifteenth century the word seems to have come to mean exclusively "peasant."[2]

Thus far it can be seen that the Russian word for peasant, used for almost six hundred years, derives from the meaning of "Christian." This etymological derivation seems to be peculiar to Russian. The words for peasant in some other major European languages are: French, *paysan*; Spanish, *campesino*; Italian, *paisano*; German, *Bauer*; Czech, *venkovan*; Croatian, *seljak*; Rumanian, *ţăran*. Every one of these is derived from the idea of country, land, or district, and the antecedent of several is Latin *paganus,* from which comes the English word "pagan."

It is wise to be circumspect about arguments from etymology, but certainly many have thought the Russian peasant to be a Christian first and foremost and have associated his religion with the most fundamental psychological features of the peasant class. Several close observers, both Russian and foreign, have however held such a view

In addition to the discussants at the conference at which a summary of this paper was presented, I should like to thank the following for the comments and corrections they provided after reading the paper in draft, without implying that they share the views expressed in the final version: Professors Ivan Avakumovic and Marc Szeftel and Dr. and Mrs. Stephen P. Dunn.

only with qualifications, and have argued that the peasantry has indeed been persistently and even stubbornly religious for many centuries, but that its religiosity has been only superficial in nature and largely confined to outward observances. A classic statement of this view is that of Sir Donald Mackenzie Wallace:

It must be admitted that the Russian people are in a certain sense religious. They go regularly to church on Sundays and holy days, cross themselves repeatedly when they pass a church or Icon, take the Holy Communion at stated seasons, rigorously abstain from animal food—not only on Wednesdays and Fridays, but also during Lent and the other long fasts—make occasional pilgrimages to holy shrines, and, in a word, fulfill punctiliously the ceremonial observance which they suppose necessary for salvation. But here their religiousness ends. They are generally profoundly ignorant of religious doctrine, and know little or nothing of Holy Writ.[3]

There is little basis in any of the available evidence for disputing the applicability of Wallace's statement to much of the Russian Orthodox peasantry in the late nineteenth century. However, such opinions are open to the charge of being as superficial as Russian peasant religiosity is alleged to have been or to be. One must go beyond the mere recording of behavior to ask several historical questions. This paper undertakes to examine the nature and extent of the religious faith of the Russian peasant by comparing the state of affairs among the majority, Orthodox peasantry with that among the Old Believers and the non-Orthodox sects; to attempt an explanation of the situation in all three groups; and to relate Russian peasant religion to the rest of Russian culture.* In this manner it is hoped that a more complete and satisfactory answer than that given by such men as Wallace will be obtained.

* No attempt will be made here to explore the oft-discussed problem of *dvoeverie* (literally, "double faith"), that is, of pagan survivals in Russian peasant consciousness and conduct. The village sorcerer survived until fairly recent times, along with the memory of the belief, if not belief itself, in a variety of animist notions. See George Vernadsky, *The Origins of Russia* (Oxford, 1959), and Nikolay Andreyev, "Pagan and Christian Elements in Old Russia," in Donald W. Treadgold, ed., *The Development of the USSR* (Seattle, 1964). "Double faith" has existed in many other peasant populations, and not only among peasants, as should be recognized in a country where side by side with the Easter feast there is celebrated the day of a marvelous rabbit that lays eggs.

The literature available on this subject is sadly deficient. Curiously enough, it is most ample on the question of the Old Believers and the sectarians, who suffered from all sorts of disabilities for centuries. There is a good deal of literature on the Russian Orthodox Church, but next to none on the main body of peasant believers at the parish level, and only one or two studies of the parish clergy. The first-hand reports of travelers are fragmentary and betray the biases of their authors; the same can be said of the reports of educated Russians, who before making their investigations were often little better acquainted with the Russian peasantry than foreigners were. Only in the work of some of the students of the sects can tourist diaries be said to yield place to something approaching anthropology. Extensive field work on peasant religion, or at any rate some systematic and well-prepared firsthand inquiry, would be desirable to furnish evidence. As far as can be discovered, virtually none was ever carried out, and if much is ever done by Soviet authorities, it is unlikely that the results will be widely disseminated.[4] The writer of this paper has encountered not a single listing that could be described as a bibliographical control of the subject. Therefore what follows is but a first attempt at organizing the issues and assembling information about them to some purpose.

The Russian Investigators of Peasant Religion

Before peasant religion could be investigated, it was necessary to identify the peasantry as a category deserving of study. Much of the credit for the acceptance of the idea of the value of studying the overwhelming mass of the Russian people must be assigned to the Slavophiles of the 1840's. In common with leaders of Romantic movements in the countries of Western and Central Europe, the Kireevskys, Aksakovs, and Khomiakov in different ways emphasized the *narod* and its importance in Russian history, and ascribed to it qualities of religious feeling. However, their "Russian people" was more of an abstraction than a concrete object for study. Haxthausen and others were discovering the *mir* or village commune for them, and they were generally content to let such men provide them with facts. They did not feel any urgent calling to investigate the peasants or the character of their religious beliefs at first hand.

Received opinions were expressed and exchanged. A notorious example was the polemic between Gogol, who had just published his *Correspondence with Friends,* and the crusading Westernizer, Belinsky. Belinsky denied Gogol's assertion that the Russian people was the most religious in the world:

That is a lie! The basis of religiousness is pietism, reverence, fear of God. Whereas the Russian man utters the name of the Lord while scratching himself somewhere. He says of the icon: "If it isn't good for praying it's good for covering the pots."
Take a closer look and you will see that it is by nature a profoundly atheistic people.... Religiousness with us appeared only among the schismatic sects who formed such a contrast in spirit to the mass of the people and were insignificant before it numerically.[5]

Thus Belinsky denied that the Russian peasant was truly religious, on moralistic grounds—he was said to be deficient in "pietism"—and argued that only among the dissenters could one find true religiosity in the peasantry. But Belinsky was only shouting, not reporting the results of study.

Serious efforts to learn about peasant religion in Russia by direct inquiry seem to have begun only with populism. Perhaps their inception may be dated from the later 1850's, when roughly at the same time A. P. Shchapov was selecting his subject for a master's thesis at the University of Kazan and V. I. Kelsiev was poring over Old Believer manuscripts given him by Herzen in London. Shchapov declared:

When I studied Ustryalov and Karamzin, it always seemed strange to me why in their histories one does not see rural Russia, a history of the masses, the so-called simple, dark people. Must the majority remain inaudible, passive, and outside of history? Has not this overwhelming majority the right to enlightenment, to historical development, to life and importance, as have the nobility and clergy?[6]

And Kelsiev wrote:

I read on and on and on. My head whirled, I stopped breathing.... In a flash I saw in front of me the peasants and bearded merchants, so scornfully despised by Europe and our educated classes.... They were not all that bad. ...On the contrary they thought, thought of the most important problems that can concern the human soul—truth and untruth, Christ and antichrist, eternity, man, salvation.[7]

Kelsiev, a young émigré populist who came from a family of poor gentry, brilliant but unable to carry anything through, traveled from London to Russia to try to meet Old Believers. Initial contacts were made, but came to nothing; the utterly nonpolitical attitude of the schismatics made the efforts of the young populists to propagandize among them useless. As for Kelsiev, he was before long converted to Christianity, gave himself up to the police in 1876, and spent the rest of his life as a writer on the Old Believers and other subjects.[8]

Shchapov came from an Old Believer family himself, so he had no trouble in communicating with the dissidents; moreover, his family had been deacons and sacristans, subordinate clerical functionaries who lived virtually as peasants and intermarried with the native population in Siberia, where they had lived since the seventeenth century. Born near Irkutsk in 1830, Shchapov went to a local clerical school, then the Irkutsk seminary (1846), and finally the Ecclesiastical Academy of Kazan (1852). During the Crimean War, the manuscript collection of the Old Believers' ancient stronghold, the Solovetsky monastery, was evacuated to Kazan, and Shchapov threw himself to work on these precious materials. His master's thesis, presented in 1858, dealt with the Schism of the seventeenth century, and explored the social and political as well as religious aspects of the dramatic events of that period. He became a professor at the Academy, and not long afterward at the University of Kazan, where he openly challenged prevailing ideas about the state in favor of *narodnost'* (making the "people" the focus of history) and *oblastnost'* (regionalism). He was arrested for publicly calling for a democratic constitution, and sent to St. Petersburg for investigation, but in 1862 was pardoned—both arrest and pardon were by personal order of Alexander II. He continued to work out his view of the Old Believers as the bearers of aspirations toward democracy and freedom, and also as the people responsible for the only genuine culture that survived among the peasantry after the Schism. The bureaucracy soon (and correctly) discerned Shchapov's political populism in his historical work, and he was accused of involvement in the London émigrés' attempt, through the dispatch of Kelsiev, to establish political ties with the Old Believers. He was soon shown not to have been involved, but he was nevertheless sent back to Siberia. In Irkutsk he turned to the natural sciences, having ceased to believe that the reconstruction of history would serve as a satisfactory intellectual basis for building a bridge between the peasantry and the intelligentsia. He was, however, attempting something beyond his powers or at least the resources available in Irkutsk, and he died in 1876, uncertain where his present path was leading.

Anther regionalist like Shchapov, N. I. Kostomarov (1817–85), did much to further the study of the peasantry and specifically of the religious dissenters, but he cannot really be counted as a specialist, for he kept the whole history of Russia as well as that of his native Ukraine in view, and he held himself more aloof than Shchapov from the political populism of the day.

In the late 1870's a new phenomenon appeared: a number of men from the populist camp set themselves the task of investigating the religious dissidents at first hand. They included A. S. Prugavin, I. V. Abramov, and I. I. Kablits.[9]

Prugavin, born in 1850 in Arkhangelsk, began his schooling at the local gymnasium and the Peter Academy of Agriculture and Forestry, but it was interrupted by his participation in student demonstrations. His interest was drawn to the sects of the North, and he began to publish articles on them in 1877. An article of 1880 attracted the attention of the Grand Duke Constantine Nikolaevich and thereby led to the liberation from solitary confinement of Adrian Pushkin, an Old Believer who thought he was a new incarnation of Christ, and three Old Believer bishops. Another article, published in 1882, on the *Siutaevtsy,* was responsible for attracting considerable attention to that sect. After several of his publications were banned, Prugavin turned in 1888 to the study of the state of peasant literacy.

Abramov used the pseudonym "Fedoseevets" (the word means an adherent to a particular wing of the Old Believers, discussed below). Born in 1858 in Stavropol in the Caucasus, he began working in the 1880's for several journals, notably *Notes of the Fatherland* (*Otechestvennye Zapiski*) in 1881–84, contributing many articles on the sectarians.

Kablits, who used the pseudonym of "Iuzov," was born to a gentry family of Kovno that was Lutheran (probably of German extraction). He was educated in Kiev at the gymnasium and university (from which he did not graduate), took part in the "going to the people" movement of the 1870's, and thereafter wandered around the country as a simple village worker. In the late 1870's he began to publish populist political articles. He had become especially interested in the Old Believers and came to believe that their movement represented something fundamental in Russian popular thought and feeling. However, unlike his fellow enthusiasts of the religious dissidents, he ended by renouncing populism. In 1882, in *The Foundations of Populism* (*Osnovy narodnichestva*), he denied that the educated classes or intelligentsia had the right to lead the common people. When he came to identify with the peasantry, he rejected the basic populist notion of an intelligentsia mission to the peasantry and along with it populism itself. His intellectual evolution reminds us that populism was not a peasant belief.

The view that while the Orthodox peasantry was not genuinely religious, the Old Believers and sects were strongly so, was conveyed to a wide public and above all to the English-speaking world by a former populist activist, S. M. Kravchinsky. Writing under the pseudonym "Stepniak" (man of the steppes) for an English audience, he published a book-length study entitled *The Russian Peasantry: Their Agrarian Condition, Social Life and Religion*. The book broke new ground and to this day can scarcely be said to have been superseded as a manual on the subject. Kravchinsky, born in 1851, had joined the Chaikovsky circle in 1872 and engaged in revolutionary propaganda among the peasantry. In 1873 he was arrested, but escaped abroad, and served as a volunteer in the rising in Bosnia-Herzegovina in 1875. Returning to St. Petersburg, he edited the journal *Land and Liberty* (*Zemlia i Volia*) for a time. Joining the terrorist current within populism, he himself assassinated Mezentsev, a high police official, and then once again fled abroad. His political commitments are evident in his book, but much of his reporting nevertheless stands on its merits.

Kravchinsky devotes a large share of his book to the problem of peasant religion. He begins his examination of the question by admitting that the peasant utters God's name at every step, uses the word "godly" (*bozheskii*?) to mean "just," prostrates himself fervently before icons, and so forth. On the other hand, he notes that pagan deities and rites survive in peasant consciousness and action (the book is dated 1888), and that whatever the official doctrine about icons, the icon to the peasant *is* the sentient body of what it portrays. As proof he cites a folktale about St. Nicholas: A priest who has struck an icon in a moment of fury is forgiven by the saint, who bids him "Go, but take care not to strike *me* with the keys on my bald pate again. Look! you have almost broken *my* skull."[10]

Kravchinsky is especially indignant about the position of the devil in popular legendry. He writes that the devil "is represented as the enemy of man, doing his best to drag him down to hell. But as this is his trade he cannot help it, and the people bear him no malice in return." Up to that point, orthodox theology may simply be overshadowed by the charity (not a bad quality by Christian standards, come to think of it) of people who have known much suffering. However, Kravchinsky presents better evidence for his views when he cites the peasant story of Noah the Godly, in which the devil is depicted as the junior brother of God, and his partner in the creation of the universe —which is not exactly the orthodox Christian view of matters. Kravchinsky also complains that the saints are treated as all too human in folklore, which again puts him on rather weak ground, since the Christian view has always been that saints are men, with the failings of men.

Kravchinsky then turns from the question of peasant religious feeling to that of the attitude of the peasantry toward the clergy:

> To put it in the most charitable way possible, the pops [village priests] are not respected by the moujiks. The orthodox clergy, as a body, have no moral influence over the masses, and enjoy no confidence among them. The extreme conservatives agree with the socialists as to this fact.[11]

He points to the undoubted fact that the white clergy have no state support aside from a little land allotted them for farming and thus are compelled to rely for subsistence mainly on fees for ecclesiastical services; he cites the resultant greed as "the chief cause" of the bad relations between the peasantry and clergy.*

---

* The "white" clergy, mainly the (married) priests attached to parishes, were always regarded as less favored than the "black" clergy or (celibate) monks; monastic properties were often substantial, and since bishops had to be celibate the monks had easier access to promotion.

The conclusion Kravchinsky reaches concerning the religious faith of the Orthodox peasantry is as follows: "If we choose to apply the name of religion to a social philosophy which is based on a system of pure ethics, with no admixture of theology, these people may certainly be called religious."[12] However, he holds that the situation is quite different as regards dissenting Christians: "Dumb and inert in the domain of politics, it is in the founding of religious sects that our peasantry has formulated its most cherished ideals and social aspirations. Here they exhibit not only great intellectual activity but also unlimited moral energy." He not only thus evaluates the intellectual and moral forces of the religious dissidents highly, but he also expects some kind of awakening from the sects. The most advanced religious groups are, in his opinion, the "rationalistic" sects, which have denied the legitimacy of governmental authority and have engaged in individual acts of passive resistance. He sees reason to hope that such may in the future become collective acts, and that an order may be constructed in which peasants can make the transition from communal cooperation to cooperation on a nationwide scale, which, he holds, is socialism. The closing sentence in his book, obviously designed to gain the sympathy of individualistic Englishmen, is: "We are not European enough to successfully imitate a progress based upon the fruition of individual interests."[13] His socialism is also coupled with atheism: the Russian intelligentsia, perhaps more "thoroughly imbued with the spirit of free thought" than the educated classes of any other nation, sooner or later ought to be able to impart the attitude of the "positive sciences" to the Russian peasantry.[14] His timetable is not quite clear, but apparently he is thinking in long-range terms about the future creation of rural socialism and the de-Christianization of the peasantry.

His view of matters in his own day is thus that the Orthodox Russian peasant is a Christian only in a superficial sense, a sense limited to the acknowledgement of Christian ethical norms. If the peasant develops genuine religious faith, it is by way of dissent from the official church: he joins either the Old Believers or one of the sects. This is similar to Belinsky's view, with an important difference: Belinsky denies the genuineness of the religious faith of the Orthodox peasant on the ground that he lacks "pietism," while Kravchinsky's criticism is that the peasant lacks theology. Perhaps the reason for the difference can be found in the change of prevailing intellectual currents from the 1840's to the 1870's and 1880's. In the former period the influence of types of thought that were heavily moralistic and pietistic was still in the air (though they had been still more influential even earlier); in the latter period the new rationalism associated with the reception of Darwin and the development of positivist currents claiming to base themselves on the discoveries of natural science was in the ascendant. In one period "pietism" seemed more important, in the other "theology." (Note that Wallace, writing at about the same time as Kravchinsky, makes about the same point he does.) There is little doubt that the ordinary Russian peasant did not have the kind of moralistic bent demanded by an early-nineteenth-century Protestant evangelical, nor the kind of intellectual understanding of his position that might have satisfied the mid-century positivist.*

Since the Russian investigators of peasant religion appear to be unanimous in holding that the dissenters provided the clearest evidence of genuine faith among the peasantry, we shall now turn our attention to them.

The Schismatics and Sectarians

The religious dissenters fall into two groups: (1) the Old Believers, who separated from the Russian Orthodox church in the seventeenth century, but who considered themselves to be the only true Orthodox and neither schismatics nor heretics, and (2) the sects, each of which developed its own doctrines and did not pretend to be Orthodox by origin, doctrine, or ritual.†

The Old Believers or Old Ritualists (*starovery, staroobriadtsy*)

---

* It may be raised as an objection here that Belinsky was not an evangelical and Kravchinsky was not a theologian. But the point is that atheists are apt to judge religion in terms of what religious people appear to consider important, and often to judge it severely by those criteria.

† There is no way of accurately determining the proportion of the Eastern Slavic peoples of the Russian Empire that belonged to the dissidents. Out of an Eastern Slavic population of 82,000,000 in 1897, estimates (some of slightly earlier date) by various hands suggest that there may have been around 13,000,000 dissidents, of which the Old Believers included about 11,000,000 (the Priestists about 3,000,000 and the Priestless about 8,000,000), the sectarians between 1,000,000 and 2,000,000. (See Frederick C. Conybeare, *Russian Dissenters,* Vol. X of *Harvard Theological Studies* [Cambridge, Mass., 1921], 242ff.) If these figures are trustworthy, the dissidents made up about 15 per cent of the Eastern Slavic population.

were, to begin with, the followers of four Russian Orthodox priests: Avvakum, Feodor, Lazar, and Epifany, who after over ten years of opposing the ecclesiastical reforms of Patriarch Nikon, were condemned by the Council of 1666–67. They were imprisoned and finally burned at the stake in 1682. The Old Believers have continued to exist, in several groups, for the three centuries since.

Various explanations for the seventeenth-century Schism in the Russian church have been advanced. In a recent illuminating article Michael Cherniavsky has distinguished an "official Orthodox" and a "liberal, populist" position.[15] The former is that ignorance and obscurantism were at the root of the schism, the latter that the main cause was social and political protest. The liberal position is represented by Shchapov and other populist writers: Prugavin, Kablits, etc., the Orthodox by N. Subbotin, E. V. Barsov, and other professors of theological academies, as well as several recent American historians that Cherniavsky proceeds to indict (six by name). Cherniavsky does not claim that his evidence disproves the assertion concerning ignorance and obscurantism, however; in fact much of his material supports it.

In order to reach a better understanding of the Old Believers, it is not necessary to attack either "school" of historians. The Old Believers were, certainly, profoundly ignorant and stubbornly obscurantist; they were also Russians who did not like Westernization, serfdom, and other things. But these social "evils" were not what they were explicitly or consciously protesting. They were engaged in a theological dispute, which very few of them were learned enough to carry on, except in terms of numbers and signs of the Apocalypse. Why? Because they were almost exclusively, in the early decades, from the uneducated peasantry. The populists accurately noted that the Old Believers, at least by the nineteenth century, were dedicated to literacy, and Kravchinsky states that a Moscow agent of the Russian Bible Society reported that most copies of the 1824 New Testament were bought up by Old Believers.[16] The same phenomenon was to be noted in the sects. An Orthodox clergyman reported: "When a common orthodox peasant goes over to the Stunda the first thing done is to teach him to read";[17] the next step was to give him the New Testament. Many illiterate Old Believers and sectarians were reported to know by heart whole chapters or books of the Bible.

However, all this, though very important in connection with the spread of popular education (in particular outside of regular civil or ecclesiastical schools), does not disprove in the slightest the contention that the Old Believers (let us for the moment postpone consideration of the sectarians) were ignorant and obscurantist. The kind of theology that is based on bare literacy and half-understood memorized passages in Scripture could not be and never has been anything else.* In *Memoirs from the House of the Dead* (*Zapiski iz mertvogo doma*) Dostoevsky characterizes a number of Old Believers who were being punished along with him: "They were highly developed people, shrewd peasants, believing pedantically and uncritically in the literal truth of their old books." It may be laboring the obvious (though Cherniavsky's article seems to suggest it may not be), but it is not sensible either to regard the Russian peasantry's ignorance as something requiring moral reprobation or to try to exculpate the peasantry by a hopeless attempt to show that it was an educated class. The peasantry was what it was, and what many peasantries have been and are. Being human and belonging (by the usual usage) to higher civilizations, peasants are educable and may rapidly reach high levels of intellectual sophistication if they have sustained contact with the world of learning. Like other people, they may, when they have traveled a more or less substantial distance up the educational ladder, either remain religious, coming to understand their religion on a new basis, or cease to be so.† But those who lack serious education cannot somehow by sheer good will or virtue compensate for their intellectual shortcomings.

Let us then turn from the pseudo-questions concerning the Old Believers to analyze the path their development followed.[18]

Patriarch Nikon's innovations (the use of three fingers in making the sign of the cross, three alleluias, and so forth) were not so much the issue as the Old Believer conviction that such innovations proved the imminent arrival or presence of Antichrist, or what some con-

---

* Anyone who has ever injudiciously opened his door to a Jehovah's Witness may offer firsthand testimony on the subject.

† We omit from consideration here those uneducated persons, akin to the "village atheist," who may sometimes operate in rural areas and elsewhere, including college campuses, and who are functional near-illiterates whose views are based on half-understood citations from atheist texts.

sidered to be the fall of Moscow, the Third Rome; hence the nearness of the Apocalypse.

Those prepared to wait a little while for the actual end of the world were the *Popovtsy,* or Priestists. Since no bishop joined the Old Believers, the inevitable solution for those who required the sacraments while waiting was to accept any Nikonian priest who abjured his "heresy." During the regency of Sophia (1682–89), a number of Priestists fled to Poland and established a center at Vetka, near Gomel. The man who soon became their leader, Feodosy, was the first to accept recanting Nikonian priests. In 1733 the troops of Anna Ivanovna crossed the Polish border and destroyed the village; it was restored, only to be finally wiped out under Catherine II in 1764. A tendency soon appeared for Priestists to think of rejoining the "Nikonian" church. A council of Priestists was held in Moscow in 1779, deciding that Orthodox converts need not be rebaptized (as had been done in some groups) but still needed chrismation (the Orthodox equivalent of confirmation, usually administered at the same time as baptism). This was not enough for one faction, which offered to return to Orthodoxy only if the 1667 decree excommunicating them were repealed and they were permitted to continue to use the old rite. The Holy Synod acquiesced, and from 1688 on many Priestists became what was then called *Edinovertsy* (literally, those holding the "one belief") under Orthodox jurisdiction. Though they were regarded by many Orthodox in somewhat the same way Roman Catholics regarded Uniats, the *Edinovertsy* grew. In 1851 they had 179 parishes; in 1900, 300; in 1917, almost 2,000. Nevertheless, the first of their priests was consecrated bishop only in 1918.

The larger share of the Priestists, however, followed the decision of their own council of 1779. Their centers included Starodub, in Chernigov province, which had existed since the 1660's but grew as some refugees from Vetka settled there. After Vetka was finally destroyed, new settlements were made on the Irgiz river in Saratov province and in Moscow; in Moscow they founded shortly after 1770 the Rogozhskoe "cemetery," which survives to this day.

Up to the time of Nicholas I (1825–55), the Priestists within the Russian Empire had experienced disabilities and annoyances oftener than persecution, but dissolutions of monasteries and arrests of priests now put them in jeopardy. The Gromovs, a merchant family of St. Petersburg, undertook to find a bishop for them outside Russia. The Austrian government agreed in 1844. The envoys of the Gromovs finally found a former bishop of Sarajevo named Amvrosy living in retirement in Constantinople who was willing to serve, and in 1846 he came to Bela Krynitsa in (Austrian) Bukovina. He was soon arrested, owing to Russian pressure, but the hierarchy survived through Cyril, one of the two bishops he had consecrated. In a few years Priestist bishops were to be found in Russia. A number were willing to rejoin the Orthodox church, and in 1862 wrote a widely circulated letter to this effect. However, they were unsuccessful. In the 1880's Kablits estimated the number of Priestists at over 3,000,000. With the other Old Believers they received freedom of worship in 1905; they have apparently about 3 million adherents today.

The tendency for the Priestists to regularize their position and to abandon the issues of 1666 is visible throughout. The wish to become respectable is a natural one; it was natural that many should have accepted the *Edinoverie* and that others wanted the whole separation to be ended. But the tendency for a sect once formed to persist is also frequent in history, and peasant tenacity may be a factor wherever this tendency is found.

The other branch of the Old Believers, the *Bezpopovtsy* or Priestless, became a category of sects rather than a unified sect. They differed from the Priestists, obviously, in believing that the true priesthood died forever when the last pre-Nikonian died, and in a sharper conviction that the Apocalypse was immediately at hand. There was also a geographical difference; while most Old Believers were Great Russians, the Priestists belonged mostly to the central provinces where clergy had been taken for granted, the Priestless to the north where laymen had long had to take over some priestly functions because of vast distances and a shortage of clergy. It was in the north that the great Solovetsky monastery provided the nucleus for resistance to the government that lasted from 1667 to 1676.

It was a monk from this monastery named Ignaty who started the first Priestless settlement, from which developed the *Pomortsy* sect. Along with Andrei Denisov, from the princely family of Myshetsky, he founded a monastery on the river Vyg in Olonets province in 1694.

Andrei and his brother Simeon Denisov were the most notable of all
the Priestless leaders.[19] Their model was apparently the monastic
ideal of Joseph of Volokolamsk, chief of the Possessors of the reigns
of Ivan III and Vasily III; since his party had identified itself with the
Muscovite autocracy, this may seem paradoxical, but it will not do to
attach any great importance to the identification, since the Old Believers also greatly venerated Maxim the Greek, the most learned of
the opposing Nonpossessor camp. Apparently what was most significant about both of these men to the Old Believers was that they lived
in an age previous to Nikon's.

Zenkovsky points out that the Denisovs' ideas began with the notion
of Moscow as the Third Rome, but replaced the city of Moscow with
Orthodox Russia as a whole, and assigned the role of custodian of ecclesiastical independence and truth not to the tsar but to "all the Russian cities and villages." Such views Zenkovsky relates to the democratic traditions of the northern Russian cities of Novgorod, Pskov,
and Viatka.

The monastery imposed celibacy on all comers, but the attempt was
soon abandoned to demand the same of the thousands who assembled
in the Vyg valley nearby. When agriculture could not provide a living
to the Vyg colonists, they resorted to handicrafts. They discovered
copper in the province, worked the mines, executed brass castings, and
began to furnish icons, crosses, and the like to Old Believers everywhere. They thrived economically, but their theology got them into
difficulties. If all priests were dead, there could be no sacraments—
except baptism and penance, which could be administered in their
view by laymen. No sacraments, no marriage; and thus there was the
choice of living as monks or nuns, as in the Danilovsky monastery,
or in what would in Anglo-Saxon countries be called common-law
marriages. But in Russia such marriages were not recognized. Scan-
dals and dissension were the result. A runaway monk from Vyg denounced the community in 1738, and an expedition to investigate was
propitiated only by the agreement of Simeon Denisov to pray for the
Empress Anna.

Toward the close of the eighteenth century the question of marriage
was tackled directly. The abbot of the monastery at Vyg, Arkhip
Dementiev, tried to hold the old line. But Vasily Emelianov, one of

the leaders of the new *Pomortsy* settlement Catherine II permitted to be founded in Moscow in 1771, arranged a kind of marriage ceremony and offered it as the solution. In the 1790's Dementiev finally gave way. Apocalypticism could not long survive such a compromise. Many *Pomortsy* became Priestists or even *Edinovertsy*. Though an official estimate of 1863 numbered them as over 2,000,000, it appears that they lost strength rather rapidly thereafter.

From Vyg came Feodosy Vasiliev, a layman originally from Vyshny Volochek, who organized the second Priestless sect. He was sent to Poland to organize the Priestless there, but in 1706 established his own sect, the *Fedoseevtsy*. Kravchinsky tells us that he attacked the *Pomortsy* for writing over the crucifix "Jesus Christ, King of Glory," and ordered the substitute inscription "Jesus, King of the Jews."[20] But the real difference, so far as it did not stem from personal ambition, was over marriage. Feodosy recognized marriages conducted by Orthodox clergy, and thus was less uncompromising than the *Pomortsy* in this respect, but his sect was stricter than they in refusing to pray for the sovereign after they gave in in 1738. In 1752 a council of the *Fedoseevtsy* took a strict line on marriage too, expelling all who had children, and prohibited marriages thenceforth. In 1762, however, a *Fedoseevets* writer, Ivan Alekseev, argued that marriage was really celebrated by God, the priest only a witness, and advised marriage in the Orthodox church, according to the old rite if that could be arranged. In 1771 the *Fedoseevtsy* were permitted (like the *Pomortsy*) to establish a center in Moscow, which became known as the *Preobrazhenskoe kladbishche* (Cemetery of the Transfiguration). A leader of this settlement, I. A. Kovylin, attacked Alekseev's position, and seems to have adopted the Catharist doctrine that open sexual unions are worse than secret ones. At any rate the *Fedoseevtsy* maintained their 1752 canons against marriage, and at a council of 1883 again expelled all who had families. Estimated at 1,000,000 in 1863, the sect was split in two by the action of 1883 and seems to have declined rapidly until the Revolution of 1917. Bolshakoff reports that it had come to include mainly better-off peasants and merchants, many of whom were liquidated by the Communists because of their social class.

The third Priestless sect was the *Filippovtsy,* whose founder also

had been a monk of Vyg. It was the introduction of prayers for Anna
Ivanovna in 1738 that led him to object to the Denisov leadership, and
such dissension resulted that the Denisovs called in the state authorities to arrest him. Filipp and seventy of his followers escaped arrest
by burning themselves to death. For a century or more the surviving
adherents of his position tried to maintain celibacy and strict avoidance of contact with the state. But fanaticism finally yielded to compromise; many went over to less rigorist groups. An Orthodox convert, Paul Prussky, finally managed to bring one of their major
centers into the *Edinovertsy* fold. The sect, if it survives, must be
insignificant in size.

Fourth was the *Stranniki* (or *Beguny*), whose leader Efim, a native
of Poltava province, defected from the *Fedoseevtsy* in the 1770's, as
usual on the grounds that the sect was compromising itself. Efim took
the doctrine of Antichrist further than any other Old Believers. In
order to avoid the state, he said, the only way was to become a nomad
or wanderer. Of course he had to compromise that doctrine immediately to establish a center of direction for the sect, which he did at
Sopelki in Yaroslavl province. His eventual solution was to divide the
group into two, one of which accepted the necessity of being less virtuous for the time being and stayed in place to offer shelter to the
other, though its members were sworn to leave home in the future;
the other was made up of endlessly moving pilgrims. In 1811 a group
of them was discovered in Tambov, and they were promptly exiled
to Siberia. After a time the Sopelki *Stranniki* came to abandon some
of their old strictness, disobeying only "un-Christian" orders of the
government and refusing passports merely because authorities insisted
on using in them the term *"Raskolnik"* to designate the passport-
holder, instead of "Orthodox Christian." A vestige of the old faith
remained, however: they strove to get out into their yards to die, so
that it could be said they had left their home.

The other *Bezpopovtsy* sects were minor. In 1870, V. Andreev reported that there were 130 known *Bezpopovtsy* sects,[21] and obviously
the creation and perhaps also the disappearance of sects was still continuing. A few more might be mentioned: the Saviorites (*Spasovo
Soglasie*), who denied any layman's right to perform a sacrament,
but baptized and married in the Orthodox church nonetheless, while

praying that God would turn the meaningless rites into true sacraments; the Purified (*Ochishchentsy*), in which each family had its
own priestess; the Nonprayers (*Nemoliaki*), founded in the 1830's by
a Don Cossack, Zimin, who had been a *Popovets* and then a *Fedoseevets,* and taught an opposition between flesh and spirit that would
persuade anyone that he had somehow come upon Manicheanism if
it had not, as Conybeare puts it, "lain buried for a thousand years at
least under the sands of Central Asia"; and the Sighers (*Vozdy-
khantsy*), who like the Nonprayers believed an Age of the Holy
Spirit had come, to be acknowledged by exhaling or "sighing," and
who seem to have appeared only in the 1870's in Kaluga province.

In their despair with the earthly (or at any rate Russian) order of
things, their expectation of the end, and their desperate attempts to
find some way of living without their sacraments and their church,
which they thought the Nikonians had defiled, the *Bezpopovtsy* sects
had much in common with each other. Many of the investigators who
have studied them have greatly admired them as people, and have
perhaps allowed their admiration to run away with them. Conybeare
goes so far as to say, concerning the *Bezpopovtsy*'s expectation of the
Apocalypse, "In their crude way these simple people had apprehended
the truth. That the present catastrophe [the Russian Revolution] is
a result of the neglect by all the Governments of Europe of the elementary moral truths enunciated in the Gospel, who can doubt?"[22]
His proposition can be doubted; but he is certainly right in saying that
these people, in their substitute-sacraments and their apocalyptic theology, "have wandered back unwittingly into a paleontological phase
of the Christian Church."[23]

If Manicheanism, or at any rate Marcionism and Gnosticism, seem
to have erupted bewilderingly in the tiny nineteenth-century Old Believer sects, then they were even more apparent in the Spiritual Christians. Here we pass from the realm of Orthodox schismatics (and
schisms within schism) to that of the sects, which did not claim to
be better Orthodox than the Orthodox but simply repudiated the historic church. It is puzzling why several of the populists, including
Kravchinsky, and such Western writers as Conybeare call these groups
"rationalistic." Bolshakoff much more plausibly calls them "Russian
'Protestant' sects." They date from the eighteenth century: the Spirit-

Wrestlers (*Dukhobortsy*; their name translates the Greek *pneumato-machoi*) were discovered by the police in the 1750's, the Milk-Drinkers (*Molokane*) seceded from them about 1770, and the Stundists were founded only about 1870.

The Spirit-Wrestlers taught that there was a spiritual Trinity, reflected in man's own spirit; the Father was Memory, the Son Reason, and the Holy Spirit Will.* What was precious in man was therefore invisible. They preached transmigration of souls and denied the resurrection of the body, but held that the soul entered the body only gradually from the ages of six to fifteen. The first known leader was Siluan Kolesnikov, a peasant from Kharkov province; a little later there appeared Illarion Pobirokhin, a peasant from Tambov province, who said that Jesus' soul was in him. The *Dukhobortsy* were peaceful citizens who paid their taxes and behaved in an exemplary way. They had no hostility toward anyone, believing that the real church is hidden and may exist among all races and religions throughout the world. These traits, which any state might find attractive, did not save them from harassment. Only Alexander I tolerated them, allowing them to establish a colony in the Crimea; Catherine II, Paul, and Nicholas I exiled and persecuted them vigorously. Their conscription was ordered by Nicholas; since they were willing to serve but not to fight, they were a problem for commanders. It seems that, after Pobirokhin, leadership (and "Jesushood") passed to his son Savely Kapustin (he took his mother's name), and in turn through Kapustin's son, grandson, and great-grandson, named Peter Kalmykov; then the latter's widow was left with the leading position, which before her death in 1886 she tried to transfer to Peter Verigin. At this point great dissension erupted. Verigin had become much influenced by Leo Tolstoy (who in turn owed much to other sectarians, as will be observed), and determined to make a new start. In 1898–99 the Verigin wing of the *Dukhobortsy,* over 7,000 in number, migrated to British Colum-

---

* Whether consciously or not, this doctrine harkened back to ancient Christian origins. St. Augustine spoke of similitudes to the Trinity that man finds in himself, and stressed the relationship of memory, intellect, and will; "the point in the case of memory, intellect and will," writes Roland H. Bainton, "is that being three they are inseparable in action as are also the members of the Trinity." See his essay, "Michael Servetus and the Trinitarian Speculation of the Middle Ages," in B. Becker, ed., *Autour de Michel Servet et de Sebastien Castellion* (Haarlem, 1953), p. 33.

bia, assisted by an oddly-assorted trio consisting of Tolstoy, Aylmer Maude, and V. Bonch-Bruevich, who was later to be Lenin's secretary. Verigin (known as "Peter the Lordly" to distinguish him from his son "Peter the Purger") lived until 1924.

A son-in-law of Pobirokhin, Semen Uklein, a tailor of the same village, fell into disagreement with him and fled to another part of Tambov province, making a bold entrance into Tambov city that resulted in the arrest of all the demonstrators. All recanted; but Uklein after he was freed continued his preaching and soon headed a sizable sect. His chief innovation was to moderate the radical spiritualism of the *Dukhobortsy,* interpreting the Bible in a commonsense rather than allegorical manner, and admitting the resurrection of the body (though the resurrected bodies were to be new ones). Just as Protestantism developed further into Unitarianism and the latter's extremists became Jews in sixteenth-century Europe, so the Spiritual Christians gave rise to similar phenomena. Uklein introduced the Mosaic dietary laws under the influence of Simeon Dalmatov, a Jewish convert, thereby rejecting Christian fasts and, among other things, drinking milk during Lent. The Orthodox dubbed them Milk-Drinkers, and they accepted the term, though some interpreted it as referring to the "milk of the Spirit." The *Molokane* split into *Subbotniki* (Saturday-observers) and *Voskresniki* (Sunday-observers). Although the former were by far the less numerous wing, they themselves produced several subgroups. Many *Subbotniki* thought of themselves as the "New Israel" and rejected the notion that Jesus was God in any sense; but they also rejected the Talmud and the notion that a Messiah was to be expected who would be a king as well as prophet.[24] In contrast, the *Subbotniki* of the Caucasus were closer to Judaism; they accepted the Talmud, expected a Messiah-king, and used Jewish prayers in Russian translation. A small group whom Kravchinsky calls the "Herrs" were fully Jewish in religion, though Russian in descent. They had born Jews as rabbis and prayed in Hebrew.* Within the *Voskresniki,* a group

---

* Klibanov reports his conviction, based on meetings with Sabbatarians of the Tambov region in 1959 and of the Voronezh region in 1964, that they were simply "followers of Judaism." However, he indicates his awareness of the probability that these small groups of survivors were different in various ways from their nineteenth-century predecessors (*Istoriia religioznogo sektantstva v Rossii . . . ,* p. 40).

following Maksim Popov, a peasant of Samara, organized a colony practicing primitive communism, which did not last long. From them another sect broke off calling itself the *Pryguny* or Jumpers, which seems to indicate an adoption of the *Khlysty* ritual. Meanwhile a disciple of Uklein, Isaiah Krylov, and a disciple of the latter's named Maslov tried to hold the *Molokane* to a moderate course, restoring communion and marriage. A group on the Don that adopted this path came to be known as the "Evangelical Christians," and not only survived but prospered after a fashion by being taken under the wing of the Baptists.

The Baptists came from the Stundists, founded in 1867. They directly reflected German Protestant influence. Stundist derives from *Stunde,* the German word for the "hours" or services held by the Germans of the colony of Rohrbach in the Ukraine. A German Nazarene pastor in the village of Liubomirka converted a couple of Ukrainian peasants, and one, Mykhailo Ratushny, became the leader of a new movement in Kherson province. He was arrested and deported, but the movement continued to spread, being influenced by other German colonies in the Ukraine, including those of the Mennonites. Meanwhile another Stundist group arose in the Caucasus, many of them converted from the *Molokane,* and under an able young preacher named Vasily Pavlov merged with the Ratushny group. Another Baptist (as we may now call the sect) group developed in St. Petersburg and enlisted the support of a colonel in the Imperial Guards, V. A. Pashkov. In 1884 Colonel Pashkov summoned a conference in the capital to attempt to unify all the Stundists, Baptists, and *Molokane,* but the *Molokane* were not much concerned with the rite of baptism, and the only result was the banishment of Pashkov and other Baptist leaders.

Another man, named Ivan Prokhanov, whose forefathers were *Molokane* but whose father was a Baptist, soon appeared to take a leading role in the Baptist movement. It was he who organized the Union of Evangelical Christians in 1908, three years after the imperial grant of toleration to the Russian dissenters (except for the "pernicious" sects *Khlysty* and *Skoptsy*). The Russian Baptist Union, following the lead of P. V. Pavlov (son of the Caucasian preacher), was much more numerous but lacked a leader of Prokhanov's aggressiveness.*

It remains to examine briefly the two sects branded "pernicious" by the law of 1905: the *Khlysty* and the *Skoptsy*. There seem to be indications that the *Khlysty,* from which the *Skoptsy* derive, were either as old as the fourteenth century or at an early stage counterfeited traditions which were that old, since their hymns commemorate martyrs who suffered under Dmitry Donskoi (1359–89) and Ivan the Terrible (1533–84). The modern sect can be traced to Danilo Filippov, a peasant of Kostroma, who proclaimed himself to be God in 1631 in Vladimir province. As "God" he was superior to the other members of the sect who were, they believed, "Christs"—a name others corrupted into *Khlysty* or "whips," that is, flagellants. It is difficult to describe them with confidence, since they had to be extremely secretive about themselves to escape the hand of the state. However, it is certain that each member believed himself to be an incarnation of God. Their organizations were congregationalist, each "ship" having its own "pilot" assisted by a woman. Ordinary services were held with the reading of the Bible and the writings of the Church Fathers, as well as sermons, but secret rites for the initiated, presided over by the woman assistant ("prophetess" or "mother of God"), were quite different. They were

---

* An agreement was signed in 1921 to merge the Evangelical Christians and the Baptists, but it was never put into effect. After the Revolution for a time Prokhanov had strong support from the Communists; his group took over most of the *Molokane* and many of the *Bezpopovtsy,* and converted numerous Orthodox. His Union grew from less than 9,000 in 1914 to more than 250,000 in 1922, and by the late 1920's its membership was about 4,000,000. During much of Stalin's period, it was persecuted along with other religious groups, but the post-1943 shift in Soviet antireligious policy led to a revival. In 1944 the Evangelical Christians and Baptists finally merged, claiming still to have about four million members. The following year the Pentecostal or Spiritual Christians, who had a loose federation of most of the remaining sects, from *Dukhobortsy* to *Khlysty,* joined this union, and the resulting Council of the United Baptists, Evangelical Christians, and Pentecostal Churches began in 1946 to publish a periodical called *Bratskii Vestnik,* or *Brotherly Messenger.* It is clear that this Council, which is government-sponsored and opposed by a number of sectarians about whom it is unwise to ask Soviet authorities, is the USSR's choice to stand for "Russian Protestantism" in international religious affairs. It is its single chapel in Moscow that is known to tourists as "the Baptist church." Plainly the group has the same problems as the Russian Orthodox Church under Soviet rule.

held at night, included both sexes, and progressed from readings and hymns to dances inducing hysteria and trances. Though the sect prohibited alcohol, sexual relations, and profanity, there were persistent tales that the end of the secret rites was often sexual relations, and students of the sect seem to differ only about whether this happened rarely or often. The particular origins of the sect cannot be established with certainty; many allege the influence of eighteenth-century German pietism and mysticism on it, and the influence seems clear: again the issue is whether it was fundamental or not. However old this sect was in uninterrupted line, it certainly incorporated a kind of ritual behavior that is found centuries or millennia earlier in the Near East, India, Egypt, and elsewhere. The established religious bodies have always known that mystical prowess was likely, if not supervised by authority, to lead to excesses.

Gregory Rasputin, confidant of the last emperor and empress, was repeatedly accused of belonging to the *Khlysty,* although the Holy Synod investigated the charge and cleared him. A recent investigator agrees that the charge was unfounded, but acknowledges that Rasputin was probably influenced by various doctrines and practices of religious dissidents he had encountered in his wanderings.[25] It is evident that in Rasputin were to be found many features of untutored Russian peasant religiosity that may explain more about his remarkable and fateful career than the political motives that have often been explicitly or implicitly attributed to him.

A clear example of the degeneration of mystical fervor was Kondraty Selivanov (his real name was Andrei Ivanov), a *Khlyst* from Orel province. The *Khlysty* forbade sexual relations and yet engaged in them; whether or not as part of the regular rites is unknown. Selivanov, about 1770, decided that the only solution was self-castration. He himself set the example, and proceeded to make converts. Arrested by order of Catherine II in 1775, he was flogged and sent to Siberia, where he pretended to be Peter III. Paul ordered him brought for a talk with him, and afterward had him placed in a lunatic asylum. In 1802 Alexander I freed him, and soon he was preaching to St. Petersburg society. A Polish convert of his, Alexis Elensky, former chamberlain of King Stanislas Poniatowski, was sent to the emperor in 1804 with a memorandum advising reforms acceptable to the *Skoptsy*. Elensky went to a Suzdal monastery for his effrontery, and in 1820 Selivanov was sent there too. He lived until 1832, when he died after being accepted back into the Orthodox church. But his followers, teaching that he was the incarnation of Christ who had reigned as Peter III, and that Christ himself had castrated himself, continued to exist. A story was current that the Tsarevich Alexis, about the turn of the twentieth century, was kidnapped and castrated by a *Skoptsy* nurse. This is almost certainly untrue; but it is certainly true that various kinds of mutilation were performed on men, women, and children by the *Skoptsy* until recent times, though it appears that many members of the sect did not interpret the injunctions about castration literally and even had to be penalized by the sect for bearing children. They may not yet be extinct.

Another offshoot of the *Khlysty* were the *Shalaput,* founded by Avvakum Kopylov, an Orthodox peasant of Tambov, in the 1820's. Abramov especially studied this sect, which offered examples of Christian communism in the northern Caucasus. Finally there were the *Siutaevtsy,* a sect founded by a certain Vasily Siutaev. He had become a religious teacher only in middle age. After spending several years as a shopkeeper in St. Petersburg he had decided such an occupation was sinful and returned to his village, near Novgorod. There he soon gave up church attendance and began to assemble followers on Sunday to read the Bible. For a time the members of his sect removed all the locks on their gates and homes as a testimony to their belief that all goods should be held in common, but eventually thievery made them restore the locks. Prugavin studied this sect, and shortly after Count Leo Tolstoy entered the throes of religious conversion he advised Tolstoy to visit Siutaev, who was living not far from friends Tolstoy was used to visiting. Tolstoy immediately acknowledged a close kinship of views with the sectarian leader: both rejected violence, the Church, and much of what state authority implied. On one occasion the two became so absorbed in conversation that Siutaev drove their cart off the road into a ditch. Tolstoy patronized Siutaev when he appeared in Moscow, and thereby gave his views currency and popularity.[26]

The sectarians, like the Old Believers of both wings, were mainly from the village. One student of the *Dukhobortsy* declared: "However far their teaching spread, it never touched people of the higher classes, but only the simple and uneducated people; there were a few merchants and tradesmen, and all the rest were peasants."[27] This statement applies also to a number of other dissident groups. Often what started as an almost entirely rural movement developed an urban component as the sect turned to trade as a means of sustaining the life of the individual believers and the continuation of the group, but none of the religious bodies discussed ever became chiefly a movement of townsmen.

It would be inaccurate to suggest that religious dissidence in Russia was only peasant in composition; it would be impossible to isolate religious elements that could be described with certainty as peasant in origin. However, in studying the psychological traits of the dissident leaders and the kinds of issues that agitated their followers, one cannot fail to recognize characteristics of the Russian peasantry as they were exhibited in its economic, social, and perhaps also political life, to the limited extent that we can say to this day that we know it. As noted above, many investigators discerned in the dissident religious groups a kind of religiosity that was more specifically and spontaneously peasant in character than that of the Orthodox Church. For this reason, given the politics or general ideological stance of several of the students concerned, they valued dissidence more highly than Orthodoxy. The moral vitality of many branches of dissidence cannot be denied. However, dissidence also suffered from severe limitations; to identify and assess them a broader approach is needed than the political one used by many observers thus far.

High and Low Culture in Russia

To the extent that Russian religious dissidence was chiefly peasant in social composition, how is it to be related to other strands in Russian cultural life? Robert Redfield may provide a basis for an answer by the distinction he draws between primitive societies and peasant communities. A primitive culture such as that of the Trobrianders, Aranda, or Zuni is "an independent and self-sufficient system," needing no outside system to function. In contrast,

The culture of a peasant community . . . is not autonomous. It is an aspect or dimension of the civilization of which it is a part. As the peasant society is a half-society, so the peasant culture is a half-culture. . . . The intellectual and often the religious and moral life of the peasant village is perpetually incomplete; the student needs also to know something of what goes on in the minds of remote teachers, priests, or philosophers whose thinking affects and perhaps is affected by the peasantry.[28]

Redfield quotes George M. Foster as saying that an obvious distinction between the two types is that the peasant (or, as Foster calls them, "folk") communities, "over hundreds of years, have had constant contact with the centers of intellectual thought and development."[29] Redfield goes on to distinguish between what he terms "great tradition" and "little tradition" (or "high culture" and "low culture"):

The great tradition is cultivated in schools or temples; the little tradition works itself out and keeps itself going in the lives of the unlettered in their village communities. The tradition of the philosopher, theologian, and literary man is a tradition consciously cultivated and handed down; that of the little people is for the most part taken for granted and not submitted to much scrutiny or considered refinement and improvement.[30]

If, then, the culture (religious or not, though no non-religious peasant cultures have been important in human history) of a peasantry is a "half-culture," if it is to be regarded as a "little tradition" dependent on a "great tradition" for completeness, an evaluation of any given example must take this into account.

Before the middle of the seventeenth century, the Eastern Slavs had a single, unified civilization. The Russians (and Ukrainians and Belorussians) had their own educated men among the clergy and to a much smaller extent outside it—for example, Prince Andrei Kurbsky, Prince Ivan Khvorostinin, and Ivan IV himself—and the mass of the people followed the same faith as the educated, with varying degrees of understanding, but most often with little if any intellectual grasp of that faith.

After the seventeenth-century Schism, a new situation arose. A sizable section of the Slavic peasantry ceased to adhere to the "reformed" Orthodox church. It was not only peasants who did so, but

the evidence available indicates that it was mainly peasants. The resulting sects exhibited many characteristics that might be expected
from the uneducated and many that filled the educated with puzzle-
ment or alarm. This was true from the start. Although the Schism
can be traced initially to a split within the so-called Friends of God
circle around Alexis, only its really evangelical members, such as
Avvakum, scornful of learning as evangelicals in all periods have
often tended to be, ended in the Old Believer camp. The marks of
the first Old Believer leaders were lack of education and a surplus of
zeal for the faith. Such marks remained on the Old Belief and on the
sectarians who during the eighteenth century took their own places
alongside the schismatics and outside the official church. Those Old
Believer leaders who were willing to reexamine their positions found
themselves prepared to accept reconciliation with the Orthodox
church, and there seems to have been a two-way movement between
the Old Belief and Orthodoxy during the eighteenth and nineteenth
centuries: a steady influx of Orthodox peasantry evangelized by the
schismatics into the Old Belief, and an irregular but significant
return of Old Believer groups under moderate leadership back into
Orthodoxy, either through the *Edinoverie* or directly. Dostoevsky, in
Memoirs from the House of the Dead, tells of an Old Believer who
was in captivity for having, along with others, burned an *Edinoverie*
church that some of his fellow schismatics were beginning to attend.

The sectarians followed a somewhat different path. Few conversions to Orthodoxy seem to have taken place, many conversions of
Orthodox to the sects; nevertheless the sects did not come to play any
large role in Russian life, partly because they continued to fragment—
one observes the same phenomenon among the *Bezpopovtsy* of the
Old Believers. They had few educated leaders; characteristically their
shepherds were devout semiliterates.

The result was that a "little tradition" or a "low culture" came to
exist separate from the high culture to a significant extent. The con-
stituents of this low culture were chiefly the peasants who followed
the *Bezpopovtsy* and the sectarians. They were proof against much
of the ferment that was going on at the higher levels of Russian
thought, though not entirely so. One of the important influences
simultaneously affecting the high and low cultures was German

Protestantism,* and the debt of the sects to such influence was obviously significant; but when one comes to the later nineteenth century, when the secularization of the Russian intelligentsia was proceeding rapidly, the sects tended to relapse into their isolation from the high culture.

The Orthodox Peasantry

The high culture went its own way; or, more accurately (and especially after the Russian Orthodox church became directly subject to the state through the control of the Holy Synod), it took several different paths. Orthodoxy had lost contact with its intellecual roots, such as they were, in the Greek churches, for the latter were subject to the rule of the sultan, and their vitality had reached a low ebb. It had lost perhaps the most devout section of its laity to the Old Believers and to the sectarians, and it was neither intellectually nor morally in a strong position to hold its own against the cultural invasion of Western religious trends and non-religious ideas that seemed to threaten its foundations. One might well have expected it to have died. Some argued that it had in fact died, yet it obviously did not, and proved after 1917 (and notably by 1943) to be at least a very lively corpse.

Of course Orthodoxy suffered from the Schism, as did the schismatics; any split in a religious or political body is apt to harm both parties to it, and leave each to a much greater degree than before at the mercy of its own weaknesses, deprived of the other's strengths, whatever they may be. Weakened by the Schism, Orthodoxy was thereafter hard hit by subjection to the state (after 1721), by the period of Protestant pietism's ascendancy as virtually an established state cult (1817–24), by the indifference of successive procurators-general of the Holy Synod, especially in the nineteenth century, and by the increasing defection of the intelligentsia after 1860.†

Post-Nikonian or, to choose an even more significant watershed for

* No attempt is made here to reproduce the detailed account of the various phases of Western influence on the high culture of Russia that I am setting forth in the Russian sections of my work-in-progress to be called "Western Thought in Russia and China."

† This paper does not purport to deal with the evolution of the Russian Orthodox Church as a whole, however, but only to explore the position of the peasant in relation to it. On the basis of available materials only a few observations are possible.

the history of the Church, post-Petrine Orthodoxy retained the allegiance of the great majority of the Russian peasantry. The peasantry was linked with the Church almost exclusively through the village clergy. The latter suffered from a variety of serious economic, social, and legal disabilities, and the consequence was cultural deprivation and impoverishment. The economic plight of the village clergy is summed up thus by Znamensky:

As in old Russia, so also in the eighteenth century up to the reign of Catherine II it [the clergy] was obliged for all means of subsistence solely to the benevolence of the parishioners, with the exception only of few and meager revenues of the Tsar's _ruga_ [the word is untranslatable, but means something like "tithe" if no specific fraction, a tenth or other, is understood] and of cadastral lands allotted to many churches, for which it was obliged to the mercy of the government.[31]

Znamensky himself later makes clear that this conclusion is overstated, and that land allotments made either by the parishes (and capable of being revised or even withdrawn) or by the state (in which case they were inalienable church property) were in practice the foundation of the village priests' maintenance. In the early eighteenth century the writer on political economy Pososhkov observed:

Among us in Russia the village priests support themselves by their own labor, and are in no way distinguishable from the peasants who till the soil; the muzhik is at the plough, the priest is at the plough; the muzhik is at the scythe, the priest is at the scythe; and the holy church and pastoral care are neglected.[32]

However, since such lands were often grossly insufficient for self-support, the _pop_ (priest) was likely to depend heavily on the fees he received from parishioners for the performance of religious ceremonies of all kinds.[33]

By the eighteenth century the clergy had become an hereditary caste, and by the late nineteenth century it was losing many of its sons to other professions without hope of replenishment (even though a law of 1869 opened the way for recruitment from other classes). It was a poverty-stricken group; many of its members were notorious for drunkenness or loose living, were objects of scorn or amusement to the villagers rather than respect, and were locked in an unending battle for an extra kopek or two with their parishioners, fellow clergy, and the state. A secret report to the Grand Duke Constantine Niko- laevich based on Nizhny Novgorod province asked:

Can the people respect the clergy when they hear how one priest stole money from below the pillow of a dying man at the moment of confession, how an- other was publicly dragged out of a house of ill-fame, how a third christened a dog, how a fourth whilst officiating at an Easter service was dragged by the hair from the altar by the deacon?[34]

Examples of misconduct by village priests are not difficult to multiply.

On the other hand, there were such priests as the one Ernest Poole learned about who had rashly married a poor girl whom he loved, had come to take up a parish in "eastern Russia" about 1890, and without complaint had set about to be a model parish priest. He had helped build a brick kiln and a schoolhouse in which his wife taught classes; he had secured the use of a bull and a stallion to improve local strains of livestock; he had obtained better quality seeds for the villagers' fields; he had persuaded a doctor living nearby to train several village girls in first-aid techniques; he had nagged a rich peasant into financ- ing the construction of a dispensary; and he had combated drunken- ness in every way he could. He remained engaged in such good works from the age of 22 to 47, when he died. The peasants had started coming to church again soon after his arrival, and became as devoted to him as he was to them. Poole reports that his successor was also a good priest.[35] C. R. Buxton happened on to a village in central Russia where a "stern, unbending" priest was in 1920 leading a united village in silent defiance of the Communist regime, obviously because he had earned the peasants' trust, in ways unknown to the author.[36]

Perhaps the soundest assessment of the pre-revolutionary parish priest was made by Williams:

Sometimes priests are hopelessly ignorant and stupid, and hold their posi- tion in spite of obvious incapacity only through the protection of powerful relatives. Sometimes they give way to drink.... The average priest is neither conspicuously devout nor conspicuously negligent. He is a hearty fellow with a broad accent, rather overburdened by the cares of his office and by family cares, not keenly intelligent, but shrewd, observant, with common sense and humour. He is not interested in theoretical questions, is sincere in his religious beliefs, takes the world as he finds it, and feels thoroughly at home in it, and able to enjoy its good things when they come to him.... There are not a few priests who delight in their office, who are full of a warm and simple faith, and who toil in poor parishes all their lives long without any other object than that of doing good. The wonder, considering all the conditions of service, is not that there are so few good priests, but that there are so many of them.[37]

What was the nature of the Orthodox peasant's faith? To begin with, he observed the sacraments: he married, baptized his children,* participated in the eucharist, and received the last rites through the clergy. If his village priest was a drunken scoundrel, that did not necessarily undermine his faith: the peasant was not a Donatist, who believed that the efficacy of the sacrament depended on the virtue of the priest, and he did not reject God because the clergyman he might see was not an admirable man. If there were examples at hand of schismatics or sectarians who were living notably upright lives and were devoted to their belief, the Orthodox peasant might become a convert of theirs.†

At various times, and indeed during the last decades before the Revolution, there were many quasi-evangelical movements within the Orthodox church. The movement led by Father John of Kronstadt was only the most noteworthy; others were started by Ivan Churikov and Father Stefan Podgorny. Such phenomena led Vladimir Bonch-Bruevich, the Bolshevik historian of Russian religious dissidence, to change the name of his great series from *Materials for the History and Study of Russian Sectarianism and Schism* to *Materials for the History and Study of Religio-Social Movements in Russia*. He had perceived increasing numbers of Orthodox who,

---

* In Leskov's story *The Enchanted Wanderer* (*Ocharovannyi strannik,* 1873, Magarshack translation) a Russian in captivity to the Tatars who has had several children by Tatar wives remarks that "as they had never received the sacraments of the Church I, for one, never considered them as my children." It must be added that his Russian hearers reproach him for lacking paternal feeling, but the anecdote is still instructive.

† In Leskov's *The Cathedral Folk* (*Soboriane,* 1872, Hapgood translation), a novel in which he portrays clergy (not rural but urban) with sympathy and discernment, a priest enters in his diary: "I have read a book about detecting the Schism. It has everything in it, but one thing is not there,—that the Schismatics live up to their errors, while we neglect our right path; and that, it strikes me, is the most important."

without breaking with the official church, were "nevertheless creating life in a certain sense according to their own lights."[38] To a considerable extent this revival of preaching was a peasant phenomenon. (There were other important stirrings in the Orthodox Church during the reign of Nicholas II, such as the formation of Religio-Philosophical Societies, but they pertained rather to the intelligentsia than to the common people.)

Whether his own parish was religiously active or moribund, the peasant retained his religious outlook. Chekhov in his story *Peasants* (*Muzhiki*; Wilson translation), written in 1897, after describing in detail the beliefs of the family central to his story, continues: "In the other families it was much the same: there were few who believed, few who understood. At the same time everyone loved the Holy Scripture, loved it with a tender, reverent love; but they had no Bible, there was no one to read it and explain it, and because Olga sometimes read them the gospel, they respected her."* Buxton noted in 1920, with some impatience, that although he was mainly interested in politics, conversation with Russian peasants was always getting "diverted" in the direction of religion; "religion in one form or another seemed to be constantly in the thoughts of these peasants."[39] Maurice Baring, several years earlier, noted that "outward manifestation of religious observance" among the people was what struck the newcomer, but "anybody who gets to know the Russian people at all well, will be struck by the unmistakable evidence of inward religious feeling which they display."[40]

The outward observance of forms and the inward conviction remained with the Orthodox peasantry. However, it must be said that during the whole Imperial period, when the Church suffered losses to the Old Belief and the sects and lay under subjection to the state, the Orthodox peasantry was deprived of the kind of cultural leadership that might have maximized his moral and intellectual development. The village priest was apt to have intellectual and moral de-

---

* Chekhov intended the story as an indictment, but it has been widely accepted as depicting at least an important part of reality. A recent Soviet émigré, writing in *Novoe Russkoe Slovo* of March 5, 1961, asserts that this story (not particularly the passage quoted) gives "the most complete idea" of what life in a remote Soviet village today is like. See Nicholas Vakar, *The Taproot of Soviet Society* (New York, 1961), p. 174.

ficiencies in leadership, partly because of his economic plight, partly because of the grave cultural and institutional problems that were besetting the hierarchy of the Church—who had to deal with the damaging effects of state control through the Holy Synod as well as the defection of the intelligentsia from Christianity throughout much of the nineteenth century.

On the other hand, the schismatic and sectarian peasantry was apt to have a leadership that was morally inspiring (let us grant that even Kondraty Selivanov had his uplifting qualities, despite the questionable morality of self-castration) but intellectually weak. Most of the dissident religious leaders lacked education, and tended to combine a minimum of literacy with superstitious and fanatical attachment to their own peculiar heresy—that the end of the world will come in a year ending with the number "6," or that marriage was impossible because the church was dead, or something similar. The disjuncture of intellectual and moral excellence, as has so often been the case in human history, produced an unstable situation. The hard-working, thrifty, monogamous schismatic or sectarian settlement, the envy of its neighbors and the despair of the authorities who worried that its example would lead to conversions, was always in peril of destroying itself through self-burning in anticipation of the Apocalypse, or the breakdown of the family through promiscuity that arose because marriage was impossible, or the failure of experiments in voluntary communism, or some such thing.

Conclusion

The history of Russia has been deeply affected by various kinds of divisions, separations, and schisms, social as well as cultural. The separation from the rest of Europe consequent on the Mongol conquest (1240), the estrangement from Constantinople before but especially after its capture by the Turks (1453), the relative isolation from the West during the whole Muscovite period (c. 1450–c. 1700), the several attempts during the imperial period to restore that isolation, and the degree of success of the Soviet authorities in reaching that objective, especially under Stalin—all these have hampered the development of Russian culture. The social gulf that existed between the Muscovite tsars and their serving-men, later the emperors and their bureaucracy on the one hand and the peasantry on the other, made the growth of a national consciousness difficult. The split that developed during the eighteenth century between the West European-ized gentry, from which the intelligentsia largely arose, and the peasantry was both social and cultural in nature.

Thus the Russian peasant for centuries was separated from the best intellectual and moral forces of his civilization. After the seventeenth century, the "low" culture of the dissidents might provoke admira-tion, but its limitations were severe. From the early nineteenth cen-tury the "high" culture of the intelligentsia was thoroughly alienated from the peasant outlook, however much the *intelligenty* might pro-claim from afar that they revered or even worshipped the peasantry. From the early eighteenth century the high culture of the Orthodox metropolitan clergy and the great monasteries was fighting a rear-guard action in order simply to preserve its own existence, was unable to reach out to the peasant millions, and left the Orthodox peasantry in a backward and undeveloped cultural condition.

Referring again to the anthropologists' categories, it is possible to go further. Redfield argues, in a passage already quoted, that a dis-tinction between primitive and peasant cultures is that the former is independent and self-sufficient while the latter is "not autonomous. It is an aspect or dimension of the civilization of which it is a part." Thus, when he distinguishes "great" and "little" tradition, or "high" and "low" culture, he presupposes a *unified* culture.

Applying these categories to Russia, it can be seen that the risk the religious dissidents ran, in their attempt to be self-sufficient, was that of lapsing from peasant culture into primitive culture. At most the schismatics persisted as a kind of living fossil of an earlier epoch, of the pre-Nikonian unified culture of old Russia; the sectarians at-tempted to create independent communities dependent on a largely imaginary past (or became virtual mission communities of Western churches).

The culture of the remainder of the Russian population also suf-fered from division. The "great tradition" was weakened by the de-fection of the intelligentsia from Orthodoxy and its adoption of West European secular thought patterns, leaving the educated portion of the Orthodox clergy, itself subjected to strong Western influences (including secular ones), to attempt to carry on the great tradition alone and under difficult conditions. The "little tradition" of the Orthodox peasantry suffered indirectly from the damage done to the "great tradition." The village priests might be insufficiently educated and the peasants deprived of effective intellectual and moral guidance precisely because the condition of the Church as a whole was unsound during the entire period of state control through the Procuratorship of the Holy Synod. The high and low cultures of the Orthodox population were both in a situation of weakness, and the relation of the two to each other became tenuous. And yet the foundations of the unified culture were not destroyed and the links between "great" and "little" traditions were not severed; a devoted priest in a given locality or the revitalized direction of a seminary might from time to time produce noteworthy even if limited results.

The low culture of the dissident peasantry was in peril of lapse into primitivism; the low culture of the Orthodox peasantry, however moribund it might appear in certain respects, still continued to function.

Did the Russian peasantry, dissident or Orthodox, cease to be religious? There seems no basis for asserting that it did, unless one is to give "religiosity" the kind of definition appropriate only to high culture, as do Wallace and Kravchinsky, inquiring whether the peasant possessed the level of theological understanding to be found only among the educated anywhere, or measuring his behavior by the standard of public conduct of the Calvinist burgher of seventeenth-century New England, and then enumerating his failures to meet the criteria so inappropriately selected. Vakar has a similar point in mind when he writes:

The standard of sophisticated piety applied to primitive rural societies has no meaning. Nor does the allegation of atheism, against a people who have never been moved to consider the existence of God theologically at all but live at a cultural level below such preconceptions and equally below such doubts.[41]

The *krest'ianin* remained *khristianin,* if not necessarily *pravoslav-nyi,* and so he remains today, provoking impatience from the Soviet authorities and scholars. Klibanov concludes his study of the sects by a call for the propagation of science, directed toward "the spiritual liberation of those Soviet people who still lie under the influence of the religious survivals of capitalism."[42] The parish priest is today rare; in his stead the collective-farm chairman sits in the midst of the villagers. Yet the icon on the wall of the Soviet peasant hut may outlast party supremacy as it outlasted Nikon, the Most Holy Governing Synod, and the October Revolution.[43]

4. The Peasant and the Army

John S. Curtiss

Because of the scarcity of sources, it is not easy to say anything significant about the peasants in the army at the end of the nineteenth century. They themselves did not express their views in print, and very few of the officers and commanders of the Imperial Army visibly concerned themselves about the attitudes of the enlisted men. If they did, they took the position that the men were a good-natured and submissive lot with no real grievances and that only the malignant influence of the Bolsheviks and other agitators finally induced them to join the Revolution. Bolshevik propaganda certainly was a factor, but in the light of social and political events after 1905 this explanation seems somewhat oversimplified. It leaves unanswered the question of why the soldiers—most of them peasants, who as a group had for centuries supported the tsars almost without question—should suddenly fall victim to revolutionary infection. There must have been additional factors that helped to subvert the peasants in army greatcoats from their loyalty to the Great White Tsar. Very few of the old officers have touched on this matter, but the comments of the few who did speak out are often quite revealing, as we shall see later.

Soviet scholars have shown little more interest in the attitudes of the peasant-soldiers around 1900. Perhaps the fact that the latter retained their traditional outlook and that, consequently, the revolutionary movement made very little headway among them before 1905 explains why there is an almost complete absence of Soviet writing on the subject. For example, a monograph on the revolutionary movement in the army in the 1905–07 period declares: "Up to 1905 the army was still a reliable support of tsarism."[1] The author of the monograph devotes less than a page to a discussion of the reasons for the rebellious conduct of many of the soldiers in 1905. Similarly, Trotsky says almost nothing on the matter in his history of the Russian Revolution, and his book on the formation of the Red Army ignores the subject completely,[2] as does his book on the Revolution of 1905.[3] And few of the soldiers of the old army who rose to high positions in the Red Army have given much information in their memoirs about the conditions of army life before 1905.

Much more information is available about conditions in the army for the period from 1905 to 1914. Where a source deals only with situations that existed solely in these years, and that were probably not characteristic of the period before 1905, it has seemed best not to use it in this study. However, when the situations and incidents described appear to be characteristic of the earlier period also, it seems justifiable to use such a source because it helps to complete the picture of conditions that peasants in the army experienced during the period at the turn of the century.

Despite the dearth of source material, I shall try to construct a semi-narrative account of the changing position of the peasants in the army in the nineteenth and early twentieth centuries. The account begins with a brief sketch of the old serf-army that was disbanded in 1855, shortly after the death of Nicholas I. Following that is a discussion of the reforms of the army during the reign of Alexander II, the effects of which were revealed most notably in the Russo-Turkish War of 1877–78. Next there is a description of the period of reaction that followed the assassination of Alexander II, during which the government openly strengthened its ties with the nobility at the expense of the other classes. (This probably caused some deterioration in the situation of the peasants in the army similar to the consequences of the reactionary policies of the government toward the peasants in civil life. It has not been possible to document this, however.) About 1900, as we shall see, the authorities began to improve the position of the enlisted men, without making any basic changes; but the behavior of the troops during the Revolution of 1905 indicates that the soldiers, most of whom were peasants, had become increasingly hostile to the authorities, in spite of the government's efforts to quiet them through suppression and mild reforms. Finally, I shall show that, although by 1907 the government had been able to restore its control over the troops, there remained a latent hostility that to some degree endured until World War I.

The pre-reform army of the first half of the nineteenth century was composed almost entirely of peasants, who were drafted at the rate of one out of seventy or eighty available men. The term of service, which at the beginning of the reign of Nicholas I was twenty-five years, was later reduced to fifteen for men with good-conduct records, with the remaining ten years to be in the reserves. (Men with poor conduct served the full term.) Even with this reduction, however, when a man was taken for the army his family bewailed him as though he were already dead, for few of them returned to their homes. If the man was married, his wife, who had little chance of seeing her husband again, was usually doomed to a life of bitter poverty. No wonder that the peasants hated military service and considered it almost as bad as penal labor for life. For some it actually was a punishment, for landlords and village communes had the right to send troublesome peasants to the army for life, and the courts sentenced minor criminals, religious offenders, vagabonds, and vicious men to serve in the ranks.[4]

This strong aversion—evidenced by suicides and desertions by recruits—was reinforced by the ferocious discipline in the army and the brutal treatment that both officers and noncommissioned officers gave them. At this time it was widely held that beating—with the fists, drumsticks, scabbards, or whatever was handy—was the most efficient way to train men. Since most of the officers had been beaten when young, many used the same method of discipline on their subordinates, and the sergeants did likewise.

The brutal behavior of the sergeants can be explained partly by the fact that many of them received their training in the notorious "stick-academies," or cantonist schools. These schools were chiefly for the children of soldiers, who were destined to lifetime careers in the army. These pitiful children, along with Jewish boys torn from their families, entered the schools at seven years of age, where, under senselessly cruel discipline, they were trained to become company clerks, musicians, tailors, shoemakers, or noncommissioned officers. Many of the soldiers' sons who survived were later assigned to army regiments as sergeants, where, as they had been taught to do, they terrorized the recruits and the other enlisted men.[5]

All of this punishment by officers and sergeants was informal, applied as each saw fit. More serious offenses, like desertion, theft, and insubordination, were handled in military court trials. These courts imposed formal punishment such as birchings and, above all, running the gauntlet. When running the gauntlet was specified, the prisoner, with back bared, marched slowly between two rows of soldiers wielding willow rods—through five hundred or one thousand men, once, twice, or even twelve times. Since few men could survive so much, the Emperor's boast that the death penalty had been abolished was hardly credible.[6]

Another unpleasant aspect of the army of Nicholas I was the military colonies, set up under Alexander I, which attempted to combine farming and soldiering. The peasants in these areas, listed as reservists once the colonies had been established, had to feed soldiers quartered in their homes, as well as to do military drill. The soldiers in the regiments assigned to the military colonies worked to clear fields and drain swamps, in addition to carrying out their military duties. Both groups hated the situation, and aides of Nicholas warned of danger. This warning proved correct when widespread revolts broke out in the military colonies in 1831 during the panic caused by a cholera epidemic. With most of the army in Poland, the reservists rose and killed many of their officers, and refused to submit even to the Tsar. Finally, after troops had arrived, the authorities wreaked terrible vengeance on the colonists. Later, however, the colonists ceased to have any military function other than that of feeding the soldiers quartered upon them, and their lot improved somewhat.[7] Eventually, during the period after the Crimean War, the government abolished the military colonies.

Apparently out of persistent fear of revolutionary outbreaks, Nicholas I made sure that his soldiers would become unthinking machines who would obey orders without question. Even when called on to suppress peasant disturbances—an increasingly frequent assignment

—they usually performed the task without demur. Doubtless the fact that the soldiers were stationed far from their native villages, amid people who were strange to them, helps to explain this obedience.[8]

Another feature of the life of the peasant-soldier was the number of parades and the guard-mounts in which he took part. The Emperor loved these displays, and he demanded nothing short of perfection. Woe to the officer whose men failed to achieve it! To prepare for these functions, the soldiers had to spend long hours in formal drill, practicing the exaggerated goose step, learning how to dress the long ranks, and following the complicated manual of arms exactly. The men hated these performances and the painstaking cleaning of equipment that preceded them, for they well knew that the fist of the sergeant was ready for those guilty of shortcomings.[9]

At parades and maneuvers the Tsar took special pride in his cavalry, mounted on beautifully matched horses, which were plump and sleek. Far from training their units for long marches, scouting, and outpost duty, the commanders emphasized elegant evolutions on the parade ground, canters, and other shortened paces that would display the horses and their well-seated riders to best advantage. The enlisted men, when not at drill, spent hours grooming their mounts, rubbing them, plucking out long hairs, and feeding them large portions of oats and mash to keep them plump.[10]

Likewise, the infantry spent little time on battle training. When maneuvers were held, the troops invariably followed the precise, inappropriate rules of the field regulation, instead of simulating actual combat. Sharpshooters in advance of the main units had to maintain alignment and keep in step, and were rarely permitted to take cover. As for musketry practice, the commanders looked on this as an unnecessary nuisance, so that many of the men did not even fire the prescribed three ball cartridges per year.[11] The artillerymen and the engineers did receive proper training and had technical skill equal to that of other armies.[12] But most of the huge Russian army was not properly trained for combat.

During the warmer months of the year the regiments usually assembled in camps for drill and maneuvers, which for the enlisted men meant a ceaseless round of training, inevitably accompanied by beatings. The soldiers learned to fear the approach of summer and to rejoice when they returned to winter quarters, where they were lodged in peasant homes. With no officers or sergeants to bother them, they could relax in familiar surroundings, occasionally helping with the family chores. Life in a strange family, however, was not always idyllic. The peasants, often poor and destitute, had the duty of feeding their soldier-lodgers, who, especially in the miserable provinces near Poland, fared poorly.[13]

Scanty rations were another of the hardships of army life, even during the summer months, for many of the officers exploited their subordinates. The colonels in command, who had the responsibility of feeding the men on sums allotted by the government, frequently bought provisions in smaller quantities and of poorer quality than they should. This practice permitted them to pocket handsome sums at the expense of their soldiers. Unscrupulous commanders also bought uniforms and other equipment of a poorer grade than officially specified, which brought them further profits at the expense of the rank and file. To this illegal income of the officers should be added the illegal profits from corruption in the management of military hospitals; improper practices in respect to the supplying of provisions, medicines, and hospital equipment yielded considerable sums.[14] Thus the peasants in uniform did not receive the care that the government considered necessary.

Inevitably these deprivations had a bad effect upon the health of the men. During the decade from 1841 to 1850, the average number of sick was officially stated as 655 per thousand, which was probably somewhat lower than the true rate. The death rate—chiefly from cholera, typhus, typhoid fever, and tuberculosis—was 37.4 per thousand, or three times that among Russian civilians of the same age groups. Even though the average mortality declined slightly from 1850 to 1854, largely because of the zealous efforts of Nicholas I to improve the feeding and the care of the soldiers, the death rate in the Russian army was substantially higher than it was in other European armies at that time.[15]

Thus the Russian peasant who was drafted into the army faced an unenviable prospect. However, in spite of the hardships that he and his fellows experienced, the military authorities succeeded in indoctrinating them sufficiently to make them loyal and submissive soldiers who gladly fought for Tsar and Fatherland. Because of the almost universal illiteracy of the soldiers, the authorities could not use the printed word to instill loyalty and patriotism, but had to rely largely on the Orthodox church. The clergy zealously exhorted the enlisted men to obey the Tsar, who was the anointed of God, and to smite his enemies in the name of the faith. Orders of the day, proclamations, and other messages from the commanders to the troops reinforced this exhortation, although few of the commanders had the ability to inspire the enthusiasm of their men. Nicholas I had this gift, and at reviews and parades he seems to have aroused great enthusiasm among the soldiers, who were trained to look on him as their friend and benefactor. The granting of medals and other honors to soldiers who distinguished themselves was another means of stimulating devotion. Perhaps the most effective means of indoctrination, however, was a sort of catechism that all soldiers had to learn by heart. Filled with edifying examples of soldierly obedience and loyalty, it hammered in the lessons of unquestioning obedience as required by the soldier's oath and the holy church, and promised reward in heaven for those who laid down their lives on the field of battle.[16] Finally, the example and teaching of old soldiers gradually instilled in the peasant recruits a pride in the great deeds of the regiment and of the army as a whole. Esprit de corps tended to develop, and the conscripts, always mindful of the soldier's proverb, "Prayer to God, and service to the Tsar, are never in vain," became submissive and often loyal soldiers. Not only did they regard fighting as a duty, but often they welcomed it as a relief from trying labors on the drillground. The informality of campaign life gave a respite from strict peacetime discipline and often produced striking exhibitions of gaiety and good spirits.[17]

In the field, the peasant soldiers displayed the traditional characteristics of Russian warriors. Their training had taught them to accept privation, disease, and death without complaining, and their ability to subsist on meager rations and to endure severe hardships was exceptional. When the real test came in the Crimea, these men— lacking in effective leadership and proper weapons—bore frightful losses, at times with little opportunity to strike back, and were still ready to renew the struggle when they were ordered to evacuate Sevastopol.[18]

This defeat ushered in an era of reforms, including that of the army, although this took much time to reach fruition. Indeed, Prince V. A. Dolgorukov, who remained as Minister of War until April 1856, and his successor, N. O. Sukhozanet, were of the old school, and the first limited reforms came largely in spite of them. These included the issue of a new uniform with red trousers, and the abolition of the military colonies and the cantonist schools. The authorities also introduced a new method of provisioning the troops that left less scope for corruption, and undertook to train the soldiers to read and write, although Sukhozanet opposed the latter step.[19] And in 1858 the term of service was reduced from fifteen years or more to seven, although men without perfect records had to serve nine years.[20]

After the appointment of D. A. Miliutin as Minister of War in 1861, the reform movement made more rapid progress. In 1863, ferocious punishments such as running the gauntlet were abolished, and flogging of soldiers was eliminated. However, enlisted men under sentence of a military court might still be given one hundred blows with the birch, and the noncommissioned officers continued to use their fists as of old.[21] Efforts to make the soldiers more literate continued, with some success, although in the 1870's not more than one-third or one-half could read and write. Even this had limited consequences, since the men had little encouragement to read, and the books that were officially approved for their use were few.[22]

In spite of the persistent financial stringency of the regime under Miliutin, the Ministry of War built numerous barracks for the troops, so that by 1870 over half of them (56 per cent) had such housing.[23] The remainder presumably had to spend the winters in peasant huts. In part because the barracks made year-long instruction of the troops possible, they received more combat training, with somewhat less stress on parades and reviews. Extended order instead of close columns in battle came into vogue, and the commanders taught the soldiers to use the terrain to secure cover from enemy fire. The infantrymen learned to entrench themselves and do other simple engineering work. Above all, the infantry gave much greater attention to musketry, although target-practice remained somewhat infrequent.[24]

These reforms resulted in large part from the efforts of D. A. Miliutin, who also dealt with the difficult problem of eliminating the common practice among regimental commanders of pocketing funds intended for their troops' provisions. (Earlier attempts to end this practice had been unsuccessful.) From 1867 on, the Ministry increased the very scanty pay of some of the colonels by substantial amounts. This improved matters noticeably, and Miliutin next sought to deal with those commanders who had not received increases in pay. The Ministry began to permit the generals of divisions to give regimental commanders an annual bonus out of the savings obtained in their regiments through proper handling of the provisioning problem. Although Miliutin felt that this was an undesirable system, he held that, because of the lack of funds for general pay increases to the colonels, it was the most expedient solution. In addition, he introduced stricter accounting for monies spent for provisions. These measures, while they did not entirely end the corruption, kept it within stricter limits. Thus, Alexander Herzen, in his newspaper, *Kolokol,* which tended to be sharply critical of the government, stated that the soldiers were "in part saved from the thieving of the commanders."[25]

The climax of the military reforms, all of which made army service less burdensome to the peasant conscripts, was the great Army Reform of 1874 that cut the term of service to six years, with considerable reductions for those who had received education before beginning their service. Although draftees were still obliged to remain in the reserves for nine more years,[26] this was not a great hardship, because it permitted them to farm and to begin family life at a fairly early age. In addition, the government sought to give military service a respectable reputation by ceasing to put criminals and outcasts into uniform as a punishment. Despite all this, few if any villagers welcomed the call to the colors.

In the light of this amelioration of military duty, it is not surprising that the peasants in army greatcoats, unlike their noble officers, showed little interest in the revolutionary movements during the decades after 1860. A. V. Fedorov, a careful Soviet scholar, explicitly states: "A broad revolutionary movement in the army, in which the chief moving force would be the masses of soldiers, did not exist [in the 1870's]."[27]

The material presented above is based upon convincing evidence from archives and other original sources. It is interesting to find it corroborated in many respects by Lt. Francis V. Greene, U.S.A., who as Military Attaché accompanied the Russian army in the Russo-Turkish War of 1877–78, from the long siege of Plevna in 1877 to the crossing of the Balkan Mountains in midwinter, and on in the hurried advance to the outskirts of Constantinople. He traveled with the advance units—at times under Turkish fire—and shared the bivouacs and field rations of the troops. While Lieutenant Greene warmly admired the Russian soldiers and some of their commanders, he was not blind to the men's failings and defects, which he set forth in an impartial appraisal. Thus his account of what he saw gives an excellent picture of the reformed Russian army in action.

The Russian soldier, Greene stated, lacked the élan of the French, and was weak in initiative and self-reliance to the point of helplessness when his officers were put out of action. He made up for this apparent stupidity by his steadfastness and his enthusiasm when led into battle. His patience and endurance were phenomenal: his cheerful acceptance of hardship and his ability to fight unfed and under difficult circumstances were "beyond all praise." He was probably "the steadiest of soldiers under defeat and adversity." Even when leaderless, a body of Russian soldiers did not disintegrate, but stayed together without panic, holding fast to the end.[28]

These qualities were displayed during the disastrous siege of Plevna in 1877* and the daring campaign that followed its capture. With Plevna taken, the Russian commanders could boldly cross the Balkan Mountains in bitter midwinter cold, having their troops haul up cannon and wagons by hand where the horses could not keep their footing on the icy roads. Once over the crest, the guns and wagons had to be carefully lowered on ropes snubbed to trees or bushes. In spite of performing this trying work twelve hours a day, sleeping in the snow without shelter or blankets, and living on scanty rations of hard black biscuits and tough meat, "the patience and good humor of the men ... was extraordinary."[29]

Following the descent, the army marched on for six hundred miles without its knapsacks, fighting, fording rivers in zero weather, still sleeping in the snow. When their boots gave out, the men cut up their

* The attackers made three costly attempts to storm the fortress. The Turks were finally starved out.

shelter tents for foot wrappings, and struggled on, at times fighting without having had food for twenty-four hours. Thanks to these remarkable exertions, they completely destroyed the Turkish armies in four months. According to Lieutenant Greene, during this extraordinary campaign, there was no insubordination, and the stragglers were far fewer than in the preceding summer.[30]

When the campaign ended, less admirable aspects of the Russians became evident. The men, without baths or change of clothes for months, were quartered in miserable villages that could shelter only half of them. The army did not observe even the rudiments of sanitation: dead animals lay rotting for weeks in the spring sun, there were few latrines, and drinking water was taken from streams fouled by troops further upstream. Naturally disease struck heavily, with malaria, typhoid fever, and typhus laying low almost half of the army. Only after energetic measures did the epidemic wane; fortunately there were not many deaths.[31]

The American also noted that harsh and even brutal treatment of the uniformed peasants by their officers, while not typical, was far too frequent. Often he heard officers, with little provocation, use abusive language to soldiers, sometimes following it with blows. On one occasion he saw a company officer strike down a first sergeant before the company in formation for some trifling misunderstanding of orders.[32] Greene also noted that the Russian soldier lacked compassion for his vanquished foes—perhaps because of his own religious fanaticism.[33]

The peasant-soldier's faith in the Tsar greatly impressed Greene. The enlisted man suspected that his generals were fools, and was sure that his commissaries were rascals, especially when his uniform proved to be shoddy, his boots went to pieces, and his biscuits were filled with weevils. But he never thought of censuring the Tsar for these abuses. In fact, he usually dismissed these manifestations with the rueful wish: "Ah, if the Tsar only knew!"—reasoning that the monarch, the best friend of the soldier, would surely correct these evils if he learned of them. But since the Tsar could not know everything, the enlisted man could expect no relief, and so he would go on doing his duty faithfully, hoping that some day things would be better.[34]

Greene was especially impressed by the close religious bond between the ruler and his subjects, which was evident at a field mass for those who had just fallen in a disastrous assault on Plevna. The upper-class Russians, he felt, were not very religious, but to the peasant class, "the religion of miracles and ceremonies which they are taught is the most real thing in their lives, and on earth it all centers on the Tsar."[35] On another occasion he watched the Emperor ride among the troops lined up for inspection, greeting the men, who answered in long shouts, and chatting with a few who had distinguished themselves. The soldiers, with awe in their faces, followed him with straining eyes, with very real, unfeigned enthusiasm: "Their expression was not so much one of joy as of absentminded, wondering veneration." Greene adds that, when they were reviewed by generals and princes at the same sort of ceremony, "the men never had the same thoughts written on their faces as they did when they saw the Tsar."[36]

Lieutenant Greene was probably correct in ascribing this reverence for the Emperor to the ancient Russian tradition that the tsar was the true friend of the people and that the people's sufferings were caused by the monarch's unworthy subordinates. There may also have been another reason, however. There is statistical evidence that the lives of the enlisted men improved during the reign of Alexander II, in large part as a result of the reforms of D. A. Miliutin. An official account of the army administrations from 1855 to 1881 shows that in the period from 1871 to 1879 alone, the number of deaths from disease in the army declined from 17.6 per thousand to 10.4 per thousand.[37] While much of this decline was probably a result of the general advances in medicine in the nineteenth century, the fact was that the soldiers probably sensed that fewer men were dying in service and gave credit for this to the Tsar. And certainly in comparison with the situation before the Crimean War, when 37.4 men per thousand had died annually, the enlisted men in 1879 had much to be grateful for.[38]

The figures for men arraigned before military courts also show a decline from 1871 to 1876. In the former year there were 28,324 enlisted men brought to trial, while in 1876, only 18,096 were tried. Similarly, the number of investigations of alleged offenses was halved —from 17,045 to 8,693.[39]

Perhaps at this time the loyalty of the army to the tsar was at its peak, for by 1900 signs of growing disaffection had appeared. For one thing, the assassination of Alexander II in 1881 produced a severe reaction under Alexander III, who strongly opposed reforms. He did not retain Miliutin as Minister of War, and he turned away from democratization of the army, instead relying greatly on the nobility. His new Minister of War was the rather mediocre P. S. Vannovsky, who made almost no significant changes in the army other than to convert Miliutin's military schools back to cadet corps (officer candidate schools), in which most of the cadets were nobles.[40]

In May 1884, General Vannovsky wrote an "extremely secret" letter to A. S. Imeretinsky, Chief of the Judicial Section of the Army, in which he emphasized the appearance of subversion among the army officers, against which the military criminal legislation had to be made more rigorous. Not only should the unreliable officers be punished, but commanders who failed to supervise their subordinates properly should also suffer penalties. Although this subversion resulted primarily from revolutionary agitation that had penetrated Russia from the West, the officer corps had "degenerated" also through the influx of non-nobles, who were far less reliable than those of noble origin.[41]

While this emphasis on the nobility as the pillar of the Empire did not directly affect the peasants in the army, the reactionary trend and the pronounced bias toward the upper class led to a far less harmonious spirit in the armed services. Although the peasantry was probably the segment of the population that was least prone to disaffection (in 1903 Gen. A. N. Kuropatkin, Minister of War, spoke of the village as the source from which came Russia's "incomparable soldiers: loyal to the fatherland, to the sovereign, brave, enduring, undemanding"),[42] the reliability of the troops was already less certain than before. In 1902 Count S. Yu. Witte told the general that the troops had been too mild in subduing riots in Rostov-on-Don. Kuropatkin rejoined that they had accomplished their purpose without massive bloodshed, and added that it was easier for the army to assault any position than to shoot into a defenseless crowd. He urged that the civil authorities try to avoid situations that might require this, for such action corrupted the troops and might bring "one of the detachments to insubordination."[43] Similarly, when V. K. Plehve, Minister of Interior, complained that the troops had inflicted unnecessarily large casualties in a disorder at Zlatoust, Kuropatkin said that the best way to prevent this was to calm the population, in order "not to spoil the troops by making them fire on an unarmed crowd."[44]

The Minister of War was also troubled because in the first years of the new century, men under indictment, who were obviously politically unreliable, were entering the army in small but increasing numbers. In 1898, 8 criminals entered the ranks; there were 30 in 1900; and by the first half of 1903, there were 73. In his report to the Emperor, Kuropatkin warned that "the infection would penetrate more and more into the army."[45] The Minister was especially disturbed over the practice of sending rebellious naval personnel into the army as a punishment,[46] which was equivalent to introducing ardent revolutionaries into the midst of the soldiers.

While these practices doubtless made the army less dependable, there were factors within the army system itself that were contributory influences, one of which was the poverty of the peasant soldiers. Gen. A. F. Rediger, Minister of War in 1905 and 1906, put this near the top of his list of causes of disorders among the troops. A private's pay was only two rubles, ten kopeks per year. The authorities recognized the great poverty of the soldiers, but they felt that this was an unavoidable evil and that any attempt to improve matters would empty the treasury.*

To make matters worse, the underwear and the shoe leather issued to the men were so poor in quality that they sold these items for what they would bring and bought better-grade articles at their own expense. Because the allowance for the boots was tiny, the men had to pay two rubles out of their pockets to have them made. "In brief, without help from home the soldier not only would be in poverty, but almost could not exist."[47] While the opportunity to hire out for wagework allowed soldiers to earn some money, not all could do this, and a soldier could retain only one-third of his earnings for him-

---

* Probably as a result of the revolutionary disturbances in the army in 1905–6, General Rediger was able to obtain, over the strong opposition of the Ministry of Finance, a substantial increase in the pay of noncommissioned officers and a small one for the privates. The ration of meat and fat was increased to a quarter of a pound (*funt*) per day, and tea and sugar were added. He also obtained blankets and bed linen for them, two towels a year, handkerchiefs, and soap, as well as a much larger allowance for making up boots (Rediger, p. 94).

self; one-third was reserved to improve the rations of the troops, and
the balance went to those who had to remain on duty without outside work.

Only if the enlisted man served under an unusually effective and
careful commander did he receive a blanket and bed linen. The government issued blankets to the soldiers only in localities with especially bad climates. Gen. A. I. Denikin, in his account of the prerevo-
lutionary army, says that the enlisted men slept on wooden benches
(*nars*) along the walls of their barrack rooms, on straw-filled mattresses and pillows, but without covers or blankets. The men covered
themselves with their overcoats, which often were wet or dirty after
drill. If they had blankets, they bought them with savings from their
food money, or with money they had received from home.[48] Denikin
adds that the army did not provide sheepskins or other warm clothing for use in severe cold, but tried to supplement the thin overcoats
of the men with extra jackets made out of old overcoats.[49]

To make matters worse, the sailors in the navy had excellent equipment, as agitators were careful to point out to the soldiers. Also the
enlisted men knew that their commanders had fine carriages and
trotting horses maintained on the regimental funds that should have
gone for the enlisted men's needs.[50]

In his memoirs, Gen. A. A. Ignatiev tells of attending lectures by
Col. A. A. Polivanov in the 1890's on military administration. (Polivanov became Minister of War in 1915.) The lecturer quietly and
without comment discussed some of the shortcomings of the Russian
army, "including the miserable state system of uniforming and feeding the soldiers." Ignatiev remarked that Polivanov had reason to
ridicule this system, under which the soldier received an issue of one
and one-half shirts a year, 35 kopeks pay per month (about 18 American cents), 3½ kopeks (per day?) to supplement his ration of food,
and "not even an issue of soap for his needs."*

Another factor that probably antagonized the peasants in the army
was the unsanitary condition of the barracks. From the report issued

---

* A. A. Ignat'ev, *50 let v stroiu* (Moscow, 1948), p. 54. General Ignatiev, who was
trained in the aristocratic Corps of Pages and rose to be a general in the Imperial
Army, accepted the Soviet regime and served in the Red Army. His memoirs, while
often critical of the old regime, do not show ideological prejudices. Apparently he
joined the Soviets as a Russian patriot rather than out of fondness for communism.

by the Chief Military-Medical Administration for 1902 it is obvious that in the St. Petersburg barracks of the Guards regiments—the elite units of the Russian army—and, indeed, in those of most troops, respiratory diseases were "a real scourge." One of the reasons for this was that the barracks provided far fewer cubic feet of air per person than the regulations called for; another was that in winter the barracks were kept at temperatures about ten degrees colder than was proper. Furthermore, the barracks had insufficient light, especially in winter. As a result, those with lung infections rarely recovered and often became incapacitated. Many who were given discharges because of illness never arrived at their homes, but died in hospitals en route.[51] Eight years later the Report for the Chief Military-Sanitary Administration for 1910, given in the Report of the Minister of War for that year, indicated that the situation had not improved. The barracks were still overcrowded, poorly heated, and had little ventilation. The latrines were primitive, cold, and usually at some distance from the barracks; if they were in the same building, the stench spread throughout the whole barracks. In the Amur Military District, especially, the barracks were very unsatisfactory; most of them were temporary structures of wood, completely unsuited to the damp climate of the Far East. Some 5 per cent of the men were not even in barracks, but lived in earth or half-earth huts or dugouts. There was much overcrowding, with almost one-third of the soldiers sleeping on double-decked *nars*. Men with infectious diseases could not be isolated, and eating and working had to be done in the main barrackrooms. Bathhouses and laundries were often inadequate.[52]

In a letter from a Major General Zhirkevich to V. A. Sukhomlinov, Minister of War in 1911, there is a series of distressing complaints about the condition of the central guardhouses, which were places of confinement for prisoners from several regiments who were awaiting trial. Because these unfortunates were separated from their units, there was no one to look after them, and the commandant's office paid little attention to the guardhouse. As a result, the inmates suffered terribly from neglect. The buildings were often bitterly cold, unventilated, filthy, and filled with foul odors and infectious vapors. The prisoners, unbathed for a month or more, were covered with vermin and had no chance to wash their clothing. In some of these insti-

tutions the mattresses were full of holes and contained rotting, stink-
ing straw. Inevitably the prisoners were embittered and corrupted by
their experiences there, and when they returned to their units, they
had a very bad effect on their comrades.[53]

Undoubtedly another reason for the increasing alienation of the
peasants in uniform was the mistreatment that they received from
their superiors. This certainly was nothing new in the Russian army,
and it has probably occurred in many other armies. General Denikin
states that discipline in the German and Austrian armies in the early
years of the twentieth century was much more cruel and brutal than
in the Russian forces, where beating of the soldiers was condemned
and prosecuted.[54] Nevertheless, he admits that relations between officers and enlisted men were not always based on proper principles.
While in many cases there was comradeship between them, there was
often rudeness and cursing, sometimes arrogance and blows in the
face. The platoon and first sergeants often were even coarser and
more brutal than the officers. This, added to the innumerable vexa-
tions of barracks life, provided abundant material for revolutionary
manifestos that termed the soldier a "victim of the gold epaulettes."[55]

In his memoirs, Ignatiev mentions in passing the beating of soldiers
by officers. Once when he called a soldier in for an interview, the
man flinched when his commander came near and averted his head,
apparently fearing the officer's fists.[56] Ignatiev suggests that this was
not unknown even in his crack regiment, for he mentions an officer,
a graduate of the Corps of Pages, who passed for a fine officer and
one destined for an excellent career. He adds, however, that after the
Revolution of 1905 the model officer had to leave the regiment because his soldiers refused to respond to his greeting when he addressed them one day at drill. "The soldiers hated him for his 'laying
on of hands,'" Ignatiev explains.[57]

It is revealing to read the account given by Gen. A. I. Spiridovich,
who became a high official in the *Okhrana,* the political police under
Nicholas II. In his memoirs he tells of his service in 1893 in what he
describes as an outstanding infantry regiment, whose commanders
and officers all devoted themselves to the well-being of their unit. The
company officers, according to Spiridovich, knew their men inti-
mately, even their secrets and the details of the families from which

they had come. During their spare time the officers read aloud to their soldiers, wrote letters home for them, showed them magic-lantern slides, or sang with them. As for discipline, "Beating, as a system, did not exist. There were individual officers, who because of irritability sometimes resorted to beating," but these were exceptional cases. It was chiefly the younger officers who beat the soldiers, and they, moreover, "soon gave up these practices."[58] It seems logical to conclude that if, in this exceptionally fine regiment, beating was occasionally inflicted by the officers on their peasant soldiers, it must have been much more frequent in ordinary regiments, where such a warm camaraderie between officers and enlisted men did not exist.

Documents published by Soviet scholars reveal that at times the complaints of the soldiers were graver than mere beating. In 1905 some soldiers of a railroad battalion in Krasnoyarsk complained to the local Social Democratic committee that their officers were abusing and degrading them, and that they actually went hungry because their commanders had pocketed their funds. Although the men had earned 3,000 rubles in hired work on the railroads, their colonel issued a statement saying that there were only 800 rubles left. A month later his aide declared that the amount on hand was only 400 rubles, and they did not even receive this amount. Later, when they complained to a general, the only result was that some of them were jailed for complaining and others suffered lesser punishment. The soldiers asserted that the colonel had set up a shop with the money from their labor and then had sold it to some merchants, who allegedly charged the enlisted men exorbitant prices for their goods.[59] There is no way of knowing how well-founded these charges were, and the source does not indicate the outcome of the dispute.

Many of the cases of cruelty to peasants in uniform, however, involved noncommissioned rather than commissioned officers. For example, in May 1909, members of a platoon of artillery of the Vladivostok garrison complained to their commander that their sergeant had forced them to jump across the barracks floor one or two hundred times after drill hours, until they were exhausted. When they refused to do any more jumps, he made them hold out their hands so he could beat them with his belt buckle. He also made them do the goose step on tiptoes around the whole barracks, with their hands on their heads. When some of them fell, he beat their hands with his belt buckle. As a result of these charges, the company commander reduced the sergeant to a private.[60]

In March 1910, a sergeant in charge of training recruits punished a young soldier by making him do jumps and run in place. When the man stopped from exhaustion, the sergeant rose from his cot and dealt the private a very painful blow on the ear. The next day he reported to the officer of the day, who sent him to the hospital, where it was found that his eardrum was broken. The sergeant was tried and reduced to the ranks for this, and was held under strict arrest for twenty days. The military court, however, found him not guilty of crippling the private.[61]

Another case involved a gunner who demanded money from young soldiers whom he was training. When one refused to pay, he made the man sit with his arms raised high for two hours, and he hit him with his fist. He beat another soldier with his belt. For this physical maltreatment, and for taking money from soldiers, he was court-martialed.[62]

A more serious case was that of a young soldier who, after having been punished for drinking, later appeared on duty without his belt. Commanded to stand at salute for two hours, he did so until his arms gave out. At this, the sergeant cursed him for not obeying orders and, when he made excuses, threw him to the floor and kicked him repeatedly. When the private threatened to report this to the commander, the sergeant swore he would drive him to his grave. The next day the man was again in trouble for forgetting a piece of minor equipment; for this mistake he had to jump for twenty-five minutes. This treatment so upset him that that night he rushed to the kitchen, where he chopped his finger with an axe five or six times. The record fails to indicate what happened to the unfortunate after that, but it does report that the sergeant who had beaten him was imprisoned in the guardhouse for one month.[63]

Self-mutilation as a means of escaping the rigors of military life, while not common in the old army, occasionally occurred. In 1896, Ignatiev, a young officer in the Cavalier Guards, had to be on duty in a district court, where he was in charge of an officer's guard. He was amazed when the indictment was read: a young peasant, on learning that he was to be drafted into the army, chopped off the forefinger of his right hand with an axe so that he would be unfit for service. The young officer followed the proceedings with horror and watched the judges, well-decorated colonels of the Guards, sentence the man to five years in penal companies. "For the first time I saw full evidence that for the Russian peasant our army was a sort of penal labor."[64]

One factor that may have alienated the peasants in the army was the scant respect that many officers had for them as individuals. Colonel Rodzianko of the crack Cavalier Guards mentions with pride that at the regimental dinner, where the officers feasted and drank, part of the entertainment was supplied by regimental singers. "When it was my squadron's turn, they marched in on their hands, singing lustily all the time. This feat invariably got great applause."[65] His patronizing attitude toward his men is also evident in his account of his work in training recruits, to whom he sometimes had to teach the alphabet, "for the men were great big children, chosen for their physique." Although they were fine specimens of manhood, and fearless hunters in their homelands, "they were dazed by Petrograd and amazingly simple."[66]

To some extent this simplicity of the peasant soldiers, insofar as it existed, came from their being treated like inferior beings who were not to think. The officers always addressed their men in the familiar *ty* (thou), chiefly used to inferiors and children, and trained them to answer in stilted formulas: "exactly so" for "yes"; "not at all" for "no"; and "I could not know" for "I don't know." The response to orders or greetings was "*radi starat' sia*" (glad to try), shouted in unison, followed by the official title of the officer. Moreover, it was not until 1917 that the enlisted men received the right to smoke on the street and in public places, to ride inside streetcars, and to become members of various societies and political unions.[67] Trotsky states that 1917 was also the first time that the peasants in army overcoats obtained the right to attend theaters and other public amusements—which some of them interpreted to mean *free* admission.[68]

A supercilious attitude toward the common soldiers was expressed also in signs on the entrances to parks and other recreational areas. In 1898 the young Ignatiev, urged by his orderly to go for a walk in the fine spring sunshine, went to the Summer Garden, where he was struck by the fact that a sign on the entrance forbade admission "to dogs and enlisted men." When he returned to his regiment he was disturbed to notice that his fine first sergeant, a veteran of several campaigns, had to be satisfied with a stroll with his children in the dusty regimental courtyard, while in the Summer Garden smooth-faced young cadets sat on comfortable benches with their young ladies.[69] Similarly, in 1909 Gen. A. A. Brusilov, who liked to walk his fox terrier in the town garden at Lublin, encountered a sign at the entrance: "Forbidden to enlisted men and dogs." He was furious at this, not because of the ban on his pet, but because of the slur on the soldiers who stood ready to fight for their country. He was able to bring the matter to the attention of the governor-general, who had the prohibition rescinded.[70] And in 1911 the Botanical Gardens in St. Petersburg posted a notice banning dogs and another stating that "enlisted men, cantonists, and common people are forbidden to enter without special permission." The Summer and Tavrida Gardens had similar regulations. These restrictions, though they originated with the civil authorities rather than with the military, indicate the low status accorded to the mass of the people, including the peasants in the army.

Whatever the reasons, the accumulated resentment of the soldiers —no doubt intensified by radical agitators—boiled over during the Revolution of 1905, when mutinies occurred in many regiments, both in the Far East and in Russia proper, so that the full breakdown of the army appeared imminent. Even the Preobrazhensky Regiment, regarded as the foremost unit of the Guards, became disobedient in June 1906, when its commander ordered it to march from Krasnoe Selo to Peterhof instead of going by rail. After a plea from the commander, it made the march. But on arriving at Peterhof, the first battalion made a disturbance, refusing to disperse and retire to quarters. The men even cursed and abused the regimental and battalion officers on duty. Only a speech by the general in command induced them to submit and to surrender the ringleaders. The regiment then marched back to Krasnoe Selo, with the first battalion disarmed.[71] This event created a great sensation in army circles. Indeed, so menacing was the widespread disaffection in the armed forces that in

1906 the Minister of War proposed that special courses for officers be set up in the military schools, so that the officers might more effectively combat the revolutionary doctrines that were penetrating the ranks of the soldiers. The proposal called for an elaborate course in political science, economics, and history to enable the officers to refute the subversive ideas that their men might encounter. Nicholas II noted on the plans for the project: "Secret and extremely urgent."[72]

The seriousness of the situation was confirmed by an article that appeared in a contemporary underground army newspaper, *Kazarma (The Barrack)*. The writer, who may have been a soldier, stated that at the height of the revolution the authorities paid the soldiers an extra fifteen kopeks per day for doing police work. As soon as the emergency was over, however, they allegedly ceased making the extra payments and providing the full meals that the soldiers had been receiving, and again fed them unpalatable food. "They make fools of us, like rams, and even call us 'gray cattle' and force us to fire on our own brothers, fathers, mothers, and sisters," which the enlisted men, "like dumb cattle," did, killing their own kith and kin. "And now, brothers, it is time for us to wake up and open our eyes and see whom we are killing and for what."[73] It is significant that this appeal was couched in homely terms that would probably appeal to soldiers drawn from the village.

There is, then, reason to believe that the peasant in the Russian army immediately before 1905 was probably more prone to disaffection and mutiny than ever before. What is remarkable about this is that life in the army, although it was still harsh, was probably not nearly as severe as it had been in earlier years. Army life under Nicholas I must have been a real nightmare for many soldiers. Things improved considerably under Dmitri Miliutin between 1861 and 1881, and although there was another difficult period for the soldiers after 1881, there is no reason to think that the life of the peasant in the army was getting worse at the turn of the century. It may even have been improving slightly. How, then, can one explain the paradox that the peasant-soldiers were considerably less submissive at this time than they were when their life was much worse?

Gen. A. I. Denikin, who led the anti-Soviet Volunteer Army in southern Russia in 1919, offers the explanation that by the twentieth century the Russian people had lost their simple religious faith and had come under the influence of material interests. As a result, the recruits "had a rather indifferent attitude toward matters of the faith and the church." The barracks regime, which tore men from their normal way of life, did not provide them with moral and spiritual guidance, but treated religion in a formal and compulsory fashion. Thus it meant much less to the soldiers than in bygone years, and hence the old formula, "For faith, tsar, and fatherland," no longer inspired devotion. Revolutionary propaganda could find fertile soil.[74]

This view probably contains some truth, but it is oversimplified, because there were many other influences on the soldiers' attitudes. The Soviet historian Fedorov puts the matter into a broader context, citing a passage from Lenin to the effect that the Russian peasants were no longer the downtrodden, submissive beings who believed the priests and feared the authorities, but a new generation, many of whom had gone off to the cities and had learned much as wage-workers. Fedorov maintains that this had a marked effect upon the army, for in it these awakened peasants met conscripts who had been workers, artisans, or students, from whom they learned new, often revolutionary, doctrines. Moreover, after three or four years, the peasant-soldiers, excited by new ideas and often literate, returned to their villages, where they often became revolutionary leaders themselves and indoctrinated subsequent conscripts from their villages.[75]

This explanation seems convincing. What it means is that it was not the conditions that they encountered in the army—distasteful though these may well have been—that caused the peasants in the ranks to be less reliable. Instead, it was largely the growth of a dissatisfied and rebellious spirit among the masses that affected the soldiers and made them less willing to give unquestioning obedience to their superiors.

In his book on the Russo-Japanese War, General Kuropatkin draws a vivid contrast between the intensely patriotic Japanese, who formed special societies to which the authorities issued thousands of rifles for target practice, and the Russians, to whom the government did not dare supply rifles, for fear of an uprising. The Russian schools, he asserts, did little to inspire patriotism, and the university students had largely turned against the government. It was "the fashion to abuse everything Russian, and military service is thought dishonorable." Kuropatkin adds that the Russian infantryman, "undersized and overloaded," was usually untidy and often dirty, and generally outfitted in a badly fitting uniform. Slouching along the street, he aroused more pity than pride among the onlookers.[76]

As a result of this widespread contempt for the military and the disaffection *within* the military, revolutionary propaganda was a serious threat. A "burning question," according to Kuropatkin, and one of ever-increasing importance, was "how to keep the destructive tenets of the revolutionary parties out of our barracks." He insisted that unless the civil authorities could destroy the subversive organizations among the people, "we can hardly expect to be able to keep the army from infection."[77]

But how could the revolutionary movement be crushed? Gen. Yu. N. Danilov, Quartermaster General during World War I, stated that by 1914 the government had lost the support of society, so that it was almost isolated, save for the monolithic officers' corps, with its deep loyalty to the fatherland. On the other hand, "the revolutionary whirlwind" had in large part affected the rank and file of the army. Unfortunately for the regime, the government had made unwise use of the army in the struggle with workers, peasants, and students, thus creating a deep chasm between the officers on the one hand and the masses of the population on the other. "The populace became accustomed to regard the armed force of the state as something strange to it and even hostile."[78] This split had become too wide and deep to heal.

Kuropatkin repeatedly stressed how dangerous it was to use the army to suppress riots. While he insisted on iron discipline, so that the soldier would always fear his officer, he held that the worst foe of discipline was the use of soldiers in the political struggle. On the one hand, the men were inevitably exposed to corrupting propaganda, and on the other, they were taken away from their military duties and used "for almost continuous police duties." This involved not only suppressing mutinies of soldiers, but also dealing with riots that the police and the gendarmes should have dealt with. Furthermore, this meant taking officers away from their units to sit in the field courts-martial, to condemn, shoot, or hang political or other offenders. As a result, the civilians hated the officers for this, while the soldiers—militarized peasants—hated both the civilians who shot at them and the officers who ordered them to kill civilians, many of whom were peasants. If riot-duty became frequent, "if the soldier sees that the government is powerless to restore order even with the aid of troops, doubts will creep into his mind as to the effectiveness of the government and as to his own commanders."[79] These doubts were probably beginning to take root in the minds of some of the peasant-soldiers even before the Revolution of 1905.

It seems clear that, although the grievances of soldiers were still significant in 1905, they were less severe than at earlier times. But the enlisted men could not be isolated from the rest of Russia. Workers—often of peasant origin—were striking and fighting on barricades in increasing numbers, and peasants were rising to attack the estates of nobles; the soldiers—most of them still peasants at heart—could not escape from the influence of these developments. Inevitably, the troops were used to suppress the riots and peasant uprisings, with consequent bloodshed and suffering for the people. This began to undermine the discipline of the troops and, although it took the horrors of World War I to complete the process, the decay of the Imperial Army of peasants had already begun by 1905.

5. The Peasant and the Village Commune

Francis M. Watters

Introduction

Any discussion of peasant life, to be complete, must ultimately become a discussion of peasant land. For nineteenth-century Russia and, most particularly, for the waning decades of the century, a discussion of the system of peasant land tenure is basic not only to an understanding of the conditions in which the peasant worked and lived, but also to an understanding of one of the most important and most pervasive issues of the time—"the peasant question." "The peasant question" referred to the broad range of problems that plagued peasant agriculture and permeated the whole life of the empire. While its causes were many, including deteriorating grain prices in the international market, the change of emphasis in agriculture from subsistence production to production for market, and the inordinate burden of taxation placed on peasant land by the state, it was the rigid and inflexible system of peasant land tenure, with its constraining effect on cultivation, that was the key element in the question.

The intensity of the controversy concerning the peasant question can hardly be overstated. It preoccupied the intellectuals of the time, forming the basis of a clash between the Slavophiles and the Westernizers. Political activists, the most prominent of whom were the *Narodniki*, found in the agrarian unrest, and in the hope of land reforms beyond those accompanying the emancipation, elements that were useful to them in their attempts to generate revolutionary momentum. The manifold aspects of the peasant question are reflected in the legislative history of the period—a long succession of decrees

This paper consists of sections of a doctoral dissertation that I submitted at the University of California at Berkeley. For their valuable comments and advice I am indebted to Professors Gregory Grossman, Henry Rosovsky, and Nicholas Riasanovsky.

pertaining to taxes, redemption payments, and the obligations and rights of occupancy. It stimulated both publicly and privately sponsored research in the field of agriculture that resulted in the compilation of vast quantities of data and the publication of a flood of books and articles. Finally, it manifested itself repeatedly in the literature of the time, indicating its importance even to those who lived in a world apart from that in which the peasant lived.

The world of the peasant cultivator was narrow: it focused almost wholly on the land and his relationship to it. It is this narrow world that is the subject of this paper. Our central topic will be the village commune, the *obshchina* or *mir*, for it was this institution that governed the life of the peasant—specifying the amount and area of land available to him, determining the crops he should plant, designating the time he should harvest, assessing his obligations, and guarding his rights.

Characteristics of Communal Land Tenure

The forms of communal land tenure in imperial Russia were too diverse and varied to permit broad generalizations. The *mir* or *obshchina* was structurally and functionally different from one locality to another. The term *mir*, Maynard tells us, refers to "rights in land [that] are held in common; but possession or cultivation is individual."[1] Kachorovsky defines the Russian land commune as an institution in which, as a result of the interaction of law and custom, the right of disposition of property belongs to the community as a whole, but the right of use belongs to each individual member.[2] These are, perhaps, definitions as precise as may be had for an institution as complex in function and diverse in pattern as was the communal village in Russia.

It is, perhaps, as difficult to generalize about the Russian *obshchina* as it is about the feudal manor. There were, however, three distinctive characteristics of the *obshchina* in European Russia in the latter half of the nineteenth century that should be noted. First, the property in land was vested not in the peasant but in the *obshchina*, a matter on which there was not universal accord, as we shall see. Second, each household within the *obshchina* had a right to an allotment of land on an equal basis with all the other member households.

These allotments were cultivated separately by the individual families. In addition to the right to an allotment of plowing land, each household had the right to use meadow and common pasture areas and to exploit forest areas according to a prescribed formula. These rights, also, were assured to each household on an equal basis with the other households. Besides the communal rights, the household held in hereditary tenure its own dwelling and adjacent garden plot. Third, the community as a whole had, in most cases, the power to repartition the land from time to time and to reapportion the quantity of land assigned to the various member households. Such a repartition would be undertaken with the object of equalizing the economic opportunities of the member households, and would be necessitated by changes in the size of the households as a result of births and deaths.[3]

Controversy over the Status of the Obshchina

Throughout the last half of the nineteenth century the *obshchina* was the subject of intense controversies concerning its origin, its legal status, its influence upon the historical development of Russia, and particularly its future role in the economic and social development of the country.

The arguments pertaining to the legal status of the *obshchina* and the property it held, vis-à-vis that of its members, arose partially from the failure of the agrarian laws to distinguish between the *obshchina* and the *sel'skoe obshchestvo* (agricultural community), the term used in legislation referring to the commune in the broadest sense, and partially from ideological differences concerning the role of the *obshchina* in the life of the empire. There was a division of opinion on whether the *obshchina* was a legal entity that owned the land itself or was merely a relationship among its individual members who were themselves the owners of the land. The former view may be designated as "organic" and the latter as "mechanistic." Pobedonostsev, the Ober-Procurator of the Holy Synod, a defender of the organic concept, regarded the *obshchina* as a corporate entity and, as such, a property owner. He argued that the individual member could not be considered the owner of land, for there was no fixed quantity of property over which he had exclusive control; rather, his claim was merely to the use of his share of the communal land, a share that could be either increased or diminished in size and could be changed from one locality to another within the area owned by the *obshchina* as the collective membership saw fit. He supported his argument by pointing out that decisions relative to the use of the land were made by the community as a whole, or a majority of it, and that therefore *obshchina* property was not private property ideologically or functionally, much less legally. Pobedonostsev distinguished between the communal property of the village and its common property. Communal property was that land which, while owned by the village as a whole, was partitioned among its member households, cultivated by them individually, and used for their individual benefit; common property, on the other hand, was open to the use of all the members and was devoted to the benefit of the community as a whole. Such areas included meadows, pastures, and roads. Pobedonostsev asserted that the right of the individual member of the community to the use and enjoyment of common property was a property right, while his right to the use of the communal lands was subject to the decision of its owner, the *obshchina*.[4]

S. V. Pakhman supported the organic view of the *obshchina* and the thesis of Pobedonostsev. He agreed that the land belonged to the *obshchina* as owner or landlord, and he further claimed for the *obshchina* an existence independent of that of the individuals comprising it; this is the organic view in its fullest sense. In Pakhman's words: "Communal land ownership presupposes that the claim to the land belongs above all to the *obshchina* itself, as the individual proprietor, self-perpetuating, that is, separate from its members, a subject of the law."[5]

The mechanistic view of the *obshchina* was apparently less widely held. As a proponent of this concept, Kavelin regarded the *obshchina* as a quasi-governmental institution and as an association of private property holders.[6] From this point of view, the members of the village commune were property owners who had formed an association for the purpose of exploiting their property in land collectively and, to this end, had imposed certain rules upon themselves limiting the rights of the individual in his control over his property in land. According to this interpretation, the *obshchina* was merely the vehicle or mechanism for the collective cultivation of the land.

The effect of the emancipation ukase of February 19, 1861, was to give official support to the organic concept of the *obshchina*. Such land as was transferred to the peasant in allotments upon his emancipation was placed at the disposition of the *obshchina* in which the ownership of the land was formally vested, along with the responsibility for the redemption obligations. It seems that attempts were made to impose this type of land tenure in localities where repartitional communal land tenure was not practiced. Apparently, however, the legal controversy persisted, as Antsiferov explains:

The ownership of allotment land, if it was not in communal tenure, was vested in the joint family, which the Supreme Court of Russia [the Senate] made attempts to interpret as a *juridical person*. It failed, however, to establish a clear distinction between the house elder as a private individual and as head of the joint family. The legal situation remained extremely confused until the legislation in 1906–1910 by M. Stolypin, when the house elder was recognized as the absolute owner of the allotment, thus depriving the junior members of the family of their claims without any indemnity.[7]

It would seem that from the functional point of view, the organic concept of the *obshchina* was the one more consonant with reality. The *obshchina* controlled the property in land and distributed it among its members. If one equates ownership with control, then it was the *obshchina* and not the individual peasant who owned the land.

Recent History of Communal Land Tenure

In addition to the dispute over the legal status of the commune, a controversy arose over its origin. This was one of the prominent issues in the grand debate between the Slavophiles and the Westernizers concerning the meaning of Russian history and the future course of Russia's political and economic development. The Westernizers saw the *obshchina* as mainly the product of recent governmental practices, while the Slavophiles insisted that it had its roots in the tribal organization of the early Slavs. This controversy has been fully described elsewhere and is not relevant here, but the history of the *obshchina* and its relation to the state, culminating in the emancipation edict of 1861, is pertinent.

The practice of communal land tenure as it existed in the nineteenth century seems to have grown and flourished in the two previous cen-

turies, and to have resulted from practices encouraged or adopted by
the landlords and the state. By the sixteenth century the *mir* had become the agent of the lord, the vehicle for implementing his direc-
tives, and, in terms of the peasants' obligations, the unit that was collectively responsible to him. In 1724 the state, by imposing the soul
tax, gave impetus to the practice of collective repartitional land tenure.
In order to be assured of the ability of the peasant to pay the soul tax,
the landlord assessed the tax on the basis of the *tiaglo*, a term that referred not only to the financial burden of the soul tax, but also to the
unit of labor responsible for the payment of the tax and to the allotment of land assigned to this unit of labor. The *tiaglo* varied from
household to household, depending upon the number of able-bodied
laborers in each. As the number of laborers in the various households
of a village community changed over time as a result of births and
deaths, a redistribution of the *tiaglo* within the community would
be undertaken to equalize the tax burden on the households and the
ability of the households to pay the tax in relation to their allotments
of land. In the eighteenth century, local officials were known to intervene in matters of land tenure to assure a sufficiently equal distribution of land to facilitate payment of the tax; by orders of such officials,
land in certain areas was confiscated or newly cleared for this purpose.
The Department of Appanage, which was created in 1797, pursued
the same general land policy with respect to the peasants within its
jurisdiction. In 1829 the Ministry of Finance directed that "black
plowing" peasant land, that is, land that had not been made the private property of a member of the upper classes was to be apportioned
among peasant households on the basis of the number of souls per
household, thereby subjecting not merely confiscated or newly cleared
land, but all peasant land of this category to repartition. Thus, in
vesting the ownership of land allotted to the peasant in the *sel'skoe
obshchestvo,* the emancipation ukase of February 19, 1861, followed
the 150-year-old practice of the state in strengthening the institution
of communal repartitional land tenure.[8]

More specifically, the effect of the emancipation edict and the process of land allotment that attended it was to make the consolidation
of the field strips, the "enclosure" of plowing lands into homestead
units, and the withdrawal of a peasant from the village commune

virtually impossible. With his freedom, the former serf also received an allotment of land, but he was required to pay a substantial sum of money to the landlord in return for the allotment he obtained. The law provided that the state would act as financial intermediary in this redemption process only if all the households of the *sel'skoe obshche-stvo* acted as a unit and assumed joint responsibility for the reimbursement of the state.[9] In the majority of cases this was the method used, and even in those communities where non-repartitional tenure had become the practice, an element of collectivity was reintroduced as a result of the emancipation. It is of interest to note that the character of land tenure was determined by the method of redemption. Thus, those communes in which property had been held in hereditary tenure, once having embarked upon collective redemption, were deemed by the law to be repartitional communes by the nature of the redemption obligation, although attempts were made by officials to preserve the hereditary nature of the allotments.

In order to ensure the ability of the commune to meet its redemption obligations, stringent conditions were imposed to discourage the withdrawal of a household from the commune and the alienation of allotment land from communal control. While individual redemption at the outset was possible, it was in practice a difficult matter for a household to obtain a single farm unit from its scattered strips and undefined rights to forest areas and common pasture. Any such consolidation or enclosure of holdings required a two-thirds vote of the assembled *mir*, which was difficult to obtain. Once the commune with hereditary non-repartitional tenure had embarked upon the redemption process as a unit with the aid of a state loan, the individual member could withdraw from the commune only under conditions that were generally very hard to satisfy: he had to pay off his debt in its entirety or find someone who would take over the allotment of land for him, along with its burden of debt. This was made difficult by the fact that the obligations frequently exceeded the value of the land.[10]

In the repartitional *obshchina*, where the communal property elements were dominant, a member could, at the time of emancipation, renounce his right to the plowing land, forest, and common pasture area and redeem his house and garden plot individually. Once the redemption process was under way, however, he could transfer the allotment and its financial burden only with the consent of a majority of the assembled *mir*. On the other hand, the individual member could withdraw from the commune while redemption was in process by surrendering his allotment to the commune, paying half the remaining obligation due on it (the precise sum was often difficult to determine, as well as to obtain), and persuading the other members of the commune to assume responsibility for the balance. If the membership of the *mir* refused to assume responsibility for the remainder of the debt, the individual could not be relieved of his membership in and obligations to the commune.

Restrictions were also placed on the *obshchina* as a whole with respect to the alienation of the allotment land. For nine years after the promulgation of the statutes, the commune could not dispose of land to any person not a member. Later, while the redemption was still in process, it could dispose of such land only upon the approval of certain *gubernia* authorities.

Robinson summarizes these confusing and complicated regulations:

It may be said that in the repartitional communes, membership and allotment holding were inseparable. So long as the land remained in repartitional tenure, it was the duty and the right of the commune to offer the allotment—and it was the right and duty of the householder to receive it; so it had to be if the system of repartition were to operate when allotment was a burden as well as an asset. If membership and allotment holding were bound up together, just so the termination of membership and the divestment of land were interlocked, and any difficulty in the way of either of these operations was therefore at the same time an obstacle to the other. That is to say, the general restrictions upon personal withdrawal acted as an additional check upon the alienation of allotment rights, while on the other hand, the difficulty of disposing of the allotment (the difficulty of getting rid of an overburdened allotment under any condition or of disposing of a profitable one at a fair value) was by all odds the most important artificial barrier to the personal separation of the peasants from the commune.[11]

Certainly herein must lie the explanation for the large percentage of the industrial labor force that still had close ties to the agricultural sector at the turn of the century, as noted by Von Laue.[12]

Succeeding agrarian legislation placed still further restrictions on the peasant and his land in what were apparently attempts to secure the peasant's position on the land. The law of June 8, 1893, placed restrictions on the sale of hereditary allotments to persons outside the peasant class. It also attempted to make the practice of redivision less frequent by specifying that redivision of the land could be undertaken only if approved by a two-thirds vote of the *mir*, and only if it had been made clear to the members by what method of accounting the land would be reapportioned and what specific amount of tax would be due from the head of each household. But once the redivision had taken place, the *mir* could not deprive a household of its allotment during the next twelve years, except in the event of death, separation from the community for penal servitude, the refusal of a household to cultivate the land, or delinquency in the payment of taxes.[13] The law also provided that at least twelve years must pass before a new redivision was undertaken. While the apparent object of the law was to reduce the frequency of repartitions, this effect was not always achieved, and in localities where the practice of repartition had all but been abandoned, the law served to stimulate its renewal. The law gave the *zemskii nachal'nik* (the land captain), whose role was to extend the control of the Ministry of the Interior in the local government, increased authority over the *obshchina* in these matters; he often interpreted the twelve-year minimum period as a maximum period also. This law, then, as interpreted and applied, had a twofold effect: on the one hand, it retarded the frequency of redivisions where this practice was the custom, and, on the other, it spread the practice of land redivision to areas where it had not been a prevalent tradition.[14]

Land Tenure Classifications: Functional and Structural

As has been stated in the above discussion, variations in the forms and practices of communal land tenure were great. The blend of private property rights and communal property rights, as well as the relationships between the village communities and their surrounding land areas, varied so greatly within the European part of the empire that any taxonomic effort is certain to be frustrated. Kachorovsky arrived at three basic—but unfortunately not very useful—categories of communal land tenure in the Russia of the late nineteenth century: (1) *obshchina* in formation, (2) *obshchina* in being, and (3) *obshchina* in deterioration. He stated that if "a line were drawn from eastern Siberia to the western *gubernias* of European Russia, then, in general, the succession goes from *obshchina* in formation to *obshchina* in being and then to *obshchina* in deterioration." This implied that in the west the equalizing function of land redistribution was tending to atrophy, and that while the *obshchina* may have been considered to own the land, individual peasants were acquiring increasingly firm holds on specific plots of the communal land. The lengthening of the periods between redivisions was evidence of this trend. Kachorovsky stated that there was a continuum between the two extreme types of *obshchina,* that is, between the type of *obshchina* in which the communal elements sharply outweighed the private elements of land ownership and the type in which the private property elements had largely suppressed the communal.[15]

Structurally the *obshchina* was no less heterogeneous an institution. V. I. Orlov set up three categories for classifying it structurally.[16] The first was the "simple *obshchina*," which was a single village owning and cultivating the land contiguous to it. The second, the "composite *obshchina*," comprised several *mirs* or agricultural communities and such land as they owned, however that land was cultivated or divided. The third type was the "distributed *obshchina*," which consisted of land that lay within the territorial confines of several agricultural communities, but was nevertheless owned and cultivated by only one of the communities. The composite and distributed *obshchinas* were more often encountered in the northern and northeastern *gubernias* than elsewhere. Functionally, the large composite *obshchina* fell at that end of the continuum where the private property elements dominated. In the composite *obshchina* usually only the haying and forest areas were managed and exploited communally: the plowing land was held in hereditary non-repartitional tenure.

Types of Land Redivision

While the jurisdiction of the *mir* encompassed the whole life of the village community, its most important decisions pertained to the redivision of the land. Here again there was great variation throughout the country, both in the frequency of redivision and in the technique of redivision. In general, however, there were three broad types of land redivision. The first type, the *korennoi peredel,* the basic or radical redivision, was one in which both the number and the sizes of the field strips comprising the communal land were changed, and a wholly new disposition of the land was made to the member households. The second type, called the *zhereb'evka,* or redivision by lot, merely redistributed the ownership of the existing field strips, which remained the same in number, size, and location. In this second type the peasants exchanged field strips among themselves on the basis of "that which is near one becomes his"; presumably, each household was left with the same quantity of land. The third category was the *pereverstka,* or "reordering redivision." Here, as in the *zhereb'evka,* the number and sizes of the field strips did not change, but the distribution of the field strips among the various households did change, with certain households losing land and others gaining.[17]

Not all redivisions of the land pertained to all of the member households or to the entire land area belonging to the *obshchina. Chastnye peredely,* or partial redivisions, referred to the repartition of a fraction of the total land area as undertaken by only a portion of the total membership of the *obshchina.* The partial redivisions were more frequent in occurrence than the *obshchina*-wide redivisions. In areas where the broader forms of redivision were no longer practiced, partial redivisions became common among related families within the commune. Between 1861 and 1882 there were reportedly more than 2.37 million such family redivisions in forty-six *gubernias.*[18]

The redivision, as a rule, pertained only to the plowed land. Garden area and the property on which the family dwelling stood was private property and could be transferred to heirs; only in very exceptional cases was it subject to redivision. Forest land was divided not on the basis of land area, but rather on the basis of the quantity and quality of timber growth, each household being given an equal right to cut a certain quantity of wood in a given period.

It was this objective of equal economic opportunity for each household that made the task of redivision a complex and taxing one. Differences in quality of soil, topography of the land, and distance of plots from the village were all factors that had to be taken into account at the time of redivision in order to make the values of the parcels of land assigned to the member households as nearly equal as possible. In

general, the practice was to divide the land of the commune into fields
that were cultivated on the basis of the three field crop rotation system.
Each of these fields, in turn, was then divided into *iarusy,* or banners,
numbering up to more than twenty, depending on the quality of the
soil and the distance of the field from the settlement. The *iarusy* were
then broken down into strips that were assigned to individual households, often by drawing lots. Each household had the right to at least
one of the strips in a field of a given quality. If land of inferior quality
was assigned to a household, compensation was made in the form of
a larger area or occasionally in the form of a direct money payment.[19]

Redivision Policies and Practices

After the tenth revision, i.e., the census of 1858, the common unit
of calculation for the redivision was the *revision soul,* a term that at the
time of the census referred to a living adult male, but in later years
became an accounting term referring to a share in the *obshchina,* that
is, a proportion of the land and of the sum of the tax obligations. As
the years passed, the composition of a village community would
change both in the number of its members and in the sizes of the various age groups comprising its membership; however, the tax payments for which the community was collectively responsible continued to be assessed on the basis of the number of taxable or revision
souls living in 1858. Thus the practice arose that each male member
of the village commune would receive land and assume a tax obligation proportionate to his share of the responsibility originally levied
on the taxable souls extant in 1858. The calculation of this share would
usually allow for the age of the worker. A ten-year-old boy, for example, would incur the obligation of one-fourth of a revision soul,
a twelve-year-old that of one-half, a fourteen-year-old that of three-
fourths. A sixteen-year-old would count as one-and-a-half revision
souls, each male between the ages of twenty and fifty-five would count
as two, and those between fifty-five and sixty as one-half. Those above
the age of sixty would be relieved of tax obligations as well as rights
to share in the land.[20]

There were also other methods used for calculating the proportionate shares of land and tax liability. In certain communes the calculation was based upon the number of all adult members. This method
was called "redivision by consumer." There was also "redivision by

agreement," a process in which the head of the household indicated how many souls' responsibility he wished to assume; the assembled *mir* decided on the acceptability of the proposal and the amount of money the peasant would have to pay, if any, for receiving extra land. A "mixed redivision" included other considerations in the calculations, such as the quantity of cattle owned by each peasant (a matter of general importance in the redivision of haying lands), the skills the peasant possessed as a craftsman, or the wages he obtained from outside work.

It was on the basis of the above considerations that the village community, at the time of redivision, determined whether a given household should have tax souls (and the attendant strips of land) "laid on" or "taken off." A variety of factors determined the frequency of redivisions. The most prominent was the change in the composition of the individual households as a result of births and deaths. When the previously assigned tax souls for given households had become either too light or too burdensome, the community "laid on" or "took off" tax souls to equalize economic opportunity and tax liability. Where land had become particularly valuable, a redivision would be undertaken to diminish the land area occupied by the boundaries that divided the field strips. As would be expected, resistance to a new redivision generally came from the wealthier peasants, who saw a threat to their economic status in this equalizing process.

No precise information exists indicating the areas where redivision was practiced or the frequency of its occurrence, save that given above concerning family redivisions. Generally, however, redivisions were more frequent in the eastern and southern steppe areas than in the central agricultural region, where in some areas the last redivision occurred at the time of the emancipation. Kachorovsky states that redivision became increasingly common in the 1870's and 1880's, and persisted until the turn of the century. The history of the legislation pertaining to the practice indicates that redivisions of allotment land were more frequent than government officials thought desirable. The law of June 8, 1893, as we have noted, restricted the practice by establishing a minimum interval of twelve years between redivisions. An earlier law (March 18, 1886) had restricted family redivisions by stipulating that they could be undertaken only with the approval of the head of the household and two-thirds of the members of the *mir*. On

July 12, 1889, this law was amended to require, in addition, the consent of the land captain.[21]

Importance of Communally Owned Land

The intense controversy concerning the political and historical role of the *obshchina* indicates its importance in the intellectual life of the time; its importance to the economy up to the Stolypin reforms is shown by statistical evidence. Kablukov states that after the emancipation there were approximately 140,000 peasant communes in European Russia, with a total membership of 22,396,069 revision souls, i.e., males of ten years and older, and that these communes owned an estimated 116,854,855 *desiatinas* of arable allotment land. (One *desiatina* equals 2.7 acres.) This comprised 57 per cent of all land at the disposition of private individuals and 80 per cent of all land in the hands of the peasant class.[22] It should be noted that Kablukov's figures do not include lands leased or purchased by *obshchinas* on their own account, and thereafter divided among their members. Not all allotment land was communally controlled, however. There were significant sections of the country where allotments were made to families and joint families, and such lands had much of the character of private property.

An indication of the importance of communally held land in relation to all land, both allotment and private, at the disposition of the peasantry is given in Table 1. This table shows that communal own-

TABLE 1

COMMUNALLY OWNED LAND AS A PERCENTAGE OF TOTAL PEASANT LAND, 1892

Region	Per Cent	Region	Per Cent
Eastern steppe	98.4%	New Russia	88.9%
Far North	98.0	Large-village Ukraine	80.4
Western Great Russia (densely populated)	97.1	Bessarabia	77.0
		White Russia	39.0
Western Great Russia (sparsely populated)	96.5	Left-bank Ukraine	33.0
		Right-bank Ukraine	13.9
Great Russia	95.8	Lithuania	0.0
Perm border	93.0	Baltic	0.0

Source: K. R. Kachorovskii, *Russkaia obshchina*, 2d ed. (Moscow, 1906), p. 74. Kachorovsky's figures are from the work of Yuzhakov; the date 1892 is highly likely but not certain.

~~ership was the predominant form of peasant landholding~~ throughout
~~European Russia in 1892, except in White Russia, the Ukraine, and
the Lithuanian and Baltic~~ *gubernias* (where it did not exist at all).
More detailed information is available concerning the cultivation or
utilization of communally owned allotment land. This type of peasant cultivation predominated throughout the empire; for the whole
of European Russia approximately three-fourths of all male peasants
utilized communally owned land, and about four-fifths of all the allotment land was thus controlled. Table 2 shows the percentages by
region of allotment land held communally in the year 1877. In Grodno and in the White Russian *gubernia* of Minsk (see map, p. 148),
the amount of such land was insignificant, and in the neighboring
province of Vitebsk it comprised less than 40 per cent of the allotment land. In the *gubernias* of the Southwest, i.e., Kiev, Podolia, and
Volynia, communally held allotment land constituted less than one-
fifth of the total.[23] But elsewhere it was predominant, in many places
almost to the exclusion of private allotment holdings.

Communal Acquisition of Private Land

The practice of periodic redivision of communally held allotment
land combined with the increasing population had the effect of re-

TABLE 2

COMMUNAL UTILIZATION OF ALLOTMENT LAND AS A PERCENTAGE OF
ALL ALLOTMENT LAND, 1877

(Figures are range of gubernia *percentages)*

Region	Per Cent	Region	Per Cent
BLACK-SOIL REGIONS:		NON-BLACK-SOIL REGIONS:	
Central Agricultural	60–96%	Industrial	Over 95%
Middle Volga	Over 95	White Russia	38–95[a]
Lower Volga	Over 97	Lithuania	None[b]
New Russia	79–95	Lake	Over 90
Southwest	5–21	Baltic	None
Little Russia	15–95	Urals	Over 94
		North	Over 80

Source: *Statisticheskiia svedeniia po zemel'nomu voprosu v Evropeiskoi Rossii* (St. Petersburg, 1906), pp. 20–23. The regions are identified on the accompanying map.
[a] Except Minsk (3%).
[b] None in Vilna and Kovno *gubernias*; negligible in Grodno.

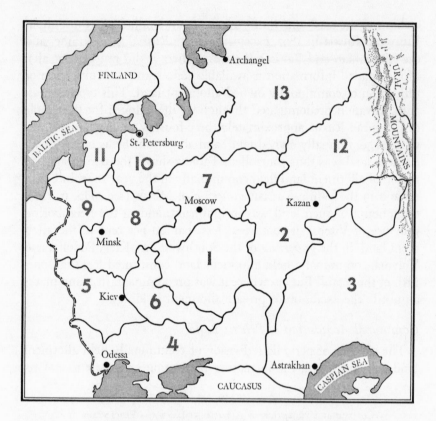

AGRICULTURAL REGIONS OF RUSSIA IN 1881

BLACK-SOIL REGIONS

1. *Central Agricultural:* Kursk, Orel, Tula, Riazan, Tambov, Voronezh.
2. *Middle Volga:* Saratov, Simbirsk, Penza, Kazan, Nizhnii Novgorod, Ufa.
3. *Lower Volga:* Samara, Orenburg, Astrakhan.
4. *New Russia:* Bessarabia, Kherson, Taurida, Ekaterinoslav, the Don Oblast.
5. *Southwest:* Podolia, Kiev, Volynia.
6. *Little Russia:* Kharkov, Chernigov, Poltava.

NON-BLACK-SOIL REGIONS

7. *Industrial:* Vladimir, Moscow, Kaluga, Tver, Iaroslavl, Kostroma.
8. *White Russia:* Mogilev, Minsk, Vitebsk, Smolensk.
9. *Lithuania:* Vilna, Kovno, Grodno.
10. *Lake:* St. Petersburg, Pskov, Novgorod, Olonets.
11. *Baltic:* Lifland, Courland, Estland.
12. *Urals:* Viatka, Perm.
13. *North:* Vologda, Archangel.

ducing the amount of such land available to each peasant cultivator. The average allotment size for European Russia declined from 5.1 *desiatinas* per male in 1860 to 2.7 *desiatinas* in 1900, a decrease of 47 per cent.[24] In response to this development, the peasants sought to increase their holdings of privately owned land. Litoshenko estimates that during the years 1863 to 1906 peasants in 44 *gubernias* bought more than 30 million *desiatinas* of land and, of this, retained approximately 20 million *desiatinas*, or about 54 million acres.[25] Most of the peasants' acquisition of privately owned land occurred after 1877. In that year they held 5.8 million *desiatinas* privately; in 1887 these holdings had increased to 12.6 million; and in 1905 there were 23.6 million *desiatinas* in private peasant holdings.[26]

Official sources list these holdings in three categories: those of private individuals, those of peasant associations and corporations, and those of peasant societies, that is, the *obshchina*. Of the 23.6 million *desiatinas* of private land listed as held by the peasants in 1905, 12.7 million were held by individual peasants; the average holding was 26.9 *desiatinas*. This was slightly more than double the 5.6 million *desiatinas* so held in 1877. A very small proportion of the peasant class participated in this type of land holding; of the total of 11.1 million peasant households in the European part of the empire in 1905, less than half a million (471,565) held privately owned plots of land.[27]

It is not possible to determine the rate of increase in the holdings of peasant associations and corporations in private land during this period, because the data concerning land ownership for the year 1877 do not distinguish between the holdings of peasant associations and corporations and those of peasant societies. By 1905, however, almost one-third of the privately owned land held by the peasants was owned by associations, that is, 7.3 million out of a total of 23.6 million *desiatinas*. Data of the Peasant Bank indicate that when land was bought by associations, the peasant household received an average of 7.8 *desiatinas* of land.[28] We may estimate, therefore, that in 1905 somewhat less than one million of the 11.1 million peasant households participated in this form of ownership.

Private holdings of peasant societies (*obshchinas*) increased almost fivefold in the period 1877 to 1905, from 741 thousand *desiatinas* to 3.6 million. The rate of increase was roughly proportional to the increase in the total of private holdings, but considerably higher than the rate of increase in the holdings of peasants as individuals. ~~The holdings of peasant societies thus comprised 16 per cent of the total of peasant holdings in private land by 1905.~~[29] According to data of the Peasant Bank, the average holding of a household in private land purchased communally was 4.4 *desiatinas.*[30] Thus about 800,000 peasant households participated in the acquisition of private land through the *obshchina.* There were, therefore, 70 per cent more households purchasing land communally than were doing so individually.

The "land hunger" created by the communal system of tenancy in allotment land and the practice of repartitioning compelled the peasants to lease significant quantities of private land. Unfortunately, data pertaining to peasant leasing of land are incomplete and, in many cases, are admittedly only rough estimates.

Estimates of the total area leased by the peasants vary widely. They range from a low of 19.5 million *desiatinas* (19 per cent of all private land) for 1900 to a high of 49.8 million *desiatinas* for the succeeding year.[31] Anfimov, who wrote what is probably the definitive work on peasant leaseholds for this period, estimates that the peasant class at the turn of the century leased some 13 million *desiatinas* of pasture and about 24 million *desiatinas* of plowing and haying land.[32] This constituted 38 per cent of all privately owned land and 24 per cent of all peasant land, allotment and private combined.

While the amount of land leased by the peasants testifies to the increasing inadequacy of the allotments, the way the land was leased indicates the continuing importance of the *obshchina* in peasant life. In the leasing of land, the peasant communes, households, and associations played almost equally important roles. Data for the year 1901 show that 32 per cent of the non-allotment land leased by peasants was contracted by households, 34.5 per cent by peasant associations, and 33.5 per cent by peasant societies or communes.[33] It should be noted, however, that this information is based on examination of the leases for only 6.8 million of the estimated 37 million *desiatinas* leased by peasants in that year. Unfortunately, there is no way of determining how representative this sample is.

In addition to its important economic functions of leasing and purchasing land, there is evidence that the village commune played an

TABLE 3

TOTAL TAX BURDEN ON LANDS OF PEASANT SOCIETIES, EXCLUDING ARREARS, 1899

Type of Tax	Amount (in rubles)
Redemption payments	92,300,000
State land taxes	6,800,000
Zemstvo levies	28,200,000
Mir levies	46,100,000
TOTAL	173,400,000

Source: P. Kh. Shvanebakh, *Nashe podatnoe delo* (St. Petersburg, 1903), pp. 139–40.

active role in the life of the peasants as a governmental unit to the turn of the century. This may be inferred from the data pertaining to the amount of taxes paid by the communes to the various echelons of government.

In the literature pertaining to this period much is made of the burden of the redemption payments on the peasantry; however, the figures in Table 3 indicate that *mir* levies, that is, the taxes of the *volost'* and the commune, constituted an amount equal to one-half the redemption payments and one-quarter of the total tax burden on peasant lands. Further, it appears that *mir* levies increased in the last years of the century. The average *mir* expenditure per *desiatina* of peasant land for European Russia rose from a figure of 28 kopeks in 1881 to 35 kopeks in 1891, an increase of 25 per cent.[34] If fiscal expenditures can be used as a rough indicator of the importance of a governmental unit, we may assume that the *volost'* and the *mir* extended their influence in the life of the peasants during this period.

An Evaluation of the Peasant Land Tenure System

In terms of land tenure alone, the data leave little doubt that the *obshchina* continued to be a dominant factor in peasant life throughout the nineteenth century. Communal land tenure applied to 80 per cent of all allotment land, and by 1905 had extended to include 34 per cent of the land leased by the peasants and 16 per cent of the land purchased by them. In sum, approximately 43 per cent of all cultivable land in European Russia was under communal control. Efforts by the peasants to expand their areas of cultivation were made to a large extent within the context of the communal control.

The disadvantages of communal land tenure were manifold. While the peasant was assured of the right to cultivate a share of the land belonging to the village, he was deprived of security in the occupancy of a specific area of land; to the extent that he lacked such security, his interest in increasing his investment in his enterprise and in preserving the fertility of the soil was correspondingly reduced. The proponents of the *obshchina* argued that it assured the peasant of his right to land and provided Russia with an avenue of development that would avoid the creation of a landless proletariat. However, it denied the peasant the security that was essential to the improvement of his lot and to the increasing productivity of agriculture in general.

In attempting to provide the peasant with the security of having an inalienable right to a certain share of the land, the legislation pertaining to the allotment resulted in a highly inflexible system that restricted the mobility of labor. This legislation, combined with the increasing burden of the financial obligations on allotment land resulting from falling grain prices, made it ever more difficult for the peasant to divest himself of his allotment and commit himself wholly to another sector of the economy. Continual references in the literature of the time to "land hunger," and the efforts of the peasants to increase the area of land at their disposal in the face of inordinately high rents and land prices, indicate the distortion in the allocation of resources that this type of tenure produced.

An optimal system of land tenure should afford the cultivator both the incentives and the opportunities to increase his output and his investment in his enterprise. High rents, confiscatory taxes, usurious interest rates, and burdensome debts all serve to impede him. All of these impediments were to be found in the peasant land system in Russia following the emancipation. It was within this highly inflexible, rigid, and restrictive pattern of land tenure—a pattern supported by government decree and buttressed by a widely held belief that it was intrinsically valuable—that the peasant faced the last decades of the nineteenth century. The history of rural Russia during these years can be characterized by two terms: "the agrarian crisis" and "the peasant question," both of which referred to the growing privation and misery of the peasant class and the mounting pressure for a change of official policy relating to the agricultural sector of the economy.

Peasant Poverty

In a narrow economic sense, the terms "the peasant question" and "the agrarian crisis" reflected the friction generated by the adherence to the traditional organization of agricultural production and the change in emphasis in the agricultural sector to production for market. The clearest manifestation of this friction was the increasing inability of the peasant to meet his financial obligations and to secure a livelihood from his progressively decreasing allotment. While a full treatment of the phenomenon of the increasing impoverishment of the peasant community is beyond the scope of this paper, a brief discussion will serve to illustrate the serious nature of the problem.

Tables 4 and 5 show how the burden of the redemption payment on an average soul allotment increased in the wheat producing black-soil *gubernia* of Kherson and the rye producing non-black-soil *gubernia* of Tver. These two *gubernias* were selected because in both cases the redemption payment and the average size of the allotment approximated the average figures for European Russia. Furthermore, specific information was available in the case of these two *gubernias* showing the effect of the Decree of December 28, 1881, which reduced the re-

TABLE 4

SOUL ALLOTMENTS, WHEAT PRICES, AND REDEMPTION PAYMENTS IN
KHERSON GUBERNIA FOR VARIOUS YEARS, 1883–1900

	1883	1887	1891	1895	1900
Average size of a soul allotment in *desiatinas*[a]	3.4	3.1	2.8	2.5	2.2
Average local autumnal price of wheat per *pud* in kopeks[b]	100	79	110	52	78
Total redemption payment in kopeks for allotment (176 kopeks for each *desiatina* less 16 per cent per Decree of December 28, 1881)[c] .	502	459	414	370	325
Total redemption payment in kopeks in terms of the price of wheat in 1883	502	581	376	712	417

[a] *Statisticheskiia svedeniia*, pp. 20–33.

[b] *Svod statisticheskikh svedenii po sel'skomu khoziaistva Rossii k kontsu XIX veka*, II, 24–25. 1 *pud* = 36.11 pounds.

[c] Iu. Ianson, *Opyt statisticheskago izsledovaniia o krest'ianskikh nadelakh i platezhakh* (St. Petersburg, 1877), p. 20 of appendix (Ianson's source was Podatnoi kommissii, Vol. XXII, Chap. III, Sect. 1); L. Khodskii, "Vykupnaia operatsia," in F. A. Brokgaus, ed., *Entsiklopedicheskii slovar*, VII (St. Petersburg, 1896), 514.

demption payments. As there is no data available showing the change in the average allotment size between the years 1883 and 1900, figures have been interpolated for the years 1887, 1891, and 1895. It should be noted that this information pertains to the former *pomeshchik* serf and not to the former appanage and state-owned serf, whose circumstances were considerably better, with respect to both the size of his land allotment and his redemption payment.

As is evident from these tables, in the thirteen-year period from 1883 to 1895 the peasant in the *gubernia* of Kherson saw the real burden of his redemption payment increase 40 per cent, while his ability to make this payment, that is, the land available for him to cultivate, diminished approximately 27 per cent. For the rye producer in the non-black-soil *gubernia* of Tver, the situation was not much better. There the average size of the land allotment decreased by about 18 per cent, while the real burden of the redemption payment increased by 30 per cent. It should be noted here, parenthetically, that 1891 was a famine year, which accounts for the extraordinarily high prices at that time.

This same general phenomenon was to be found throughout all of European Russia during these years; it constituted the economic basis of the agrarian crisis, resulting in accumulating arrears in taxes

TABLE 5

Soul Allotments, Rye Prices, and Redemption Payments in Tver Gubernia
for Various Years, 1883–1900

	1883	1887	1891	1895	1900
Average size of a soul allotment in *desiatinas*[a]	3.4	3.2	3.0	2.8	2.6
Average local autumnal price of rye per *pud* in kopeks[b]	83	48	123	50	63
Total redemption payment in kopeks for allotment (172 kopeks for each *desiatina* less one ruble for entire allotment per Decree of December 28, 1881)[c]	485	450	416	382	348
Total redemption payment in kopeks in terms of the price of rye in 1883	485	778	281	634	458

[a] *Statisticheskiia svedeniia*, pp. 20–33.
[b] *Svod statisticheskikh svedenii*, II, 30–31.
[c] Ianson, p. 20 of appendix; Khodskii, p. 514.

and redemption payments, and reducing the peasant class to abject misery. Some indication of the sense of despair and the brooding awareness of injustice on the part of the peasants is shown by Shvanebakh in the following anecdote concerning a peasant in the *gubernia* of Tula, as reported by a certain Madam Bers:

"Consider, madam," said an old man to me, "my little *desiatina* gave me 39 *puds* of oats; for seed there were 12, for the calf on meal 2, I sold a cart of 25 *puds* at 40 kopeks; that came to ten rubles. But I paid 25 rubles in taxes. Mine is an allotment for one soul. Consequently, I work in vain; to horses after their work is left some straw, but I paid 15 rubles more. My son lives as a laborer to help me, an old man; look, madam, he gave me half his earnings. Is that right?"[35]

However, it would be too facile and superficial an explanation of the peasant problem of this period to attribute it solely to falling grain prices. Declining prices no doubt compounded the problem and deepened the penury of the peasant, but strong evidence exists that the basic cause of the "peasant problem" was the system of peasant land tenure as it grew out of legislation promulgated pursuant to the emancipation.

Writing from the perspective of the early 1870's, at a time when the impact of falling grain prices could not have been foreseen, Ianson pronounced the Decree of 1861 to be inadequate as it applied to the economic life of the liberated serfs. It had been explicitly stated in the decree that, in addition to his freedom, the serf was to receive an allotment of land that would enable him to feed his household, to make his payments (*obrok*) to the landlord during the period of "temporary obligation," and, subsequently, to fulfill his financial obligations to the government once the redemption of the allotment had been formally undertaken. Ianson was able to conclude that (1) "the allotment did not secure the way of life of the peasant, even for the number that had been specified in the late revision" (the census of 1858), (2) "the peasant is, in fact, almost attached to the allotment," and (3) "payments and obligations on the land are not altogether in proportion ... to income received from the allotment."[36] His study of the peasant land system and the obligations on that land led him to call for further reforms:

The tax system and our agrarian legislation cannot long remain in the present form without serious danger for the well-being of present and future generations. A change in the tax system on the part of the government has long been in order, and we hold it correct to desire a rapid and radical transformation to consummate what was begun by the great reform of the present reign.[37]

Vasilchikov, also writing in the early 1870's, observed that the agricultural taxes in Russia at that time consumed virtually all the peasant income in most areas (and in some actually exceeded it), leaving, as he put it,

not a single kopek from the gross income of a *desiatina* for the surplus of the owner. In all the *gubernias,* excluding only Astrakhan, two *uezds* of Voronezh *gubernia,* and Bessarabia, the government and *gubernia* offices made formal testimonies formulated thus: that the income from the land has been found, for agricultural land owners of taxable condition, inadequate for the payment of their taxes, or that the existing tax rates are not commensurate with peasant means.[38]

As a result of the accumulation of arrears in redemption payments and the evident distress caused by these payments, the government, by the Decree of December 28, 1881, directed that they be reduced for the *pomeshchik* peasants; the decree also provided for a special reduction in those villages and localities that had experienced severe economic adversities. In aggregate these reductions amounted to 27 per cent of the total yearly obligation of this type of peasant; however, the variations from *gubernia* to *gubernia* were very great, ranging from a reported 16 per cent reduction in Kherson to one of 92 per cent in Olonets.[39] It is clear, however, that except in those *gubernias* such as Olonets, where the reductions were very substantial, the ameliorative effect of this decree on the peasant economy was more than negated by the precipitously falling grain prices.

From time to time the imperial government took further cognizance of the plight of the peasants by forgiving arrears and by other tax reductions, notably the abolition of the poll tax in 1886. However, these reductions were at least partially offset by increases in the taxes of the *gubernia* and *uezd* governments and by increasing *mir* expenditures. Corrective fiscal measures, while no doubt welcome, were inadequate to break the grip of poverty on the peasant class. What was needed was a more radical and fundamental change that would introduce flexibility into the system of peasant land tenure and enable the peasant to rationalize his economic life. In this sense, the Russian peasant had to wait until the first decade of the twentieth century for his emancipation.

In summary: Given the importance of the *obshchina* as an economic and political unit, and as an intellectual shibboleth, it is essential, in interpreting the economic history of rural Russia in the late nineteenth century, not to discount the influence of the peasant commune. While further research is needed to determine the precise influence of this institution on peasant productivity, some tentative conclusions can be offered here.

The *obshchina* prevented the introduction of rational policies in agriculture, policies that would have resulted in a more flexible allocation of human and non-human resources and, no doubt, would have led to technological improvements and increased output. The efforts of the peasants to supplement their allotment holdings by leasing and purchasing land stand as testimony to the need for a less rigid system of land tenure.

At the time of the emancipation, and in the succeeding legislation pertaining to the agricultural communities, the government in effect substituted the authority of the *obshchina* for that of the former serf owner. In defining this authority it severely limited the area within which the peasantry could make adjustments to changing economic conditions. These constraints, combined with the terms of the land allotment to the peasantry, the great burden of taxes and redemption payments on peasant land, and adverse developments in the market for grain commodities, condemned the peasants to increasing poverty in the last decades of the nineteenth century. This poverty was the price the peasants paid for the continued rigid control of rural Russia by the autocracy through the *obshchina* and the land captain, as well as for the government-sponsored programs of economic development for which this period is so well known.

6. The Peasant and the Factory

Reginald E. Zelnik

In a recent thought-provoking article,[1] the historian Theodore Von Laue aptly describes the intermediate status between peasantry and proletariat, between agriculture and industry, that was occupied by the vast majority of Russian workers during the "Witte period."* "His tastes and appetites," Von Laue writes, referring to the "peasant-come-to-the-factory," "were those of the village, but his outward life was that of the factory. There was no harmony between the two."[2] Von Laue makes no attempt to draw any political conclusions from his analysis of the ambiguous status of the peasant-worker at the turn of the century, but Leopold Haimson, in an article which appeared shortly after Von Laue's, addresses himself primarily to the political implications.[3] Haimson shifts the discussion a decade into the future, into the period immediately preceding the beginning of World War I. Rejecting both the stubbornly-held contention of Soviet Marxist historians that a direct correlation exists between advanced proletarian class consciousness and revolutionary élan, and the belief of some Western historians that a more or less linear progression of working-class integration into modern industrial life was taking place in Russia, he focuses on what might be called the "hyphenated" character of most Russian workers, that is, their continued rural ties, their failure to accept urban industrial life, as an explanation for their openness to extreme appeals under the confusing circumstances of rapid industrialization and urbanization.

Each of these authors is, of course, dealing with a period of Russian history that was characterized by exceptionally dynamic industrial

---

* Essentially the years 1892–1903, the period during which Count S. Yu. Witte served as Russian Minister of Finance.

growth, and a correspondingly rapid transformation of Russian peasants into part-time or full-time industrial workers. It goes almost
without saying that an economically "backward" country that is undergoing intensive industrialization will inevitably find an inordinate
proportion of its labor force among the peasantry, and that for a temporary period, at least, this condition will have a significant influence
on the life, habits, and attitudes of factory workers. What is particularly interesting about the history of industrial labor in Russia, however, is the extent to which the "peasant-in-the-factory" phenomenon
pervaded Russian manufacturing virtually from its very origins—that
is, beginning with the reign of Peter the Great, if not earlier.

It has become a commonplace to state that the Russian working
class of the late nineteenth and early twentieth centuries lacked the
background and traditions that the independent artisan-guilds had
grafted onto the history of the working classes of Western Europe,
particularly England. Commentators on Russian social history with
political postures as diverse as those of Miliukov and Trotsky have
been quick to stress the weakness of the Russian city as a factor contributing to the unique historical development of the nation; the
absence within the industrial labor force of any urban artisan tradition
is only a particular manifestation of this. But the absence of such a
tradition should not lead one to the conclusion that the industrial
workers of the late nineteenth and early twentieth centuries were
without any tradition at all. For the peasant characteristics of Russian factory labor described by Von Laue and Haimson were a later
expression of a two-centuries-old phenomenon. Here our purpose is
to assess this phenomenon in its earlier eighteenth- and nineteenth-
century contexts.

For all intents and purposes, the history of Russian factory labor
begins with the reign of Peter the Great. Factories of various sorts had
appeared here and there in sixteenth- and seventeenth-century Russia
—the first sign of industrial revival since the collapse of the Kievan
artisan industry that followed the Mongol invasions of the thirteenth
century. But such industrial activity as there was had been only
sporadic in nature.* Undoubtedly, when Peter the Great embarked

---

* Thus, in the course of the period from 1576 to 1673, only four paper mills were
erected; the extraction of metals was fairly common in the sixteenth century, but the

upon his policy of forced industrialization, there was a nucleus of industry on which to build, but the nucleus was too small to have any long-range significance, and most of the industrial problems encountered by Peter turned out to be new problems for Russia.

Chief among these problems, from our point of view, was to find a source of labor power for Russia's new factories. Enserfed peasants were the natural choice. The vast majority of the Russian population was already tied to the land, and inasmuch as the strengthening of that bond was a fundamental policy of Peter's regime, the creation of a free labor force for Russia's new industries would have been a historical anomaly, running counter to the basic currents of the Petrine period. Moreover, insofar as industrialization was a state policy, instituted primarily to serve immediate military needs, it was essential to state interests that the supplying of industrial labor be carried out as systematically as possible, under governmental supervision, and that it not be subject to the unpredictable vacillation of a freely functioning labor market. In one form or another, bondage appeared to be the safest mechanism for the accomplishment of this purpose.

The precise form that the use of forced labor for industrial production would take, however, was bound to vary with the situation of the particular industrial enterprise. If the factory in question was the private property of a serf-owning noble, located on his estates, no particular problem of labor supply existed, for the principle of *barshchina* was structurally as adaptable to factory work as it was to field work. During the reign of Peter, however, the manorial factory was still very atypical. The merchants, foreigners, and adventurers who were called upon by the state to assume the new entrepreneurial functions lacked the direct access of the nobleman to serf labor, and such labor had to be supplied from other sources.

Under these circumstances, the institution of what later came to be known as "possessional" workers or peasants was a logical solution. This approach to the problem was not entirely new. In the seventeenth century the government had used a similar method to supply labor to the country's young and struggling metallurgical works, al-

---

first high furnace appeared in Russia only in 1628; Russia's first wool cloth factory was established as late as 1684 (Bertrand Gille, *Histoire économique et sociale de la Russie du moyen age au XXᵉ siècle* [Paris, 1949], pp. 67–69).

though at that time the assigning of peasants to particular factories was mainly for the purpose of carrying out auxiliary functions, rather than the actual factory work. By the early eighteenth century, however, the scale of the problem had increased to the point where the compulsory assignment of large numbers of peasants to permanent factory work was the only available method whereby non-noble enterprises could be maintained. The possessional method was formally institutionalized by an Imperial ukase.[4] This ukase permitted persons of non-noble origin, merchants in particular, to purchase whole villages of peasants for their factories. The peasants, however, were to become the inalienable property not of the factory owner, but of the factory itself as it passed from owner to owner. What this meant, in effect, was the creation of a new and special category of serfs —factory serfs—whose freedom of movement would, if anything, be less than that of their manorial counterparts and whose ambiguous peasant-worker status, as we shall see, was bound to give rise to serious and continuous tensions.

The ukase of 1721 underwent several modifications in the course of the next hundred years. The first significant change was introduced in 1752, when, for the first time, strict limitations were placed on the acquisition of forced peasant labor by non-noble manufacturers. Limits were placed on the number of peasants that could be acquired by the various types of factories (the number depending upon their size and equipment), and requirements were set forth that limited the percentage of peasants attached to each factory who could actually be used for factory labor as opposed to performing agricultural or auxiliary functions.[5]

It can readily be seen that these modifications had a dual effect upon the status of factory serfs. On the one hand, they placed limitations on the disposition and employment of factory serfs that were considerably narrower than those which applied to ordinary manorial peasants (although we shall see that the use of manorial serfs by *noble* manufacturers was also subjected to certain restrictions by the government). These new restrictions were therefore a step in the direction of transforming factory serfs into a distinct and circumscribed social group. On the other hand, the specific content of the 1752 ukase was such as to reemphasize and even to place a positive value upon the continued peasant character of the factory serfs. Limiting the use of factory serfs in actual factory work was tantamount to recognizing that factory labor was less than desirable from the peasant's point of view. It was a form of governmental protection for the peasants, and there is ample reason to believe, as shall be indicated, that it was viewed as such by the peasants themselves. The ukase of 1752, judging by later developments, probably had its origins in noble fears of merchant usurpation of what the nobles felt to be their own prerogatives, but its main effect was to reinforce the peasant-worker tension already inherent in the factory serf's position.

The government's discomfiture with the factory serf system culminated in Peter III's ukase of March 1762, which was confirmed shortly thereafter by Catherine II. This legislation prohibited the further acquisition of serf villages by factories, whether noble- or non-noble-owned.[6] However, the ukase raised more questions than it resolved. Specifically, it had nothing new to say about the situation of factory serfs who were already ascribed to factories at the time. It should be emphasized that these included not only those who had been acquired by merchant-manufacturers in recent years, but also the descendants of all those peasants who had been transformed into factory serfs since the reign of Peter the Great—a grand total of some 67,000 peasants at that time. The legislation of 1762 in effect placed an official onus upon the situation of these peasants, while failing to relieve it in any way. In so doing, it effectively condemned the descendants of the 67,000 peasants whose lives it failed to affect to a life that was apparently considered sufficiently intolerable to warrant the prohibition of further purchases.

Furthermore, given the scant labor supply that existed in Russia at the time, and the weaknesses in the functioning of the free labor market, the legislation evaded the question of where new sources of labor were to be found if industry was to continue to develop, even modestly. Under these circumstances, the new legislation could only serve to encourage evasive and illegal tactics on the part of manufacturers in obtaining new factory serfs, and, in so doing, heighten the tensions which had always inhered in the position of factory serfs. From the point of view of the peasants themselves, this was important, in that the official decrees now legitimized their efforts to resolve this tension in favor of their original peasant-agrarian status. The appeal to legitimacy, as will be demonstrated, was a permanent aspect of peasant protest against factory conditions and worker status throughout much of the eighteenth and nineteenth centuries.

Catherine the Great was content to maintain the middle ground established in 1762, freezing de jure, but not necessarily de facto, the position of factory serfs. To back away from the prohibition of new acquisitions would undoubtedly have disturbed the nobility, while to abolish forced factory labor altogether was too drastic a measure to contemplate, given the still precarious situation of Russian industry. Paul I, however, was much less reluctant than his mother to violate the sensibilities of the noble class, and chose to extricate himself from the dilemma by returning, more or less, to the status quo of 1752.

Beginning in 1798, it again became legal for manufacturers to purchase peasant villages and attach them to factories, as long as they adhered to the restrictions that had been established in 1752.[7] Certain additional stipulations did, however, place further limitations on the degree to which manufacturers could make use of their factory serfs: the new law strictly prohibited the transfer of such peasants from factory to factory or village to village, and prohibited the resale of such peasants, individually or collectively, except in conjunction with the sale of the factory itself. Finally, as a rather strangely conceived corollary of Paul's decree of the previous year limiting *barshchina* labor to three days per week, or one half the number of workdays, the 1798 decree limited the number of factory serfs that could be used in actual factory work to one half the number of peasants attached to the given factory. This stipulation, like the ukase from which it was derived, was rarely enforced in practice. Its significance lies first of all in the outlook that it reflected, which equated the situation of the factory peasant with that of the agricultural peasant, and, second, in the fact that it introduced yet another principle on the basis of which peasants could legitimately protest against factory labor.

Paul's prohibition of the transfer of factory peasants from region to region was broadened in 1802 by Alexander I, who pushed this principle one step further by prohibiting the purchase of serfs for factory employment unless the villages involved were located in the vicinity of the factory to which the peasants were to be assigned.[8] This attempt to prevent the undermining of the traditional life of the peasantry obviously placed an all but complete limitation on the manufacturers' source of bonded labor power. The law of 1802 was followed by a series of individual acts restricting the rights of manufacturers to acquire factory serfs in individual branches of industry.* Finally, in 1816, Alexander came around to the position of Catherine II and placed a nearly absolute prohibition on the purchase of peasants for factories, with or without land.[10] By this time the use of freely-hired labor had increased significantly, and the use of forced labor had begun to lose credit in Russian economic thought. Nevertheless, as had been the case in 1762, the possessional system was allowed to remain in force where it already existed. With the exception of an 1840 law which encouraged the voluntary transformation of possessional factories into fully private enterprises, no significant formal modifications were made in the system until the Great Reforms of Alexander II.

Possessional peasants, or factory serfs, as we have called them here, comprised the single most important category of factory workers at the turn of the eighteenth century, and the huge majority of workers in the Ural mining and metallurgical region. However, they existed side by side with three other categories of workers, each of which, in different ways, participated in the peasant-worker, agrarian-industrial tension to which we have alluded. These were: (1) those state peasants who, from the time of Peter the Great and in some cases earlier, labored in state-owned factories; (2) the so-called freely-hired workers, whose importance dates primarily from the second half of the eighteenth century; (3) the serfs who labored in the manorial factories of their lords, likewise dating primarily from the second half of the eighteenth century.

The first of these categories, state peasants working in state fac-

---

* E.g. in 1807 the purchase of whole villages by the proprietors of mining works (*gornye zavody*) in the Ural region was prohibited, the number of individual peasants that could be purchased by them was drastically reduced, and the restrictions under which new peasants could be acquired were tightened; in 1808 a decree was issued that provided that the government had to approve each individual purchase of peasants for factories in the wool cloth industry, and that further tightened the restrictions governing such purchases. It should be pointed out, however, that in both cases the restrictions were connected with the granting of exceptions to the law prohibiting the purchase of peasants from distant locations.[9]

tories, will concern us here only insofar as their fate crossed paths with that of the factory serfs. We shall see that to the extent that the government was willing to transfer these state peasants to private manufacturers in the capacity of factory serfs (a practice that was particularly frequent during the reign of Catherine the Great, once the legislation of 1762 had eliminated private purchases of peasants as a source of labor power) it contributed to the creation of one typically Russian form of labor protest, which was based on the enserfed worker's demand to be restored to what he considered to be his rightful status as a state peasant. This claim paralleled the Russian peasant's traditional preference for the status of state peasant to that of manorial serf.

The second category, the freely-hired worker, is of particular interest. First of all, by the early nineteenth century it had surpassed in numbers the category of possessional laborers for Russia as a whole. (As early as the eighteenth century it was the most important form of factory labor in such urban industrial centers as Moscow and St. Petersburg.) Second, of the various forms of factory labor that existed in Russia, it was the one that most closely approximated free labor as understood, say, in nineteenth-century Western Europe, so that whatever peasant-worker tensions prevailed in *this* segment of the laboring population sharply illustrate the peculiar circumstances of Russian factory labor. While estimates vary considerably and accuracy is out of the question, it is the view of one leading authority on Russian labor history that such freely-hired workers composed some 40 per cent of the Russian labor force by 1769, if mining and extraction are excluded from the calculations.[11] The salient characteristic of freely-hired labor in Russia, as is well known, is that despite the name, the freely-hired labor force consisted primarily of manorial serfs, who were working in factories with the permission of their lords, and were using their wages in order to pay off their annual *obrok*. Such workers were "free" only insofar as they were at liberty to conclude their own contracts with the factory owner, but throughout the eighteenth century and the first third of the nineteenth century, they were always subject to recall to their estates at the will of their lords. Moreover, the government tended to look upon the freely-hired worker as a special category of serf. A clear illustration of this attitude in the eighteenth century may be found in the official policy that equated unauthorized departures from the factory by freely-hired workers with the crime of flight from the manorial estate.[12]

The last category of worker was the manorial peasant who worked in the manorial factory of his lord. Although this type of factory was on the rise throughout the post-Petrine years of the eighteenth century, it was never quantitatively very significant. Of 554 enterprises that fell within the jurisdiction of the College of Manufactures in 1769, only 71 belonged to nobles, and this number had decreased by the middle of Catherine's reign. In the metallurgical industries, which fell within the jurisdiction of the College of Mines, noble participation was of even less significance. By the nineteenth century, except in the area of the manufacture of spirits, where they were buttressed by the government, noble manufacturers found it virtually impossible to compete with other types of enterprises.[13] It should be noted, however, that not all factories owned by nobles were necessarily manorial factories, that is, factories established on the nobleman's estate and operated on the basis of *barshchina* labor. In some cases individual noblemen became the proprietors of possessional factories or of capitalist enterprises operated on the basis of freely-hired labor. For our purposes, such cases may be subsumed into those two categories respectively.

The pioneer work on labor unrest in the Russian factory of the eighteenth century is Volume I of V. I. Semevsky's *Krest'iane v tsarstvovanie Imperatritsy Ekateriny II*.[14] Semevsky presents us with a detailed and well-documented discussion of some of the more important cases of unrest among factory peasants in the eighteenth century, including many significant quotes from archival materials. While Semevsky's work is mainly descriptive, and does not deal specifically with the problem we are attempting to raise in this paper, the information he presents is most pertinent to our discussion.

In discussing unrest in the eighteenth century among agricultural serfs, Semevsky makes the point that such disorders occurred very frequently on the occasion of the transfer of landed property and villages from one owner to another.[15] His prototype for this type of unrest is the sale of an estate to a nobleman who has a reputation for cruelty, and the consequent refusal of the peasants to accept the change in ownership. In its broadest outlines, this prototype can be usefully applied to unrest among factory peasants during the same period, except that the introduction of factory work complicates the matter to varying degrees. The simplest situation is that of the sale of villages by one noble to another, where the purchaser is a factory owner. In this case the alleged cruelty of the purchaser is either compounded by or identified with the potential danger of being shifted from agricultural work to factory labor as a result of the transfer.

A case in point is the purchase of several hundred villagers by the Demidov family in 1756. Nikita Demidov was the owner of several iron factories in the Tula province and in the Ural region. Fearing assignment to factory work in the Tula factories, the recently purchased peasants engaged in various forms of both passive and violent resistance for several years rather than be torn away from work on the land. If there was any principle involved in this case, on the peasants' side, it was the customary peasant attitude that the land they tilled was their own, or God's, from which it followed that the substitution of factory work for work on their land was an injustice. This customary peasant outlook was not, however, sanctioned by authority, which never questioned the compatibility of factory work as such with serfdom. As the State Senate put it in 1762, after having investigated the case in question: "When they are his serfs, he has power over them in this respect."[16]

Considerably more complex, as well as more frequent, were cases of unrest among factory serfs in the possessional category. Such cases were further removed from the prototype referred to above in that not only were ownership and occupation transformed, but a basic change took place in the peasants' juridical status as well. The quality of this transformation enabled the peasants to seek and find validating principles for their protests which transcended beliefs in the right to land usage and specific grievances regarding life in the factory, although both these factors were often present. Nevertheless, these cases shared the basic characteristic of the others insofar as it was almost always a transfer of peasant personnel that precipitated the protest, or that was used to justify it in retrospect.

Such cases were most frequent among peasants who had been purchased for permanent ascription to the private metallurgical factories of the Ural mining region. According to the archives of the Ministry of Justice, there were some 45,000 peasant workers in this category in 1769.[17] Typical in this regard was a series of incidents which took place in Perm province in the early 1770's, that is, after the prohibition on the purchase of peasants for factories had been put into effect. The incidents originated in an attempt on the part of a Perm nobleman to ascribe some 5,000 of his own villagers to a recently acquired metallurgical factory. Although such an action was clearly in violation of the law of 1762, which applied to nobles as well as non-nobles, he was able to obtain special permission from the College of Mines to carry out his plans. Whatever objections the peasants may have had to this change in their status were not expressed until the transaction was compounded by the owner selling the factory, together with some 4,000 of the peasants, to a private party. The new owner, in turn, received special permission from the College of Mines to transfer peasants to some of his other factories. These two steps—their original sale as possessional workers and the subsequent attempt to move them to another region—drove home to the peasants the ultimate significance of their change in status, but they were unable to formulate their grievances in any sophisticated fashion. Their first step of protest, which was to complain that they were being ripped away from the land without even being given the opportunity to gather the harvest and dispose of their livestock, strongly implied a preference for the status of agricultural serf to that of possessional worker.

When complaints to responsible officials failed to alter their situation, the peasants were prepared to turn to armed resistance; only the intervention of the State Senate, which ordered that the peasants not be transferred until the matter had been clarified, averted a bloody clash between the peasants and government troops.[18] (The case dragged on for several years, with the government finally ruling that the peasants' grievances had been justified.)

Peasants who resisted attachment to factories in the name of the right to remain in their traditional status were not necessarily manorial peasants. More often than not, protesting workers were former state peasants who had been turned over to private manufacturers by the government in order to meet the needs of production. This situation sometimes provided a curious twist to peasant resistance. Insofar as the social outlook of eighteenth- and early nineteenth-century Russians had not yet been penetrated by fine conceptual distinctions between workers and peasants, and in view of the fact that the exertion of maximum control inherent in the serf system was a rational approach to operating a pre-modern factory from the point of view of the manufacturer, factory owners, particularly nobles whose chief experience had been with serf labor, were prone to assimilate their non-serf factory hands to the same status. In and of themselves, such attempts could not provide a rationale for protest to workers who, like those mentioned above, were of immediate serf origin. For the ex-manorial serf, it was not "serf-like" treatment in the factory which was likely to become the focus of his discontent, for such peasants tended to look upon their lives as manorial serfs as being more desirable than their lives as workers. For the ex-state peasant, on the other hand, the disadvantages of transfer to a factory were multiplied to the extent that he also felt himself being transformed into a serf in the process. Indeed, even if the former state peasant had been employed as a laborer in a state factory prior to being turned over to a private manufacturer, thus neutralizing factory life per se as an element in his discontent, the complaint that the private manufacturer was treating him like a serf was sufficient cause for a number of incidents of rather strenuous protest. We will not belabor the fact that all things being equal, state peasants found themselves in a considerably more tolerable position than manorial serfs in pre-Reform Russia. What is important here is the extent to which a parallel situation existed between state peasants who worked in state factories and those peasants whom we referred to earlier as factory serfs. A few illustrations follow.

In 1755 three state-owned ironworks in Azov province were turned over by the government to Prince P. I. Repnin, together with some 900 former state workers. Although Repnin was already a serf-owner, it was clearly understood at the time that his newly-acquired workers were not to be assimilated into his villages, were not to be given the status of manorial serfs working in factories, but were to become, in effect, possessional peasants attached to the factories. They could not be transferred to other locales, and they could only be used by Repnin for factory work. In short, they were to be treated in roughly the same way as the state had treated them in previous years.

In practice, however, Repnin's administrators soon began to treat the new workers as if they were Repnin's serfs: their pay was lowered, they were forced to engage in non-factory work, they were paid in goods instead of cash, and they were subjected to punishments from which they had been immune when they worked for the state. The workers soon began a long struggle to prevent their de facto reduction to the status of manorial serfs. Their methods included the petitioning of high officials, small-scale clashes with government troops, and the total repudiation of the authority of the factory administration. Neither whippings, beatings, nor the exile of petitioners would deter them from their course. Even the threat of capital punishment, originating in the State Senate, failed to move them. In the end their persistence was rewarded. In 1769, at the initiative of the Empress herself, the factories were reclaimed by the state, Repnin was compensated for his loss, and the workers were restored to their former status.[19]

A similar situation arose when, again in 1755, the government turned over the Krasnoselskaia state paper factory, with its state workers, to a high-ranking nobleman, Count Sivers. Again the agreement was that the situation of the workers would remain basically unchanged: their wages were not to be lowered, they could not be transferred from the factory, Sivers could not exercise judicial powers over them (as he could over his own serfs), and so on. Some time later, after Sivers had passed away, his widow violated these terms by transferring six of the workers to her manorial estates to perform serf labor on a permanent basis. This act was followed by a period of unrest and conflict, which was accelerated by the sale of the factory in 1775 to a family of nobles that began to introduce various changes in the circumstances of the workers, including, for example, the introduction of non-factory work. This was followed by a pattern of protest, petition, disobedience, and repression generally similar to what took place among the Repnin workers. At first, it would seem, the workers' resistance to these policies was carried out in the name of the restoration of the status quo as it existed under Sivers, but it was not long before the dichotomy of state people (*kazennye liudi*) versus serfs asserted itself in the workers' consciousness. In one instance, for example, when a factory overseer threatened to report a worker to the owners for disobedience, the worker responded angrily: "They are not my lords, and we are not their serfs!"

The question of enserfment grew more complicated, however, when it turned out that the deed which had been concluded between Countess Sivers and the new owners had indeed referred to the workers as if they were serfs. Thus, the deed being legal, the new policies that were being introduced ceased to be illegitimate. To this new development the workers responded with considerable sophistication, by arguing in several petitions that insofar as they retained the status of state people under Sivers, the deed which transferred them to the new owners in the capacity of serfs was itself null and void. The State Senate, however, still found it difficult to accept these distinctions, and ruled against the workers. The decision, which was taken in 1785, remained unaltered for another ten years. Then, in 1796, shortly before her death, Catherine the Great, for reasons which remain obscure, decided to reverse the ruling of the Senate in favor of the workers, maintaining that the various owners of the factory were obliged to maintain the original status of the workers as state people. The decision was put into effect over the next few years. It should be emphasized, of course, that in succeeding to rid themselves of the serf status that the owners had attempted to impose, the workers became, in effect, factory serfs, with both the restrictions and the privileges that this status implied. They did so, however, in the name of their original rights as state people.[20]

In a few cases the feeling of lost status was so strong that the struggle against assimilation to serf status extended over several generations. Thus in the 1770's, workers at the Kopninskaia paper factory still recalled that when their ancestors had been assigned to the factory by the government some thirty years earlier, they had been state peasants and not serfs. On this basis they resisted attempts by the *pomeshchik* who owned the factory to apply to them laws that were meant to apply only to serfs and not to possessional peasants. Again many years went by before the government recognized the distinction in the name of which they were protesting, and it was not until after the turn of the century that the workers received (partial) satisfaction.[21]

A series of events in the Ural mining region differed from the above cases only in that it combined resistance to enserfment with resistance to factory work per se on the part of a large number of former state peasants. In this case nearly a thousand peasants had been assigned to the metallurgical factories of N. Demidov early in the reign of Peter

the Great. As came to be customary, they were attached to the factories under very strict conditions that circumscribed the freedom of
action of the owner. Some of these peasants had belonged to monasteries prior to their transfer to the factories by the state. As the years
went by, and Demidov and his heirs began to follow the apparently
inevitable trend of slowly converting the workers into their personal
peasant property, resistance to enserfment and memories of non-
industrial life began to merge in the minds of many of the peasants.
As late as 1762, sixty years after the original transfer, the descendants
of the first group were petitioning the government to be returned to
their old monastery. Pending a positive response, they refused to
engage in any factory work. Unrest, arrests, and armed clashes with
soldiers were to follow before the position of the peasants received
official sanction in the form of recognition of their status as state
peasants.[22]

One could cite other examples to illustrate the above themes. Each
case had its own variations, but for our purposes the common features
are more important. In nearly all cases the peasant-workers were resisting either a recent or a past change in status; although resistance
was inevitably set in motion by a particular grievance, the legitimizing principle, whether implicit or explicit, was found in an alternative social role that was essentially traditional, whether it involved former serfs demanding to be returned to the land or former
state peasants—including state factory workers—resisting de facto
enserfment. In almost all cases both the government and the manufacturers involved were less conscious of or sensitive to the distinctions
that underlay the activities of the protesting workers than were the
workers themselves, but in the case of the government at least, prolonged activity on the part of the workers frequently led to recognition of the legitimacy of their demands. We are not arguing that any
of this was particularly surprising or even unique. In a basically preindustrial society it was only natural that the introduction of factory
labor would draw upon elements of society who were conscious of
alternative social roles that were steeped in tradition, or to put it more
directly, who were conscious of the fact that they simultaneously belonged to a social group *other* than the one whose functions they were
performing. What was particularly interesting about this phenom-

enon in Russia, however, was the degree to which the pattern was repeated decade after decade, generation after generation, and, with some significant modifications and variations, well into the nineteenth century and through Russia's exposure to the effects of the industrial revolution.

The chief characteristic of the Russian labor force in the nineteenth century, as far as broad secular trends are concerned, was the steady displacement of the factory serf by the freely-hired laborer. It is virtually impossible to talk in terms of absolute numbers of factory workers for the pre-Reform period, since the term *factory* was so broadly defined as to include enterprises that were minute in scope. What can be said, however, is that as the number of factories and factory workers multiplied, the proportion of freely-hired workers rapidly increased, exceeding 50 per cent of all industrial workers by the reign of Nicholas I, exceeding 80 per cent by the reign of Alexander II, and finally, of course, encompassing all factory workers in the post-Emancipation period.[23] The reasons for this trend were manifold, but constitute a separate topic from the one with which we are dealing in this essay. What we shall attempt to demonstrate here is, first of all, the continuation into the nineteenth century of the patterns that have been outlined above in the contracting manorial and possessional sectors of industry. Second, we shall show that certain patterns may be extrapolated from the expanding free labor sector that in their own way recreate the peasant-worker, agrarian-industrial dualism of the past. These patterns will be linked with the themes discussed by Von Laue with respect to the industrial upsurge of the 1890's.

We have spoken of the eighteenth-century phenomenon of peasant resistance against sale to undesirable masters, and the special case of this phenomenon which arose when the master in question was a factory owner and the peasants had formerly been confined to agricultural and related work. Such a case arose again on a very significant scale during the reign of Alexander I, and in the course of time became a major object of government attention. In 1811 some 1,600 male serfs and their families from the Novgorod and Vologda estates of the famous Dashkov family were sold to A. I. Yakovlev, the scion of a family of noble entrepreneurs of *meshchanin* background and the

owner of iron factories in the Viatka province, located about 800 versts
from the purchased villages. These peasants had been particularly
prosperous and well-off, thanks to the excellent treatment they had
received at the hands of their former masters. Under these circumstances, any transfer of ownership, even if factory labor had not been
involved, would probably have come as a blow to the peasants. But
when it was learned that many of the peasants would be sent to the
far-off factories, they responded by announcing their total rejection
of Yakovlev's authority.

It will be recalled that a law had been passed in 1802 that prohibited
the purchase of serfs for employment in factories that were not located
in the vicinity of the peasants' villages. Shortly after Yakovlev began to
transfer some of the peasants against their will, they became cognizant
of this prohibition, which now gave them a legal as well as a moral
source of support for resistance. There followed an extensive and
oftentimes confusing pattern of non-cooperation, petition, reprisals,
and punishment. Various branches of the government wavered as to
which side they would support in the dispute. For reasons that will
shortly be clarified, the main tendency within the government was to
withhold support from the peasants' position. Rather than curtail the
peasants' resistance, however, this policy only served to heighten their
sense of frustration. In the course of time, passive resistance was transformed into an armed rebellion of some 600 men.

It was only in 1813, after the peasants had been temporarily pacified
and certain high-ranking officials had shifted to their side, that Yakovlev was ordered by the Committee of Ministers to desist from sending
any more peasants to the factories, and to return to their villages those
peasants who were already in the factories.

The controversy, however, was far from ended. The peasants had
been deeply scarred by the two-year struggle, and they were now further embittered both by the horror stories about factory life that were
related by their returning comrades and by the government's decision
to prosecute some of the rebellious leaders even after having ruled that
their cause was just. Yakovlev, on the other hand, whose factories were
floundering for lack of labor, was still determined to bring about a reversal in the course of events.

In the following year, roughly the same history began to repeat itself when Yakovlev purchased several hundred new peasants in the Viatka province. This time, however, Yakovlev took considerably greater pains to remain within the letter of the law. Again the government withheld support from the peasants, and again the peasants, this time inspired by the earlier actions of their counterparts in Vologda and Novgorod, resisted with arms. The peasants were finally subdued and, after some hesitation, the government upheld the position of their master (this despite the fact that the entire incident became the occasion for the Tsar's promulgation of the 1816 law that reestablished the 1762 position on the purchase of peasants for factories). As was the custom, "instigators" were punished. The only positive effect of the entire episode from the peasants' standpoint was that thereafter the government took a great interest in the situation of Yakovlev's factories and peasants and corrected certain abuses on his part that were subsequently discovered.[24]

Two particularly interesting aspects of the Yakovlev case were the solidarity displayed by peasants from different villages and even different regions, and the government's motives in hesitating to support the position of the peasants. As to the first, there was apparently clear evidence of collaboration between Yakovlev's peasants in Vologda and Novgorod, as well as general support from local villages that were not directly involved in the controversy. Furthermore, there was evidence that the Viatka peasants, although they had no direct connection with the peasants from Vologda and Novgorod, were directly inspired by their earlier actions. It is safe to assume that the factories themselves were the source of contact that enabled the news to be disseminated among peasants from distant locations. If so, we have here a very early foreshadowing of the factory's future role as a unifying force among discontented peasants from far-flung regions, somewhat but not entirely along the lines described in Haimson's article.

The government's reluctance to assert the justice of the peasants' claims seems paradoxical, (a) in view of the fact that such conflict had frequently been resolved in favor of the peasants in the eighteenth century, and (b) when contrasted with Alexander I's apparent desire to abort the forced transformation of peasants into factory workers, as reflected in the legislation mentioned earlier. In view of these considerations, Gessen's explanation appears to be the only logical one:

Yakovlev's factories were producing badly needed goods for the government. Yet without the transferred peasants, in the absence of any other labor supply in the vicinity of the factories, production at the factories would have ground to a halt. Thus the immediate needs of the government—probably of a military character, given the nature of the factories—turned the balance against the social policies of the Tsar in this particular instance. Here we have not so much a foreshadowing of a future government-industrialist alliance against the interests of the lower classes (for there were cases as late as the early twentieth century of government support of workers against the interests of industrialists) as an anticipation of the conflict which later arose within the government between the desire to preserve the peasant character of Russian workers for social and political reasons, and the need to provide industry with a skilled and culturally advanced labor force in order to meet the industrial needs of the state. We shall see that this conflict became particularly acute after the accession to the throne of Alexander II.

Possessional labor was clearly a declining institution in the first half of the nineteenth century. Its economic decline was reinforced by government measures such as the legislation of 1816, which outlawed the future acquisition of new possessional peasants in all branches of industry except metallurgy. Further laws enacted during the reign of Nicholas I contributed to the undermining of possessional labor as an institution.[25]

Even as the possessional factory declined, however, the problem of attempts by manufacturers to reduce possessional workers to the status of serfs, and resistance to these attempts by the workers, persevered. Quite naturally, the issue of transformation of status was much less clear-cut than it once had been, if only for the reason that the workers were several generations further removed from their non-possessional status. Nevertheless, in some cases at least, consciousness of the previous status apparently persisted. Thus a series of conflicts at the Kiritsky iron foundry in Riazan province during the years 1824–26*

---

* The particular issue that precipitated these conflicts was the manufacturer's practice of turning over some of his workers as military recruits. As possessional peasants they should have been immune from this treatment, which was legal only with regard to serfs. The government, however, supported the manufacturer.

culminated with the declaration on the part of the workers that they did not consider themselves to be the property of the factory owner; rather, they insisted, they were "free State workers, ascribed to the factory."[26]

That the struggle to ward off de facto enserfment was fairly pervasive among possessional peasants, at least in the Ural metallurgical region, is confirmed indirectly by a memorandum "On the Situation of Factories of the Ural Range," which was submitted to the Chief of the Third Section by an unnamed industrialist in 1828. The author of the memorandum insisted that in order to root out the unruly elements who, he claimed, were responsible for the unrest that prevailed among the workers of many privately-owned Ural factories, it was necessary that the factory owners be given the full rights of *pomeshchiki* over their workers. If this advice were followed, he argued, the workers "would cease to be seduced by false ideas about their so-called rights and would remain in a proper state of obedience."[27] If this point of view was at all representative, then evidently workers' attempts to safeguard their status by claiming the traditional rights of possessional peasants were only serving to increase the efforts of their employers to do away with those rights and integrate the workers into serf or semi-serf status.

One of the rights of possessional workers—which clearly distinguished them from serfs—was the degree of government protection to which they were entitled. It is well known that with the exception of certain definite proscriptions, the fate of a manorial peasant under serfdom was almost entirely in the hands of the *pomeshchik*. As we have already had occasion to see, this was not the case for peasants in possessional factories. Because the possessional factory was considered to be subsidized by the government, the idea of state responsibility for what went on inside the factory was never completely abandoned, however vacillating the government may have been in applying this idea in practice. That this concept often penetrated the workers' consciousness, and helped legitimize their protests, we have already noted. The memorandum cited above bears witness to the extent to which some manufacturers saw this concept as a threat to their authority in the factory, for in addition to claiming *pomeshchik* rights over the workers, the author specifically adopted as a corollary to this position the proposal that governmental agencies, the Mining Department

(*Gornoe nachal'stvo*) in particular, exclude itself from any intervention in factory affairs. We shall see that this question recurred in a somewhat different form with regard to the situation of freely-hired workers.

If we turn to the late 1850's, to the years immediately prior to the emancipation, we find a few noteworthy changes in the situation described here. A few of the more important incidents of labor unrest in possessional factories during those years, particularly in the Orenburg province, a major center of metallurgical industry, are described in some Soviet studies published in the early 1920's.[28] Rather than relate these in any detail, we shall confine ourselves to a few general comments. There can be no doubt that as the emancipation approached, and particularly as news and rumors of the impending change began to spread, the labor protest of possessional peasants began to change correspondingly in character. By this time the appeal to traditional rights as such began to lose its cogency, and in some cases was replaced by the claim to the right of freedom, in large part because such a claim had been legitimized prospectively by the rumors concerning the government's future plans. In addition, there was a greater tendency than in the past for dissatisfied workers to concentrate their demands on specific grievances rather than on past rights. The government, for its part—and most particularly the Ministry of Internal Affairs—grew more and more inclined to resort to such extreme measures in defense of the workers as declaring a factory to be under state guardianship, although this practice was by no means without precedent. This shift in policy apparently reflected the mood and spirit of a government that was about to embark on far-reaching reforms directly affecting the status of the masses in general. It should be added, however, that this rather strict posture toward the owners of possessional factories was resisted to a great extent by the Ministry of Finance and its subordinate institutions.

Much has been said in the past to explain the rather persistent conflict in nineteenth-century Russia between the Ministry of Finance and the Ministry of Internal Affairs over labor matters, a conflict traces of which can be found as early as the reign of Alexander I and as late as that of Nicholas II. Without necessarily disputing what has been said on this topic in the past, I should simply like to add that the conflict may also be seen as a reflection of the peasant-worker tension that has frequently been referred to in this paper. If the laborer was pulled both by traditional agrarian and new industrial forces, it was in a sense the Ministry of Internal Affairs that saw him most as a traditional peasant, in need of protection by a benign autocracy from vulgar new bourgeois developments, while the Ministry of Finance saw him in his capacity as worker, and, in the interests of the smoothness of production, hesitated to deny the manufacturer full authority over his labor force. We will now discuss the ways in which these divergent views were reflected in the position of freely-hired workers, a category which, after the Great Reforms, encompassed virtually all Russian industrial laborers. Our discussion of this aspect of the problem will be confined to the workers of the city that became Russia's most important working class center—St. Petersburg.

St. Petersburg was the region of Russia where factories resembling the mechanized capitalist enterprises of the Western European industrial revolution appeared the earliest and gained the most rapid predominance. Steam engines manufactured in Western Europe, probably England, had been introduced in St. Petersburg textile industry on a small scale during the reign of Alexander I.[29] Between the 1830's and the beginning of the Crimean War, the mechanization of St. Petersburg cotton mills proceeded rather rapidly, a development that was stimulated by the decision of the British government in 1842 to lift its restrictions on the export of machinery. At a time when hand-weaving still dominated in the textile factories of Central Russia, mechanical looms were already beginning to play an important role in the capital.[30]

In addition to their mechanization, many of the newer factories differed from the traditional private factories we have been discussing thus far in that they were neither possessional factories nor the private property of noble families, but rather were organized and founded as European-type joint-stock companies. The introduction of this principle on a significant scale coincided roughly in time with the spread of mechanization. Both qualitatively and quantitatively, then, there were concrete signs that during the reign of Nicholas I, the industrial revolution, and not just industry, was penetrating into at least some areas of Russia. Until the Crimean War, these developments, which took place independently of any conscious government policy, were largely confined to the textile industry. One of the important effects of the war was the extension of these aspects of the industrial revolution, this time as a matter of conscious government policy, into the metallurgical and machine industries.[31]

The free capitalist enterprise mechanized and financially organized on a sophisticated Western European model was thus beginning to point to a new economic future for Russia. The question immediately arises as to whether or not there took place a corresponding transformation in the nature of the labor force that manned these factories. As industry became both more complex and more highly rationalized in its operations, a permanent, highly skilled labor force, with no ambiguity as to where it belonged in the socioeconomic schema of the nation, grew increasingly essential. Such had been the case in the social and economic development of England, Europe's industrially most-advanced nation. In England the industrial revolution had been characterized by an identity crisis among the lower classes, by conflict and tensions between traditional social roles and the demands of the new era. In that country it was primarily the traditional status of the independent artisan that was at stake, rather than that of the peasantry. Whatever the social cost, which has been depicted with great sensitivity in E. P. Thompson's recent study *The Making of the English Working Class,* the final outcome was the emergence of a new and distinct stratum of society—the industrial proletariat—whose social, economic, and political impact on British history has been enormous. In Russia, where the independent artisan tradition was extremely weak, if indeed it existed at all, the corresponding tensions were between peasant and worker status, and, I would argue, no clear victory for the latter ever emerged. The social, economic, and political consequences of these tensions were as great in Russia as they had been in England, but of a completely different nature.

In discussing the freely-hired worker of the eighteenth century, we stressed the fact that most of these workers were actually peasant-serfs, closely tied to their villages and obliged to pay *obrok* to their landlords from their earned wages. The freely-hired workers of St. Petersburg industry in the first half of the nineteenth century presented a similar picture. So rustic were their habits, and so close were their ties to the land, that the St. Petersburg police rarely differentiated between peasants and workers in the reports that they issued prior to the reign of Alexander II.[32]

As St. Petersburg industry began to modernize and expand in the 1830's and 1840's, it was the expansion rather than the modernization that affected the labor force. To put it another way, the effect on the workers was quantitative rather than qualitative. By the mid-1840's, precisely the same category of peasant-workers was manning the factories as had been doing so at the turn of the century, but their numbers had more than doubled (from about 5000 to about 11,600), and their numbers would continue to expand as the emancipation approached.[33]

The ties of these peasant-workers to lord and village were only one way in which peasant status, as opposed to worker status, was reinforced. It was also reinforced by the urban industrial center itself. In part because their sojourn in the city was temporary, and in part because of other obstacles, the peasant-workers rarely assimilated to urban life. As serfs they did not possess the legal right to own immovable property in the city; their participation in the municipal educational system was almost nil even on the eve of the emancipation; and most of them had no family life to speak of in the city.[34] Even finding living quarters in the city was often a difficult problem.

Why were there almost no attempts to alter this situation in the first half of the nineteenth century, to convert the freely-hired peasant-worker into a full-time, permanently-employed industrial laborer? In a sense, to ask this question is tantamount to asking why the serfs were not emancipated earlier, for emancipation was a necessary (but not a sufficient, as the post-emancipation period would demonstrate) condition for such a conversion, if it were to be complete. Part of the answer is to be found in the deep hostility toward urban industrial development, and ultimately toward the development of an urban proletariat, that was rooted both in Russian society and in the government. The history of this attitude is a topic unto itself, and we will pause here only to point to a few examples.[35]

During the reign of Nicholas I, with the exception of some of the "Westernizers" of the 1840's, intellectuals as well as officials looked askance at the results of Western industrialization. Hostile attitudes toward the introduction of mechanized urban industries could be found among persons as divergent as Slavophile theoreticians and Finance Minister E. Kankrin, although their respective motivations were quite different. However divergent the motives, the general view prevailed that precisely because he was not completely a worker, either for his own sake or from the point of view of state security, the Russian laborer was in a much more desirable situation than his European counterpart. Kankrin stated it as follows:

In Russia factory workers and other workers come from the villages, which ... has great value in that it prevents the excessive growth of an urban factory class which falls into poverty when work is not available. The peasant returns to the village on such occasions, and ... he at least has a roof and his daily nourishment: our factory class does not combine for the purpose of extorting raises in pay.[36]

This rationale for preserving the peasant character of factory workers was bound to clash with the realities of industrial needs. Although several decades would elapse before the government began to grasp the full significance of this conflict, legislation was introduced as early as 1835 which, had it been fully implemented in practice, would have had the effect of regularizing the contractual relationships between freely-hired workers and their employers, and of undercutting the *pomeshchik*'s control over the travel of serfs engaged in urban factory work. The motives for this proposal involved not economic development but social stability. Nevertheless, the fact that it was even considered pointed toward a new situation in which state interests would no longer be so clearly served by preserving the peasant-worker duality.[37]

This isolated occurrence would have no sequel before the advent of Alexander II, particularly since the European revolutions of 1848 solidified official thinking about the desirability of avoiding the development of a European-type proletariat in Russia. The Crimean War, however, ushered in a new era in Russian history, an era which witnessed not only the abolition of serfdom and the introduction of the Great Reforms, but also the growth and development of railroads, banks, joint-stock companies, and machine industry. Possessional and serf labor soon ceased to be sources of industrial manpower, and were replaced by the adoption of the free labor system throughout the Empire. The question of whether or not the Russian worker should or could become an urban proletarian assumed a new order of magnitude.

Public discussion of the status of the Russian worker began during the first years of Alexander II's reign, shortly after the termination of the war. Defeat had focused attention on Russia's economic backwardness, and among the most conspicuous factors were the illiteracy of the masses and their lack of advanced industrial skills. There was a new undercurrent of opinion, especially among persons of moderate liberal persuasion, that the Western European, and especially the English, worker should be looked upon as a model for Russia rather than as a foil. Such views could be found, for example, in Mikhail Katkov's *Russkii vestnik*,[38] and in some of the new economic journals such as *Vestnik promyshlennosti* and *Promyshlennost'*. Those who held this view did not, of course, wish to see the Russian workers undergo the suffering which the industrial revolution had inflicted upon their Western counterparts, but they were hopeful that pro-labor institutions that had recently been adopted in England could be transferred to Russia before matters had gone that far. Likewise, some commentators turned toward a novel approach that combined the older belief in the unique peasant character of the Russian worker with an acceptance of the positive value of urban industry. The synthesis was made possible by the belief that the two could be combined by the principle of cooperative association, which was seen to be inherent in the peasant institution of *artel'*.[39] In either case the eventual separation of the Russian worker from the village was assumed.

Both approaches were destined to fail. The labor *artel'* never played a significant role in the urban industry of nineteenth-century Russia, except on the level of employment, and the model of the free English factory worker never became viable in urban Russia.

The most important single reason for the failure to adopt the English model was the persistence of the quasi-Slavophile and proto-Populist position toward labor in government circles, already noted in the earlier quotation from Kankrin, which saw the land and the village as a safer solution to the problem of proletarianization than any approaches which might be worked out in the urban industrial context. Of the utmost importance in this regard were the terms of the emancipation itself, with the cumbersome restrictions it placed on peasant mobility and the well-known difficult conditions that had to be met in order for a peasant who was interested in permanent urban employment to sever himself from his commune. Over and beyond this basic factor, however, which provided the general context for all discussion about labor policy, there was the question of the extent to which effective steps could be taken to assimilate the peasant-worker to urban industrial life.

Two approaches were possible. One, based on the assumption that the peasant-worker was and should continue to be essentially a peasant, was for the government to continue to exercise patriarchic and paternalistic control, and to interfere on behalf of the workers when their situation became excessively burdensome and led to unrest. The other approach was based on the assumption that the peasant-worker was (at least potentially) an urban worker, and involved, *maximally,* positive steps by the government to encourage the development of institutional channels through which workers' grievances could be aired and educational institutions through which workers could acquire urban culture and industrial skills. Minimally, it involved a willingness to tolerate private efforts to achieve the same goals.

On these issues the government of Alexander II was divided, and the division, at first glance, would seem to reflect a reversal of ministerial roles from the earlier half of the century, although this reversal was more apparent than real. At least in the earlier years of Alexander II's reign, it was the Ministry of Finance that was most enthusiastic about introducing legislation aimed at protecting the position of the peasant-workers as workers, effectively granting them status as an organized social group with legitimate class interests.[40] If one interpreted the attitude of the Ministry toward possessional workers under Nicholas I in simple terms of pro- or anti-labor attitudes, this would seem to be a significant about-face in the posture of the Ministry. But if we return to our earlier point concerning the Ministry's tendency to distinguish itself from other branches of the government by viewing the peasant-worker in his worker status rather than in his traditional role, then the contradiction disappears, for in the late 1850's and early 1860's there existed the possibility not only to emphasize that status but to institutionalize it. Until the 1880's, however, all the effort of the Ministry in this direction floundered on the rock of the autocracy's fear of legitimizing the existence of an urban working class in Russia. Until the Ministry of Bunge in the 1880's, all efforts were in vain, and even Bunge's victory, as is well known, proved to be of short-lived and dubious value. By the time the autocracy was willing to make even semi-serious efforts in the direction of assisting labor to shape itself as a clearly delineated and independent class, the problem had reached the unmanageable proportions that are depicted by Von Laue.

In the area of working-class education, as I have attempted to show elsewhere,[41] developments were rather similar. In fact, in this and other areas affecting the life of the peasant-worker, not even the minimal condition of tolerating private efforts to integrate the peasant-worker into urban life was met by the regime. At best such efforts were tolerated occasionally, and then only in a guarded and hyper-cautious manner that smacked of what has come to be known as tokenism. It was during the first six years of Alexander II's reign that the possibility that such efforts would be tolerated looked brightest, and yet every effort that was made during those years ended in dismal failure if not outright suppression. No new channels were developed, either public or private, through which the peasant-workers might be integrated into modern industrial life. That life began to develop in Russia, but left the workers behind. By the time of the emancipation, many educated Russians, both within and without the government, had come to the conclusion that Russia could develop a modern factory labor force that would not be subjected to the hardships experienced by their counterparts in Western Europe, and this belief was based in part on the assumption that Europe's experience could provide Russia with formulas that would mitigate the workers' plight before the alienation of labor set in. By the end of 1862, the government had rejected the most important of these formulas, offering as a substitute the preservation of the workers' ties to the soil, to the village commune, qualified only by the tenuous right of the peasant-worker to enroll in the ranks of the urban *meshchanstvo*, a right that existed mainly on paper. This system was preserved even while the government moved ahead with its policy of encouraging the development of modern mechanized industry, and the result, not unexpectedly, proved unsatisfactory on both counts.

On the one hand the industrial skills of the peasant-worker developed all too slowly, thanks to the barriers that existed to his total assimilation to the urban industrial situation. On the other hand, industry developed sufficiently before the 1890's to attract an increasing number of peasant-workers for fairly protracted periods. These peasants were subjected to the factory situation at its worst—that is, without the presence of mitigating influences such as effective labor legislation, recognized channels for the adjustment of grievances, or private philanthropic assistance from society. Under these circumstances, the factory worker did not remain the half-peasant, half-worker of the official ideal, but became instead the shadow of that ideal—the alienated quasi-proletarian, unable to return to his traditional life and unable to adjust to his new one. The more industrialization progressed, the more this process accelerated.

St. Petersburg in the 1860's provides us with a picture of a steadily increasing number of employed factory workers and their growing concentration in fewer and larger factories.[42] In addition to this growing number of employed workers, there was a rapidly increasing number of new peasant arrivals from the countryside—some of them unable, some of them unwilling, to find factory employment. The population of the city, and particularly the peasant population, grew enormously during the second half of the decade. Increased mechanization accompanied the concentration of larger numbers of workers in single factories. This was true primarily in St. Petersburg's two leading industries: cotton spinning and the manufacture of heavy metal products. An intermediate group of factories played important roles in the city's economy, but were unmechanized. However, in sheer numbers, the smaller, more primitive workshop continued to prevail. Thus the new peasant arrival found himself in a city of contradictions and contrasts. Side by side with unfamiliar modern factories were tiny workshops. There were alcoves in the city where the intimacies of village life could be reproduced, and there were impersonal conglomerations of human labor and machines that foreshadowed the twentieth century. Most of the big factories were located on the outskirts of the city, and thus geographically accentuated the peasant-worker's separation from urban life. In a very real sense, the peasant-worker employed in the city did not belong to the city at all.

Despite the modest industrial growth of the 1860's, the overall impression one gleans is that the peasants who came to the city were entering a rather competitive and fairly unstable labor market, one in which just enough temporary and semi-permanent employment was available to justify a temporary break with the countryside. The fact that the labor market was unstable, however, was not necessarily a discouraging situation for the peasant immigrant: a simultaneous rise in factory jobs and decline in artisan work, the liquidation of smaller factories in favor of larger ones, the displacement of men by machines even while employment figures rose—all served to keep the employment situation fluid, to encourage a large and rapid turnover, and thus to increase the possibility of his gaining short-term employment at any given moment. However, it was not so much industrial expansion as it was agricultural problems that were pushing the peasant population into the cities. As the years passed, St. Petersburg was becoming not less but more of a city of peasants than it had been earlier: peasant-artisans, peasant-tradesmen, peasant-coachmen, peasant-workers —over 30 per cent of the population were "hyphenated" peasants with multiple ties to their native villages. Among them, a large majority of the men lived in the city without their families, the largest proportion of these being found among the peasants of the city's most industrial districts.

Because so large a segment of the labor force consisted of temporarily uprooted peasants who continued to have ties, however unrewarding, with the countryside, and because the still rather chaotic nature of early industrial development also contributed to the lack of permanence in industrial employment, the roots of the peasant-worker in the city continued to be shallow and easily severed. The retention of communal ties and the irregularity of movement in and out of the city made it easy for many observers to persist in their belief in the unique and special character of Russian factory labor. Conservative government officials who believed in the peasant-worker concept as the key to the preservation of the country from the Western illness of proletarian unrest had reason to brag; they could still take pride in the country's ability to make substantial, albeit not dramatic, industrial progress without having generated a real urban proletariat. This situation, and the near absence of serious labor unrest in the large cities, fed the complacency of the government, and this complacency in turn prolonged the uprootedness of the peasant-workers. Those voices outside the government that attempted to point to the long-run weaknesses of the government's approach—humanitarian physicians who pointed to the possible social consequences, business-oriented specialists and technicians and a few enlightened industrialists who pointed to the obstacles that this type of labor force placed before any truly dynamic industrial development—remained unheeded, although a few honorific gestures were made in their direction.[43]

By the end of the decade, technical experts, academics, some industrialists, and even foreign observers were pointing to the low productivity of Russian labor and to the poor work habits of the laborer and his lack of moral and economic purposefulness. To a varying extent, many commentators blamed these conditions precisely on the semi-peasant existence of the workers, which continued to obtain official sanction. More and more saw the need for the creation of a distinct and independent working class in Russia, unfettered by the peasant commune and other vestigial institutions, as a means of reducing high production costs which made it difficult for Russia to compete on a reasonable footing with European industry. In short, there was a growing awareness of the need to bring the status of factory workers into line with the requirements of modern industry.

This point of view was put forth publicly and even dramatically by the first all-Russian industrial congress of 1870. At least some elements within the government were prepared to take its suggestions seriously. But it was precisely at this time that the patience of St. Petersburg workers began to run out. Beginning in 1870 and throughout the following decade, the quantity and intensity of labor unrest in St. Petersburg and neighboring regions mounted steadily, and although there were many official deliberations on possible changes in policy, the main thrust of government policy was to quell these disturbances with police methods. As the population and industry of the city continued to expand, as more and more peasants arrived to join the ranks of employed and unemployed labor, and, perhaps above all, as Russian industry was increasingly subjected to the vicissitudes of the international business cycle, the integration of the factory workers into the urban environment became ever more problematical. To all this must be added the fact that there were several unprecedented aspects to the labor unrest of the seventies: it was the first sustained wave of protest carried out by freely-hired workers in a Russian city, it was not (nor could it any longer be at this juncture) carried out in the name of rights derived from a traditional status, and it had a political coloration insofar as many of the workers involved came under the influence of Populist radicals. These circumstances combined to make the government even more hesitant to adopt an open, innovative, and experimental approach to labor questions than it had been a decade earlier. And with the government having failed to take the necessary steps toward the conversion of the peasant-workers into a modern working class, and having allowed nearly insurmountable obstacles to integration into urban life to accumulate, the field was left open for the influence of the Populist intelligentsia to penetrate the milieu of the workers. It goes almost without saying that, to the Populists, the integration of the peasant-worker into urban industrial life was anathema, and in a strange, almost perverse way, the Populist influence complemented the attitudes of the government.

When labor legislation was finally introduced in Russia, in the mid-1880's, the industrial workers of St. Petersburg had already experienced a decade of contact with the revolutionary intelligentsia in a context that provided no real recourse for the redress of grievances. The legislation that was introduced was a halfway house. The main body of legislation was introduced as a concession to the largest, most militant strike by freely-hired workers in Russian history, and yet the concessions did not even include the right of workers to organize independently or otherwise develop class organizations. Much of the legislation, moreover, proved to have little value to the workers in practice.

Such was the situation when the great industrialization spurt of the 1890's began under Witte, when thousands of the raw peasants described by Von Laue began to enter the workshops of St. Petersburg and other cities for the first time. By now the older generation was more worker than peasant, but it was still not fully at home in urban industrial life. The new recruits, on the other hand, were still much more peasant than worker. In both cases—as among the Russian workers of the eighteenth and early nineteenth centuries—there were deep ambiguities and psychological tensions as to where they properly belonged, and in the case of the new recruits, much disorientation brought about by their strange new way of life. The Populist answer —that they were really peasants in a country where urban industry was doomed—was no longer meaningful. The Marxist answer—that they were really industrial workers whose distress stemmed from production relationships and not from industrial life as such—was much more appealing in a period when tensions could no longer be resolved by an appeal to tradition.

7. The Peasant in Nineteenth-Century Historiography

Michael B. Petrovich

Although pre-emancipation Russia was a predominantly agrarian country, few Russian historians before 1861 devoted special attention to the history of the peasantry. Indeed, though Russian industry was still in its infancy in the first half of the nineteenth century, there were more works on the history of Russian industry written during this period than on the history of Russian agriculture.[1] There were at least two major reasons for this anomaly—one technical, the other political.

The technical reason may be summed up in the classical phrase *pas de documents, pas d'histoire.* As late as 1881 the distinguished historian Vasily I. Semevsky found it necessary to write an article entitled "Is It Not Time to Write a History of the Peasants in Russia?" In this article he warned:

The nonspecialist reader may conclude that much has already been done, and that there remains only to collate the facts obtained by individual researchers and then to put together a complete history of the peasants in Russia. But this is quite wrong.[2]

In undertaking to write a history of the Russian peasantry during the reign of Catherine II, an important period in the history of Russian serfdom, Semevsky found himself forced, as late as the 1870's, to begin his task almost from scratch. Of the half-dozen or so survey works in the field of agrarian history before Semevsky, most were based almost exclusively on published sources. A vast fund of archival material relating to the peasantry lay virtually untouched well into the nineteenth century.

For example, cadastral registers had been kept for several centuries by the Russian government. Yet the first scholar to suggest that they were valuable as historical sources was V. N. Berkh, the historian of Russian geographical exploration, who published a book in 1821 concerning an expedition to the cis-Ural towns of Cherdyn and Solikamsk. In that work he called attention to two old cadastral registers that he had found, and observed, "It is very sad that not one of our historians has thought of making use of cadastral registers. From these old documents one could easily compile a statistic (*statistika*) of Russia in the sixteenth and seventeenth centuries."[3] (In those days *statistika* usually meant a description of the national economy.) It was not until late in the century that historians followed this advice at all systematically. To give a similar example, the whole tangled question in Russian historiography of the origins of Russian serfdom came eventually to concern interpretations of the same few sources. The discussion took a different turn only in 1895, when S. A. Adrianov's attention was caught by the phrase "prohibited years" in a charter of 1592, which had been recently published.[4] (See pp. 228–29.)

One of the chief reasons that historians of agriculture in pre-emancipation Russia had fewer sources to draw upon than historians of Russian industry was that both groups concerned themselves mainly with government measures, and the Russian government had intervened far more in industry and commerce than it had in agriculture. In general, the government was content to leave agricultural matters to the landowners to a great degree.[5]

Historians who were more interested in the social development of the peasantry than in the strictly technical aspects of agricultural history found themselves confronted with an additional handicap: in 1818 the Minister of Public Education issued an order forbidding periodicals or individual works from expressing anything either in defense of peasant rights or against them. This prohibition remained in effect until 1858, when the government felt obliged to open the entire question of the liberation of the serfs.[6] How far this ban went may be judged by the fact that when Konstantin S. Aksakov wrote an article in the newspaper *Molva* about American Negro slavery in which he hinted that free labor had certain advantages over slave labor, he was reprimanded by the Deputy Minister of Education, Prince P. A. Vyazemsky.[7] If Alexander Pushkin was able to publish at least an expurgated version of his *History of Pugachëv*, it was thanks to the unperceptiveness of his personal censor—Tsar Nicholas I.[8] The book might well have suffered a worse fate at the hands of a less exalted and more fearful censor.

The first scholarly monograph on the history of Russian agriculture was that by O. Turchinovich, *The History of the Agrarian Economy of Russia*; though its title page bore no date, it is known to have been published in 1854, in St. Petersburg.[9] This pioneer work avoided any discussion of serfdom that might have offended the authorities. The author's approach was defined in his preface thus: "The condition of the agrarian economy in every state depends in the largest part on the measures that the government has taken in the direction and perfection of this branch of industry."[10] The book was, then, a survey of government policies with respect to agriculture. The first part encompassed all of Russian agricultural history from the ninth century to the reign of Peter I. The second part, which comprised three-quarters of the book, skipped lightly over the eighteenth century and was almost wholly devoted to the first half of the nineteenth century. It dealt with such diverse topics as credit for landowners, measures for obtaining better agricultural machinery and tools, the organization of provincial fairs, the settlement of foreign colonists, grain exports, and the roles of the Free Economic Society and of various state agencies, especially the Ministry of State Lands.

The next two books to appear on the same subject, in 1856 and 1858, were similar to Turchinovich's in their emphasis on government measures. The first, by a professor of agriculture at the University of Kiev, S. M. Khodetsky, was entitled *A Review of Successes in Agriculture in Russia, with a Historical Presentation of Government Measures for the Improvement of the Economy*.[11] The second was by a professor of technology at the University of Kazan, A. K. Chugunov; it was entitled *A Historical Survey of Government Measures for the Development of Agriculture in Russia*.[12]

Once Alexander II decided, after the Crimean debacle, to confront the question of the emancipation of the serfs, and the decree forbidding public discussion of the topic was annulled, a stream of journalistic works on the peasant began to appear. However, the number of scholarly monographs on peasant history remained small before and during the period of the Great Reforms, and nearly all were concerned with the legal and administrative aspects of the subject.

Among the more noteworthy of these efforts was an early work by Konstantin P. Pobedonostsev (1827–1907). In 1858, just before he became a professor of civil law at Moscow University, Pobedonostsev wrote a survey of the history of Russian serfdom in *Russkii Vestnik*.[13] With the first half of the seventeenth century as its end point, Pobedonostsev's study dealt with legal aspects almost to the exclusion of economic factors. Nevertheless, when Semevsky assessed the state of Russian historiography on the peasant question up to 1881, he praised Pobedonostsev's work.[14] In 1861 Pobedonostsev wrote a sequel, on serfdom in eighteenth-century Russia, which was also published in *Russkii Vestnik*.[15]

Other writers at the time also stressed legal factors. A good example is V. I. Veshnyakov, whose articles of 1857 and 1859 in the journal of the Ministry of State Lands were all concerned with legal nomenclature and classification of various forms of land tenure, and were based almost entirely on the *Complete Collection of Laws of the Russian Empire*.[16] The same legalistic or administrative emphasis marked later and broader works, including, for example, those by A. V. Romanovich-Slavatinsky, who published a valuable monograph in 1870 on the gentry from the beginning of the eighteenth century to the emancipation, and M. I. Gorchakov, who in 1871 published a work on Russian Church lands from 988 to 1738.[17]

Such works could hardly satisfy the growing ranks of those who called for a history of the Russian *people* rather than of the Russian *state*. The persistence of this demand throughout the nineteenth century is a particularly interesting phenomenon in Russian intellectual history. Undoubtedly much of the impulse behind it came from the romantic nationalism of the post-Napoleonic period, which produced a whole new vocabulary of such untranslatable words as *narodnost'* and *samobytnost'*. (Both terms were influenced by German thought. *Narodnost'*, meaning roughly "nationality," was used in the cultural sense of *Volkstümlichkeit*; *samobytnost'* meant "individuality" in the sense of the German *Eigenart*.) It is especially interesting that although Karamzin's famous *History of the Russian State* was a monument to Russian patriotism, it was precisely this work that critics cited as the kind of history they did not want. They identified nationalism not with the state but with the people. It was in this spirit that Nikolai A. Polevoi (1796–1846) wrote his six-volume *History of the Russian People* (1830–33)—to counteract Karamzin's emphasis on the state as the prime mover in Russian history. The Slavophiles went even further by defining the people (the *narod*) as preeminently the Russian peasantry.

It was, fittingly enough, a Slavophile—Konstantin S. Aksakov—who was among the first to call for a history of the Russian peasantry. He seized the opportunity in his review of the seventh volume of the monumental *History of Russia from Earliest Times* by Sergei M. Solovyov (1821–79), which appeared in 1858. Chiding Solovyov for devoting only six pages of the volume to the peasantry as such, even though he was discussing the very period in which serfdom became established, Aksakov wrote:

In the *History of Russia,* the author has omitted just one thing: the Russian people. Karamzin did not take note of the Russian people either, but one could hardly expect that then, as one might in our own time. Besides, Karamzin called his history the *History of the Russian State.* The *History of Russia,* the subject of the present work, may also be called with complete justice the *History of the Russian State,* nothing else; the land, the people—the reader will not find them there.[18]

It was, of course, not only the Slavophiles who felt this way. The same thought was repeated again and again by liberals and revolutionaries of all persuasions. Take, for example, Dobrolyubov's bitter question:

How many historians of the people have there appeared in Europe who would look upon events from the standpoint of popular interests, who would observe what the people have gained or lost in a given epoch, where it went badly with the masses, for people in general, and not just for a few titled individuals, conquering generals, and the like?[19]

And Pisarev pointed out, "The active force lies always and everywhere not in individuals, nor in circles, nor in literary productions, but in the general, and preeminently economic, conditions of the life of the popular masses."[20] Because of his interest in the village commune, Chernyshevsky had a particular reason for wishing to see the

limits of historical study expanded to include the economic and social life of the peasantry. Yet however interested these social thinkers,
publicists, and revolutionaries were in history, they were not themselves historians.

There was one group of historians who had special cause to concern themselves with popular as distinct from political history—the
Regionalists or Federalists. Whether their particular region was Siberia, the Ukraine, or some other part of the empire, each of these historians stressed the element of local popular autonomy as against the
centralizing tendencies of the capital.

Afanasy P. Shchapov (1830–76), a rebel *raznochinets* par excellence, was the son of a Siberian deacon and a Buriat mother. He devoted most of his historical work to his native Siberia and such popular movements of the past as the Old Believers. Shchapov once described his motivation for pursuing such studies in the following
terms:

When I studied Ustryalov and Karamzin, it always seemed strange to me
why in their histories one did not see our rural Russia, a history of the
masses, the so-called simple, dark people. Is this majority of our citizenry
to be eternally voiceless, passive, inactive? Does not this vast majority have
a right to enlightenment, historical development, to life and significance,
as much as the gentry and the clergy? ... Yet read the chronicles or the historical records up to the eighteenth century: who built, founded, and popu-
lated the Russian land, cleared the soil of forests and marshes? Who if not
the communal peasant?[21]

Nikolai I. Kostomarov (1817–85), another Federalist historian and
a champion of Ukrainian autonomy, asked similarly, "How is it
that all histories speak of eminent statesmen, and sometimes about
laws and institutions, but somehow pass over the life of the popular
masses? The poor muzhik—the toiling tiller of the soil—seems not
to exist for history."[22] In a lecture delivered in 1863 on "The Relation of Russian History to Geography and Ethnography," Kostomarov rebuked Karamzin and others for ignoring "the untouched life
of the popular masses, their social and domestic life, their habits, customs, conceptions, upbringing, sympathies, vices, and aspirations."[23]
Being especially interested in what he called "the spirit of the people"
and their "spiritual physiognomy," Kostomarov turned to a study of

ethnography, and particularly folklore, as a historical source. Some of his work was superficial and colorful at the expense of historical truth. Nevertheless, he did much to broaden the historian's scope to include the popular element. This is especially evident in his works dealing with peasant rebellions. Mass movements in the "Time of Troubles" or Stenka Razin's revolt fascinated him as moments in history when the common people, the peasantry, were left to act on their own.

There were other historians who were interested in the history of rural Russia no less than the Slavophiles: these included revolutionary democrats and socialists, as well as Federalists. However, they denied the possibility of writing peasant history, at least in the manner envisaged by its romantic proponents, as something distinct from the history of the state.

The most eminent of these historians was Sergei M. Solovyov, the man whose *History of Russia* so displeased Aksakov. In an essay entitled "Observations on the Historical Life of Peoples," Solovyov declared, "A government, no matter what its form, represents its people; the people are personified in it, and thus it has been, is, and ever shall be of primary interest to the historian." In Hegelian fashion, he divided peoples into "historic" and "non-historic." He extended this classification to social classes as well. For him the peasants, as such, were "non-historic." As he put it:

History deals only with that which visibly moves, which acts and manifests itself, and thus history has no way of dealing with the popular masses; it deals only with representatives of the people, no matter in what form the government may express itself; and even when the popular masses are set in motion, it is the leaders, the directors of that movement, who are of primary interest and with whom history is and should be primarily concerned.[24]

Konstantin D. Kavelin (1818–85), legal historian and founder of the Statist school of Russian historiography, was certainly not hostile to the peasantry; on the contrary, as a liberal Westernizer he was an ardent champion of their emancipation. He considered the archetype of the Great Russian to be the landowning peasant of the past—the *domovladyka*—whose whole conception of governmental and social life was rooted in his village. Kavelin greatly admired "this people, who created a state, who bore on their backs the brunt of all the adversities of history, and who were paid for their service to the fatherland with serfdom."[25] Nevertheless, as a historian, Kavelin could see in the Russian peasantry nothing but an "ethnographic protoplasm" that was still but in the process of being molded.[26]

Despite this attitude, or perhaps because of it, it was precisely the Statist historians who did some of the best pioneer work in the history of Russian agrarian institutions. Notable among these was Boris N. Chicherin (1828–1904), who was a professor of law at the University of Moscow until 1868, when he resigned in protest against administration policies. Whereas the Slavophiles stressed the spontaneous formation and aboriginality of Russian peasant institutions such as the commune, Chicherin assigned a determining role to the state as the organizer of economic and social life. His first noteworthy work in this field was an article, in 1856, in which he reviewed the historical background of the village commune in Russia.[27] This was among the earliest such studies in all of Russian historiography. His second article, which also appeared in 1856, was a study of slaves and peasants in Russia from earliest times to the sixteenth century.[28] More will be said about these articles later.

The foremost contributor to the history of the peasantry on the Slavophile side was Ivan D. Belyaev (1810–73). A professor of history at the University of Moscow, Belyaev became known for his work on Russian social history in the Muscovite period. His first important work in this field was a modest article on agriculture in early Russia, published in 1855 in the Moscow *Vremennik* of the Society of Russian History and Antiquities.[29] This was followed, in 1860, by a major work—*The Peasants of Rus'*—which was not only the chief Slavophile contribution to the history of the Russian peasantry, but the first serious scholarly survey of this subject in Russian historiography.[30]

The outstanding Russian historian of the nineteenth century, Vasily O. Klyuchevsky (1841–1911), is in a class by himself. Like his teacher Solovyov, Klyuchevsky possessed an encyclopedic knowledge of Russian history, but his particular contribution was his success in synthesizing this knowledge and placing it in a broad socioeconomic perspective. Klyuchevsky's works merged economic history with social history; he went beyond the conventional documentary sources to the travel accounts of foreign visitors, the lives of saints, and anything that would help him reconstruct the total environment of the past. While he resembled Shchapov and Kostomarov in this respect, he originally followed Solovyov and the Statists in his view that the state rather than the people was the prime mover in Russian history.

However, in his later work, beginning in the late 1870's—particularly in a series of works on the Russian peasantry—he stressed the role of economic factors in history. In 1879 he wrote an article entitled "The Serf Question on the Eve of Legislative Action," which was inspired by the appearance of the second volume of Yury F. Samarin's work on *The Peasant Question up to the Imperial Decree of November 20, 1857.*[31] Klyuchevsky followed this with a whole series of studies in the 1880's: "Law and Fact in the History of the Peasant Question" (1881);[32] "The Origin of Serfdom in Russia" (1885);[33] and "The Capitation Tax and the Abolition of Slavery in Russia" (1885).[34] In these works Klyuchevsky turned away from the Statists by attributing the origins of serfdom not to state policy but to economic conditions as reflected in the contractual relations between lord and peasant. Nevertheless, his basic framework remained legalistic; he merely took the question of serfdom out of the realm of public law and treated it as an aspect of civil law. It is indicative of Klyuchevsky's lasting interest in the history of the peasantry that one of his very last works, left unfinished at his death in 1911, was an article prepared for the fiftieth anniversary of the emancipation.

It was natural that the Populist historians should have been among the chief contributors to Russian peasant history. Like the Slavophiles before them, the Populists had a special ideological interest in the subject. The Populists saw the peasantry as the basic force behind any Russian revolution, and they regarded the village commune as the hallmark of an indigenous Russian socialism. They saw at the foundation of the Russian historical process a tension between two conflicting principles—the autocratic state and popular freedom, the latter having the village commune as its institutional base. Their belief in the inevitability of popular revolution gave their historians a particular interest in the history of peasant rebellions. Above all, they were interested in serfdom, its development and its abolition.

In all of these respects the works of Vasily I. Semevsky (1848–1916) are not only the most distinguished examples of Populist historiography, but milestones in Russian historiography as a whole. Early in his student days at the University of St. Petersburg, Semevsky chose the history of the Russian peasantry as his special field. The first result of his labors came in 1876, when he published an article in *Russkaia Starina* on serfdom in the reign of Catherine II.[35] This was but the beginning of a series of published studies that culminated in his capital work, *The Peasantry in the Reign of the Empress Catherine II*.[36] Semevsky presented this work in 1880 as his master's dissertation, but Professor K. N. Bestuzhev-Riumin blocked its acceptance in 1881, just after the assassination of Emperor Alexander II, on the grounds that Semevsky's preface was critical of the Great Reform of the Tsar-Liberator.[37] In 1882 Semevsky presented his dissertation to the University of Moscow, where it was accepted. On that occasion Semevsky delivered a stirring address calling upon other historians to heed the tocsin, as he put it, and to devote more work to the history of the Russian peasantry.[38] It was obvious from this expression of self-dedication that the writing of peasant history was for Semevsky a scholar's way of "going to the people."

Semevsky's work *The Peasantry in the Reign of the Empress Catherine II* was undoubtedly the most solid piece of original research on a single period in the history of the Russian peasantry to appear up to that time. It was based on the painstaking labors of a decade, often in hitherto unexploited archives—for example, the 230 tomes of the Land Survey Office in Moscow, with their wealth of statistics, district by district. Semevsky made use of a great variety of sources: travel accounts, peasant testimony before investigating commissions, unpublished family papers such as those of the Sheremetievs or Kurakins, the reports of Catherine's provincial procurators published by the Free Economic Society, court records, reports by the delegates to Catherine's famous Great Commission in 1767, the archives of the various Collegia and the Senate, and many others.[39] Semevsky's book was especially valuable inasmuch as it dealt with a period that had been neglected by other historians. This neglect is all the more astonishing when one considers that Russian serfdom reached its complete form during the reign of Catherine II. Semevsky continued work on this period all his life; the second volume of his study appeared twenty years after the first, in 1901. There was to have been a third volume, but he died before completing it.

Semevsky's second great work in the history of rural Russia was his two-volume survey *The Peasant Question in Russia in the Eighteenth and First Half of the Nineteenth Century,* published in St. Petersburg in 1888.[40] It was this work that won him a doctor's degree from Moscow University, the Uvarov Prize of the Academy of Science, and the Great Gold Medal awarded by the Free Economic Society. "Here, for the first time," reported the prize commission of the Free Economic Society, "there has been presented, in the fullest possible manner, the question of the gradual development of official and unofficial measures toward the restriction of serfdom and its eventual end."[41] It is still regarded as "the fundamental study of serfdom in post-Petrine Russia."[42]

Basically Semevsky's work was not so much economic history as it was social history—indeed, intellectual history; and widely disparate historians have criticized Semevsky for this. As Klyuchevsky wrote in a review article, "His book has turned out to be not so much a history of the peasant question as a chronological enumeration of opinions and programs concerning the peasant question."[43] The Soviet historian N. L. Rubinstein has similarly observed that "for Semevsky the peasant question appeared to be an ideological problem," so that "the history of social movements is transformed by Semevsky into the history of social ideas."[44] Apparently one of the reasons for this criticism is that Semevsky found it impossible to demonstrate statistically that serfdom had outlived its profitability, and so he stressed political and humanitarian factors behind the emancipation. This, of course, ran against the materialistic interpretation that, as Lazar Volin has pointed out, "had become intellectually fashionable long before it gained the monopolistic exclusiveness of a political orthodoxy after the Revolution."[45] Certainly in our own day Jerome Blum has reached the conclusion, in his *Lord and Peasant in Russia,* that the economic reasons often given for the emancipation are not convincing by themselves and in the light of hard facts; he himself points to *raisons d'état* and to the influence of humanitarianism as being more decisive than economic factors.[46]

Besides Semevsky, there were more than a few other important economic and social historians of Populist persuasion whose studies on the peasant question in their own time comprise some of the best works available on the latter half of the nineteenth century. A pioneer who preceded Semevsky was Vasily V. Bervi (1829–1918), also known by his pseudonym N. Flerovsky, whose monograph *The Position of the Working Class in Russia* was first published in 1869. In this work, Bervi discussed urban laborers, but he gave his attention primarily to the peasantry, which he regarded as the most important segment of the working class. The book was an indictment of the emancipation in that it portrayed the progressive pauperization of the freed peasants after 1861.[47] Mikhail I. Venyukov (1832–1901) prepared a four-volume survey entitled *Historical Outlines of Russia from the Time of the Crimean War to the Conclusion of the Treaty of Berlin, 1855–1878*; the volumes were published in 1879 and 1880 in Leipzig and Prague, which was a wise precaution in view of their criticism of the tsarist regime. The fourth volume dealt with the plight of the Russian peasantry before and after the emancipation, which Venyukov characterized as "concealed serfdom."[48]

There was also a whole group of later Populist economic historians who were interested in showing what they believed to be the special noncapitalist development of the Russian economy. Their works naturally concentrated on the role of agriculture and the village commune. Among the most important writers of this group were Vasily P. Vorontsov (1847–1918), who often signed himself simply V.V.; Nikolai F. Danielson (1844–1918), who signed himself Nikolai —on; and Sergei N. Yuzhakov (1849–1910).

There are several Populist historians who merit special attention for their works on the history of agrarian communes. The first is Pavel A. Sokolovsky (1842–1906), whose best known works were his *Outline of the History of the Village Commune in the North of Russia* (1877) and *The Economic Way of Life of the Agricultural Population of Russia and the Colonization of the Southeastern Steppes before Serfdom* (1878).[49] Both works were favorable toward peasant communes and directed against the Statists, especially Chicherin. Alexandra Ia. Efimenko (1848–1918), a Ukrainian scholar, is remembered especially for her work entitled *Investigations into the Life of the People* (1884), as well as for her studies of land tenure in the Ukraine.[50] Her independence as a scholar is shown by her readiness to challenge a favorite tenet of the Populists—the ancient origin and unbroken development of Russian agrarian communes. Alexander A. Kaufman (1864–1919) made an important contribution to the discussion of communes with his monograph *The Peasant Commune in Siberia* (1897), as well as his later work entitled *The Russian Commune during the Process of Its Inception and Rise* (1908).[51]

Another group of historians interested in the peasantry from a special point of view consisted of those writing on Russian law and legal institutions. Professionally most were professors of law at various universities. One of the earliest of these was Ivan D. Belyaev, whose work *The Peasants of Rus'* we have already cited; however, it is appropriate to mention here that Belyaev's textbook *Lectures on the History of Russian Legislation* (1879) is full of references to the peasantry and their legal status in various periods of Russian history.[52] Another such legal historian was Vasily I. Sergeevich (1835–1911), a professor at the University of St. Petersburg, who was a founder of the Juridical school of Russian historiography. The third volume of his work *Russian Legal Antiquities* was devoted entirely to the subject of land ownership,[53] and his textbook entitled *Lectures and Investigations in the Ancient History of Russian Law* was a highly original survey of pre-Petrine law and institutions that included a discussion of the agrarian problem.[54] The Kievan scholar Mikhail F. Vladimirsky-Budanov (1838–1916) was the author not only of a standard and often republished survey of the history of Russian law, but also of several important works on the Ukraine, all of which deal with the peasant question.[55] Mikhail A. Dyakonov (1855–1919) was a specialist in the history of the peasantry in sixteenth- and seventeenth-century Muscovy. A major work of his—*Sketches on the History of the Peasant Population in the Muscovite State in the XVI–XVII Centuries* (1898)—was based on a collection of primary sources that he had published previously, under the title of *Documents Concerning the History of the Taxed Population in the Muscovite State*.[56] His work on this period was carried on by another prominent legal historian, Stepan B. Veselovsky (1876–1952), who, like Dyakonov, deserves special recognition for publishing so many primary sources, in this case cadastral registers.[57] Nikolai P. Pavlov-Silvansky (1869–1908), a legal historian from the University of St. Petersburg, strongly reflected the influence of Sergeevich and the Juridical school in his writings, notably in his monograph *Feudalism in Appanage Russia,* begun in 1897, but not published until 1910.[58]

During the nineteenth century, Marxist historians offered little of note on peasant history. Of course there were only a very few Marxist historians in the nineteenth century, and they came to the fore very late. Moreover, they had more ideological interest in the urban workers than in the peasantry. During the entire nineteenth century there were only three Marxists who wrote about the Russian peasantry in the past—Fedoseev, Rozhkov, and Struve—and all three are doubtful cases in one way or another.

Nikolai E. Fedoseev (1871–98) did not live long enough to fully establish himself as a historian. However, Soviet surveys of Russian historiography credit him with being a pioneer of Marxist historiography in Russia. In the history of Russian Communism he is remembered as the organizer of the first Marxist circle at the University of Kazan. As a historian he is remembered, at least by Russian Marxists, for two works—"On the Village Commune" and "On the Causes of the Fall of Serfdom in Russia." The manuscripts of both works have been lost, though excerpts from the latter were published in 1897 in the *Samarskii Vestnik.*[59] It is known, however, that the manuscripts were read by others, including Lenin, who valued them highly.[60] Fedoseev's insistence that Russian Marxists pay more attention to the history of Russian serfdom did not find much response in Plekhanov and other members of the Liberation of Labor group.

Nikolai A. Rozhkov (1868–1927) wrote a master's thesis titled "The Agrarian Economy of Muscovite Russia in the Sixteenth Century."[61] He defended the thesis successfully at the University of Moscow in 1899. Rozhkov's aims were to write a study of the technical aspects of agricultural production in sixteenth-century Russia and to trace the influences of this system of production on the social and political structure. The most noteworthy feature of this work was Rozhkov's attempt to apply some of the newest methods of economic research, including statistical methods, to the earlier periods of Russian history. However, in his analysis there was much more of the

Statist school than there was of Marx. In 1901 Rozhkov publicly repented his Statist bias, and declared that he should have looked further into the broader aspects of economic relations in general.[62]

It is difficult to know how to classify Pyotr B. Struve (1870–1944), either professionally or ideologically. He was more of an economist and sociologist than historian. Yet his work *The Serf Economy: Investigations into the Economic History of Russia in the Eighteenth and Nineteenth Centuries* is a noteworthy contribution to Russian historiography.[63] As for his ideological stance, it is well known that he was probably the leading theorist of Marxism in Russia during the 1890's as well as the author of the manifesto accepted by the newly formed Russian Social Democratic Labor Party at its first congress in 1898. He is generally described as a Legal Marxist in this period. Later he turned to the Constitutional Democrats, then joined other erstwhile Marxists in the Vekhi group, and ended his days abroad as an anti-Bolshevik adherent of the moderate right.

Though his book *The Serf Economy* was published in 1913, the author himself noted that it was an elaboration of a study he had done around the turn of the century. Perhaps the principal theoretical feature of the work was Struve's contention that serfdom was not a brake on the Russian economy but a prime driving force. Making a comparison between peasant farm agriculture and an economy based on large estates, Struve concluded that the latter was the more progressive in that it was linked to a market and a money economy. He declared that serfdom had been ended precisely at the time when it was at its height as the mainstay of a productive estate economy.[64] Struve even used the notorious indebtedness of the estate owners as a sign not of a financial crisis but of a healthy expansion in capital investment. Thus Struve saw no economic justification for the abolition of serfdom, but regarded it as an artificial measure imposed by the state. "From this proceeds the fact," he wrote, "that all the agrarian economy of post-reform Russia bears within itself the traces of serf economy."[65] It is not hard to see why Soviet critics have regarded Struve as a standard bearer of capitalist rather than Marxist thought. (In his work *The Development of Capitalism in Russia* Lenin left no doubt as to his own opinion that serfdom was abolished because it retarded the development of the capitalist economy in Russia.)

It has not been our aim in the foregoing résumé to present a biblio-graphical survey of all significant works dealing with the peasantry in nineteenth-century Russian historiography. That would be too large a task, at least in the framework of this study. Our purpose has been, rather, to show that Russian historians began relatively late in the nineteenth century to pay special attention to the past of the Russian peasantry. Serious research in this area was hampered for a long time by a lack or insufficient use of primary sources. In addition, during the first half of the century, work on the peasantry was dis-couraged because the government would not permit free and open discussion of the peasant question. In the latter half of the century, as monographic studies concerning the past of the peasantry began to appear, they conformed to no single approach or methodology. Most, if not all, of the historians wrote from the standpoint of a par-ticular intellectual position, whether Slavophile, Westernizing, Popu-list, Marxist, or some other. Each also stressed some particular aspect of history, usually at the expense of others—for example, juridical or legal, socioeconomic, or intellectual. In any case, Russian historical scholarship concerning the peasantry did not develop in the un-troubled atmosphere of the study but in a milieu in which the "peas-ant question" was one of the two or three most vital issues facing Rus-sian society. Russian historiography in the period between the post-Crimean era of the Great Reforms and the First World War clearly reflected public concern over the peasant question. The marvel is that all these pressures should have permitted the high quality of much of the Russian historical scholarship that dealt with the peasant past.

There were several topics that attracted historians more than other aspects of peasant history. The most important of these were the ori-gins and development of the Russian agrarian commune, the origins of Russian serfdom, the history of peasant rebellions, and, more re-cently, the causes and aftermath of the emancipation of the serfs. Each of these topics involved issues whose importance transcended the limits of purely academic discussion. We shall deal here with only the first two of these topics.

There is probably no subject in Russian agrarian history about which so much has been written and yet about which so little is

known as the origins and historical development of the rural commune. The basic problem is that very few facts are known about the
commune in medieval Russian history, while there is a great variety
of opinion as to what communes were like even in later times, such
as the sixteenth and seventeenth centuries, for which there are source
materials. Also of importance is the difficulty—some would say inability—of establishing a genetic link between the earliest communes
of medieval Rus' and the communes of early-modern Muscovy. Were
the latter the result of an unbroken development arising from a naturally evolving and ancient peasant way of life, or was the early-
modern commune a newly established institution created artificially
in response to some pressure from outside the peasant way of life, in
particular the state?

   This question that seemed at first purely academic assumed an importance in the second half of the nineteenth century that went beyond scholarly interests. It became the subject of a dispute that arose
at the end of the Crimean War, when the question of the abolition
of serfdom was opened. In this tense and exciting period, when great
changes were in the air, the discussion of the origin and development
of agrarian communes in Russia was related to basic attitudes toward
such currently vital questions as the proper role of the state in Russian
society, and the rights and abilities of the peasants—the largest part
of the Russian population—to have a voice in their own government.
The discussion was also linked to the broader problem of the nature
of Russia's social development. Was the rural commune a sign of Russia's backwardness and an impediment to its progress, or was it the
expression of some unique and indigenous Russian way of life and
the promise of a better future than even Western Europe could hope
for?

   The question of the origin of the commune among the early Slavs
is complex. Apart from casual comments, Russian historians of the
eighteenth and early nineteenth centuries had no systematic theories
or conclusions to offer. The first attempt at a theory in Russian historiography was made by Johann Philipp Gustav Ewers (1781–1830),
a student of Schlözer's at Göttingen, who made his home in Russia
in 1803. In his work *Das älteste Reich der Russen in seiner geschicht-
lichen Entwicklung* (1826), which appeared in a Russian translation

in 1835, Ewers advanced the theory of an original clan society (*rodovoi byt*) of Eastern Slavs from which the state evolved as a result of their amalgamation and development, replacing the earlier institutions of their primitive patriarchal society.[66] This theory was later accepted and developed by Solovyov and the Statists, notably Kavelin and Chicherin.

Another German scholar, Baron August von Haxthausen, proposed a different theory in his three-volume work *Studien über die innern Zustände, das Volksleben und insbesondere die ländlichen Einrichtungen Russlands* (1847–52). As a result of his journey through Russia in 1843, Haxthausen made many observations on the rural commune. He idealized it as "an organically free republic whose whole independence was limited only by its payment of a fixed rent to the lord." The commune distinguished Russia from Western Europe, Haxthausen declared, in that it preserved Russian society from "the cancer of a proletariat."[67]

The scholarly debate over the origins of the commune among Russian historians arose in 1856 with an article by Chicherin entitled "A Review of the Historical Development of the Rural Commune in Russia," which was published in *Russkii Vestnik*.[68] Chicherin argued here, and in a series of polemical articles that followed, that the rural commune as it was known in modern Russia was not the organic product of a misty ancient past; there may well have been communes of some sort among the early East Slavs, as among the other Slavs, he conceded, but these had probably disappeared by the time the Varangians arrived in Russia. Modern village communes, he declared, arose at the end of the sixteenth century as the result of government regulations binding the peasants to their place of residence as a tax measure. Furthermore, the principle of repartitional land tenure, in which the commune periodically equalized land holdings among its members through reallotment, was no ancient principle arising from a primitive socialism, but a practical response to meet the obligation of the state's capitation tax, imposed by Peter I.

Chicherin based his conclusions essentially on two facts: first, that earlier evidence pointed to the ability of freeholding peasants to dispose of their plots without reference to any commune; and, second, that there was no evidence of repartitional tenure before the imposition of the capitation tax. Chicherin argued that, because the capitation tax imposed a burden on all peasants alike, there was an obligation to provide all peasants with a plot of land from which to pay their tax; furthermore, since the tax was equal for all, the land holdings had to be equalized. As inequities arose because of births, deaths, and migrations, it was necessary to reallot the land periodically. The commune was the collective agency that carried this out and that was responsible for the paying of the tax. Also, the commune saw to it that all its tax-paying members remained on their plots so that none could escape the tax. (It should be remembered that all the land of the commune belonged to a single noble owner, while the peasants had only *use* of the land.) This communal system evolved at first on private estates, and then gradually, by government decrees (particularly the regulations of 1754 and 1766), was extended to include state peasants and freeholding farmers. Chicherin concluded his article thus: "The institutions of our communes are the products of modern times, and to compare them with the patriarchal communes of other peoples is to deny our historical development."

The Slavophile Konstantin Aksakov opposed this conception with the counterclaim that the society of ancient Russia was based not on clans but on a communal structure (*Obshchinnoe ustroistvo*). "The Russian land," he insisted, "was from the beginning least of all patriarchal and above all a communal land."[69] Unfortunately his definition of a commune as "a natural union of men" was as imprecise as his opponents' conception of clans. However, of one thing Aksakov was certain: the communal principle was at the base of the Russian historical process from the dawn of history to the present.

Among the Slavophiles, the most authoritative voice on matters of history was that of the only professional historian among them—Ivan D. Belyaev. It was his critical review of Chicherin's article, published in the first issue of *Russkaia Beseda,* in 1856, that set off a public debate between Chicherin and himself. This debate was carried on in a round of articles, with Chicherin being joined by both Solovyov and Kavelin.[70] Belyaev's arguments, and those of the Slavophile camp as a whole, may be summed up in the following points: (1) the Russian commune was not a patriarchal, clan, or state institution, but a corporate entity; (2) it resembled the commune of the other early

Slavs; (3) it had always differed from Western communes in that the Russian communes were self-governing; and (4) the present Russian commune had a continuous existence from earliest history and was not the creation of the state.[71] Out of Belyaev's investigations came his monograph entitled *The Peasants of Rus'*, cited earlier in this study. Despite its scholarship, this work suffered from an obvious sympathy with the Slavophile mystique, which Solovyov branded as "anti-historical" and Chicherin as "mystico-fantastical."

Despite this criticism, Belyaev was joined by another Slavophile sympathizer, Vasily Nikolaevich Leshkov (1810–81), whose works on early Russian history advanced the theory that the basis of government in Kievan Rus' was the territorial commune.[72] He identified this commune with the *verv'* (meaning an association of neighbors in a country district) in the medieval *Russkaia Pravda*.[73]

Actually, the trouble was that both sides were groping in the darkness of a time in Russian history on which there were very few or no documents to shed any light. For example, Belyaev could offer only one document, and that from as late as the sixteenth century, to show the existence of repartitional tenure in earlier times.[74] Whereas the Slavophiles resorted to imagination, logical deduction, analogies with the history of kindred people, and amateur anthropology, the more literal-minded Statists found it to their advantage to deny the existence of something for which no documentary proofs existed. Theirs was the easier task, inasmuch as they dealt with a more recent period, for which there were documentary sources. And yet there were other scholars, good scholars, who were not convinced that the main Slavophile contentions were wrong, regardless of the Slavophile mystique or the lack of documentary evidence.

It must be stressed that, particularly in the 1850's and 1860's, the dispute over the origin of communes touched some vital current issues. The proponents of the antiquity of the Russian commune, especially the Slavophiles (and later the Populists), saw in the commune a guarantee against the penetration of capitalism into the village and against the creation of a Russian proletariat on the land. Their Westernizing opponents (and later the Marxists) saw the commune as but a stage in Russia's social development—as an institution that had also existed in Western society but had passed away with time, as it surely would in Russia as the country caught up with Western development.

Another issue was raised by the manner in which both camps regarded the relationship between the people and the state. The Slavophiles (and later Populists) perceived in the peasant commune an autochthonous principle of a submerged popular sovereignty; the Populists especially saw this principle as one suppressed by the alien power of the state, but as one that was nonetheless vital and waiting to be fulfilled. The Westernizers (and later the Marxists) saw the state as the dominant element in the organization of the economic life of the country, while the commune was an institution which the state had created and which presumably the state could destroy.

In 1872 a civil servant named Lalosh was assigned to the northern province of Olonets, between Lakes Ladoga and Onega. He was surprised to discover, upon his arrival, that peasants in that region owned their own land in hereditary tenure, and yet communes existed there. Furthermore, these communes had ultimate control over certain lands, which originally had belonged to no one. Some of this communal land, Lalosh found, was being tilled by peasants who treated it as though it were their own, though they recognized the commune's claim to it and the commune's right to repartition it. Still another portion of this land consisted of common pasture. Lalosh concluded that what he was observing was, in fact, different stages, side by side, in the natural development of the communal order. This was the gist of a study he published on his observations. His findings tended, of course, to dispute the validity of some of Chicherin's basic assumptions.[75]

It was the historian P. A. Sokolovsky who first attempted to apply Lalosh's observations to his own historical research. Out of this came his monograph *Outline of the History of the Agrarian Commune in the North of Russia,* which was published in 1877.[76] As a liberal Populist, Sokolovsky was predisposed to believe in the antiquity of communes in Russia. He found in the contemporary communes of northern European Russia a confirmation of his theory that Muscovite Russia had been settled not by whole clans of East Slavs but by small families who banded together as they carved villages out of the wilderness. With equal rights to the land, these settlers took plots for themselves with full freedom of disposing of them by sale, rent, inheritance, or division, as long as the commune retained control. If there was no repartitional tenure, Sokolovsky argued, it was only because there was no need for it, since there was an abundance of uncultivated land for everyone. *Volost'*, or country district, communes existed from earliest times in Rus', Sokolovsky claimed, but disappeared gradually in those central regions in which the patrimonial estates of the nobles took over. There village communes came to replace the *volost'* communes, but in the north, for example, the old *volost'* commune survived.[77]

It should be noted that Sokolovsky did not limit his evidence to northern Russia. In 1878 he published a book entitled *The Economic Way of Life of the Agricultural Population of Russia and the Colonization of the Southeastern Steppes before Serfdom*.[78] Here, too, he presented the commune as a primeval social form in Russia, one that had been violated by the intervention of the state, but that survived away from the central government.

Sokolovsky, like other Russian proponents of the antiquity of the commune, was influenced in part by West European scholarship on the subject, especially by the German scholar Georg Ludwig von Maurer (1790–1872). Basing his claims on the writings of ancient authors, notably Caesar and Tacitus, Maurer insisted upon the antiquity of the German commune or *Mark*, which allegedly characterized the earliest nomadic tribal society of the Germans and continued in the agricultural stage until it gave way to village organization and separate farms under feudalism.[79] Sokolovsky accepted Maurer's theory, but argued that, whereas in Germany the *Mark* disappeared, in Russia the *volost'* commune merely changed into another form of communal organization—the village commune.[80] In any event, it was especially Maurer's work that led certain Russians to the conclusion that the communal order was characteristic of all societies in a certain stage of development from a nomadic to a sedentary agricultural way of life.

However, there were both Western and Russian scholars who disputed Maurer's thesis from the start. Among the latter an early critic was the then young scholar Vasily I. Sergeevich. In general Maurer's opponents began with the supposition that the land was originally settled by already formed clans and tribes that cultivated it as organized groups. Furthermore, Maurer's opponents assumed that in this stage there was neither private nor communal property but simply the free use of an ample supply of land by all who wished to till it. These steadily cultivated plowlands eventually became the private property of those who tilled them. However, as the supply of free land became more limited, communes were set up to regulate the use of the land. The commune, Sergeevich concluded, was not so much a form of *social* organization as it was a primary form of *state* authority.[81]

It was hardly surprising that the Statists challenged Sokolovsky, but it was a fellow Populist, Alexandra Efimenko, who dealt the most serious blow to his theory. Moreover, she did so on the basis of her research in the north of Russia, out of which was to come her major work, *Investigations of Popular Life,* published in Moscow in 1884.[82] Without denying the existence of a *volost'* commune or *Mark* among the early Slavs or Germans, Mrs. Efimenko declared categorically that she could find no evidence of its ever having existed in the Russian north. Relying especially on family and church archives, she wrote, "In our hands there are hundreds of facts that not only attest to the existence of the village as an individual agricultural unit, but also present a very detailed picture of its organization, whereas there is not a single document that would indicate the existence of a larger agricultural unit—the *volost'*."[83] Besides, she asked, what purpose could a *volost'* commune have served when all cultivated land was centered on the village? In the entire north, she averred, cultivated lands were enclosed from time immemorial, while all the land beyond was accessible to all.

Although Mrs. Efimenko denied that land tenure in Muscovite Russia was communal in form, she did not believe that it was based on private homesteads. Rather she advanced the theory of a third form of land tenure that she called *dolevoi* (from the word *dolia,* meaning "part," "portion," or "share"), which combined the elements of both the commune and the homestead, in that the village comprised an agricultural unit whose arable land was divided into fields, with each household having plots in each field. This system allegedly arose with the breakup and division of the large family, the *pechishche* (or the Russian equivalent of the South Slavic *zadruga*), in which each separate household got its share or *dolia*.[84] The village arose originally from this kinship group, which apportioned lots to members of the larger family, lots that became the property of the owners, even though all recognized that the entire land was the patrimony of the Grand Prince. Eventually, with the proliferation of the kinship group, the rise of inequalities among its members, and the influx of strangers, there was a loss of kinship ties. In some cases—particularly in the north—private ownership of lots was maintained; in others—notably in the central regions of Russia—ownership rights passed from the agriculturalists to the state, and collective forms then took over. Where the latter happened, Mrs. Efimenko declared, there was not the slightest reason to suppose that either the state or the noble landowner had created the commune; the peasants created it themselves, to equalize landholdings to correspond to their equal obligations.

Thus Mrs. Efimenko agreed with Chicherin in concluding that the modern agrarian commune in Russia was not linked with the communes of the ancient Slavs. On the other hand, she denied his claim that the modern communal form had been imposed from above by the state purely for fiscal reasons. While communes in the north may have been established by the state, in other regions they could have developed naturally, by evolution, through the division of large kinship groups.[85]

After this, the dispute took a different turn. In 1880 S. A. Priklonsky, a talented publicist rather than a scholar, published an article in *Russkie Vedomosti* in which he asserted that the principle of equal use rather than of common rights to the land was the basis of agrarian communes. The first settlers in the north, he wrote, had no need of communes to allot land; there was plenty of land for everyone. There was neither a sense of common property nor of private property. It was all "God's land," there for the taking by all who wished to till it. But the boyars of Novgorod began taking lands, especially forests. The peasants then banded together when their common interests were threatened, and formed *volosti* with established borders.[86]

Sergeevich took this argument a step further by claiming that the *volost'* communes arose when the princes of Moscow confiscated the lands of the Novgorod boyars and left them to the use of the peasants in exchange for fixed financial obligations. It was, Sergeevich agreed, the equal capitation tax imposed by the state that led to repartitional tenure.[87]

It will be noted that an important issue in the discussion was whether the earliest known forms of unions in medieval Kievan Rus' were based on kinship or whether they were territorial. The import of the argument seemed to be that if the commune was based on kinship ties, it must have preceded the state, and if it was territorial, it must have been created by the state. As often happens in such cases, it was discovered that the extremes did not necessarily exclude each other.

A whole group of scholars—F. I. Leontovich, A. Efimenko, G. F. Blumenfeld, and K. N. Bestuzhev-Riumin—held that the *verv'* of the *Russkaia Pravda* was not a neighborhood commune but a family commune. Leontovich, the first in this group to take up this theory, gave the discussion of the 1850's a quite different turn. While acknowledging the merit of the sociological approach of his predecessors, he disagreed with them, notably with Solovyov, on the existence of clans among the early Slavs before statehood. Leontovich equated clan societies with primitive nomadic military hordes. Inasmuch as the earliest known Slavs were sedentary farmers, their form of social organization was different. Taking the *zadruga* or extended family commune of the Balkan Slavs as an analogy, Leontovich described Russian society before Rurik as being based on family communes. This is how he identified the *verv'* in the *Russkaia Pravda*. In time, he held, the patriarchal blood ties gave way to contractual relations among the members, and the family commune became a territorial association, bound together by the authority of the state.[88]

A different view was held by another group of scholars—V. Leshkov, N. P. Pavlov-Silvansky, M. F. Vladimirsky-Budanov, and later A. E. Presniakov, to name a few.[89] All of them insisted that the *verv'* of the *Russkaia Pravda* was a local territorial commune and was not based on kinship. While this opinion cast doubt on the "organic" origins of the commune, it by no means damaged the claim concerning the antiquity of the commune. Pavlov-Silvansky dissociated himself from the Statists with his pronouncement that laws did not create social relations, but social relations created laws. Though he did not regard the commune as a family union, neither did he think it had been established by the state. Linking the commune with the early medieval institutions of the *verv'*, *sotnia*, and *pogost'*, he asserted that all these, down to the *volost'* organization of the sixteenth century, were the products of a given stage of social development and not the political creations of state legislation.[90]

From the standpoint of scientific scholarship, northern Russia was not, despite its abundance of documentary materials, ideal for trying to reconstruct the development of the commune. The state had interrupted what might have been the natural evolution of the commune through its tax measures, thus forcing the previously nonrepartitional commune to resort to repartitional tenure. What was needed was to study the commune in a region where government intervention was not a factor. Siberia seemed to be such a region.

Of the scholars who investigated this aspect of the problem, the most significant was the liberal Populist scholar A. A. Kaufman. His book *The Peasant Commune in Siberia According to Local Investigations 1886–1892* appeared in 1897.[91] Kaufman hoped that by studying the contemporary communes of Siberia, rather than documents from the past, he could observe the "living history" of communal development in Russia. "In many localities in Siberia," Kaufman reported, "in the course of local investigations one could actually see with his own eyes instances of the establishment of new peasant settlements."[92]

What made Siberia so much like ancient Rus' was that land was plentiful. Since it belonged to no one but the state, anyone could simply choose a plot of suitable ground and cultivate it without interfering with anyone else. Settlers naturally clustered in villages that grew until everyone had all the land he could till, or until the borders of one settlement met the borders of the next settlement's lands. There was no question of whose land it was since in the beginning there was enough for all. Thus the primary fact in nineteenth-century Siberian land tenure was not *ownership* but *use* of the land. This circumstance recalled the theories of certain historians, both West Europeans and Russians, concerning the origin of the earliest *Marken* or communes. Here was a case of a primary stage of land tenure in which two elements were lacking: (1) any defined form of landownership, and (2) any regulation of the use of the land.

Kaufman could also see the next stage, where land was no longer free for the taking, and where it became hard to find suitable land for division into plots. In this stage, a village became a naturally established communal territory, or, as Kaufman put it, "a social unit closed to the outside and united within through ownership and use of the land." The peasants formed *volost'* communes in which various lands were apportioned to members. Kaufman noted here the existence of mixed communal ownership in which, instead of a single commune, there were various and territorially overlapping associations of a functional nature. For example, one association managed pastures, another hayfields, and so on. This particularly interested Kaufman in that it pointed to the natural origins of such unions, corresponding to the particular use of the land.

The next stage Kaufman observed was the dissolution of these territorial communes into simple village communes. However, regulation went on, with the need, first of all, to supervise the use of hayfields and meadows, and then to gather the harvest. That use rather than ownership was primary could be seen from the fact that plots that were left uncultivated for any period of time were simply handed over to anyone who would cultivate them. The length of periods in which plots could go uncultivated got shorter as land became scarcer. The basic principle was maximum use of the land. The next step was repartitional tenure, in which the commune took land from large landholders who were not able to till all their land by themselves, and assigned it to small landholders who could cultivate more land than they possessed. All of this happened without any state intervention.

This study of Siberian communes appeared to demonstrate two points concerning the origin of communes: (1) the earliest communes were not repartitional because land was plentiful, and (2) where the prince (that is, the state) was the ultimate owner, it did not matter which peasants occupied which land, as long as they were producing income. Perhaps this is best summed up in Sergeevich's statement that "ownership was communal, and use of the land was private." The next stage was repartitional tenure.

From this, the Populist writer V. V. Vorontsov concluded that, on the basis of both Mrs. Efimenko's and Kaufman's research, it was ultimately state policy that determined whether the path of development from the earliest pre-repartitional communes would lead to single farms, as in Germany and the Ukraine, or to communal tenure, as in Great Russia, Siberia, and the Cossack lands. Wherever the government maintained its position as owner, even passively, the commune was strengthened.[93]

We have touched on but a few aspects of this important issue in Russian historiography in the nineteenth century. The origin and development of the agrarian commune in Russia was being discussed at a time when that institution was undergoing a steady dissolution, at least in the central regions, under the pressure of new economic forces. The Stolypin reforms were but the culmination of this process. In the early twentieth century it seemed that those who looked upon the commune as a passing phase in Russian history were right. However, the discussion is not over. In 1921, the Soviet historian A. E. Presniakov wrote that the question of the origins of the commune in Russia was still an open one,[94] and it is open even today. Still, those scholars who have sought to answer it have contributed much to our knowledge of the role of the peasantry in Russian history.

The question of the origin of serfdom was first raised in Russian historiography by the eighteenth-century historian Vasily N. Tatishchev (1686–1750). In going through some old manuscripts, he came across the Law Code of 1550, the *Sudebnik* of Tsar Ivan the Terrible. Tatishchev's attention was drawn to the following wording in Article 88 of the Code: "And it is forbidden for peasants [to go] from district to district or village to village except during one period in the year: during the week before St. George's in autumn and one week after St. George's in autumn."[95] This was the official statement of the traditional right of peasants to change lords in November, after the harvest. However, Tatishchev noted among the addenda to the Law Code of 1550 a decree of November 21, 1597, which stated that any peasant who had fled from any estate within the previous five years was to be brought to trial. Tatishchev therefore concluded that the peasants had been deprived of their right to change lords some time between 1550 and 1597, probably in 1592, that is, five years before the decree of 1597. In a special study on the Law Code of 1550, Tatishchev asserted that such a decree of 1592 existed, and that he hoped that it would some day be found.[96]

Tatishchev thus held that Russian peasants were free to live where they pleased until the time of Tsar Theodore, during the regency of Boris Godunov. Other documents, specifically Tsar Boris's decree of 1601 and Basil Shuisky's decree of 1607 made him conclude that, probably as a result of popular discontent, Boris had restored the right of St. George's Day, but pressure from the nobles caused the "Boyars' Tsar" Basil Shuisky to impose permanent serfdom. Tatishchev did not say directly what prompted the abolition of the right of St. George's Day, but it may be concluded from his remarks that he ascribed the putative decree of 1592 to the Crown's desire to please the middle and lesser gentry by assuring them a steady labor supply. He also indicated his own approval of the measure, insofar as it sought to restore order, by putting an end to disruptive wandering by fugitive peasants.[97]

Tatishchev's views on the origins of Russian serfdom became known to the public in 1768, after his death, when Gerhardt-Friedrich Müller, a German scholar in Russia, published Tatishchev's work under the title *The Law Code of the Sovereign Tsar and Grand Prince Ivan Vasil'evich....*[98] Subsequently, historians in the eighteenth century generally accepted Tatishchev's conjectures, even when they disagreed with his interpretation.[99]

The first nineteenth-century historian in Russia to take up the question was Johann Ewers. In his *Geschichte der Russen,* published in Dorpat in 1816, Ewers differed with Tatishchev on several points. First, he did not accept Tatishchev's guess about the existence of a decree of 1592, but rather took the decree of November 21, 1597, as the beginning of serfdom. Second, he disagreed with the opinions of Tatishchev, Boltin, and Shcherbatov that the right of the Russian peasants to change lords had been an ancient custom and that Article 88 of the Law Code of 1550 was only an attempt to define and limit that right. Ewers pointed out that in earlier centuries, before the Tatar invasion, the only peasants who enjoyed personal freedom were the *smerdy* (i.e., landowning peasants), and even they found themselves bound to the soil and progressively burdened by their obligations to the landlords. To Ewers the legislation of Ivan the Terrible regarding St. George's Day was a favor to the peasantry that guaranteed to them some right to change masters. Thus, he rejected the conception of a once-free peasantry suddenly enserfed by some royal decree at the end of the sixteenth century, and stressed, rather, the gradual enserfment of the peasantry as a historical process. However shaky some of Ewers' deductions may have been, he indicated a very fruitful approach to the problem.[100]

In 1823 Nikolai M. Karamzin published the tenth volume of his monumental *History of the Russian State.* Ignoring Ewers' analysis, Karamzin wrote:

We know that peasants in Russia had civil freedom from earliest times, though without ownership of real property; they had the freedom to move during a specified term from place to place, from owner to owner, with the provision that they could cultivate one part of the land for themselves, the other for the lord, or pay him rent.[101]

He also followed Tatishchev's interpretation of the decree of 1597 when he agreed that the peasant's right to transfer from estate to estate was abrogated in 1592 or 1593. However, Karamzin was not entirely uncritical in his attitude toward Tatishchev's findings. For one thing, he doubted the authenticity of Shuisky's decree of 1607 because of its seemingly anachronistic language. However, he agreed with Tatishchev's suggestion that a decree of 1592 (or 1593) had to exist.[102] Essentially the same interpretation was accepted by Nikolai G. Ustryalov (1805–70) in his *Russian History,* published in 1839.[103] This book became an official textbook in Russian history.

Nevertheless, by the second quarter of the nineteenth century the failure of anyone to find a single copy of the decree of 1592 became embarrassing, especially in view of increasing activity on the part of various official and unofficial searchers for documents. Two of the most active pioneers in this effort were Pavel M. Stroev (1796–1876) and K. F. Kalaidovich (1792–1832). Beginning with an expedition in 1817, these two partners devoted their entire lives to finding and publishing historical documents. Some of the most valuable sources of Russian history were first brought to light by them—the Law Code of Ivan III, the St. Sophia Annals, the Slavic text of George Hamartolus, and many other rare items.[104] In 1836 they published the first volume of *Acts of the Archeographic Expedition,* which included the original of a decree of 1602 that confirmed the authenticity of the decree of 1597 found by Tatishchev. However, Stroev felt obliged to

deny the existence of any decree of 1592.[105] One of the first historians
to accept Stroev's doubts was N. S. Artsybashev (1773–1841), a disciple of Kachenovsky's Critical school, who in 1843 published the
third volume of his *History of Russia*.[106]

The failure to find any decree of 1592 stimulated a fresh approach
to the problem. Instead of attributing Russian serfdom to specific decrees, students of the question began to look upon serfdom as a gradual historical process resulting from many causes. At first it was not
the historians but the government administrators who, perhaps because of their experience with the practical contemporary aspects of
the problem, adopted this more pragmatic approach. In 1836 Mikhail
M. Speransky (1772–1839) wrote a study entitled "A Historical Survey of Changes in the Right of Land Ownership and the Status of
the Peasantry." This manuscript was not accessible to readers until it
became a part of the collection of the St. Petersburg Public Library
in 1856, after the author's death. It was published in 1859.[107] Speransky disagreed with the allegation that the right of St. George's Day
had been abolished by Boris Godunov. According to him, the decree
of 1597 affected only those fugitive peasants who left their lords'
estates in violation of the procedure set by the Law Code. The right
of St. George's Day was never formally abolished, Speransky insisted;
it fell into disuse naturally when peasants could no longer take advantage of it because of indebtedness. The legal right of peasants to move
from estate to estate remained until the census of 1721. Thus Speransky saw the origins of serfdom "not in any abuse, nor in the arbitrary will of the landowner, nor in the intervention of the government." He believed, rather, that "it was first founded on custom, then
law."[108]

This approach was also reflected in a memorandum entitled "On
the Status of the Peasantry in Russia," which A. Zabolotsky-Desyatov-
sky wrote in 1841 in connection with the preparation of some legislation on peasant obligations. The author held that the *smerdy* of
medieval Russia had been free farmers, and that serfdom became
established during the late sixteenth and the early seventeenth centuries. However, he attributed serfdom not so much to the immediate pressure of that time as to two earlier and extended conditions in Russian history: (1) the existence of personal slavery, and

(2) the change from the system of *votchiny,* or patrimonial estates, to the *pomestia,* or estates of the service gentry. Zabolotsky-Desyatov-sky suggested that the status of free peasants fell when slaves and indentured servants, who had originally been used only as courtyard servants, were assigned to cultivate the land as well. Many of these became bound to the soil by custom, from generation to generation. Eventually there was a fusion between these bondsmen and free peasants, and the change from a customary status to a legal status was an easy step, once the need arose.[109]

In the five years between the end of the Crimean War and the emancipation, a whole series of writers published studies on the origins of serfdom in Russia. From the standpoint of this discussion, the most noteworthy were Chicherin, Solovyov, Pogodin, Konstantin Aksakov, Pobedonostsev, Kostomarov, and Belyaev.

The views of the Statist school of Russian historiography on this question first came to the fore in 1856, when B. N. Chicherin published an article in *Russkii Vestnik* entitled "Conditions of Servitude in Early Russia."[110] Like Speransky, Chicherin reached the conclusion that the peasants were enserfed on state lands before they were on private estates. Whereas Speransky had placed this at the time of the Tatar conquest and attributed it to the need to collect the Tatar tribute, Chicherin placed it in the sixteenth century and ascribed it to the policies of Ivan the Terrible. Basic to Chicherin's argument was his claim that the Crown made all classes of the population subject to the service of the state—nobles and peasants alike. Just as the service demanded of the nobles necessitated their mobility, so the obligations to be paid by the peasants required that they be bound to the soil. As Chicherin put it, "Every subject had to carry out his obligation to the state according to his place, an idea which lies at the basis of the enserfment of the peasants."[111]

Later documents show that Speransky and Chicherin were both wrong in asserting that state peasants became enserfed before peasants on private lands. However, Chicherin's most telling point was that enserfment came about because of the coercive power of the state and its interests. The right of peasants to move about freely from estate to estate was recognized in Kievan times, he wrote, but it was the appanage princes who first encroached on this freedom. In the fourteenth and fifteenth centuries the state began to place restrictions on peasants to ensure the regular payment of taxes. As the need for taxes increased, so did the restrictions, said Chicherin, until by the time of Ivan the Terrible all taxed peasants were already bound to the soil. Chicherin believed that this found its legal expression in a decree of 1592 or 1593 under Boris Godunov. Both state serfs and private serfs became involved in the same obligation to the state, whose main concern was to replenish its treasury and to provide the service nobility with a steady labor force. Other historians of the Statist school, particularly A. D. Gradovsky (1841–89) and K. D. Kavelin (1818–85) agreed with Chicherin's appraisal.[112]

In his *History of Russia,* Solovyov stressed still another aspect of the problem. Unlike Chicherin, Solovyov did not believe that the peasants had been enserfed by a single legal measure. Nor was he entirely convinced by Chicherin's suggestion that enserfment came as a part of a general binding of all social classes to the service of the state. He felt that the state was primarily interested in assuring the middling gentry—the new service nobility—of the kind of steady labor supply that the older patrimonial estates of the blood nobility already had but were themselves losing because of unsettled conditions. As Solovyov put it, "There was much land, but few hands."[113] Peasants, he emphasized, were fleeing en masse for the fringelands of the Urals, Siberia, and the steppes, leaving deserted villages in their wake. Thus the Crown made common cause with the class it needed most, and the price of the alliance was serfdom for the peasantry.

A historian close to the Slavophiles, Mikhail P. Pogodin (1800–75), was the most emphatic opponent of the idea that serfdom had come about by an act of the state. In an article that he published in 1858, in *Russkaia Beseda,* he asked the question in the title: "Should Boris Godunov be considered the Founder of Serfdom?"[114] His reply was a decided "no." He then asked:

> Who, then, was the founder of serfdom among us?
> No one.
> Whom should one blame for its spread?
> Circumstances.[115]

The Soviet economic historian K. A. Pazhitnov argues that certain details of Pogodin's argument are too similar to Speransky's previously cited memorandum to be mere chance. Among the four similarities of detail that Pazhitnov notes is the especially interesting reference both Speransky and Pogodin made to English history, namely, that just as no one can point to a single time when English serfs became free, so no one can determine exactly when Russian free peasants became serfs.[116]

In denying the existence of a decree of 1592, Pogodin made much of the fact that no copy of such a decree existed. Pointing to the thousands of documents of the period that had been found, Pogodin argued that it was not a question of finding the one original manuscript copy of the decree, for there must have been many copies of so important a law as one which defined so drastically the status of the most numerous part of the population. And even if all these copies should have been destroyed, was it not fair to expect at least some reference to the decree in other contemporary or near-contemporary writings?

What Pogodin advanced as his main argument came to be known as the environmental theory (*bytovaia teoriia*)—from the word *byt,* meaning "way of life." He claimed that serfdom developed gradually and in the natural course of events. He also insisted that the freedom of peasants to transfer from one estate to another continued to exist throughout the seventeenth century and most of the first quarter of the eighteenth century. However, he did admit that the state from time to time felt it necessary to limit the movement of peasants, especially so as to ensure a steady labor supply for the gentry. Unlike Speransky, Pogodin did not stress the factor of peasant indebtedness. Whether later historians agreed with Pogodin or not, his presentation did help to produce one general result: few historians after him insisted any longer on the existence of a decree of 1592.

The Slavophile Aksakov also rejected Tatishchev's view that the right of St. George's Day had been abrogated in 1592. He insisted that there were fugitive peasants even before that date, and peasants who moved about freely from estate to estate even after that date, judging by certain cadastral registers, as late as in 1632. Aksakov blamed the enserfment of the peasantry on the reforms of Peter I. In typical Slavophile fashion, he noted the difference in style between the Muscovite *gosudar',* the pre-Petrine term for landowning lord, and *barin,* the later designation. Whereas the former term denoted to him a patriarchal relation, the latter designated a state juridical relationship between peasant and lord.[117]

In 1858 Pobedonostsev came very close to Pogodin's position, in an article that he published in *Russkii Vestnik*. He also held that the lord's power over the peasantry took place gradually and "independently of legal measures."[118] Moreover, even after the peasants were bound to the soil by law, they did not become the property of the landlords until the eighteenth century.

Kostomarov, who agreed with the interpretation by Tatishchev and Karamzin, presented a convincing critique of Pogodin's arguments. He interpreted the decree of November 21, 1597, as requiring the prosecution of only those peasants who had left their estates during the previous five years; as for peasants who had left before that time, Kostomarov understood that they were not touched by the decree. Thus, he concluded, there must have been a new regulation in 1592 or 1593 annulling the provisions of the Law Code of 1550. He fully accepted the validity of Tsar Basil Shuisky's decree of 1607 and used it as supporting evidence. Turning to Aksakov's study, Kostomarov rejected the Slavophile's claim that peasants were generally still free to leave their lord's estates even after 1592; these were, he said, special cases involving agreements between the previous landlord and the new landlord. The law forbade landlords from entering into agreements directly with the peasants of other landlords, Kostomarov claimed, but the landlords had full right to deal with one another over their peasants.[119]

In 1861 Belyaev came out with one of the first solid monographs on peasant history in Russian historiography, *Peasants of Rus'*. This book presents an interesting confrontation between Belyaev's Slavophile inclinations and his scholarly methodology, which, by virtue of his interest in the history of law, had much in common with the Statist and Juridical schools. On the one hand, he leaned toward the view that the peasants had been free until the end of the sixteenth century; on the other hand, he accepted the existence of a law in the 1590's annulling the right of St. George's Day.

Belyaev treated the problem of serfdom in three stages. During the first stage, from earliest recorded history to the end of the sixteenth century, the peasants enjoyed the right to transfer freely from one landowner to another. Then, from the end of the sixteenth century to the second decade of the eighteenth century, the peasants were legally bound to the soil, though they continued to enjoy all other rights as free men. Finally, after the first census, under Peter I (in 1721), the peasant began to lose his other rights as well, and became the property of the landowner.

Belyaev did not accept Pogodin's account of the origin of serfdom, even though he was Pogodin's student. Belyaev admitted that he did not know when serfdom began or how it was promulgated, but it is evident that he believed it was done by a particular act of state. He was even willing to guess that this act took place "in the first years of the reign of Tsar Theodore Ivanovich." In any event, he clearly rejected Tatishchev's theory about a decree in 1592, for he specifically denied that the decree of 1597 pointed to the time of first enserfment; it merely indicated a five-year period involving fugitive peasants who could be brought to justice. On the other hand, he contradicted himself when he admitted, on the basis of a monastic charter of dubious authenticity, that enserfment could not have taken place before 1590, inasmuch as another charter of that year still recognized the right of free transfer by peasants. Finally, Belyaev stated later in his book, quite unaccountably, that serfdom must have been inaugurated in 1591.

As for a motivation, Belyaev stressed the financial crisis, which he attributed especially to the wars of Ivan the Terrible. "The extremely disorganized state of financial affairs and the burdening of the people finally compelled the Moscow government to a new and previously unheard-of measure—a general binding of free peasants to the land."[120] It is interesting that Belyaev felt that the enserfment of the peasants was as burdensome on the landlords as on the peasants themselves; no longer could landlords dismiss unsuitable peasants and attract better ones. Indeed, Belyaev wrote, the nobles would not cooperate at first with the government's efforts to enforce the law against fugitive peasants; it was only upon coming into contact with the Polish lords during the "Time of Troubles" that they changed their minds and took the side of the new order.[121]

After the emancipation of the serfs in 1861 and during the period of the Great Reforms, interest in the historical aspects of serfdom lessened. There was a far greater concern with serfdom as a contemporary problem. However, just as thoughtful men saw that the Great Reforms had not solved all the problems linked with serfdom, so historians were increasingly struck by the realization that the historical origins of serfdom had not been satisfactorily explained. This feeling grew as more and more primary sources came to light. Thus there took place, some two decades after the Emancipation of 1861, a revival in historical writing on the subject. Some writers clung to the traditional view, but most new contributions were characterized by the gradualist genetic or environmentalist approach of Speransky and Pogodin.

It was a German scholar at the University of Dorpat, J. Engelmann, whose work *Die Leibeigenschaft in Russland* (Dorpat, 1884) revived interest in this approach. He completely rejected the Tatishchev-Karamzin view regarding the annulment of the right of St. George's Day, either in 1592 or earlier. Rather Engelmann believed that serfdom began, not directly but indirectly, by the decree of 1597, and in the following manner: In 1592 cadastral registers (*pistsovye knigi*) were compiled, registering the landlords' holdings and the names of the peasants who tilled these holdings. When the decree of 1597 gave landlords the right to prosecute fugitive peasants, the landlord proved his rights on the basis of these cadastral registers.

It was in response to Engelmann's work that V. O. Klyuchevsky wrote an article entitled "The Origin of Serfdom in Russia," which appeared in *Russkaia Mysl'* in 1885.[122] Klyuchevsky argued that the basis for serfdom did not lie in the state's binding the peasant to the soil, but in the peasant's personal indebtedness to the landlord, to the point of slavery. In this respect Klyuchevsky traced the origins of modern Russian serfdom all the way back to early Russian slavery and debt servitude (*kabala*). He argued that whereas a distinction had been made originally between free tenants who entered into contracts with the lord and chattel slaves who sold themselves to the lord to pay off a debt, eventually both categories became merged as the free peasants fell more and more into debt, so much so that by the middle of the sixteenth century there was no way out of the debt. This explanation of the origin of serfdom was virtually the same as the one Pogodin had advanced many years before. Most significantly Klyuchevsky did not see the state as the prime mover behind enserfment; rather he believed that the state's laws merely recorded and defined existing economic relations between peasant and lord, to protect the interests not only of the lords but also of the state treasury and even of the peasants themselves.

One of Klyuchevsky's ablest supporters was M. A. Dyakonov, whose approach was based on a broad synthesis of legal history and general history. In his *Outlines of the Social and Political Organization of Early Russia* Dyakonov asserted that peasant indebtedness rather than state policy was the real basis for serfdom.[123] He saw as the first serfs in Russian history the *starozhil'tsy,* or peasant tenants, of Muscovite times, who remained indefinitely under the same lord. Provoking Sergeevich's strenuous protests, Dyakonov alleged that the Muscovite state was not given to legal creativity and that many of its laws merely defined what had already become established practice. What actually happened, he claimed, was that even though the right of St. George's Day had not been annulled, by the end of the sixteenth century the indebted peasants simply were not able to take advantage of it. What they did do was to rid themselves of their obligations by fleeing from central Russia altogether.

Pavel N. Miliukov (1859–1943) adopted a similar position, very neatly summarized in his article on "Peasants in Russia" in the *Entsiklopedicheskii Slovar'.*[124] He also believed that serfdom in Russia began long before the close of the sixteenth century, and without any particular intervention by the state. He ascribed the rise of serfdom to three circumstances: (1) peasant indebtedness, (2) *starozhil'stvo,* or choosing to remain indefinitely on a lord's estate, and (3) immobilization of the peasants for tax purposes. Miliukov concluded that the right of St. George's Day played a minor role in the mobility of the peasants.

This is where the dispute stood when it took a new turn, at the very end of the nineteenth century, with the introduction of new primary sources. The discussion now revolved about a new element—the so-called "prohibited years" (*zapovednye gody*). The first reference in print to the "prohibited years" was made in 1895 by S. A. Adrianov, in an article in the journal of the Ministry of Public Education.[125] He found the phrase in a document of 1592, published in Volume XIV of the *Russkaia Istoricheskaia Biblioteka,* which dealt with a search for peasants who had fled from the lands of St. Nicholas Korelsky Monastery. He did not know what conclusion to draw from this phrase, but he realized that it required attention.

The answer was provided by D. M. Odynets, in 1908, in an article in the journal of the Ministry of Justice.[126] The "prohibited years," Odynets explained, were years in which the state authorities forbade the departure of peasants from their lords' estates. Such a prohibition, Odynets held, proved the state's intervention in enserfing the peasants.

After Odynets' article there appeared a goodly number of documents dealing with "prohibited years" that were published in 1909 by D. Ia. Samokvasov in the second volume of his *Archival Material*.[127] The documents showed convincingly that the year 7090, that is, from September 1, 1581, to September 1, 1582, was a prohibited year, and so was the following year. Other documents, not included by Samokvasov, pointed to 1591, 1592, and 1596 as prohibited years. All this led Samokvasov to conjecture that just as West European scholars had been unable to find specific laws instituting serfdom in the West, so Russian scholars could not find any such law because it did not exist. What did exist were state measures involving cadastral registers and tax obligations. Ivan the Terrible put an end to quarrels among landlords over migrant peasants by having the peasants registered on tax rolls by estate and forbidding their moving about. This law, which was among newly discovered archival materials, was called the Decree on Prohibited Years. Two years before the death of Ivan the Terrible the migration of peasants during the term around St. George's Day was forbidden by law.

At about the same time that Samokvasov wrote, P. E. Mikhailov offered a useful corrective to the whole emphasis on peasant indebtedness in the views of Pogodin, Klyuchevsky, Dyakonov and their supporters. In two studies on the *starozhil'tsy,* published in 1910 and 1912 in the journal of the Ministry of Public Education, Mikhailov dealt a serious blow to Dyakonov's claim that the *starozhil'tsy* could be considered the first real serfs in Russian history, by virtue of their being bound to their lords' estates through their indebtedness.[128] Mikhailov observed that the *starozhil'tsy* were not indebted paupers but were more apt to be the most prosperous peasants. If they chose not to move, it was because things were going well for them. Mikhailov asked his readers to understand that he was not condoning serfdom, but that he merely wished to show that historians erred when they ignored the psychological aspect. As for the debate on the origins of serfdom, Mikhailov stressed that the binding of the *starozhil'tsy* to their lords' lands came not from their dependence on the lords, but from the desire of the state to assure the stability of the national economy in a time of financial crisis.

With this began a new phase of the discussion, which was carried on in the decade or so after the outbreak of the First World War, and which is beyond the scope of this study. The discussion was ably furthered by such scholars as V. E. Geiman, S. B. Veselovsky, and especially B. D. Grekov. As a result of the labors of all these generations of scholars, it is generally accepted today that there was a decree in the last years of the reign of Ivan the Terrible, probably in the fall of 1581, but in any case not earlier than 1580, which prohibited the movement of peasants. Though no term was specified, this prohibition was temporary and was meant to remain in force until a new decree was issued. This period of so-called "prohibited years" was in fact interspersed by years in which peasants could move about, in accordance with the earlier provisions of the Law Code. However, with Tsar Basil Shuisky's decree of 1607, no further free movement of peasants was permitted.[129]

And so, what has taken place is a synthesis of the several different interpretations of how serfdom became established in Russia. Both the genetic, or environmental, approach and the Statist approach have been brought together after much sifting and winnowing by Russian scholars.

Whoever has had the patience to follow even so condensed a summary as this of the labors of Russian historians in dealing with only two problems in the history of the Russian peasantry—the origins of communes and the rise of serfdom—must come away with a feeling of respect for the scholars who have worked so diligently to answer fundamental questions in Russian history.

8. The Peasant in Literature

Donald Fanger

Literature is a part of history, but an autonomous part; its truths may parallel what we take to be historical truth, but they are not to be confused with it. Starting from this notion of literature as an institution, I propose to examine the work of some of its most notable practitioners in nineteenth-century Russia (largely in the field of fiction), seeking not external correspondences but internal ones, asking not what they show about the problem of the peasant but how they pose it.

The first thing that strikes the investigator in this field is the almost complete absence of works depicting peasant life from the inside. The Soviet *Literary Encyclopedia* of the 1930's, in a long article entitled "Peasant Literature," ruefully notes that the majority of writers from peasant backgrounds in the nineteenth century tended to produce works that follow hackneyed (and often outright reactionary) conventions and stereotypes; the new *Literary Encyclopedia,* now being issued, omits the topic altogether. The result was hardly more impressive when a host of writers in the middle of the last century sought to simulate the "insider's" view through careful documentation. As Pypin comments: "The pursuit of authentic peasant atmosphere [*kolorit*] went so far that the heroes of stories spoke a muzhik-language, fractured to the point of incomprehensibility; it was impossible to read certain storytellers... without the Provincial Dictionary (*Oblastnoi Slovar*) in one's hands." Annenkov was even driven to declare irreconcilable the depiction of the "real, hard course of peasant life" and the demands of art.[1]

In any case, the great age of the Russian novel shows us not a single significant novel of peasant life.[2] Plekhanov, discussing the reasons for this lack, found the primary explanation in the uniformity of peasant life, in the "ocean of people," where only the sum total of individual existences has meaning:

Gleb Uspensky himself says that "to isolate a single entity from this mass of millions and try to understand it is an impossible task" and that "Semyon Nikitich, the Elder, can be understood only in a heap of other Semyon Nikitiches." Therefore to depict Semyon Nikitich is possible only "in a heap of other Semyon Nikitiches." But this is far from rewarding work for an artist. Shakespeare himself would stop in perplexity before a peasant mass in which the muzhiks are just like one another, and their women are just like one another, with the same uniform thoughts, costumes, with the same uniform songs, and so on. The only milieu that lends itself well to artistic representation is one in which human individuality has already reached a certain degree of development. The triumph of artistic creation is the depiction of individuals who are participating in the great progressive movement of mankind, who are serving as the bearers of great universal ideas. But it goes without saying that such an individual cannot be "the Elder, Semyon Nikitich," whose whole environment serves as an expression not of his own thought and will, but of one outside him and utterly alien to him.[3]

Annenkov had made a similar point some decades before. In an article on "Novels and Stories from the Life of the Common People in 1853" he remarked, apropos of an unsuccessful peasant novel by Grigorovich: "It is easy to see what a difficult task the author faced: to develop in the artistic form of a novel a life so uncomplicated that the first word of each character contains within itself all the rest of his speeches and his first thought already reflects the whole series of the sort of thoughts that will occur to him in the course of his whole existence."[4]

The peasant, then, cannot speak for himself in nineteenth-century literature, nor can his way of life inspire a long, coherent work. He can only be approached from outside, by writers who, because they have *chosen* him as a subject, must find some significance in his existence. That significance is the writer's own invention or discovery; it answers *his* needs and is a part of *his* moral life. Thus the story of the peasant in Russian literature is the story of the changing moods and attitudes of the most influential segment of educated society, and it tells us much more about that society than about the peasant himself. In other words, as far as imaginative literature is concerned, the peasant is—in the best and most serious sense of the word—a myth.

The Eighteenth Century: Radishchev and Karamzin

Radishchev is the ancestor of all the nineteenth-century writers on the peasant—hardly an approach or an attitude turns up in the next hundred years that is not adumbrated somewhere in his *Journey from Petersburg to Moscow*—yet his position is so peculiar that he can only be seen as part of the "prehistory" of our subject. The reasons for this go beyond chronology, and even beyond the fact that his literary conventions are largely of the eighteenth century. His is a lonely, isolated voice. Turned down by all the regular publishers, his book was finally printed in the spring of 1790 by Radishchev himself, on his own printing press. The twenty-five copies he put on sale at the Gostiny Dvor were enough to produce a search of his home, the burning of most of the remaining 575 copies, and the arrest and exile of the writer. The book was only republished in 1858, by Herzen, in London; it was still banned in Russia. When, in 1872, one P. Efremov printed a two-volume edition of Radishchev's works, including the *Journey,* it was promptly seized by the government and destroyed. Two limited editions, designed for bibliophiles, were allowed in 1888 and 1899, but the 2900 copies published by P. A. Kartavov in 1902 were destroyed by the government. By the time the book could be freely issued, the nineteenth century was over.

Radishchev was not the first to bespeak sympathy for abused serfs. In 1772 Novikov's "The Painter" (*Zhivopisets*) pointed out how landowners often showed more pity for their horses and dogs than for people; the point is underlined by the speech of one crude squire who justifies himself in this fashion:

The painter says that landowners torment their peasants, but the damn fool doesn't even know that in times gone by the tyrants were the unbaptized ones, and tortured the saints. . . . But our muzhiks aren't saints, after all— so how can we be tyrants? . . . Surely he can't want the muzhiks to get rich when we, the gentlemen, grow poor, 'cause the Lord didn't command that sort of thing: any rich man, or landowner, or peasant has to be [what he is] —after all, every monk can't be an abbot. Even in the Holy Scripture it says: carry each other's burdens and so you will fulfill Christ's law. They work for us, and we whip them if they start getting lazy; so we're equal; what else are they peasants for? That's the sort of job he has—to work without rest. Go give them freedom, and who knows what they'll cook up?[5]

Here—and in other such works of the eighteenth century—the emphasis is on seignorial turpitude; the peasant is pitied not because he is a serf but because he may have a bad master. Catherine the Great herself, in a play entitled *O Time!,* takes note of seignorial interference with the marriage choices of peasants, along with other arbitrary and whimsical abuses of power. When, in Fonvizin's *Adolescent* (1783), Eremeevna says that her wages are "five rubles a year and five slaps a day," the point is the same one that Prostakova makes in boasting about her own ceaseless activity from morning to evening— "either scolding or beating: that's what keeps the house going." Even when, as in Krylov's *Spirit Post* (*Pochta Dukhov,* 1789), the indictment is broader and more abstract, the peasant remains the shadowy victim of a vice (selfishness, bad management) that seems ultimately to be more moral than institutional. One gentleman, showing a right hand bedecked with rings, boasts: "On these fingers sits my village, Ostashkovo; on my feet I am wearing two villages, Bezzhitova and Grablenaia; in this expensive watch you see my beloved village Chastodavovo; my coach and four horses remind me of my beautiful estate, Pustyshka; in short, I cannot now glance at a single caftan or livery of mine without being put in mind of a mortgaged settlement, or village, or group of house-serfs, sold as recruits." To which a Frenchwoman, the owner of a store, adds: "Our store alone can ruin in a year up to a hundred thousand peasants."

But to such examples as these, the official response in the late eighteenth century remained more or less as it had been stated in *The Antidote,* a book published in French in 1768, in which the Empress herself had a hand: "This alleged poverty does not exist in Russia; the Russian peasant is a hundred times happier and better off than your French peasants." It was observed that the Russian peasant, unlike the French, was not taxed beyond his abilities. And in any case "good or bad treatment of domestic servants depends much more on the good or bad morality of the masters than on the laws of the country."[6]

The novelty of Radishchev's *Journey* rests on his refusal to dissociate morality and laws; castigating inhumane officials and serfowners, he castigates at the same time an institutional structure that encourages such inhumanity. Every instance he cites of corruption or cruelty is an item in a single long indictment, and each is accompanied by reflections that spell out its importance and implications. Small wonder that Catherine found him "worse than Pugachev."

Radishchev's book is basically sentimental in tone and rhetorical in purpose. "I looked around me," he writes in the dedication, "and my heart was wounded with the sufferings of humanity. I turned my glances inward—and saw that man's woes arise from man, and often only from the fact that he does not look straight at the objects around him." The key terms of this dedication are the favorite ones of the Enlightenment: reason, heart, the voice of nature, sensitivity (*chuvstvitel'nost'*), compassion. And they make it clear that he is seeking, through the conventional form of a journey in his own country—laced with meditations, dream allegories, and interpolated essays on a variety of subjects—to soften the hearts and enlighten the minds of his countrymen.

His book, then, is a tract in the guise of a travel book; the guiding impulse is not the reporter's curious eye (of twenty-five episodes, only eight involve the author as witness or participant), but the moralist's pursuit of the single broad theme set forth in the dedication. There is what we can call "straight" reporting, and description of ways and customs; but both are occasional and subordinate to the author's dominant concerns. The description of a peasant's hut in "Peshki" is a case in point:

For the first time I surveyed attentively all the equipment of a peasant hut. For the first time I turned my heart toward what had hitherto only glided over its surface. Four walls, half covered, as was the whole of the ceiling, with soot; the floor full of cracks and at least two inches in accumulated dirt; the stove without a chimney, but the best protection from cold; and smoke, every morning, winter and summer, filling the hut; window holes, in which a stretched bladder would let through a darkling light at midday; some two or three pots (happy is the hut if there is some thin cabbage soup in one of them every day!). A wooden bowl and some vessels called plates; a table, hewn with an axe, which is scraped off on holidays. A trough to feed the pigs or calves if there are any; sleeping together with them, swallowing air in which a burning candle appears to be shrouded in fog or behind a curtain. With luck, a barrel of *kvas* that tastes like vinegar, and a bathhouse in the yard in which, if no one is steaming himself, the cattle sleep. A homespun shirt, the footwear nature gives, or leggings and bast shoes for going out.

This whole description is new and striking, but it is not there to speak for itself. It is what the exemplum was to the medieval sermon. Radishchev goes on:

Here is what is with justice considered the source of the national wealth, energy, and might; but here also are evident the weakness, shortcomings, and abuses of the laws, and, so to speak, their rough side. Here is evident the greed of the gentry, our robbery and tyranny, and the defenseless condition of poverty. Greedy beasts, insatiable leeches, what do we leave for the peasant? Only what we cannot take away: the air.... On the one hand, near omnipotence; on the other, defenseless impotence.

These denunciations continue for another half page, and the chapter ends with a list of offenses that trails off into a string of etceteras.

It is the situation of the peasant that Radishchev emphasizes throughout. No need here to catalogue the abuses he mentions—the forced marriages, forced separations, rapes, beatings, and the rest. History records them as well. Catherine herself commented, apropos of Radishchev's account of a squire who had violated sixty peasant girls, "It is all but the story of Alexander Vasilievich Saltykov." In the middle of the next century Turgenev and others were still recording them.

What is most noteworthy in Radishchev's treatment of the peasant is not so much his sympathy, or even his reiterated conviction that "one man is born into the world equal in all respects to any other" ("Zaytsovo"); it is his fundamentally Rousseauistic point of view. The peasants are seen as primordial human beings, suffering from the corruption of their masters, but themselves uncorrupted. When the peasants gathered to see off the conscripts in "Gorodnya" speak in a language as elegantly artificial as that of the cultivated narrator, it is not because Radishchev was unaware of the way they really spoke, but because eighteenth-century literary decorum required a lofty style for the expression of serious sentiments. So when a peasant mother apostrophizes her departing son in phrases full of Church Slavonicisms, inversions, parallelism, and chiasmus, her language is no more than a sign that she is to be taken with full seriousness; the apparatus of elegance is in effect a democratic cue, signifying that her feelings are universal human ones, independent of class.

Paradoxically, the style comes closest to realism when Radishchev goes beyond egalitarianism to make his Rousseauistic points. In "Edrovo," for example, he comes upon a crowd of "rustic beauties" (he later refers to them as "rural nymphs") and expands invidiously on their freshness as compared with that of aristocratic city girls. The smiles and laughter of these girls reveal "a row of teeth whiter than the purest ivory. Teeth that would drive our smart society women out of their minds." And this, he notes, is achieved without dentists or toothbrushes. "Stand mouth to mouth with any of them you like," Radishchev invites the young ladies of Moscow and Petersburg; "not a single one of them will infect your lungs with her breath." But the young lady from the city may well be the carrier of hereditary syphilis, contracted by her mother or father in any of a variety of standard ways (which he spells out). The city corrupts, and its corruption threatens not only the wellborn. When Anna, a peasant girl, mentions that her Vanyukha means to work his way to St. Petersburg, Radishchev exclaims: "Don't let him go, dear Anyutushka, don't let him go; he is going to his ruin. There he will learn to drink, to squander his money, to eat fancy things, to dislike farm work—and most of all, he will cease to love you."

The dangers of the country are, by contrast, external. Anna has resisted pressures to marry a ten-year-old boy. Girls like her have been humiliated, violated, sold. Yet internally, they remain for Radishchev pure gold. Just as the high style in other sections has screened the actual peasant from us, leaving only an impression of his dignity; just as elsewhere the sufferings of the peasant have been explored, but not their moral or psychological effects on the victim; so here, when Anna and her mother are presented in all their canniness, speaking a persuasively racy and quite unliterary Russian, the element of abstraction enters in the narrator's inevitable reflections on what he has reported: "Anyuta, Anyuta," he cries, "you have set my head in a whirl! Why could I not have known you fifteen years ago? Your frank innocence, inaccessible to any sensualist's audacity, would have taught me to walk in the paths of chastity.... O, my Anyutushka, sit forever by the gate and give us precepts through the example of your unconstrained innocence." At the end of a long disquisition on the ideal union of man and woman, he invokes her name again: "These, Anyuta, are the virtuous thoughts with which you have inspired me. Farewell, my dear Anyutushka, your teachings shall remain forever engraved on my heart, and the sons of my sons shall have them as an inheritance."*

It is easy to smile at such naïve idealization, but what evokes the smile is the naïveté, not the idealization. Almost a century later, a writer so far from simplicity as Dostoevsky could make an article of faith out of such an attitude—as, indeed, could Tolstoy. Radishchev's many-sided picture of the Russian peasant may be incomplete because it is uncritical, but the work of almost every writer on the subject over the next hundred years can be seen as a variation on some theme in his book.

Catherine had been troubled that some passages in the book tended to incite peasants against their masters. There was small danger of this, as Radishchev pointed out in his own defense: "Our common people do not read books." Besides, this one was "written in a style incomprehensible to the people." Literature over the next century was to continue to involve the peasant in just this way: it would be written about him, but not by him or for him. It would use him as an instrument, the image varying with the writer's social and moral pre-occupations—and with his designs on the reader.

Karamzin's "Poor Liza" (1792), in its brevity and simplicity, offers perhaps the most extreme illustration of this point.† It *tells* us

---

* Here and throughout, all quotations from literary works are in my own translation.

† It may be worth noting that Karamzin's attitude toward the peasant was mixed: as a writer of fiction he could admire the charms of country life and country people, but as a political writer he could be coolly practical, wary of any change in the peasants' condition. In his *Vestnik Evropy* for 1803, for example, he writes that peasants are lazy not because of serfdom, but naturally and habitually. See A. N. Pypin, *Istoriia russkoj etnografii,* I (St. Petersburg, 1891), 208–18.

nothing about the peasant: Karamzin's sentimental-pastoral convention filters out everything that is not "pleasant" (his favorite word in this story) or "touching." Yet, where Radishchev exclaims with admiring surprise to his seventeen-year-old Anyuta, "You already know how to love!," Karamzin generalizes the point, and gives it a manifesto ring: "Peasant women, too, know how to love!" This point may seem less than revolutionary, but there is no doubt that "Poor Liza" (and the vogue it inspired) did soften the hearts of readers—for what that may have been worth. A whole generation was moved to exclaim with Karamzin: "Ah, I love those objects which move my heart and force me to shed tears of tender grief." (As late as 1876 an edition of 12,000 copies was printed.) Moreover, in purely literary terms the story is a landmark in the development of a style that could eventually treat life in more realistic terms. Karamzin's is a stylistic clearing action; his naïve simplicity replaces the tortured convolutions of plot and language common in the Russian fiction of his time.

The Early Nineteenth Century: Minor Writers

The influence of Karamzin and Radishchev, both separately and in combination, dominates the drama and fiction of the opening decades of the new century. A host of works, deservedly forgotten, nevertheless have a certain curiosity value, and can at least remind us how rapid was the rise of serious attention to the peasant in the following period.

The peasant, a comic figure in the theater of the eighteenth century, now appears in a sentimental light; he may be no more complex, but he is cleaner and nobler—and audiences, as S. T. Aksakov testified, literally dissolved in tears at the spectacle. One Vasily Fyodorov adapts "Poor Liza" for the stage, and "improves" it by having Liza fished out of the pond in which she has tried to drown herself, revived, and married to the repentant Erast. N. I. Ilin writes "Liza, or the Triumph of Gratitude" (1801), as well as "Magnanimity, or the Levy of Recruits" (1803). In the former, a young peasant, Kremnev, has just returned from service; since he is a good lad, he has not plundered, and so returns without booty, carrying only his rifle. His father, Fedot, greets him:

FEDOT: Faithful comrade of my Osip! Let me embrace you. [He moves to embrace the rifle, but suddenly stops.] Tell me the truth, Osip: has much blood flowed down this bayonet?

KREMNEV: Much, father!

FEDOT: Then throw it away, Osip; my eyes will grow dim looking at it. [He unscrews the bayonet.] Or—no, let us have it reforged into a scythe; the dew of morning is sharp: it will take off all the blood and will make it clean again.

KREMNEV: As you wish, progenitor.[7]

The same sentimental strain marks the rash of journeys written in imitation of Radishchev's during the opening decade of the century. The Karamzinian filter leaves only sweetness in these accounts, and, if the traveler must report unhappy events, he tends to do so not with indignation but with obvious pride in his capacity for fellow-feeling. An article in the *Journal of Russian Literature (Zhurnal Rossiiskoi Slovesnosti)* for 1805 complains of a new epidemic disease in literature: the author calls it "swelling of the heart."[8]

The prevalence of idyllic pictures of popular life can be variously explained; it was not, of course, only a Russian phenomenon. But whatever the positive encouragement for such an attitude, there was also a negative encouragement, coming from the censorship. Pnin's "Essay on Enlightenment" (*Opyt o prosveshchenii*)—openly criticizing serfdom as an institution—proved such a good seller when it came out in 1804 that the censor not only refused to allow a second edition, but even ordered the confiscation of all copies of the first that could still be found in the bookstores. The main charge was that "the author complains with ardor and enthusiasm of the unfortunate condition of the Russian peasants, whose property, freedom, and life itself, in his opinion, are in the hands of some capricious pasha." The official reviewer warned: "To incite the minds and inflame the passions of such a class of people as our peasants is tantamount to collecting a ruinous black cloud over Russia." Fourteen years later Prince Galitsyn went so far as "to call the attention of the censor to the journals and other works being published, in order that there not appear in them, under any guise whatsoever, anything either in defense or condemnation of the freedom or slavery of the peasants, not only native but also foreign."[9]

This is not to suggest that the censor was stifling Russian fiction in the first quarter of the century, for (with the exception of Narezhny, whose original satiric novels constitute a bestiary of wild Russian landowners) there was hardly any Russian fiction to stifle at the time. When a few noteworthy writers of prose begin to publish around 1830, their work shows the influence of European romanticism, with its interest in the life of the people (*das Volk, narod*), as well as in the problem of the artist, who appears in the guise of a peasant in more than one Russian story.

The writers who take up the peasant theme in the 1820's and 1830's are, significantly, *raznochintsy:* Pogodin, Polevoi, Pavlov. And however imperfectly their common attitude may have been embodied in the stories they produced, its emphasis is worth noting: literature has not explored peasant life. "We do not know Russian villages," Polevoi insists in his "Bag of Gold" (1829), and he contrasts the sentimental picture of happy shepherds and shepherdesses with the dirt, drunkenness, and poverty of the real scene. Pavlov makes the point even more tellingly in "The Name-Day," where the hero is a literate and gifted serf. "I took greedily to books," he says, "but, while satisfying my curiosity, they offended me: they all told me about others, and never about myself.... I was a being excluded from the literary census, not worth attention, uninteresting, incapable of inspiring thoughts, about whom there was nothing to say, impossible to remember." Pavlov's own answer to such an attitude amounts to a manifesto for realism: "Man is everywhere equally worthy of attention, because in the life of every man, whoever he is, however he has spent his life, we will meet feelings, or a word, or an event that will cause any head accustomed to reflection to droop."[10]

"The Name-Day" is the story of a serf who, thanks to his musical talent, rises above his station for a time. Chosen as a flutist for the amusement of his masters, he finds a sympathetic patron who makes it possible for him to continue his education. But the more he develops, the more false his position becomes. With the fact of his birth kept secret, he dines with the guests of his patron and hears one guest exclaim: "I made a fine deal today; I sold two musicians for a thousand rubles each." To which his neighbor comments *sotto voce:* "You can tell who's not a musician right away! I wouldn't take even two thousand for one of mine." Eventually, the hero's requited love for a noble girl proves his undoing. He confesses that he is a serf; she faints. His hope for buying his freedom disappears when his master—who had been ready to free him for 10,000 rubles—loses him at cards, together with a whole village. The musician runs away, is caught, becomes a soldier: "No longer threatened by a master's whim, I became the servant not of people but of death."[11] The same tragic theme of the peasant-artist is to be found in Timofeev's "The Artist" (1833), and a decade later in Herzen's "Soroka-Vorovka."

What such stories do is to ennoble the peasant without idealizing him: the implicit critical statement is more modest than Radishchev's, since it suggests nothing about the inherent qualities of the class—about "peasantness." Instead, we have a working-out of the influential theme of Gray's "Elegy Written in a Country Churchyard," whose translation by Zhukovsky in 1802 marks the beginning of a whole new tendency in Russian literature:

> Let not Ambition mock their useful toil,
> Their homely joys, and destiny obscure;
> Nor Grandeur hear with a disdainful smile,
> The short and simple annals of the poor.

This is the general starting point for Polevoi and Pogodin, and it will be the axiom of Grigorovich and Turgenev later. Pavlov, Timofeev, and Herzen in their stories of peasant artists draw on the view expressed in Gray's subsequent lines:

> Perhaps in this neglected spot is laid
> Some heart once pregnant with celestial fire;
> Hands, that the rod of empire might have sway'd,
> Or wak'd to ecstasy the living lyre.

> But Knowledge to their eyes her ample page
> Rich with the spoils of time did ne'er unroll;
> Chill Penury repress'd their noble rage,
> And froze the genial current of the soul.

These stories concern the lifting of gifted peasants out of their milieu, only to show the "genial currents" of their souls being frozen once again—and so to attack the institution that permits this. In Turgenev, a more realistic treatment of the same theme will discover the flowering of esthetic, philosophical, and even administrative talents within the peasant milieu, with quite different effects.

Before we move on to the 1840's, a word must be said about Pushkin and Gogol. That word can be brief. The peasant in the work of both men is a marginal figure, who makes no more than sporadic appearances. In Pushkin's case, his poem "The Village" sums up the whole problem. Written in 1819, it begins by celebrating the peace, quiet, and inspiration awaiting the poet, "freed from the fetters of vanity," in the bosom of nature. The first half of the poem develops these themes; the second half, beginning "But here a horrible thought darkens my soul," sketches the obverse side of the idyllic picture: "Here a savage gentry, without feeling and without law / Has appropriated to itself with the rod of violence / The labor, and the property, and the time of the tiller of the soil." Specifying the miseries of the people in this situation, he concludes: "Shall I ever see, O friends, the people unoppressed / And Slavery, fallen by the will of the Tsar, / And will the beautiful dawn of enlightened Freedom / Ever rise over my native land?"

At one point in the second half, Pushkin exclaims: "O, if my voice were able to stir hearts! / Why does a fruitless ardor burn in my breast, / And why has fate not given me the awesome gift of eloquence?" These lines, I think, must be taken at face value. It was less the censorship, which kept the whole second half of the poem from appearing in print until 1870, than the fundamental nature of Pushkin's genius that explains his avoidance of the peasant theme (together with the fact that the literary conventions within which he worked could not easily accommodate it). Proof of this may be seen in his "History of the Village of Goriukhino," where something like Chekhov's view of the unchanging nature of peasant life is suggested in the entry: "9 May, rain and snow. Grishka beaten for drunkenness on account of the weather." Could literature work with such material? "Goriukhino" is, in fact, based on this question, and the work is among those that Pushkin abandoned halfway through.

As for Gogol, after the puppet-show and comic-opera countryfolk of *Evenings on a Farm near Dikanka,* the peasant is noticeable in his work mainly for his absence. We could mention the "two Russian [*sic*] muzhiks" whose laconic speculations on Chichikov's carriage wheel open *Dead Souls,* and half a dozen others who materialize briefly in the course of that book—but we could not discuss them. Gogol's attention, as we see also in *Selected Passages,* is concentrated almost exclusively on the landowner. The peasants are there to work and show respect; the landowner is there to dispose of the products of their work and to demonstrate wisdom—that is, to try to be worthy of his privilege. Beyond this—to use one of Gogol's favorite expressions—everything becomes shrouded in fog. The rest is a matter of mystery and faith. The symbolic Russian troika, for which other nations make way in awe at the end of *Dead Souls,* draws a vehicle that is the work of some no less symbolic Yaroslav muzhik; but who he is or what he stands for is as unknown as the meaning of the speeding troika and its destination.

The "Natural School": Grigorovich and Turgenev

By the middle of the 1840's, the literary situation had changed markedly in Russia. An intelligentsia takes shape; many of the writers whose names mark the golden age of the Russian novel begin publishing; and a new generation of readers, schooled in German idealist philosophy, appears on the scene. Social thought, under the guise of literary criticism—largely in the person of Belinsky—makes new demands upon literature, which is assigned no less a role than expression of the national identity. "Art and literature in our day have become more than ever before the expression of social problems," Belinsky writes, combining prescription with description. "Substance," he finds, "is now more important than form."

It is the substance rather than the form of Grigorovich's "The Village" (1846) that explains its great contemporary success. "Grigorovich has written a physiology," Dostoevsky writes his brother in December 1846, "which is here creating a *furore*." The reference is to a new genre made popular by the French—the so-called physiological sketch—a half-journalistic description of the ways (*byt*) of the lower classes. A collection of such sketches called *Les Français peints par eux-mêmes* had been translated into Russian in 1840 and quickly gave rise to imitations, among them Nekrasov's *Physiology of St. Peters-*

burg (1844). It was thus in response to the new spirit of the age that the young Grigorovich used the occasion of a trip to his provincial home to explore, notebook in hand, the life of his peasants.

The result was the first "inside" account of peasants to be written by an outsider, and the inevitable element of factitiousness was largely concealed by the quasi-documentary character of the mode, together with the humane tendency of the story. Where the untutored peasants of Radishchev and Karamzin had spoken a Russian considerably more elegant than that of Pavlov's educated serf-musician, Grigorovich now offered conversations whose authenticity seemed guaranteed by their frequent unreadability (thanks to the proliferation of peasant dialect terms). This speech was clearly not meant to be colorful, nor were the characters.

As the title makes clear, "The Village" is a study of a milieu. A narrative bristling with proverbs takes us to peasant huts to hear long conversations; to a rural wedding, exhaustively described; to a village tavern in the early hours of the morning. The story follows Akulina, a peasant girl, from her birth to a dying cattle-tender, through her life with dull and grudging foster-parents, to her marriage—arranged at the whim of a crudely caricatured landowner's wife—to a drunken lout of a husband, and then to her early but merciful death. "There are people," Grigorovich comments near the end, "who seem foredoomed by fate to lifelong misery." Akulina is one such. Like the title character in Grigorovich's other peasant tale of the same period, "Hapless Anton," she is pure victim (in the double sense of the adjective), and the story is not so much about her as it is about the process of her victimization. The real subject is the environment that crushes her.

For all its stark detail, then—and the atmosphere of thickening gloom is quite unrelieved—"The Village" is, in effect, another sentimental tale. It is true, as one historian of literature notes, that this is the first portrayal in Russian of "the shocking story of one female life in the country"; and it is equally true that "all this was new, unheard-of and in sharp contrast to the peasant idylls of Dahl, Sollogub, and other 'lovers of the people.' "[12] But this is only to say that a new image of the peasant had been created—one whose life was a continual round of brutalization. Akulina is not herself brutalized; in this

ability to remain pure, sensitive, and unsullied, as Grigorovich hints
at the opening, she resembles Oliver Twist, and so her vulnerability
must make her doubly pathetic. There is evidence that contemporaries wept over this story just as their grandfathers had wept over
"Poor Liza," and Shchedrin himself was to compare the book's effect
to a "spring rain": "These were the first good humane tears, and
from ... Grigorovich the thought took firm hold in Russian literature
and Russian society that the peasant is a human being."[13]

Grigorovich's Akulina and Anton compel sympathy through their
unalloyed goodness and their unequal battle with an environment
that seems bent on destroying them. But it is only their situations that
are memorable; as characters, they are mute, inexpressive, minimally
individualized. If, therefore, Shchedrin is right in the remark just
quoted, that remark must be understood in a narrowly chronological
sense. The larger achievement in this line—more varied and more
subtle—was Turgenev's in *A Sportsman's Sketches*.

Where Grigorovich plunges us into the peasant milieu, Turgenev's
wandering narrator serves as a sensitive link between his readers and
the gallery of portraits he is presenting. The chance nature of his en-
counters, the absence of anything like plot in most of the sketches,
the constant emphasis on nature and the freedom of the hunter's life
—all dispel the occasional impression of tendentiousness. Despite the
famous retrospective remark about his youthful "Hannibal's oath" to
fight serfdom, Turgenev seems to have had no further purpose in
mind in writing the first of these sketches, "Khor and Kalinich," than
the settling of an argument he had been having with his mother. The
notion of a hunter's sketches was an addition of Panaev's—a subtitle
to attract readers. In some of the other sketches, the influence of Belinsky's indignant "Letter to Gogol" is evident, but in general Turgenev's later confession must be taken at face value: "I not only don't
want to, but absolutely cannot, write anything with a preconceived
thought or aim, in demonstration of one idea or another. With me, a
literary work takes shape the way grass grows."[14]

A Sportsman's Sketches, then, is a poetic statement about the Russian people and the Russian landscape, by turns lyrical, melancholy,
and ironical, whose fineness of observation is the warrant of its un-
biased truthfulness. The abuses and injustices of serfdom—most of
them familiar from Radishchev—form part of the picture, but only

part. Nor is the ethnographic description at the beginning of the first sketch the main thing. The historical importance of this work comes rather from the fact that Khor can be identified as "an administrator, a rationalist" ("his cast of face resembled Socrates"), while Kalinich belongs "to the category of idealists, romantics, enthusiasts, and dreamers" (in the first draft he resembles Schiller). This is a far cry from the discovery that peasants know how to love or create or play the flute. The whole book amounts to a demonstration of the deep and many-sided humanity of the Russian peasant, as expressed in the normal course of his life. No story gives point to these portraits. Khor and Kalinich are simply what they are; "The Singers" manifest astonishing artistic gifts, but these gifts prompt no reflections on their station in life; the peasant boys in "Bezhin Meadow" are simply and triumphantly boys; the memorable "Wolf" shows himself capable of facing a moral problem; Lukerya in "The Living Relic" demonstrates a touching sensitivity to nature and a humble love of life; Kasyan, an eccentric, speaks the language of birds. In the selection of subjects for these sketches, and in their collective force, one Soviet critic has plausibly seen a sort of mirror image of *Dead Souls,* a largely positive gallery of peasant types to match Gogol's negative gallery of landowners, and a concrete specification of what Gogol left vague in his numerous digressions on the strength and character of the people.[15]

A Sportsman's Sketches is a landmark, and it is small wonder that two young men, meeting Turgenev on a train from Orel to Moscow, should have bowed to him and thanked him "in the name of the whole Russian people." The battle for sympathy had been won; Turgenev had established the image of the Russian peasant as a fully human being, spiritually, at least, as much a citizen of his country as anyone else. To do so, however, he had removed him from his natural milieu, from the village and the land.[16] Looked at unsentimentally in that milieu, the peasant was to appear problematic in a new way.

The Peasant Milieu: The Powerlessness of the Masters (Tolstoy)

The censor, in forbidding a second edition of Turgenev's book, had objected that the author had shown that "the peasants are oppressed, that the landowners behave themselves indecently and illegally."[17] Since Radishchev, such demonstrations had been the rule. A victim always implies a villain. The following understated scene from Turgenev's "The Bailiff" (*Burmistr*) is typical of countless stories on the peasant theme:

Having breakfasted solidly and with visible pleasure, Arkady Pavlich poured himself a glass of red wine, lifted it to his lips and suddenly frowned.

"Why isn't the wine warmed?" he asked one of the serving-men in a somewhat sharp voice.

The man grew confused, stopped, as if rooted to the spot, and blanched.

"My dear fellow, I am asking you a question," Arkady Pavlich continued calmly, without taking his eyes off him.

The unhappy servant stood irresolutely in his place, twisted his napkin, and said not a word. Arkady Pavlich lowered his head and looked at him thoughtfully from under his eyebrows.

"*Pardon, mon cher,*" he said with a pleasant smile, touching my knee in a friendly way with his hand and staring again at the servant. "All right, go," he added after a short silence, lifted his eyebrows, and rang.

A stout, swarthy, black-haired man with a low forehead and eyes quite swimming in fat came in.

"About Fedor...take steps," said Arkady Pavlich in a low voice and with utter self-possession.

"Yes, sir," replied the stout one and went out.

"*Voilà, mon cher, les désagréments de la campagne,*" Arkady Pavlich observed cheerfully.

Tolstoy breaks new ground by exploring the opposite situation. In "A Landowner's Morning" (*Utro Pomeshchika,* 1856), he introduces nineteen-year-old Prince Nekhliudov, who, on a visit to his estate, discovers things "in indescribable disorder" and finds that "the chief evil lies in the most pitiable and disastrous condition of the muzhiks." But this evil, he thinks, can be corrected by work and patience. He will therefore remain on the estate and devote himself to its correction. "Is not mine," he asks, "the holy and direct obligation to care for the happiness of these 700 people, for whom I must answer to God?"

The story deals with one round of visits to his peasants. The careful description of the first, Ivan Churis, could come from Turgenev: the face is healthy, intelligent, and expressive. But a single detail—his smile shows "quiet self-confidence and a somewhat mocking indifference to everything around him"—signals a new type and a new complication. These individuals are intractable. They will not take the aid that is offered; they do not want schools for their children; they will not use the new hospital Nekhliudov has set up; they will not cooperate in progressive reforms; they will not, in short, change their ways. The poor turn out to seem irremediably poor; the well-off resist propositions to further their independence.

Nekhliudov had already known for a long time, not through rumors, not by hearsay, but in actual fact, the extreme degree of poverty in which his peasants lived; but the whole reality of it was so incongruous with his whole upbringing, cast of mind, and way of life, that he kept inadvertently forgetting the truth, and each time that, as now, he was palpably and at first hand reminded of it, his heart became intolerably heavy and sad, as if the recollection of some accomplished and irredeemable crime were torturing him.

"Why are you so poor?" he said, involuntarily giving voice to his thought.

Prejudice, cruelty, and neglect had been easier targets for writers. Now, in Nekhliudov's unanswered question, the image of the peasant becomes as enigmatic as the task of improving his lot. The lesson —"This peasant is a man!"—had been urged by writers since Radishchev, and urged in terms familiar to educated readers. Now that it was accepted, the serious attention it made possible led to a disconcerting discovery: *This man was a peasant!*

After 1861 he was no longer a serf. What was he? What could be done for him? What could he do for himself, and for Russia? Droves of writers approached him, particularly in the populist 'seventies, with such questions in mind, and every answer was at once an image, a theory, and a myth. Many, following the example of Grigorovich's peasant idylls of the 1850's, idealized him anew, finding in the peasant commune those bases for a just social organization which gave Zlatovratsky the title for a once-celebrated novel (*Ustoi, Istoriia odnoi derevni*).[18] Others, no less morally inspired, sought to understand and depict the peasant in "scientific" terms. Of the latter, Gleb Uspensky was unquestionably the most gifted.

The Power of the Land

Much of Uspensky's work is an updating of Tolstoy's theme: the gulf between the peasant and the intelligentsia. He begins with the high hopes and utopian dreams of the populist intellectuals of his time, anxious to redeem their inherited debt and guilt toward the people, and traces, in detail, their inevitable disillusionment. The peasant turns out to be a totally alien being, a different genus, with a distinct psychology and a morality quite unlike the one invented for him by an enthusiastic intelligentsia. In place of the myth of the happy peasant, the superior individuality formed by the commune, capable of inspiring and teaching his city-corrupted brothers, Uspensky, toward the end of his career, formulates a pessimistic counter-theory, based on "the power of the land":

This secret is truly an enormous one, and, I think, it lies in the fact that the enormous mass of the Russian people is patient and mighty in misfortunes, is young in soul, manful in its strength and childlike in its meekness ... so long as the *power of earth* governs it, so long as at the very root of its existence lies the *impossibility* of *disobeying* its *commands,* so long as they have power over its mind and conscience, so long as they fill its whole existence .... Tear the peasant from the land, from those cares which it imposes on him, from those interests by which it moves the peasant, get him to forget "the peasantry"—and that people ceases to exist, as does its world view, as does that warmth it exudes. There remains only the empty apparatus of an empty human organism. Spiritual vacuity sets in, "full freedom"—that is, an unknown empty distance, a boundless empty breadth, a terrible "Go wherever you will...."

The land, about whose unlimited ... power over the people I am speaking, is not something allegorical or abstract, but just that very earth which you have brought in from the street on your galoshes in the form of mud, the same earth that is in your flower pots, black and raw—in short, the most ordinary, natural earth.

Uspensky instances the importance of a blade of grass to the peasant, argues his dependence upon it. Its growth can bring the peasant a healthy chunk of bread—or it can fail to grow, being itself "in the power of every cloud, every breeze, every ray of sun." Not only that: "For this blade of grass ... to be able to provide nourishment, a mass of adjustments is necessary, a mass of labor, a mass of attention in mutual human relations. A hard-working wife is needed." And what, he asks, would happen if, reckoning the results in money, we were to give any peasant household three times the amount of money it earns in a year? The peasant, losing his dependence on nature, would lose the main support of his dignity, of his unique culture, of the tradition that gives him his special character.

Thus in the tiller of the soil there is not a step, not an action, not a thought which does not belong to the earth. He is in complete bondage to the little green blade of grass. To such an extent is it impossible for him to tear himself free from this power, that when he is asked, "What do you want, imprisonment or flogging?" he will always prefer to be flogged, to suffer physical torture, only in order that he may be immediately free—because his master, the earth, will not wait: the mowing must be done, the cattle need hay, the earth needs cattle. And it is precisely in this constant dependence, in this massive burden, under which the man himself cannot even move—precisely in this lies that unusual *easiness* [*legkost'*] of existence, thanks to which the muzhik Selianinovich [in the *bylina* about Sviatogor] could say: "My mother, the raw earth, *loves* me" [*menia liubit mat' syra zemlia*].

And "loves" is the word: she has taken him entirely into her hands.... But in return *he is not responsible* for a thing, not for a single step he takes. Once he acts as his mistress, the earth, *commands,* he is answerable for nothing. He has killed a man who was stealing his horse—and is guiltless, since without the horse he cannot work the land. All his children have died —again, he is not at fault; the land did not bring forth, there was nothing to feed them with. He has driven this wife of his into the grave—and is innocent: she, the fool, was a poor housekeeper and lazy; through her the whole thing, the work, came to a standstill. And their mistress, the earth, demands this work; it will not wait. In a word, if he only heeds what the earth commands, he is guiltless in everything; and the main thing is—what happiness not to be inventing a life for oneself, not to be seeking for interests and sensations, since they appear of themselves every day, as soon as you have opened your eyes! If it's rained outside—you *must* sit at home; if it's a warm, dry day, you *must* go mowing, harvesting, etc. *Responsible* for nothing, *devising* nothing himself, a man lives only *obeying,* and that obedience—every minute, every second—when expressed in constant work, forms a *life* that has no apparent result (what they earn they consume), but that has a result precisely in itself.

Why is this oak tree growing? What use is there in its taking up juices from the ground for a hundred years? What interest can it have in covering itself with leaves every year, then losing them, and finally feeding pigs with its acorns? The whole utility and interest of the life of this oak lies precisely in the fact that it *simply grows,* simply turns green, as it does, without knowing why. The life of the peasant tiller of the soil is the same thing: everlasting labor—that is life and the interest of life; and the result is a zero.[19]

Uspensky's double-edged theory is a key statement in the evolution of the myth of the peasant in Russian literature. It not only marks a break with the assumptions underlying most previous depictions; it also marks, with unusual clarity and cogency, the basis for the last memorable attempt to see the peasant as a figure whose enigmatic, alien nature contains some secret of great import for Russia. Tolstoy and Dostoevsky offer the models here.

The Peasant as Teacher: Tolstoy and Dostoevsky

It should be clear by now that this account of the peasant is in good part the story of the intellectuals' struggle to come to terms with the peasant as an idea, to find a satisfactory conception of him. At first a disadvantaged brother, he becomes in the second half of the century (and especially after the emancipation) a separate figure whose kinship to the educated observer is highly problematical. And what seemed to be his disadvantages begin, as Uspensky shows, to look like advantages. Seen in his absolute otherness, the peasant appeals to the intelligentsia's nostalgia for a life without the burden of ideas and choice: "If he only heeds what the earth commands, he is guiltless in everything.... What happiness not to be inventing a life for oneself, not to be seeking for interests and sensations, since they appear of themselves, every day, as soon as you have opened your eyes!" Here, perhaps, is a value in its own right. Tolstoy, in each of his novels, shows his hero discovering and applying aspects of this value to his own spiritual quest.

War and Peace is the first and most important instance; there the exemplary peasant is named Plato, and he has much to teach Pierre Bezukhov about the meaning of life. Platon Karataev balances and finally outweighs the other representative peasant figure, Tikhon Shcherbaty. Shcherbaty, who has killed a landowner, is the peasant armed, the partisan, defender of the homeland. Karataev, although a soldier, shows few signs of his military experience; he is meant to incarnate, simply and fully, peasant wisdom. For Pierre he is "the ineffable, full and eternal embodiment of the spirit of simplicity and

truth,... the personification of everything Russian, good and full"
(IV, I, 13). He seems proof against fatigue and illness; his speech is
always to the point and studded with proverbs (which Tolstoy had
painstakingly copied out of Dahl's collection); he is imperturbable
and indiscriminate in his benevolent contact with the world. Everyone he addresses is "my brother," "dear man," "friend," "my good
friend." Here—at this stage of the writer's development—is Tolstoy's
"ideal, his position, his philosophy."[20] And this philosophy rests on
the belief that man is to be viewed in terms of his whole organic society, the individual expressing the laws of his species unconsciously.
Karataev is attractive precisely in his spontaneity, his directness, his
unselfconsciousness—less a personality than a random expression of
the poetry of peasant life we have seen Uspensky hint at in passing.*

Attachments, friendship, love, in the sense that Pierre understood them,
Karataev did not have at all; but he loved and lived lovingly with everything that his life brought him in contact with, and particularly with man—
not with any particular man, but with those people who were there in
front of his eyes.... He did not understand and could not grasp the meaning of words taken apart from speech. Each word and each action was the
manifestation of an activity unknown to him, which was his life. But his
life, as he himself regarded it, did not have a sense as a separate life. It had
a sense only as a part of some whole which he constantly felt (IV, I, 13).

In this new attitude, which emphasizes love not for the individual
so much as for the qualities of all his fellows, almost accidentally
crystallized in him, there is a lesson. Pierre learns it from Karataev
because he is ready to; so too is Levin, in *Anna Karenina,* brought to
the high point in his quest for a spiritually viable life by the chance
remark of a peasant, which, "like an electric spark, had transformed
and condensed a whole swarm of disparate, impotent separate
thoughts that had never ceased to concern him (VIII, 2)."

Dostoevsky, after close observation of "the people" in his Siberian
prison, also sought the highest national and human truths in the
peasant—but the very intensity of his faith left his demonstrations less
than convincing. *The House of the Dead* is too complex—and too in-

---

* In his postscript to *Vlast' zemli,* Uspensky, in fact, praises Karataev as a figure "in
which, in the best sense, is concentrated *one* of the most fundamental groups of the
most characteristic popular qualities."

direct—to reward brief discussion; the same might be said of *A Raw Youth,* which, in the person of the narrator's father, offers the fullest symbolic image of the peasant that Dostoevsky ever achieved in his fiction. Dostoevsky's mystical convictions were evidently unarguable as well. His sketch "Vlas" (in *The Diary of a Writer,* 1873) contains the flat assertion that "different [peasant] 'Vlases,' the repentant and non-repentant ones ... will show us a new road and a new way out of all our apparently insoluble difficulties." "For," he goes on—making clear the negative basis of this faith—"it will not be Petersburg that finally settles the Russian destiny." The piece ends with a characteristically vague restatement: "Light and salvation will come from below (in a form, perhaps, completely unanticipated by our liberals, and there will be much comedy in that). There are even some hints of this surprise; even now facts are turning up .... However, we may say something about this later." He did not—but an episode reported by Leskov, involving Dostoevsky and Tolstoy, may serve as a summary of this climactic phase of the myth of the peasant in nineteenth-century Russian literature—which coincides with the end of an era, the so-called Golden Age.

The story concerns Dostoevsky in the middle 1870's. At the beginning of his career he had been shy in aristocratic salons, but now, near the height of his success, he was very much his own man. He would sit, unapproachable and silent, much of the time; when he spoke it was in prophetic tones. Meeting the highly intelligent Yulia Zasetskaia (daughter of Denis Davydov), who made no secret of her conversion to Lutheranism, Dostoevsky tried over the course of a whole winter to convince her of her mistake. Unfortunately, the lady turned out to know her Bible better than he did, not to mention the more important works of English and German biblical scholars. As a result, in religious discussions he revealed "more passion than knowledge." In the face of repeated forensic defeats, Dostoevsky turned to a new tactic—riddles, enigmatic utterances he would refuse to argue or explain, relying on his reputation to give them weight—and out of this tactic came what was to become a celebrated expression: the "kitchen muzhik" (*kufel'ny muzhik,* a colloquial corruption of *kukhonny muzhik*).

During one heated exchange, Zasetskaia confessed that she could not understand what was better in Russia than in other countries, or why the Russian should be considered better than any other nationality. *Everything* Russian was better, Dostoevsky insisted, and, when she replied that she did not see why, he suggested that was because no one had taught her to. "So teach me!" she challenged him. He remained silent; she persisted. Finally, nettled by the insistence of the other ladies present, Dostoevsky exclaimed in anger: "You don't know whom to go to for teaching! Fine! Go to your kitchen muzhik —he'll teach you!" When one of the ladies called this nonsense, Dostoevsky rose and, addressing himself in turn to each, repeated: "And you go to your kitchen muzhik, and you...." Asked what the kitchen muzhik would teach them, he could only answer: "Everything, everything, everything." In another house, the same scene was repeated that same evening—only this time, when pressed as to what "everything" might mean, Dostoevsky added: "To live and to die." Unable to elaborate, he tried to send one incredulous young lady through the door that led to the kitchen, for which she thanked him, but suggested that he should precede her, and should, first of all, seek a lesson in politeness.

For a decade after, the term "kitchen muzhik" enjoyed a certain enigmatic notoriety in the aristocratic houses of both capitals. Many were worried that Dostoevsky was warning darkly of some danger from the kitchen, some incursion into the rest of the house; others asserted that there was no danger, that the kitchen servant would never be allowed into the other rooms and would remain forever with the pots and pans. Only in 1886 was the whole argument laid to rest, in an unexpected way, with the appearance of Tolstoy's *The Death of Ivan Ilyich*. What Dostoevsky, an outsider in the houses of the wealthy, had only threatened, Tolstoy accomplished. Leskov writes:

As a familiar, knowing all the entrances and exits in the house, he made way for the kitchen muzhik and led him into the apartments. What people enjoying the strength of life and expending it in concern for their careers had rejected, the torments of dying had forced one of them to admit into his presence. Ivan Ilyich, deserted by everyone, having become a burden even to those closest to him, found real (in the spirit of the people) compassion and help only in his kitchen muzhik.... The master had himself asked the peasant to come to him, and here before the open grave the kitchen muzhik had taught his master to appreciate genuine sympathy, which made what society people bring to each other at such times look insignificant and repugnant.

Ivan Ilyich had learned *what can be learned* from the kitchen muzhik, and—made healthy by that teaching—he died.[21]

In other words, Tolstoy had answered the question that Dostoevsky, having provoked, proved unable to answer—and Leskov suggests that he may well have done so deliberately. In any case, Leskov confirms the authenticity of Tolstoy's depiction by citing the observations of one I. A. Rosenstrauch, who, in his capacity as evangelist, had witnessed many deaths among Russians of all classes, and had left descriptions showing how the peasants accepted the inevitability of death and sought traditionally to help the dying and their families. The upper classes, by contrast, tended to evince repugnance, panic, and indifference in such situations.[22] This is precisely the case with the muzhik Gerasim and Ivan Ilyich's family and friends in Tolstoy's work; the choice of the kitchen muzhik, rather than merely any old family retainer, in its very seeming casualness, makes it clear that Gerasim's ability to comfort and teach his master comes precisely from the fact that he is a peasant.

In this last major positive image of the peasant in the nineteenth century, Tolstoy is making a claim all the more profound for its limitation. The peasant is the custodian neither of rectitude nor of wisdom; but he *is* the custodian of a truth that must underlie any higher morality. His humane acceptance of death alone makes possible a humane use of life. The intelligentsia, in the person of Ivan Ilyich, can learn from him—not about the conditions of the good life, but about its preconditions, something both less and more than an idealized image might have taught.

Chekhov, Bunin, Gorky: The Peasant without Tears

In Chekhov and Gorky, we find for the first time in the century a thoroughly prosaic image of the peasant, without the pathos of either great expectations or lost illusions. In Bunin, the view is similarly dispirited, but Bunin, essentially a poet, manages to invest even such an unlikely theme with a kind of dark lyricism, a poetry of fatigue as much as of repulsion.

One reviewer of Chekhov's "Peasants" (*Muzhiki*), at the time of its appearance in 1897, noted:

As the author presents the matter, not only learning from the people, but even teaching them appears almost impossible. What ideals, in fact, live in the soul of Kiriak (the waiter's drunken brother), of the toothless old woman, spitefully grumbling at everyone, of the beaten-down Maria, or the licentious Fekla? All these characters are represented as somehow rudely possessed by a life that gives neither time for reflection nor freedom for demonstrating anything except purely instinctive urges with unusually faint glimmerings of human reason.[23]

Chekhov's story of the sick Moscow waiter who returns to his native village with his family, only to be resented for bringing another set of mouths to feed, is based on an actual occurrence; the setting is his own Melikhovo. This is the village in decline, emancipated from tradition.

Previously, fifteen or twenty years ago and earlier, the conversations in Zhukovo were much more interesting. Then every old man had the air of keeping some secret, of knowing something and waiting for something; they talked about a document with a gold seal, about sharing out, about new lands, about treasures; they hinted at something. But now the Zhukovites had no secrets; their whole life was open to general view, and they could speak only about need and feed, about how there was no snow.

Chekhov's peasants are in no position to teach anyone, because history has caught up with them, and they are now as much the victims of a time of transition as those who once looked to them for lessons (compare *The Cherry Orchard* of seven years later). So it is hardly surprising that there is no important representative of a different class to contrast with the peasants—as there has been in every work discussed so far. The peasants are seen in their own milieu, without persecutors or disciples, without any sort of special pleading, alien, spiritually deprived, gray, depressing. Olga, newly widowed, thinks as she leaves her dead husband's village:

In the course of the summer and winter there had been hours and days when it had seemed that these people lived worse than cattle, when it had been terrible to live with them; they were coarse, not honest; filthy, not sober; they lived in discord, quarreling constantly, because they did not respect but feared and suspected one another. Who keeps the tavern and makes the people drunkards? A peasant. Who embezzles and drinks up the communal school and church funds? A peasant. Who has stolen from his neighbor, committed arson, given false testimony in court for a bottle of vodka? Who at *zemstvo* and other meetings is the first to declaim against the peasants? A peasant. Yes, to live with them was terrible, yet all the same they were people; they suffered and wept as people do; and in their lives there was nothing for which excuse might not be found.

The novelty of these reflections lies in the priority of emphasis: whatever the reasons, *this* is what the peasant is like. Well might a populist critic complain that the artist had "blasphemously disparaged millions of people, forgetting about the fact that this people has the soul of a child."[24] The myth had been suddenly deflated, the very mythological apparatus apparently dismantled, and another critic (a radical) had grounds for declaring that this story was "an event, marking an era in fiction, as [Grigorovich's] *Hapless Anton* (incomparably weaker) or *A Sportsman's Sketches* (not more powerful) had done."[25]

Such an estimate took Chekhov's generalizing title seriously—and properly so. Tolstoy's complaint—that readers seemed unaware that Chekhov's peasant characters belonged only to a certain area near Moscow and were by no means typical—appears disingenuous by contrast. The intelligentsia, Tolstoy said, neither knew nor wanted to know the peasants, needing them only as an abstraction for polemical purposes.[26] But this is the inevitable reaction of a writer who had spent nearly half a century finding meaning in the peasant toward a younger writer who could find none. Rozanov sums up the difficulty of Chekhov's story by comparing it to Tolstoy's *The Power of Darkness.* Tolstoy had painted a harrowing picture of peasant life for the sake of "Christian example"; Chekhov had painted an equally dark picture —not for the sake of any example, but simply as a demonstration of "what is." "This 'what is' upset and offended the intelligentsia because it did not know how to respond to [Chekhov's story]. One can clearly 'love' only what is sympathetic—but here ... ?"[27]

In the same decade Gorky published his celebrated "Chelkash," and the emphasis of that story is similarly on the meanness of the traditional peasant. Korolenko, on reading the manuscript, had praised Gorky for being a realist ("You appreciate man as he is"), but had added with a smile that he was at the same time a romantic.[28] What he seems to have had in mind is the central opposition between the hobo Chelkash and his casual accomplice, the peasant Gavrila, who in the end becomes Chelkash's murderer. Gorky's theme is spiritual freedom. Chelkash, conscripted from his peasant village never to return, has become a tramp and a thief, has denied his roots in the land and learned to love freedom and its symbol, the sea. Gavrila, by contrast, is a peasant who has been working as a hired laborer; his ties with his native village have been weakened, but his nostalgia tends homeward, away from freedom, to possessions and security. Chelkash's initial attraction to "this healthy, good-natured lad with the bright childlike eyes" turns gradually to contempt as he perceives the truth about him. "You beggar!" Chelkash exclaims near the end, "how can you torture yourself so for money? Fool! Greedy devils!" And staring at the boy's face, "distorted by the elation of greed," he feels that he himself, "a thief, an idler, a man who had severed all ties, could never be so greedy, so base, so without dignity."

Mikhailovsky, the populist editor of *Russian Wealth,* the journal to which Gorky had submitted the story, took predictable exception to the character of Gavrila. The psychology, he said, was comprehensible, but the ethnographic detail was unconvincing.[29] The objection recalls Tolstoy's objection to Chekhov's "Peasants"—and amounts, as Tolstoy's did, to a rejection of the new programmatic statement implicit in both stories. Gorky, of course, is doing more than simply identifying the peasant's attachment to the soil with a perverse unfitness for spiritual freedom. He is suggesting that the peasant must now be seen in terms of his inevitable deracination. Not those who stay in the village are important, but those who leave it; hence it is not the traditional village values that are important, but rather the courage to seek new ones. Gorky is romantic in his attraction to the strong and individual, rather than to the typical and unremarkable, but he is at one with Chekhov and Bunin in denying the century-long fascination with the muzhik, and in finding that new times have advanced a new peasant. When Bunin considers him a decade and a half later, the very length of his sustained attention to this dismal phenomenon makes his work a kind of epitaph to the whole varied mythology we have been considering.

Bunin's novella "The Village" dates from 1910 and is set in the

period of the 1905 revolution. Its three main parts are devoted respectively to the ex-peasant tavern-keeper Tikhon Ilyich Krasov, his
brother Kuzma (a would-be intellectual), and a composite portrait of
the village itself—not accidentally named Durnovo (from *durnoi*:
"bad," "rotten"). The bright side of Pushkin's "Village" is absent, as
is the tendentious side of Grigorovich's. This is a view from within.

It opens with a historical perspective. The great-grandfather of the
Krasovs, a serf, had been torn to pieces by dogs for successful sexual
rivalry with his master. The grandfather had been freed, and moved
to town, where he became a famous thief. The father had been a
petty tradesman in the village. Now Tikhon Ilyich, a shrewder and
more forceful development of the type of Gorky's Gavrila, runs his
establishment there—lonely, bored, childless, grasping, hated. He has
just enough conscience to wonder at this situation and to feel its hopeless boredom and lack of meaning ("It's a prison!"). There is no story
of Tikhon's life, properly speaking; instead, what we get is a kaleido-
scopic picture of a certain kind of existence. When Kuzma suggests
mockingly that his brother's biography should be written, Tikhon
resents the mockery, finding the idea reasonable. But when it occurs
to him later, he is forced to see the truth: "And what was there to
describe? Nothing. There was either nothing, or nothing worth the
trouble. Even he himself remembered nothing of this life." As for
Kuzma, who dabbles in poetry, "he had dreamed all his life of studying and writing. What were his verses! He had only 'indulged himself' with verses. What he wanted to tell was how he had come to
ruin, to depict, with unheard-of pitilessness, his poverty and that way
of life, terrible in its ordinariness, that had crippled him and made
him a 'barren tree.'"

Alongside Tikhon Ilyich's house runs the railroad track, "a reminder that there are cities in the world, and people, newspapers,
news." The reminder is fruitless. Here in the village everything is
senseless, hermetic routine. Tikhon's aspirations to wealth, Kuzma's
to literature, the peasants' to sufficiency—all are without reward or
meaning. "God, what a region! Black soil a yard and a half down—
and such soil! Yet five years doesn't pass without a famine. The town
is famous throughout Russia for its grain trade—and a hundred men
in the whole town can eat their fill of this grain. And the fair? Beg-

gars, fools, blind men, and cripples—all of them the kind that it is terrible and nauseating to look on—and a regular regiment of them!" Throughout the region, estates are gone to ruin, the peasants pauperized. Bunin's eye for telling detail is unerring, and all the detail tells the same story. The sky lowers, the chill wind blows, people live like animals: the work is built impressionistically, relentlessly, a lugubrious tone poem. And its subject is not merely a single village; Balashkin, the local wise man, insists that *all of Russia is a village!*"

Bunin's work, no more ideological than Chekhov's "Peasants," is simply a long, unblinking look at a banal and sordid picture. Echoing the words of Conrad's Kurtz, who had seen into the heart of darkness in primitive Africa, Bunin himself would run from his room while writing "The Village" to cry, "The horror! the horror!"—and then go back to his desk.[30] His view of the peasant and his environment is perhaps the darkest in Russian literature, terrible, as Kuzma realized, precisely in its ordinariness. Pushkin had reacted to the first chapters of *Dead Souls* by exclaiming, "God, how sad our Russia is!" Gorky's reaction to "The Village" went even deeper; he found this work provoked reflection "not about the muzhik, not about the people, but about the strict question: Is Russia to be or not to be?"[31] To the extent that Bunin's despairing farewell to a tradition can be said to be about the peasant at all, its contribution is probably the only one left to make: the peasant is fundamentally uninteresting.

"Where, then, is that good-natured, thoughtful, Russian peasant, that tireless seeker after truth and justice, about whom Russian literature of the nineteenth century told the world so convincingly and beautifully?" The words are Gorky's, in 1922. "In my youth, I sought diligently for such a man through the villages of Russia—and did not find him." The bitterness comes not simply from this disillusionment, but from revolution and civil war and the reflections they provoked "about my country, more specifically, about the Russian people, about its majority, the peasantry." This is a class, Gorky finds, that has no moral traditions, preserves no memory of its heroes (or, indeed, of anything), is given to unspeakable cynicism and cruelty, and seems to have triumphed: "One can say now with assurance that, at the price of the ruin of the intelligentsia and the working class, the Russian peasantry has been reborn."[32] Gorky's pamphlet *On the Russian*

Peasantry is a long shudder of revulsion at his country's suffering, and it casts the peasant for the first time in the role of villain—if not evil himself, then the historical agent of evil. And yet, even if this view were "true," the validity of the preceding incarnations of the peasant would remain untouched—because the only kind of validity they can properly claim is a literary one. Gorky's own fiction hardly gives a more balanced or accurate account of life. Nor should it: that, even in Russia, never was the business of literature.

Afterword: The Problem of the Peasant

Nicholas V. Riasanovsky

The Russian people is marvelous, but marvelous
so far only in potentiality. In actuality it is low, horrid, and beastly.
Mikhail Pogodin[1]

Nineteenth-century Russia was a land of peasants. Population statistics for 1796 indicate that then 34,700,000 or 96.4 per cent of its inhabitants were rural and only 1,300,000 or 3.6 per cent were urban. A hundred years later, in 1897, the countryside contained 112,700,000 or 87.4 per cent of the total population, while the towns sheltered the remaining 16,300,000 or 12.6 per cent.[2] With a minor discount for the gentry and the clergy, this rural sea of people consisted of peasants. Moreover, many residents of the towns maintained close contacts with their native villages and remained, both legally and in terms of their own view of themselves, peasants like their forefathers.

To say that in nineteenth-century Russia peasants were not represented in proportion to their numbers in the government, administration, politics, social life, education, or culture of their country would be euphemistic to the point of nonsense. Rather, a student of the subject is brought to the realization that the entity known as imperial Russia consisted of two separate worlds: the world of the educated and that of the illiterate, of government and "society" on the one hand and of the masses on the other, of the city or town and of the village, of the rich and of the poor, of the exploiters and of the exploited, of the active and of the passive, of the dynamic and of the static. All this, of course, is common knowledge, although the nuances and the qualifications might well vary with each particular observer. Also, one hardly needs to be reminded that the division between the elite and the masses in Russia paralleled similar divisions in other countries. Still, the Russian split was not quite like the others, or at least it represented a more extreme species of the same genus. In this, as in so many other cases, the evolution of Russia seems to offer a sharper and cruder version of what happened to the west of it.

"A satiated man is not a comrade of a hungry one," a Russian proverb asserts, and this bit of folk wisdom has undeniable relevance for Russian history. In imperial Russia, some of the satiated tended to be satiated to the full, while the hungry ones went very hungry. During the nineteenth century, Russia possessed the most splendid court and perhaps the most palatial and magnificent capital city in Europe, as well as an exquisite literature and a glorious ballet, but most of its people endured a marginal existence with every drought threatening starvation. A dreadful famine swept much of the country as late in the century as 1891. Not only did the satiated and the hungry worlds coexist, but the first oppressed and exploited the second in a particularly blatant and obvious manner. Indeed in the period before 1861, for roughly half of the Russian peasants this exploitation took the form of serfdom, an odious quasi-slavery that made many millions of Russians virtual chattels of their masters. The resulting social and economic gulf between the upper classes and the masses needs no further comment, but it does not tell the whole story. For there existed yet another basic cleavage between the two sides, a more specifically Russian one: the cultural. To be sure, the landlords and the administrators were always likely to be better educated than their serfs or even than the state peasants, and this was already true of Muscovite Russia. However, with Peter the Great and his determined Westernization of his native land the nature of education in Russia changed from fundamentally religious and medieval to essentially secular and modern. Education also became better-organized and gradually much more widespread and demanding. The new education, and the whole new outlook on which it was based, were entirely foreign to the Russian peasant. It was after Peter the Great, and especially as broader and broader layers of the officialdom and the gentry became Westernized, that the pattern of the two worlds emerged in full: two separate societies and two separate cultures that seemed to have little if anything in common.[3]

The world of the upper classes could not entirely fail to notice the world of the peasants, because, after all, the peasants did all the work in the fields, as well as supplied soldiers for the army and servants and artisans for the households of the gentry. But to their social betters the peasants looked all too often like an inarticulate and inert, when not a recalcitrant or even threatening, mass, outside the light of reason or the course of history. To many educated nineteenth-century Russians the concept of peasant culture, as distinct from peasant ignorance and peasant backwardness, would have been a contradiction in terms. Yet that culture did exist, and any discussion of the Russian peasantry in the nineteenth century omits reference to it at its own peril.

Therefore, possibly the central essay in the present volume is Professor Mary Matossian's study of the Russian peasant way of life in the nineteenth century, where the author, using the approaches of modern anthropology, does her inspired best to understand Russian peasant culture in its own terms. Following her Ivanovs from cradle to grave, after having set minutely and precisely the stage for their activities, Professor Matossian reconstructs traditional peasant existence with its working schedules directly related to the seasons, its established ways of behavior for almost every occasion, its very numerous rites and rituals, its joys and sorrows. Far from being inert, undifferentiated, or meaningless, Russian peasant life emerges as a complex, thoroughly integrated, and, so to speak, organic form of human existence. Indeed the author apparently finds it to be more natural, meaningful, and attractive than life in industrial society.

Important aspects of Russian peasant culture that Professor Matossian mentions only in passing, as they entered the lives of the Ivanovs, included folk literature and folk art. It was especially in the nineteenth century that educated Russians discovered the treasures of popular artistic creation, which came to affect the creative culture of the upper classes, whether in Pushkin's tales or Moussorgsky's music. Above all, there was the Russian language itself to testify to the creative and artistic energies of the masses.

The peasants had not only literature and the arts, but also religion. Professor Matossian states this fact as follows: "The Russian peasants acted out the drama of life in a world whose central focus was the church in the *selo*. The church was the meeting place for heaven, earth, and the world underground. From heaven to the altar and down into the crypt: this was the peasant *axis mundi*."[4] Professor Donald Treadgold treats the subject of the Russian peasant and religion in the large, and in the framework of a historical evolution. One is compelled to agree with his main emphases, and in particular with his stress on the importance of religion, in the first place Orthodoxy, in the lives of the Russian peasants. The issue, as Professor Treadgold realizes so well, is not the presence or absence of religious superstition and ignorance among the peasants: of course, the peasants were superstitious and ignorant, and this has been denounced, above all by churchmen, at least from the time of St. Theodosius in the eleventh century. The issues are rather the great role of religion and religious observance in the daily lives of the peasants and also, although this is a very difficult subject indeed, the nature of Christianity itself. For Christianity, in particular Orthodox Christianity, is not primarily an enlightened ethical code or a scholarly philosophical doctrine, but a belief in the eternal life in Christ and in the transfiguration of the world. Its main dogma is the Incarnation. Precisely because of this supernatural claim of Christianity, it found itself from the start in contact and contest with the abundance of superstition and magic among the Russian peasants. Yet, Christianity being what it is, those who criticize the Russian peasants for not being truly Christian might themselves be farther removed from Christianity than the most superstitious and coarse inhabitants of a Russian village. In any case, as Professor Treadgold indicates, they are hardly in a position to judge the distances involved.

Russian peasants even possessed a well-established and firmly held political theory. In brief, they were staunch monarchists, convinced believers in the uniquely valid authority of the rightful tsar. Peasant political theory remained unaffected by the developing split between the government and the educated public in Russia in the nineteenth century, and it became the despair of numerous revolutionaries when they tried to pursue their activities among the masses. Not that the peasants were always docile. But, in order to oppose authority, whether in the "Time of Troubles" or in 1861, they had either to proclaim the reigning monarch a usurper and act in the name of an alleged true tsar, or, more modestly, assert that they were carrying out the wishes of the ruler that were being thwarted and misrepresented by evil landlords and bureaucrats. One of several contributions of Professor Terence Emmons' paper on the peasant and the abolition of serfdom is the remarkable picture he draws of this peasant political theory in action. Other scholars, too, from Klyuchevsky to Professor Emmons' teacher, the leading contemporary specialist on the emancipation, Professor P. A. Zaionchkovsky, have noted the peculiar need of the Russian peasants to buttress their causes with the supreme authority of the tsar. Thus, throughout his fundamental study of the emancipation, Professor Zaionchkovsky indicates how peasant disturbances were invariably linked to claims of a suppression or a perversion of the monarch's will.[5] One is further reminded of the testimony of Lieutenant Greene, presented in Professor John Curtiss' paper on the peasant in the army, and of countless other accounts of the devotion of Russian peasants, or peasants as soldiers, to the tsar. Lieutenant Greene, it will be remembered, observed the emperor reviewing his troops: "Their expression was not so much one of joy as of absentminded, wondering veneration. [Whether reviewed by generals or by princes] the men never had the same thoughts written on their faces as they did when they saw the Tsar."[6] In fact, an important problem of Russian history is the elucidation of the circumstances and the time of the loss of the peasant loyalty by the Crown, a subject to which Professor Curtiss, concentrating on the army, can give no more than passing attention.

Yet Professor Curtiss' judicious essay has significance beyond its subject matter, important as this subject matter is. To a student of the Russian peasantry the imperial army provides an extremely rich source of observation of this peasantry, although, to be sure, under special circumstances; it also provides another illustration of the split between the elite and the masses, the division between the two worlds. It has been generally recognized that the Russian soldiers knew how to die. On the field of Borodino, in Sevastopol, or around Plevna they stood their ground until they prevailed over the enemy, were wiped out, or were ordered by their superiors to retreat. Interestingly, this ability to face death, this, in a sense, acceptance of death, mentioned by so many military observers as characteristic of Russian soldiers, was also noted by some of the greatest Russian writers, including Turgenev, Dostoevsky, and Tolstoy, as a remarkable trait of the common people of Russia, that is, of the Russian peasants. Tolstoy, who was both a writer and an army officer, left in the *Sevastopol Tales* and elsewhere some of the most tantalizing images available of the soldier and peasant mentality in its relationship to life and to death.

If death in the service often lay at the end of a soldier's road, the hallmark of the entire way was endurance. Russian soldiers endured heat and cold, hunger and epidemics, penury and exhaustion, brutal company officers and stupid generals. Time and again they demonstrated not only a dogged ability to survive, but also a remarkable resilience, as in the Balkan campaigns against Turkey, both in the late twenties and the late seventies, when decimated and exhausted Russian armies came back to win the wars. It is probably the same capacity to persevere and preserve one's own identity that enabled the Russian peasant to survive the rigors of urban industrialization while remaining to an astonishing extent essentially a peasant. Professor Reginald Zelnik's imaginative study of "the Russian peasant as factory worker" thus complements that of Professor Curtiss in more ways than one. The author's conclusion, drawn as a parallel to the British development, deserves particular attention: "In Russia, where the independent artisan tradition was extremely weak, if indeed it existed at all, the corresponding tensions were between peasant and worker status, and, I would argue, no clear victory for the latter ever emerged. The social, economic, and political consequences were as great in Russia as they had been in England, but of a completely different nature."[7] The same peasant tenacity gave strength to peasant institutions, notably the celebrated *obshchina,* whose stranglehold on the Russian countryside has been so effectively depicted by Professor Francis Watters in his contribution to the present volume.

Peasant as soldier shared, of course, the weaknesses as well as the strengths of peasant as peasant. The same observers who admired the endurance and even heroism of Russian troops frequently deplored their laziness, stolidity, and lack of initiative. The men who could not be dislodged from the Fourth Bastion in Sevastopol or from the Shipka Pass had the greatest of difficulties in observing elementary sanitary regulations and in responding on their own to quite minor unforeseen problems and challenges. Beyond that (and this was apparently an important consideration in the background of the emancipation), they looked like poor candidates for the modernization and technical improvement required of nineteenth- and twentieth-century armies. The "big children" mentioned in Professor Curtiss' essay simply would not grow up. And it would seem that these and other such complaints by imperial officers and officials were largely justified. To a historian, however, their main burden is not to condemn Russian soldiers in any absolute sense, but to emphasize once more the cleavage between what Prince N. Trubetskoy called the upper and the lower layers of Russian culture. For endurance and death belonged to the peasant world, modernization and technical improvement did not. The imperial Russian army, even more than the gentry estate—because, after all, officers fought and died with their men— represented a peculiar pragmatic combination of two separate societies that could not really understand each other. Under the circumstances, it performed above and beyond reasonable expectations.

As the above observations suggest, the Russian peasant possessed his own way of life, indeed his own culture, and he also apparently developed certain character traits deeply embedded in that culture. The upper classes could not entirely ignore the peasant world and its values. Romantic enthusiasts were fascinated to discover folk traditions, literature, and art. Officers came to rely on the sterling qualities of their men and to be aware of their limitations. The Church, of course, united in some manner all Orthodox Russians, from the emperor to the last village tramp. The government declared that a boundless devotion to the tsar was the distinguishing mark of all true Russians, and thus in a way took cognizance of and approved peasant political theory. Administrators came to know something about the people they administered. The landlords continued to be engaged, in a sense, in a joint enterprise with their serfs.[8]

And yet there was very little understanding between the two sides, few effective bridges across the chasm. Educated Russians were appalled by the hardness, misery, ignorance, and brutality, not to say bestiality, of peasant life. Even the minority among them who romantically admired folk spirit or folk culture had in fact no more rapport with the common people than the majority who ignored the peasants as best they could or recoiled from them in sadness, horror, or disgust. Misunderstanding, indeed a total lack of comprehension, prevailed, even when authorities or landlords tried to be helpful.

In the course of the cholera epidemic in St. Petersburg in the summer of 1832, after a crazed mob stormed a temporary hospital, killed several doctors, and routed Count Peter Essen, the governor-general of the city who tried to restore order, Emperor Nicholas I himself

proceeded to the center of rioting in Haymarket Square. The daunt-
less sovereign—assisted, no doubt, by the veneration of the tsar mentioned earlier—brought the crowd of some five thousand people to
their knees, upbraided them in his most sweeping manner, and obtained docile obedience from them. But when the Emperor made a
rhetorical contrast in his address between the rebellious French and
Poles and the traditionally loyal Russians, his listeners concluded that
he confirmed their suspicions that they were being poisoned by the
French and the Poles, and they reacted by catching and bringing to
police headquarters, confident that they were executing the will of
their tsar, foreigners and other suspicious-looking individuals.[9]

Near the end of the century Chekhov wrote a remarkable, sad short
story, "The Malefactor."[10] A peasant brought to court for stealing a
bolt from the railroad tracks to weight his fishing tackle totally fails
to see his guilt, and in describing his activities constantly refers to
"we," meaning the peasants of his locality, the people. "Bah! Look
how many years we, the entire village, have been removing bolts and
God preserved us, and here [you are talking about] a crash ... people
killed.... We do not remove all of them ... we leave [some].... We
do not act without thinking ... we understand."[11]

The incomprehension in Haymarket Square and in Chekhov's
courtroom was evident throughout the wide expanses of Russia. It
appeared that the Russian peasants, and the entire economic and social system based on them, could at best maintain their routine existence, but could not respond effectively to new demands or opportunities. Whether in the matter of industrialization or of modernization of the army, old rural Russia and its ways loomed as an almost
insuperable obstacle. Nor was the established system safe even in its
routine operation. The two above-mentioned examples themselves
deal respectively with a murderous riot and with an unwitting sabo-
tage of railroad tracks. More characteristically, serfs rose against their
masters, killing them and setting manor houses on fire, or at least refusing to perform their obligations or trying to escape. Soviet scholars
in particular have paid close attention to evidences of rural unrest in
imperial Russia. In fact, these two characteristics of the peasant world
—its rejection of change and the threat it posed to the landlords and
the state—have been adduced most frequently, alternately or in conjunction, as the explanation for the most important measure dis-

mantling old Russia, the emancipation of the serfs.[12] But the emancipation came only in 1861, and, to put it in its proper perspective, one has first to consider briefly other attitudes and approaches to the peasant problem on the part of the educated public and the government.

A deep gulf separated the government and the educated public from the peasants, "society" from the "people," in nineteenth-century Russia, causing manifold and fundamental problems and dangers. Logically there could be three distinct reactions to the inescapable reality of the chasm, and all three had their exponents in imperial Russia. One alternative was to demand that the educated classes abandon their separate culture and join the peasants; another, to maintain and defend the existing situation; a third, to try to lead the peasants to Westernization and modernization.

The first would-be solution—joining the common people—was of course purely utopian. Yet it blazed a trail in Russian thought and was not without significance in the general history of the country. Its original and most important proponents were the Slavophiles of the eighteen-forties and fifties, who creatively applied the ideology of romanticism and German idealism to their native land.[13] In the writings of Khomyakov, Ivan Kireevsky, and other members of the circle, the fundamental romantic dichotomy between the integrating full understanding and the isolating, egoistic, and superficial reason became the dichotomy between Russia and the West. Russia represented true religion, vital tradition, an organic and harmonious historical development. The West stood for a denial of God, revolution, division, and mortal struggle. Peter the Great, tragically, turned to the West, introducing the West into Russia. After him, the Russian upper classes fell into the bondage of the false Western principles, while the common people, the peasants, remained faithful to their heritage. It was the task of the Slavophiles to make educated Russians conscious of their own true principles preserved by the common people, and thus restore ancient Russia, but on a higher, because fully conscious and articulate, plane.

In order to appreciate the profound and basic Slavophile admiration of the Russian peasant world, and especially of the peasant commune, it is important to realize that Slavophilism was essentially a vision of integration, peace, and harmony among men. This vision found its theological embodiment in Khomyakov's concept of *sobor-*

nost, an association in love, freedom, and truth of all believers; it found its social embodiment primarily in the Slavophile view of the peasant commune. In the words of Konstantin Aksakov:

A commune is a union of the people who have renounced their egoism, their individuality, and who express their common accord; this is an act of love, a noble Christian act, which expresses itself more or less clearly also in its various other manifestations. A commune thus represents a moral choir, and just as in a choir a voice is not lost, but follows the general pattern and is heard in the harmony of all voices, so in the commune the individual is not lost, but renounces his exclusiveness in favor of the general accord—and there arises the noble phenomenon of harmonious, joint existence of rational beings (consciousnesses), there arises a brotherhood, a commune, a triumph of human spirit.[14]

It was apparently the Slavophile apotheosis of the peasant commune that came to Alexander Herzen's mind when, disillusioned with the West, the great Westernizer turned to his native land for consolation and hope. Through Herzen and Mikhail Bakunin the peasant commune and its supreme virtue and value for the future of Russia became a treasured belief of later generations of radicals and revolutionaries. Indeed, broadly speaking, the entire populist orientation, so prominent in Russia between the emancipation of the serfs and the Communist seizure of power in 1917, can be interpreted as an effort to join the people, or at least to buttress and promote those peasant qualities and institutions on which the future of the country would presumably depend. The classic "going to the people" of 1874 was only a particularly striking and revealing instance of a major trend. At the end of the century Nikolai Mikhailovsky still affirmed that the Russian peasant constituted a higher type of man than a typical denizen of the West, though at a lower level of development. It is worth noting that the radical championing of the peasant commune represented, even in its more extreme forms, a truncated (because secularized and made more pragmatic) version of the original Slavophile vision, a development quite common in the history of modern thought.*

* Considerations of space prevent me from doing anything like justice to the varied views of Russian radicals and populists concerning the peasants and the peasant commune. Suffice it to say that, in my opinion, while these views by no means simply proceeded from those of the Slavophiles, the Slavophile connection was important.

As Professor Donald Fanger's sparkling contribution to this volume so well indicates, appreciation and even admiration of the peasant also entered the imaginative literature of the educated classes. However (to follow Professor Fanger's perceptive analysis), this attitude frequently reflected the needs and fancies of the writers themselves rather than any peasant reality. It bears reminding that this turning to rural Russia, its way of life, beliefs, and values, was by no means limited to some literary hacks or to representatives of certain narrow ideologies—for example, populism, in the stricter sense of the term. Indeed such independent giants of Russian literature as Dostoevsky and Tolstoy looked to the Russian peasant for enlightenment, for answers to the crucial questions of life and death, and, in the case of Dostoevsky, for insight into the mission and destiny of Russia. It was Tolstoy in particular who made a heroic effort to join the common people, *oprostit'sia,* trying to abandon fame, Westernized culture, and literature itself in order to work, live, and, he hoped, believe and die like a peasant—a gigantic simplifier in an immense peasant land.

But in spite of such dedicated men as Konstantin Aksakov and Leo Tolstoy, turning to the peasant way of life provided no real solution for the Russian intellectual even on the personal plane, and it had nothing to offer in the broader terms of the historical evolution of Russia. At the beginning of the nineteenth century, the Russian government and society could choose only one of the remaining two ways: to maintain the chasm and the two worlds on its opposite banks, that is, "to keep the peasants in their place," or to try to bring them over to Westernization and modernization. Alexander I and his advisers spoke much of the second alternative but in essence practiced the first. There is little doubt that the brilliant, exciting, springlike quality of Alexander's reign was in part due to the fact that in that reign the fundamental problems of Russia were at least discussed, that new horizons seemed to open, that new solutions beckoned. The abolition of serfdom appeared to be a possibility, and with it a transformation of Russia from top to bottom. Yet when late in 1825 Alexander I died, very little had been changed. Most important of all, the problem of the peasant in Russia remained almost exactly what it had been at the time of the emperor's accession to the throne twenty-five years earlier.

Emperor Nicholas I brought words into conformity with deeds. His thirty-year reign gave classic expression to the conservative alternative: to hold the line. The liberal aspirations of the time of Alexander I were replaced by an explicitly reactionary ideology that came to be known as the doctrine of Official Nationality.[15] The three principles of this creed—Orthodoxy, autocracy, and nationality—stood as an emphatic endorsement and defense of the established order of things in Russia: autocracy, serfdom, stifling censorship, and all. It has been pointed out that the reign of Nicholas I did not mean mere stagnation. In fact the sovereign worked devotedly, even desperately, to improve the functioning of the government and the condition of his subjects. The codification of law and the reorganization of the state peasants testify to the important results achieved where able men took charge. But it was precisely a fundamental change in the existing system that ceased being a possibility once Nicholas I replaced his brother on the Russian throne.

To be sure, Nicholas I did not like serfdom personally. He had at least some awareness of its burden on the people and of its attendant evils; also, in contrast to a number of his predecessors, he felt no particular sympathy for the gentry class and its almost unlimited power and authority in the countryside. However, emancipation, or even measures pointing in that direction, would have been, in the opinion of the Emperor, a step much too dangerous to take. As he explained the matter in 1842 to the State Council: "There is no doubt that serfdom, as it exists at present in our land, is an evil palpable and obvious to all. But to touch it *now* would be a still more disastrous evil.... The Pugachev rebellion proved how far popular rage can go."[16] More exactly, Nicholas I and his government were afraid of two different revolutions that could be unleashed, in their view, by the shock of the emancipation: another Pugachev rebellion (in other words, an elemental, popular uprising) and a bid by the gentry, perhaps in the manner of the Decembrists, to obtain a constitution once they had been deprived of their serfs. Count Sergei Uvarov, the minister of education and the creator of the doctrine of Official Nationality, presented the problem in an unmistakable manner: *"Political religion, just as Christian religion, has its inviolable dogmas; in our case they are: autocracy and serfdom."*[17] And on another occasion:

The question of serfdom is closely linked to the question of autocracy and even monarchy.

These are two parallel forces which have developed together.

Both have the same historical beginning; both have equal legality....

Serfdom, whatever one may think of it, does exist. Abolition of it will lead to the dissatisfaction of the gentry class, which will start looking for compensations for itself somewhere, and there is nowhere to look except in the domain of autocracy.... Peter I's edifice will be shaken....

Serfdom is a tree which has spread its roots afar: it shelters both the Church and the Throne.[18]

Nicholas I kept appointing characteristically secret and repetitious committees to deal with various aspects of serfdom, but, in contrast to what was accomplished for the state peasants,* their busy work—not surprisingly, given the orientation of the Emperor—produced almost no results.

The doctrine of Official Nationality had considerable support in Russia in the second quarter of the nineteenth century.[19] Moreover, those who adhered to it at least in part included some great literary figures and prominent professors as well as the bureaucratic apparatus and the official or semi-official press. True, in the case of men of genius, as well as in the case of others, the support often went to the power, position, or even alleged historic mission of the Russian state rather than to the condition and treatment of the lower classes, let alone to serfdom as such. Thus, though Pushkin came very close to the official doctrine in his resounding praise of the work of Peter the Great and the glory of the Petrine state, he retained from his earlier liberalism a tragic sense of the cost of this glory. Somewhat similarly, Tiutchev attached to his appreciation of the Russian autocracy the hope that it would assume the leadership of all the Slavs and resolve in the Pan-Slav sense the outstanding problems of eastern and central Europe.

---

* Count P. Kiselev's important reorganization of the state peasants has traditionally received great praise in Russian historiography. For a recent major assessment of it, which is highly critical, see N. Druzhinin, *Gosudarstvennye krestiane i reforma P. D. Kiseleva,* 2 vols. (Moscow-Leningrad, 1946–58). It should be noted that while Kiselev meant to improve the condition of the state peasants, his reform did not challenge the hierarchical and stratified nature of the Russian system, with the state peasants restricted to their particular enclave in it.

Others gave a still more sweeping and unqualified support to the conservative orientation of the government, a support that explicitly included the policy of the government to keep the peasants in their place. For example, as late as 1859 the grammarian, writer, and journalist Grech echoed Nicholas I on the subject of the emancipation: "The liberation of wild slaves, under conditions of complete moral disorder, of a lack of true, spiritual religion, and of the corruption of our minor officials, will bring upon Russia complete ruin and countless misfortunes."[20]

But to return to great writers, it was Gogol who provided, in his *Selected Passages from Correspondence with Friends,* published in 1847, a naïve, direct, and unforgettable formulation of the conservative or reactionary point of view as it applied to Russian society. Consider, for instance, his celebrated advice to the landlord:

Take up the task of a landlord as it should be taken up in the true and lawful sense. First of all, gather the peasants and explain to them what you are and what they are: that you are the landlord over them not because you want to rule and be a landlord, but because you are already a landlord, because you were born a landlord, because God will punish you if you were to exchange this condition for any other, because everyone must serve God in his own place, not someone else's, just as they, having been born under authority, must submit to the same authority under which they were born, for there is no authority which is not from God. And right then show it to them in the Gospel so that they all down to the last one will see it. After that tell them that you force them to labor and work not at all because you need money for your pleasures, and, as a proof, burn right there in front of them some bills, and make it so that they actually see that money means nothing to you. Tell them that you force them to work because God decreed that man earn his bread in labor and sweat, and right there read it to them in Holy Writ so that they will see it. Tell them the whole truth: that God will make you answer for the last scoundrel in the village, and that, therefore, you will all the more see to it that they work honestly not only for you, but also for themselves; for you know, and they know it too, that, once he has become lazy, a peasant is capable of anything—he will turn a thief and a drunkard, he will ruin his soul, and also make you answerable to God. And everything that you tell them confirm on the spot with words from Holy Writ; point with your finger to the very letters with which it is written; make each one first cross himself, bow to the ground and kiss the book itself in which it is written. In one word, make them see clearly that in everything that concerns them you are acting in accordance with the will of God and not in accordance with some European or other fancies of your own.[21]

No wonder that Gogol also decided that peasants should not be educated at all, that the words of a priest were more useful to them than all the books, and that learning should be provided only for those few among them who had the ability and the urge "to read the books in which is inscribed God's law for man."[22]

Gogol's obscurantist views, delivered in the moral tones of a director of conscience, produced a scandal highlighted by the critic Vissarion Belinsky's devastating attack on the writer. Yet it should be said on Gogol's behalf (Belinsky's assertions to the contrary notwithstanding) not only that he had remained true to himself while writing the *Selected Passages,* but also that his opinions reflected very well, in a sense, both Russian reality and the less openly expressed thoughts and attitudes of many of his contemporaries. Gogol simply made an all-out attempt to defend, indeed almost to sanctify, the conservative or reactionary alternative in modern Russian history with its central effort of preserving the separate worlds of the peasants and the educated with the chasm between them.

Nor did the proponents of this alternative disappear with the death of Gogol, or of Nicholas I, or even with the emancipation of the serfs. Perhaps not surprisingly, the most extreme and remarkable reactionary ideologists wrote late in the century, when the established order was in the process of dissolution. It was then that the statesman, professor, and thinker of the right, Konstantin Pobedonostsev (1827–1907), tried to stem by word and deed the flood of change, wishing even "to keep people from inventing things," while the writer and ideologist Konstantin Leontiev (1831–91) proclaimed it as his greatest desideratum "to freeze everything." Both Pobedonostsev and Leontiev, it should be added, placed their greatest hopes (declining hopes to be sure) in the power of the religious principle among the common Russian people, in what Leontiev considered to be the Byzantine element in old Russia.

Such Slavophiles as Khomyakov and Aksakov wanted "to join the common people." Proponents of Official Nationality of the Uvarov type were determined to keep this people in its place. Certain Russian intellectuals, however, were affected by both approaches and tried to combine them in some manner. A striking example of this syncretism is provided by the thought of Mikhail Pogodin, a publicist of the school of Official Nationality and a prominent historian, who stood close to the Slavophiles, admired Schelling, and accepted the intellectual premises of German romanticism.[23] Pogodin had himself emerged from a serf background, was professionally preoccupied all his adult life with problems of Russian history, and was distinguished for bluntness and a certain crudity. His brutal formula reflected well various intellectual crosscurrents, as well as the great dilemma that the peasant world presented to many educated Russians: "The Russian people is marvelous, but marvelous so far only in potentiality. In actuality it is low, horrid, and beastly."[24]

In the long run Uvarov's solution proved to be as utopian as Aksakov's: it was no more possible to hold the peasants in their place indefinitely than it was for the educated classes to join them. After the death of Nicholas I and the defeat in the Crimean War, the Russian government and a considerable segment of the upper layers of Russian society were ready for a change. The third alternative resolution to the problem of the peasant in nineteenth-century Russia, that of raising the peasant toward the level of the other classes, came to the fore.

Yet, although the emancipation of the serfs and the subsequent reforms struck Russia with a sudden and explosive force, reform had been prepared in advance, and in more ways than one. As far as the educated public was concerned, interest in the well-being of the peasants and a desire to improve their lot dated at least from the eighteenth century. Alexander Radishchev in particular has been called both the founder and the precursor of the Russian critical intelligentsia for his devastating attack on serfdom in *A Journey from St. Petersburg to Moscow,* which was published in 1790 and sent its author to Siberia. In the first half of the nineteenth century, the Decembrists, the Westernizers—as well as the Slavophiles as a group—and the Fourierist *Petrashevtsy,* together with many educated Russians who belonged to no distinct school of thought, desired emancipation. They saw the appalling contrast between their own conditions of life and those of the masses, and they were influenced by the example of the apparently happier countries in the West. It was especially among the Westernizers that interest in improving the lot of the common people became prominent, developing in two directions. Most Westernizers, moderates such as Timothy Granovsky, but also in large part the radical Belinsky, believed that Russia would and should follow the historical evolution of Western Europe with the growth of a middle class and the eventual transformation of the entire society. They took a wholly negative view of peasant life and rested their hopes on its ultimate transformation into a civilized existence. A few radical Westernizers, however, notably Alexander Herzen and Mikhail Bakunin, assumed, under the Slavophile influence, a more positive attitude toward the peasant world, and in particular toward the peasant commune. They and their later followers, the populists of all sorts, manifested a peculiarly Russian combination of aims by trying to elevate the peasant while preserving his style of life and institutions. The Granovsky approach and the Herzen approach to the transformation of Russia, and specifically to the solution of the peasant problem, competed for the allegiance of the Russian intelligentsia from the middle of the nineteenth century to the revolutions of 1917. The Marxist version of the solution represented, in its low estimate of the peasants and in its determination to abolish them altogether by eliminating the difference between town and country and between intellectual and physical work, an extreme form of the majoritarian Westernizer thought.

During the years preceding the emancipation, many educated Russians, whatever their specific views, had become convinced that it was time to abolish serfdom and to try to lift the masses to a better life. The abolishing and the lifting had to be done by the government, certainly not by the peasants themselves. With the almost unique exception of Bakunin, no Russian before the emancipation advocated a peasant revolution. Indeed the Decembrists, even when staging their own rebellion, were careful not to provoke the masses into action, while some of the gravest warnings of the dangers of a popular uprising were issued by Herzen.[25]

The reaction of the government to the problem of the peasant in nineteenth-century Russia cannot be entirely separated from that of the educated public to which the members of the government belonged. Growing humanitarian sentiment with its condemnation of serfdom penetrated high bureaucratic and court circles. Nevertheless, the authorities were likely to be even more impressed by state issues and needs. After the defeat in the Crimean War these needs became only too apparent: as already indicated, serfdom obstructed modernization in the army and in the country; in addition, the disturbances that it provoked represented a constant threat to law and order. Once the new Emperor, Alexander II, and his advisers became convinced of all this, they set the wheels of emancipation in motion. On the nineteenth of February, 1861, serfdom was abolished in Russia.

The emancipation of the serfs by Alexander II has been called the greatest legislative act in the history of mankind. It has also been mercilessly criticized as misguided, insufficient, and altogether disastrous. Considering the magnitude of the measure and its attendant legislation, and especially the dimensions of the problem, both points of view might be correct at the same time. The present volume contains Professor Emmons' important study, based on original research, of the great reform, which constitutes essential background for several other contributions. Without retracing the ground, it bears pointing out that the liberation of the serfs meant the irrevocable choice of what has been mentioned as the third solution to the problem of the peasant in nineteenth-century Russia: the lifting of the peasant toward the upper, educated layers of society. The liberation of the serfs was accompanied by a change in the status of the state peasants, and it thus affected fundamentally all tillers of the soil in Russia. Moreover, it made other "great reforms" meaningful and, indeed, possible. These included the establishment of local self-government, usually referred to as the *zemstvo* reform of 1864, the fundamental reform of the judiciary in the same year, the reform of city government in 1870, and the military reform of 1874, together with numerous other less striking measures in areas ranging from finance to the censorship. Russia was finally on the move.

For the ultimate failure of this movement to solve the pressing problems, and for the collapse of imperial Russia in a catastrophe, a number of reasons have been offered. Central, of course, were the scope, complexity, and difficulty of the issues involved. Although peasants received land at the time of the emancipation, and although they purchased more land in subsequent decades, their rapidly increasing numbers made the land shortage ever more acute and in particular contributed heavily to what came to be known as "the pauperization of the center." While Russian industry finally made great advances in the eighteen-nineties and again on the eve of the First World War, these advances were purchased by squeezing the peasant further and deepening penury in the countryside. Whereas industrialization and urban growth, together with the desperate rural situation, brought crowds of peasants into towns, the integration of the newcomers into city life proved to be slow and difficult. For that matter, the industrial workers themselves were not successfully integrated into Russian society before 1917. While after the *zemstvo* reform and many later measures education finally acquired a mass basis in Russia, a little more than half of the tsar's subjects were still illiterate at the time of the Revolution. And the political advance, which became prominent with the revolution of 1905 and the ensuing constitution, introduced grave new problems into Russian life. Finally, the ill-prepared empire of the Romanovs had to engage in a mortal struggle with a number of other powers, including the much more modern and efficient Germany. Professor Watters' grim picture of the condition of the country in the last decades of tsarist rule looks convincing on the whole. In fact, many historians, including the entire Marxist school, have judged that imperial Russia was doomed long before the fatal shot was fired in Sarajevo.

Perhaps, therefore, no successful outcome was possible for the Russian government when it gave up its policy of holding the line and made an effort to bring the peasants into modern life. Even then the way in which the government proceeded, the style, so to speak, of its defeat, deserves the attention of historians. And this attention is bound to increase as one allows more for voluntarism, for contingencies, for the fluid complexity and unpredictability of history. In terms of our analysis, it should be emphasized that the change of government policy in 1861 was decisive, but never complete. Indeed it was impossible to return to serfdom, to keeping peasants strictly in their former place. Yet the old policy of maintaining the status quo, of defending the established order of things, remained at least as an undercurrent to the new bid for change. Moreover, time and again, as in the reign of Alexander III and parts of the reign of Nicholas II, the old approach came to dominate government activity—aiming grotesquely to freeze the evolution of Russia at a given fluid moment of history. Nicholas I's and Uvarov's positions had at least been of longer duration and much better prepared.

In general, the reforming activity of the Russian government lacked ideology and vision. Alexander II had been a dutiful son of Nicholas I and an arch-conservative before he introduced, apparently out of what he considered to be sheer necessity, his epochal reforms. His enlightened assistants, such as the celebrated Miliutin brothers, can best be described as intelligent conservatives dedicated to the well-being of the existing autocratic state and its people. Sergei Witte, the chief modernizer of Russian economic life, was quite conservative in many of his other views. The point of this observation is not to condemn Witte or the Miliutins, who combined realism with enlightenment and managed to translate many of their useful ideas into practice, but to indicate certain limits to a reform effort that had no more extreme champions than these. To put it differently, if Uvarov was the most articulate ideologist of the Russian state in the first half of the nineteenth century, when the government was defending the status quo, its outstanding ideologist in the second half, when change came, was an even more determined representative of the extreme right, the already mentioned Pobedonostsev. No Russian sovereign of the second half of the nineteenth century, certainly not Alexander III or Nicholas II, showed as interested and favorable an attitude towards liberalism as had Alexander I. In fact, the government often moved to the right as public opinion shifted to the left.

Even when the government did introduce change, it frequently found it difficult to decide what change and how much of it would be most appropriate for the peasants. As in the case of the populists and of broad layers of the Russian educated public in general, the recurring issue was that of the preservation of the peasant way of life and institutions as against a modernization and transformation of rural Russia. Time and again the government opted for preservation, at least as long as this was at all feasible. Thus, to mention the crucial instance, the emancipation reform gave land to the peasant commune wherever it existed, not to individual peasants or peasant families. Professor Michael Petrovich's study provides a learned account of the origins and evolution of the peasant commune, and also of the opinions of educated Russians concerning that commune as well as concerning the history of the Russian peasantry in general. Professor Francis Watters' contribution analyzes comprehensively its operation in post-reform Russia. We are left with the impression of a genuinely native, if not necessarily immemorial, institution, which could be defended and upheld on many counts, but which nevertheless represented a major obstacle to the economic development and modernization of Russia. The authorities finally realized some of the drawbacks of the peasant commune in the years immediately preceding the First World War, when Pyotr Stolypin introduced his crucial but belated legislation to break it up. Somewhat similarly, the government for a long time did little to educate the peasant, or tried to confine him largely to parish schools, until, on the eve of the Revolution, the demand in the country for general education became simply too strong. In the legal field, emancipated serfs and other peasants were left subject to their own customary law, the excellent modern reform of the judiciary in 1864 thus remaining inapplicable to most Russians on most relevant occasions. That this was probably the most intelligent and even the only possible arrangement merely underlines the gravity of the basic problem.

History is rarely kind to logical schemes. Logically there could be three basic attitudes toward the chasm separating the Russian educated classes from Russian peasants, to the dichotomy of "society" and "people" in Russia. The first, for the educated classes "to join the people," remained purely utopian, although, like other utopias, it left a certain imprint on "real life." The second, to maintain the division, was the policy of the Russian government until the middle of the nineteenth century, but it proved untenable in the end. The third, to raise the peasants to the level of the educated classes, began with the emancipation of 1861 and was central to subsequent Russian history. Yet, delayed by the persisting force of reaction within the government, by the characteristic difficulty of determining the desirable peasant role in Russia, and, of course, by the enormity of the task itself, it was merely well begun when war and revolution brought imperial Russia crashing down. Professor Matossian's Ivanovs, buffeted and baffled by it all, nevertheless survived largely intact to present a major problem to the Soviet government, just as they had presented one to the government of the tsars. Their Soviet fate, however, belongs to another conference.

Notes

Notes

Introduction

1. V. I. Lenin, *Sochineniia,* 4th ed. (Moscow, 1946), VI, 325–96.
2. Moskva Institut marksisma-leninisma, *Vospominaniia o Vladimire Il'iche Lenine* (Moscow, 1956), I, 381.
3. Nicholas Vakar, *The Taproot of Soviet Society* (New York, 1961), p. 41.
4. Donald Mackenzie Wallace, *Russia* (New York, 1877), p. 501.
5. Vakar, p. 40.
6. Wallace, p. 88.
7. Vakar, pp. 34–37.
8. Robert E. MacMaster, *Danilevsky: A Russian Totalitarian Philosopher* (Cambridge, Mass., 1967), p. 50.
9. Franco Venturi's *Roots of Revolution* (New York, 1960), though inadequate in some respects, is still the best available work in English on the intellectual trends of this period.
10. I. M. Strakhovskii, *Krest'ianskii stroi* (St. Petersburg, 1905), I, 388.
11. Lenin, *Sochineniia* (Moscow, 1949), XXVI, 229.
12. Barrington Moore, Jr., *Social Origins of Dictatorship and Democracy* (Boston, 1966), p. 481.
13. Basile Kerblay, "The Peasant," *Survey,* No. 64 (July 1967), 99–107.
14. On the archival materials, published documents, and studies concerning the peasant disturbances in Russia in the nineteenth century and the beginning of the twentieth, see E. S. Paina, *Krest'ianskoe dvizhenie v Rossii v. XIX-nachale XX v.v.* (Moscow, 1963).
15. N. M. Druzhinin, *Gosudarstvennie krestiane i reforma P. D. Kiseleva* (Moscow, 1963).
16. P. A. Zaionchkovskii, *Provedenie v zhizn' krest'ianskoi reformy 1861 g.* (Moscow, 1958).
17. *Ezhegodnik po agrarnoi istorii vostochnoi Evropy* (Moscow, 1958). This volume contains materials of the sessions of Mezh respublikanskii simposium po agrarnoi istorii vostochnoi Evropy; since 1959 the *Ezhegodnik* has been published under the auspices of Akademiia nauk SSSR, Institut istorii.
18. The bulk of the ethnographic and anthropological work is done under the auspices of the Institut etnografii im. N. N. Miklukho-Maklaia in the Soviet Academy of Sciences. The Institute publishes separate monographs and symposia, as well as the series *Materialy po istorii zemledeliia SSSR,* 6 vols. (Moscow, 1952–1965). The studies purport to show how the forms of "national culture are being replaced by new ones, corresponding more closely to socialist social relations." Important ethnographic journals include *Sovetskaia etnografiia* and *Sbornik museia antropologii i etnografii.* On the ethnographic investigations in Russia since the founding of ethnography as a dis-

cipline in the beginning of the 1860's, see *Ocherk istorii russkoi etnografii, fol'kloristiki i antropologii,* Akademiia nauk SSSR, Trudy Instituta etnografii im. N. N. Miklukho-Maklaia (Moscow, 1956).

19. Anatole Leroy-Beaulieu, *The Empire of the Tsars and the Russians* (New York, 1893–96).

20. For publication data, see Note 4.

21. Geroid T. Robinson, *Rural Russia Under the Old Regime* (London, 1932).

22. Sir John Maynard, *The Russian Peasant and Other Studies* (London, 1942).

23. Cyril E. Black, ed., *The Transformation of Russian Society* (Cambridge, Mass., 1960).

24. Jerome Blum, *Lord and Peasant in Russia from the Ninth to the Nineteenth Century* (Princeton, 1961).

1. The Peasant Way of Life

1. Wright Miller, *The Russians as People* (New York, 1961), p. 64; A. F. L. M. Haxthausen, *The Russian Empire* (London, 1856), p. 21, and S. A. Tokarev, *Etnografiia narodov SSR: Istoricheskie osnovy byta i kul'tury* (Moscow, 1958), p. 51.

2. S. P. Tolstoi, *et al.,* eds. for the Akademiia nauk SSSR, Institut etnografii, *Narody Mira: Narody evropeiskoi chasti SSSR,* I (Moscow, 1964), 283–90. Hereafter cited as *Narody Mira.*

3. *Narody Mira,* pp. 298–303, and Tokarev, p. 85.

4. *Narody Mira,* pp. 305–10, and Haxthausen, p. 101.

5. Tokarev, pp. 57–59 and 69.

6. *Narody Mira,* pp. 309–10, and Haxthausen, p. 101.

7. Harold W. Williams, *Russia and the Russians* (New York, 1914), pp. 336–37; *Narody Mira,* p. 311; Tokarev, p. 65; and Wright Miller, p. 26.

8. Volodymyr Kubijovyc, ed., *Ukraine: A Concise Encyclopedia* (Toronto, 1963), pp. 306–7, and *Narody Mira,* p. 311.

9. *Narody Mira,* pp. 156–57.   10. *Ibid.,* p. 166.

11. *Ibid.,* pp. 106 and 170.   12. *Ibid.,* pp. 170–72.

13. *Ibid.,* pp. 167–83.

14. *Ibid.,* pp. 185–89, and W. R. S. Ralston, *Songs of the Russian People, As Illustrative of Slavic Mythology and Russian Social Life,* 2d ed. (London, 1872), p. 396.

15. *Narody Mira,* pp. 222–30, and Tokarev, *Etnografiia . . . ,* pp. 48–49.

16. *Narody Mira,* pp. 363–64.

17. John Maynard, *Russia in Flux* (New York, 1962), p. 52.

18. *Narody Mira,* pp. 393–99.

19. *Ibid.,* pp. 371 and 376, and Tokarev, pp. 71–72 and 76–77.

20. *Narody Mira,* pp. 371–76, and Tokarev, pp. 71–78.

21. *Narody Mira,* pp. 462–64, and Tokarev, p. 28.

22. Vera Sandomirsky Dunham, "The Strong-Woman Motif," in Cyril Black, ed., *Transformation of Russian Society* (Cambridge, Mass., 1960), pp. 459–83.

23. Eric Wolf, *Peasants* (Englewood Cliffs, N.J., 1966), pp. 65–70, and *Narody Mira,* p. 468.

24. Lev A. Tikhomirov, *Russia, Political and Social,* I (London, 1888), 187, and Haxthausen, *The Russian Empire,* p. 123.

25. Y. M. Sokolov, *Russian Folklore* (New York, 1950), p. 163; Tokarev, *Etnografiia*..., p. 86; and Ralston, *Songs of the Russian People*..., pp. 134–38.

26. *Narody Mira*, p. 408, and Ralston, pp. 126–27, 135, and 138.

27. Sokolov, pp. 164–66.

28. For descriptions of difficult deliveries see Anton Chekhov, "The Name-Day Party," and John Rickman, "Placenta Praevia" in *The People of Great Russia* (New York, 1962).

29. Tokarev, p. 85, and *Narody Mira*, pp. 467–68.

30. *Narody Mira*, pp. 408–9, 468–69, and 187.

31. *Ibid.*, p. 469.   32. Sokolov, p. 216.

33. *Narody Mira*, pp. 497 and 879.

34. The foregoing account of the wedding ritual is drawn mainly from *Narody Mira*, pp. 469–72, with contributions from Tokarev, *Etnografiia*..., pp. 83–84, and Sokolov, p. 206.

35. *Narody Mira*, pp. 472–73; Tokarev, p. 85; Sokolov, *Russian Folklore*, pp. 224–25; Ralston, pp. 309–19; and *Ukraine Encyclopedia*, pp. 345–46.

36. *Narody Mira*, pp. 170 and 406–8.

37. *Ibid.*, p. 410.   38. *Ibid.*, pp. 163 and 199.

39. *Ibid.*, pp. 394 and 413–14.   40. *Ibid.*, p. 399.

41. Ralston, *Songs of the Russian People*..., pp. 200–201 and 283–84.

42. Angelo S. Rappoport, *Home Life in Russia* (New York, 1913), p. 64, and *Narody Mira*, p. 414.

43. *Ibid.*, p. 414.

44. *Ibid.*, p. 163.

45. *Narody Mira*, pp. 394 and 415, and Sokolov, *Russian Folklore*, pp. 191–92. Rappoport says that the "spirit of Maslenitsa" was represented by a drunken man in a dirty cart bristling with brooms. The cart was pulled by ten horses, each with a rider dressed in rags, his face blackened with soot, and carrying a whip, broom, or other household tool. The cart went from one *derevnia* to another announcing the end of Maslenitsa (*Home Life in Russia*, p. 38).

46. *Narody Mira*, pp. 394 and 415, and Sokolov, pp. 191–92.

47. Miller, *The Russians as People*, pp. 27–29.

48. *Narody Mira*, pp. 394 and 415.   49. *Ibid.*, pp. 182–83.

50. *Ibid.*, p. 186.   51. *Ibid.*, p. 163; Miller, p. 30.

52. Sokolov, pp. 195–96; *Narody Mira*, p. 416; and Ralston, pp. 239–40 and 391.

53. Sokolov, p. 195, and Ralston, pp. 143–44 and 244–45.

54. Sokolov, p. 196; and *Narody Mira*, p. 186. In the Ukraine this is the day for the "maiden fair." The girls of the *selo* and its satellite *derevni* promenade in the center of town in the hope of catching the eye and heart of a desirable young man (*Ukraine Encyclopedia*, p. 331).

55. *Narody Mira*, pp. 174–77; Sokolov, p. 198; and Ralston, pp. 249–50.

56. *Narody Mira*, p. 186.

57. *Ibid.*, p. 188.

58. Ralston, *Songs of the Russian People*..., pp. 254–55.

59. Sokolov, *Russian Folklore*, p. 200.

60. Sokolov, pp. 198–99; Ralston, p. 251; *Narody Mira*, p. 174.

61. *Narody Mira*, pp. 177–80.

62. *Ibid.*, p. 416, and Ralston, p. 256.

2. The Peasant and the Emancipation

1. *Materialy dlia istorii uprazdneniia krepostnogo sostoianiia pomeshchich'ikh krest'ian v Rossii v tsarstvovanie Imperatora Aleksandra II* (Berlin, 1860), I, 113–14.

2. N. Tsagolov, *Ocherki russkoi ekonomicheskoi mysli perioda padeniia krepostnogo prava* (Moscow, 1956), pp. 27–28.

3. M. Confino, *Domaines et seigneurs en Russie vers la fin du XVIIIe siècle* (Paris, 1963).

4. Cf. M. Tugan-Baranovskii, *Russkaia fabrika v proshlom i nastoiashchem,* 7th ed. (Moscow, 1938), pp. 423–25; and Alexander Gerschenkron, "Agrarian Policies and Industrialization, Russia 1861–1917," in *Cambridge Economic History of Europe,* Vol. VI, part 2 (Cambridge, 1965), pp. 707–12.

5. Cf. A. Skerpan, "The Russian National Economy and Emancipation," in A. Ferguson and Alfred Levin, eds., *Essays in Russian History. A Collection Dedicated to George Vernadsky* (Hamden, Conn., 1964), pp. 165–68.

6. See below, p. 49.

7. This was the message of an important memorandum presented to Alexander II in October 1856, by one of the chief architects of the reform legislation, Nicholas Miliutin (*Tsentralnyi gosudarstvennyi istoricheskii arkhiv SSSR, g. Leningrad,* f. 1180, No. 85, pp. 437–57).

8. Cf. P. Péchoux, "L'ombre de Pugačev," in R. Portal, ed., *Le statut des paysans libérés du servage, 1861–1961* (Paris and The Hague, 1962), pp. 128–52.

9. Quoted in P. A. Zaionchkovskii, *Otmena krepostnogo prava v. Rosii* (Moscow, 1954), p. 48.

10. A. I. Koshelev, *Zapiski. (1812–1883)* (Berlin, 1884), p. 90.

11. This was the general import of what was in fact a complex of rumors with differing details. Cf. I. Ignatovich, "Krest'ianskie volneniia," in *Velikaia reforma. Russkoe obshchestvo i krest'ianskii vopros v proshlom i v nastoiashchem,* (Moscow, 1911), III, 55–61.

12. For an introduction to the controversy, compare the treatments of P. Liashchenko, *History of the National Economy of Russia to the 1917 Revolution* (New York, 1949); and J. Blum, *Lord and Peasant in Russia from the Ninth to the Nineteenth Century* (Princeton, 1961).

13. Zaionchkovskii, *Otmena krepostnogo prava,* p. 93.

14. *Ibid.,* p. 48.

15. *Tsentralnyi gosudarstvennyi arkhiv Oktiabr'skoi revoliutsii,* Moscow. (Hereafter cited as *TsGAOR.*) *Otchet III otdeleniia za 1858 g., pp. 126–26a.* Cf. V. A. Fedorov, "Trebovaniia krest'ianskogo dvizheniia v nachale revoliutsionnoi situatsii," in *Revoliutsionnaia situatsiia v Rossii v 1859–1861 gg.* (Moscow, 1960), pp. 133–48.

16. Zaionchkovskii, *Otmena krepostnogo prava,* pp. 92–93.

17. Cf. Ignatovich, "Krest'ianskie volneniia," pp. 63–64.

18. *TsGAOR, Otchet III otdeleniia za 1858 g.,* p. 126.

19. I. Ignatovich, "Otrazhenie v Rossii krest'ianskogo dvizheniia v Galitsii 1846 goda," in *Sbornik trudov professorov i prepodavatelei gos. Irkutskogo universiteta. Vypusk V* (1923), 161–208.

20. Fedorov, "Trebovaniia," p. 143.

21. *TsGAOR, Otchet . . . za 1858 g.,* p. 126a.

22. This argument was used extensively in the writings of such liberal publicists

as K. D. Kavelin, A. I. Koshelev, and B. I. Chicherin between 1855–57, and was subsequently adopted by those landed-gentry deputies who, when called upon by the government to discuss reform, proposed that land be given with emancipation.

23. Fedorov, "Trebovaniia," pp. 137ff.

24. G. Dzhanshiev, *Epokha velikikh reform* (Moscow, 1900), pp. 39–42.

25. P. A. Zaionchkovskii, *Provedenie v zhizn' krest'ianskoi reformy 1861 g.* (Moscow, 1958), pp. 24ff.

26. These reports, which have been published, form one of the main sources of information about the peasant reaction to the emancipation: *Krest'ianskoe dvizhenie v 1861 godu posle otmeny krepostnogo prava. Chast' I i II. Doneseniia svitshikh generalov i fligel' -ad'iutantov, gubernskikh prokurorov i uezdnikh striapchikh* (Moscow and Leningrad, 1949).

27. *Krest'ianskaia reforma v Rossii. Sbornik zakonodatel'skikh aktov* (Moscow, 1954), pp. 47–66, 135–58.

28. *Otmena krepostnogo prava. Doklady ministrov vnutrennikh del o provedenii krest'ianskoi reformy 1861–1862* (Moscow and Leningrad, 1950); E. A. Morokhovets, ed., *Krest'ianskoe dvizhenie 1827–1869. Vypusk II* (Moscow and Leningrad, 1931); *Krest'ianskoe dvizhenie v Rossii v 1857–mae 1861 gg.* (Moscow, 1963).

29. Zaionchkovskii, *Provedenie v zhizn'*, p. 64.

30. *Ibid.*, p. 65.

31. *Krest'ianskoe dvizhenie, 1827–1869*, II, 20–21.

32. *Krest'ianskoe dvizhenie v Rossii v 1857–mae 1861 gg.*, pp. 569–736; *Krest'ianskoe dvizhenie v Rossii v 1861–1869 gg.* (Moscow, 1964), pp. 599–697.

33. *Krest'ianskoe dvizhenie v Rossii v 1857–mae 1861 g.*, "Khronika."

34. From peasant testimony before the commission, quoted in I. Ignatovich, "Bezdna," *Velikaia reforma*, V, 212.

35. *Ibid.*

36. *Krest'ianskoe dvizhenie v Rossii v 1857–mae 1861 g.*, p. 358.

37. *Ibid.*   38. *Ibid.*, p. 360.

39. Zaionchkovskii, *Provedenie v zhizn'*, p. 68.

40. Quoted in Zaionchkovskii, *Provedenie v zhizn'*, p. 72.

41. *Krest' ianskoe dvizhenie v Rossii v 1857–mae 1861 gg.*, pp. 430–33.

42. Zaionchkovskii, *Provedenie v zhizn'*, p. 74.

43. V. A. Fedorov, "Lozungi krest'ianskoi bor'by v 1861–1863 gg.," in *Revoliutsionnaia situatsiia v Rossii v 1859–1861 gg.* (Moscow, 1963), pp. 245ff.

44. *Ibid.*, pp. 245–46.

45. F. Venturi, *Roots of Revolution* (New York, 1960), p. 310.

46. *Krest'ianskoe dvizhenie v Rossii v 1861–1869 gg.*, "Khronika."

47. Fedorov, "Lozungi krest'ianskoi bor'by," p. 246.

48. Quoted in Zaionchkovskii, *Provedenie v zhizn'*, p. 97.

49. *Krest'ianskoe dvizhenie v Rossii v 1861–1869 gg.*, pp. 798–800.

50. *Krest'ianskoe dvizhenie v 1857–mae 1861 gg.*, p. 736; *Krest'ianskoe dvizhenie v 1861–1869 gg.*, pp. 798–800.

51. Zaionchkovskii, *Provedenie v zhizn'*, pp. 107–8.

52. *Ibid.*, pp. 103–4.

53. Soviet historians have, by and large, emphasized the "class-*pomeshchik*" character of the activities of the mediators. Cf. *ibid.*, pp. 88–93; M. Naidenov, *Klassovaia bor'ba v poreformennoi derevne (1861–1863 gg.)* (Moscow, 1955), pp. 170–91.

54. A. Kornilov, "Deiatel'nost' mirovykh posrednikov," *Velikaia reforma,* V, 237–52.

55. Fedorov, "Lozungi krest'ianskoi bor'by," p. 247.

56. I. Miller, " 'Slushnyi chas' i taktika russkoi revoliutsionnoi partii v 1861–1863 gg.," in *Revoliutsionnaia situatsiia v Rossii v 1859–1861 gg.* (Moscow, 1963), p. 148.

57. Cf. Zaionchkovskii, *Provedenie v zhizn',* pp. 104–5; Fedorov, "Lozungi krest'ianskoi bor'by," pp. 247–50; Naidenov, *Klassovaia bor'ba,* pp. 214–29.

58. Quoted in Zaionchkovskii, *Provdenie v zhizn',* pp. 99–100.

59. *Krest'ianskoe dvizhenie v Rossii v 1861–1869 gg.,* "Khronika."

60. Zaionchkovskii, *Provedenie v zhizn',* p. 104.

61. Naidenov, *Klassovaia bor'ba,* p. 307.

62. *TsGAOR, Otchet III otdeleniia za 1862 g.,* p. 92a.

63. Naidenov, *Klassovaia bor'ba,* pp. 307–13; *Krest'ianskoe dvizhenie v Rossii v 1861–1869 gg.,* "Khronika."

64. *Velikaia reforma,* VI, 84.

65. *Otmena krepostnogo prava,* p. 68.

66. *Krest'ianskoe dvizhenie, 1827–1869 gg.,* p. 22.

67. N. Vakar, *The Taproot of Soviet Society* (New York, 1961), pp. 40–41.

68. M. Cherniavsky, *Tsar and People: Studies in Russian Myths* (New Haven and London, 1961), p. 95.

3. The Peasant and Religion

1. I. I. Sreznevskii, *Materialy dlia slovaria drevnerusskogo iazyka* (Photoreproduction of 1893 edition, Moscow, n.d.), I, cols. 1343–44.

2. A. G. Preobrazhensky, *Etymological Dictionary of the Russian Language* (New York, 1951), p. 384, and Max Vasmer, *Russisches etymologisches Wörterbuch,* 3 vols. (Heidelberg, 1953–58), I, 662.

3. Donald M. Wallace, *Russia: On the Eve of War and Revolution,* Cyril E. Black, ed. (New York, 1961), p. 385. The first edition appeared in 1877.

4. Apparently there have been only two serious studies of Great Russian villages: P. I. Kushner, *Selo Viriatino v proshlom i nastoiashchem: Opyt etnograficheskogo izucheniia russkoi kolkhoznoi derevni* (Moscow, 1958), and L. A. Anokhina and M. N. Shmeleva, *Kul'tura i byt kolkhoznikov Kalininskoi oblasti* (Moscow, 1964). Neither study pays any perceptible attention to religion. The Kushner book is discussed in Stephen P. Dunn and Ethel Dunn, "The Great Russian Peasant: Culture Change or Cultural Development," *Ethnology,* II (July 1963), 320–38; the Anokhina-Shmeleva book has been extensively used, the authors inform me, in the forthcoming book by Dr. and Mrs. Dunn entitled *The Peasants of Central Russia.*

5. V. G. Belinsky, *Selected Philosophical Works* (Moscow, 1956), p. 540.

6. Quoted from *Istorik-Marksist,* III (1927), 9–10, by Anatole G. Mazour, *Modern Russian Historiography,* 2d ed. (Princeton, 1958), p. 147.

7. *"Ispoved' "* V. I. Kel'sieva in *Literaturnoe nasledstvo,* Nos. 41–42 (Moscow, 1941), 285, as quoted in Franco Venturi, *Roots of Revolution,* trans., Francis Haskell (New York, 1960), p. 115.

8. Nicolas Zernov, *The Russian Religious Renaissance of the Twentieth Century* (New York and Evanston, 1963), p. 18.

9. See the articles in Brockhaus-Efron, *Entsiklopedicheskii Slovar',* entitled "Iakov Vasilevich Abramov," Aleksandr Stepanovich Prugavin," and "Iosif Ivanovich Kab-

lits." Additional examples are given in A. I. Klibanov, *Istoriia religioznogo sektantstva v Rossii (60-e gody xix v.-1917 g.)*, Izdatel'stvo "Nauka" (Moscow, 1965), pp. 17–18.

10. Cited in Stepniak, *The Russian Peasantry* (New York, 1888), pp. 221–22. Kravchinsky's italics.

11. *Ibid.*, p. 229.　　　　　　　　12. *Ibid.*, p. 210.

13. *Ibid.*, pp. 374 and 394–95.　　　14. *Ibid.*, pp. 234–35.

15. Michael Cherniavsky, "The Old Believers and the New Religion," *Slavic Review*, XXV (March 1966), 1–39.

16. See Stepniak, p. 354.

17. In the *Kherson Diocesan Messenger,* as quoted in *ibid.*, p. 351.

18. For the discussion which follows, facts were drawn from the following, except where otherwise noted: F. C. Conybeare, *Russian Dissenters* (Cambridge, Mass., 1921); Serge Bolshakoff, *Russian Nonconformity* (Philadelphia, 1950); Stepniak, *The Russian Peasantry*; and for the sects alone (the Old Believers are not included), A. I. Klibanov, *Istoriia religioznogo sektantstva v Rossii.* The dependability of the first two may be illustrated by the fact that Conybeare speaks of the "English Methodist, Young Stilling" (p. 322) when he means the German mystic Jung (Stilling), and that Bolshakoff speaks of Vladimir Soloviev as a Roman Catholic (pp. 117–18); moreover, Conybeare makes no pretense whatever to objectivity. Klibanov's scholarship is painstaking, but his analysis seldom rises above the level of such statements as: "Baptism was where capitalism was, where the village was producing a kulak upper crust at the expense of the impoverishment and pauperization of the majority of the peasants" (p. 193). A scholarly account of Russian religious dissidence up to the present or even up to the Revolution apparently remains to be written.

19. See Serge A. Zenkovsky, "The Ideological World of the Denisov Brothers," *Harvard Slavic Studies,* III (Cambridge, Mass., 1957), 49–66.

20. Stepniak, p. 276.

21. V. V. Andreev, *Raskol i ego znachenie v narodnoi russkoi istorii* (Photoreproduction of 1870 edition; Osnabrück, 1965), pp. 188–89.

22. Conybeare, p. 177.　　　　　　　23. *Ibid.*, p. 184.

24. See Vladimir Bonch-Bruevich, ed., *Materialy k istorii i izucheniiu russkago sektantstva i raskola,* IV (St. Petersburg, 1911), "Novyi Izrail'."

25. Martin Kilcoyne, "The Political Influence of Rasputin." Unpublished dissertation, University of Washington, 1961, pp. 23–31. See the interesting observations of George Katkov, *Russia 1917: The February Revolution* (New York, 1967), pp. 204–7.

26. Ernest J. Simmons, *Leo Tolstoy* (London, 1949), pp. 393–400.

27. Novitskii, *O dukhobortsakh* (Kiev, 1832), as quoted by "Iu.," "Dukhovnye khristiane," *Viestnik Evropy,* Nov. 1880, p. 8.

28. Robert Redfield, *Peasant Society and Culture: An Anthropological Approach to Civilization* (Chicago, 1956), p. 68.

29. George M. Foster, "What is Folk Culture?," *American Anthropologist,* LV, No. 2, Pt. 1 (April–June 1953), p. 164; as quoted in Redfield, p. 69.

30. *Ibid.*, p. 70.

31. P. Znamensky, *Prikhodnoe dukhovenstvo v Rossii so vremeni reformy Petra* (Kazan, 1873), p. 669.

32. Quoted in *ibid.*, pp. 720–21.

33. *Ibid.*, p. 670.

34. Quoted in Wallace, *Russia: On the Eve . . .*, p. 379.

35. Ernest Poole, *The Village: Russian Impressions* (New York, 1919), pp. 155–63.

36. Charles Roden Buxton, *In a Russian Village* (London, 1922), p. 75.
37. Harold Whitmore Williams, *Russia of the Russians* (London, 1917), pp. 147–48.
38. Bonch-Bruevich, ed., *Materialy k istorii i izucheniiu russkago sektantstva i raskola,* VII (St. Petersburg, 1916), xxvii.
39. Buxton, p. 36.
40. Maurice Baring, *The Russian People,* 2d ed. (London, n.d.), p. 350.
41. Nicholas Vakar, *The Taproot of Soviet Society* (New York, 1961), p. 120. Vakar was obviously not using the term "primitive" in Redfield's sense.
42. Klibanov, *Istoriia religioznogo . . . ,* p. 335.
43. In 1961 in the village of Konstantinovka, Petrovsky *raion,* Stavropol *krai,* 57 per cent of the homes had icons; in the village of Strigovo, Kobrinsky *raion,* Mogilev *oblast,* seven out of eight homes had them. (I. P. Tsamerian *et al.,* eds., *Stroitel'stvo kommunizma i preodolenie religioznykh perezhitkov,* Izd. "Nauka" [Moscow, 1966]. The original was unavailable to me at the time of writing, and the facts came from the U.S. Joint Publications Research Service translation of excerpts, p. 41.)

4. The Peasant and the Army

1. Kh. I. Muratov. *Revoliutsionnoe dvizhenie v Russkoi armii v 1905–1907 gg.* (Moscow, 1955), pp. 8–9.
2. Lev Trotskii, *Kak vooruzhalas' revoliutsiia,* 3 vols. in 5 (Moscow, 1923–25).
3. Lev Trotskii, *1905: Perspektivy russkoi revoliutsii,* 2d ed. (Moscow, 1922).
4. John S. Curtiss, *The Russian Army under Nicholas I, 1825–1855* (Durham, N.C., 1965), pp. 232–37.
5. *Ibid.,* pp. 240–42.
6. *Ibid.,* pp. 238–44.
7. *Ibid.,* pp. 277–85.
8. *Ibid.,* pp. 273–78.
9. *Ibid.,* pp. 111–19.
10. *Ibid.,* pp. 131–36.
11. *Ibid.,* pp. 120–23.
12. *Ibid.,* pp. 145–51.
13. *Ibid.,* pp. 246–47.
14. *Ibid.,* pp. 212–18, 220–24.
15. *Ibid.,* pp. 242–52.
16. *Ibid.,* pp. 255–62.
17. *Ibid.,* pp. 267–72.
18. *Ibid.,* pp. 355–58.
19. P. A. Zaionchkovskii, *Voennye reformy 1860–1870 godov v Rossii* (Moscow, 1952), pp. 47–49.
20. A. V. Fedorov, *Russkaia armiia v 50–70 gg. XIX veka. Ocherki* (Leningrad, 1959), p. 274.
21. Zaionchkovskii, pp. 214–15.
22. *Ibid.,* pp. 211–13.
23. *Ibid.,* pp. 218–19.
24. *Ibid.,* pp. 187–91.
25. *Ibid.,* pp. 124–25.
26. Fedorov, p. 274.
27. *Ibid.,* p. 281.
28. F. V. Greene, *Sketches of Army Life in Russia* (New York, 1881), pp. 25–26.
29. *Ibid.,* pp. 328–29.
30. *Ibid.,* p. 369.
31. *Ibid.,* pp. 201–2.
32. *Ibid.,* pp. 22–23.
33. *Ibid.,* p. 87.
34. *Ibid.,* p. 27.
35. *Ibid.,* pp. 12–13.
36. *Ibid.,* pp. 10–11.
37. M. I. Bogdanovich, *Istoricheskii ocherk deiatel'nosti voennago upravleniia v Rossii v pervoe dvadtsatipiatiletie blagopoluchnago tsarstvovaniia gosudaria imperatora Aleksandra Nikolaevicha (1855–1880)* (St. Petersburg, 1879–81), VI, *Prilozhenie,* 118.

38. Curtiss, *The Russian Army*, p. 250.

39. Bogdanovich, VI, 400–406.

40. Fedorov, *Russkaia armiia*, p. 280; see also N. N. Golovine, *The Russian Army in the World War* (New Haven, 1931), p. 11.

41. M. Akhum and D. Zinevich, "Iz istorii bor'by samoderzhaviia s revoliutsionnym dvizheniem v armii v 80-kh gg. XIX veka," *Krasnyi Arkhiv*, II (1922), 19–20.

42. [A. N. Kuropatkin], "Dnevnik Kuropatkina," *Krasnyi Arkhiv*, II (1922), 19–20.

43. *Ibid.*, p. 13.   44. *Ibid.*, p. 40.

45. *Ibid.*, pp. 52–53.

46. A. N. Kuropatkin, *The Russian Army and the Japanese War*, I (London, 1909), 297.

47. *Ibid.*

48. A. I. Denikin, *Put' Russkogo ofitsera* (New York, 1953), p. 120.

49. *Ibid.*

50. A. F. Rediger, "Zapiski o 1905 g.," *Krasnyi Arkhiv*, XLV (1931), 92.

51. M. Semin, "Zhizn' soldatov v tsarskoi armii," *Krasnyi Arkhiv*, XCVIII (1940), 147–48.

52. *Ibid.*, pp. 160–61.

53. *Ibid.*, pp. 161–63.

54. Denikin, *Put' Russkogo ofitsera*, pp. 121–22.

55. A. I. Denikin, *Ocherki Russkoi smuty*, I (Paris and Berlin, 1922–26), Part I, pp. 24–25.

56. A. A. Ignat'ev, *50 let v stroiu* (Moscow, 1948), p. 150.

57. *Ibid.*, p. 146.

58. A. I. Spiridovich, "Pri tsarskom rezhime," *Arkhiv russkoi revoliutsii*, XV, 105.

59. Semin, "Zhizn' soldatov," pp. 148–49.

60. *Ibid.*, p. 157.   61. *Ibid.*, pp. 158–59.

62. *Ibid.*, pp. 164–65.   63. *Ibid.*, pp. 165–67.

64. Ignat'ev, *50 let v stroiu*, p. 72.

65. Paul Rodzianko, *Tattered Banners* (London, 1939), p. 87.

66. *Ibid.*, pp. 83–84.

67. Robert P. Browder and Alexander F. Kerensky, eds., *The Russian Provisional Government, 1917: Documents*, II (Stanford, 1961), 848 and 853.

68. Leon Trotsky, *The Russian Revolution*, I (New York, 1932), 259.

69. Ignat'ev, pp. 95–96.

70. A. A. Brusilov, *Moi vospominaniia* (Moscow, 1963), pp. 47–48.

71. [A. F. Rediger], "Iz zapisok A. F. Redigera," *Krasnyi Arkhiv*, Vol. V (Vol. LX, old series) (1933), p. 117.

72. "Iz istorii 'ideologicheskoi' bor'by samoderzhaviia s revoliutsionnym dvizheniem v armii," *Krasnyi Arkhiv*, XLIV (1931), 167–70.

73. Muratov, *Revoliutsionnoe dvizhenie*, p. 60.

74. Denikin, *Ocherki*, I, Part I, pp. 8–9.

75. Fedorov, *Russkaia armiia*, pp. 281–82.

76. Kuropatkin, *The Russian Army*, II, 122–23.

77. *Ibid.*, II, 116.

78. Iu. N. Danilov, *Rossiia v mirovoi voine, 1914–1915 gg.* (Berlin, 1924), p. 27.

79. Kuropatkin, *The Russian Army*, II, 124.

5. The Peasant and the Village Commune

1. Sir John Maynard, *Russia in Flux* (London, 1949), p. 23.
2. K. R. Kachorovskii, *Russkaia obshchina,* 2d ed. (Moscow, 1906), p. 71.
3. Lazar Volin, "The Peasant Household under the Mir and the Kolkhoz in Modern Russian History," in Caroline F. Ware, ed., *The Cultural Approach to History* (New York, 1940), pp. 125ff.
4. A. Leont'ev, "Obshchinnoe zemlevladenie," in F. A. Brokgaus, ed., *Novyi entsiklopedicheskii slovar,* XXIX (Petrograd, 1916), 182.
5. *Ibid.*
6. *Ibid.,* pp. 182–83.
7. Alexis N. Antsiferov *et al., Russian Agriculture during the War* (New Haven, Conn., 1930), p. 20.
8. Jerome Blum, *Lord and Peasant in Russia from the Ninth to the Nineteenth Century* (Princeton, N.J., 1961), pp. 512ff.
9. Geroid T. Robinson, *Rural Russia under the Old Regime* (New York, 1932), p. 74.
10. *Ibid.*
11. *Ibid.*
12. Theodore H. Von Laue, "Russian Peasants in the Factory, 1892–1904," *Journal of Economic History,* XXI, 1 (March 1961), 65.
13. A. Kaufman, "Pozemel'naia obshchina," in Brokgaus, ed., *Entsiklopedicheskii slovar,* XXIV (St. Petersburg, 1898), 207.
14. Robinson, p. 121.
15. Kachorovskii, *Russkaia obshchina,* pp. 77–78.
16. Kaufman, p. 215.
17. F. L. Barikov *et al., Sbornik materialov dlia izucheniia sel'skoi pozemel'noi obshchiny* (St. Petersburg, 1880), pp. 9ff.
18. *Svod trudov mestnykh komitetov po 49 guberniam Evropeiskoi Rossii* (St. Petersburg, 1902–5), II, 78, as quoted in Harry Dorosh, *The Russian Agrarian Reform* (Philadelphia, 1937), p. 8.
19. Kaufman, p. 217.
20. *Ibid.*
21. Dorosh, *The Russian Agrarian Reform,* p. 8.
22. N. Kablukov, *Ob usloviiakh razvitiia krest'ianskogo khoziaistva v Rossii,* 2d ed. (Moscow, 1908), pp. 210–18.
23. It follows that Blum is not altogether accurate in his statement that communal land tenure was "conspicuously absent in the Little Russian provinces of Chernigov, Poltava, and parts of Kharkov" (*Lord and Peasant in Russia,* p. 522).
24. *Statisticheskiia svedeniia po zemel'nomu voprosu v Evropeiskoi Rossii* (St. Petersburg, 1906), pp. 20–33.
25. Leo Litoshenko, "Landed Property in Russia," *Russian Review,* II, 4 (1913), 200.
26. *Svod statisticheskikh svedenii po sel'skomu khoziaistva Rossii k kontsu XIX veka,* I (St. Petersburg, 1902), 27. The figure for 1877 omits the Don Oblast; the figure for 1887 omits the *gubernias* of Penza, Astrakhan, and Lifland, and the Don Oblast. *Statistika zemlevladeniia 1905 g.* (St. Petersburg, 1906), Vols. I through L, pp. 10–14 of each volume, excluding Vols. I, IX, XXVII, and L, which were missing from the Hoover Library. The figure for 1905 was computed from *gubernia* data from this

source by the author. *Gubernias* for which data are lacking for 1905 are Podolia, Vitebsk, Lifland, Moscow, and Courland.

27. *Statistika zemlevladeniia,* pp. 11–13 of each volume.

28. Litoshenko, p. 201.

29. *Statistika zemlevladeniia.*

30. Litoshenko, p. 201.

31. Dorosh, *The Russian Agrarian Reform,* p. 11.

32. A. M. Anfimov, *Zemel'naia arenda v Rossii v nachale XX veka* (Moscow, 1961), p. 13.

33. *Statisticheskiia svedeniia,* pp. 37–41.

34. A. Diadichenko and L. Chermak, *Statisticheskii spravochnik,* II (St. Petersburg, 1906), 89–93.

35. P. Kh. Shvanebakh, *Nashe podatnoe delo* (St. Petersburg, 1903), pp. 159–60.

36. Iu. Ianson, *Opyt statisticheskago izsledovaniia o krest'ianskikh nadelakh i platezhakh* (St. Petersburg, 1877), pp. 123–24.

37. *Ibid.,* p. 120.

38. Aleksandr I. Vasil'chikov, *Zemlevladenie i zemledelie v Rossii i v drugikh Evropeiskikh gosudarstvakh* (St. Petersburg, 1876), p. 545.

39. L. Khodskii, "Vykupnaia operatsia," in F. A. Brokgaus, ed., *Entsiklopedicheskii slovar,* VII (St. Petersburg, 1896), 514–15.

6. The Peasant and the Factory

1. "Russian Labor Between Field and Factory, 1892–1903," *California Slavic Studies,* III, 1964, pp. 33–65.

2. *Ibid.,* p. 64.

3. "The Problem of Social Stability in Urban Russia, 1905–1917," Part 1, *Slavic Review,* XXIII, No. 4 (Dec. 1964), pp. 619–42.

4. *Polnoe sobranie zakonov Rossiiskoi Imperii,* 1st Series, VI, No. 3711 (hereafter cited in footnotes as *PSZ*). See also Iu. Gessen, "Prinuditel'noe obrashchenie pomeshchich'ikh krest'ian v gornozavodskie rabochie," *Arkhiv istorii truda v Rossii,* I (1921), p. 48; V. I. Semevskii, *Krest'iane v tsarstvovanie Imperatritsy Ekateriny II,* I (St. Petersburg, 1881), pp. 393–94; Bertrand Gille, *Histoire économique et sociale de la Russie du moyen age au XXᵉ siècle* (Paris, 1949), p. 88.

5. *PSZ,* XIII, No. 9954; Semevskii, p. 394; Gessen, pp. 48–49.

6. *PSZ,* XV, 11490; Gessen, p. 49; Semevskii, pp. 394–95.

7. *PSZ,* XXV, No. 18442; Semevskii, p. 393; Gessen, p. 49.

8. *PSZ,* XXVII, No. 20352; Semevskii, pp. 396–97.

9. *PSZ,* XXIX, No. 22498; *PSZ,* XXX, No. 23132.

10. *PSZ,* XXXIII, No. 26504. Certain categories of factories were excepted. In theory, this prohibition was a temporary measure.

11. K. A. Pazhitnov, *Polozhenie rabochego klassa v Rossii* I (Petrograd, 1923), 47.

12. See M. P. Viatkin, ed., *Ocherki istorii Leningrada,* I (Moscow and Leningrad, 1955), 279–80.

13. N. I. Pavlenko, "K voprosu ob evoliutsii dvorianstva v XVII–XVIII vv.," in V. V. Mavrodin, ed., *Voprosy genezisa kapitalizma v Rossii* (Leningrad, 1960), pp. 70–75.

14. I refer specifically to chapters I through V of the section entitled "Possessional Peasants," as well as to Semevskii's general chapter on serf unrest. Semevskii's study has not been superseded in either pre-Soviet or Soviet historiography, although the latter has dealt fairly extensively with the general question of Russian industry in the eighteenth century. See for example, P. G. Liubomirov, *Ocherki po istorii russkoi promyshlennosti XVII, XVIII i nachala XIX veka* (Moscow, 1947). No collection of documents comparable to Pankratova's multi-volume *Rabochee dvizhenie v Rossii v XIX veke* has been put together by Soviet experts on the eighteenth century.

15. Semevskii, pp. 353, 374.
16. *Ibid.*, pp. 353–58.
17. *Ibid.*, p. 449n.
18. *Ibid.*, pp. 450–52.
19. *Ibid.*, pp. 413–23.
20. *Ibid.*, pp. 423–31.
21. *Ibid.*, pp. 431–36.
22. *Ibid.*, pp. 436–42.

23. P. I. Liashchenko, *Istoriia narodnogo khoziaistva SSSR*, I (3rd ed.; Moscow, 1952), 531.

24. Gessen, "Prinuditel'noe obraschchenie pomeshchich'ikh krest'ian . . . ," pp. 50–62.

25. See M. Tugan-Baranovskii, *Russkaia fabrika v proshlem i nastoiashchem*, 3rd ed. (St. Petersburg, 1907), pp. 125–40; Gille, *Histoire économique et sociale de la Russie . . .*, p. 147.

26. K. Pazhitnov, "Volneniia sredi farichno-zavodskikh rabochikh (s 1824 g. po 1860 g.)," Part 1, in *Arkhiv istorii truda v Rossii*, I (1921), pp. 86–87.

27. *Ibid.*, p. 88.

28. Pazhitnov, "Volneniia . . . ," Part 2, in *Arkhiv istorii truda v Rossii*, II (1921), pp. 135–37; L. Aizenberg, "Byt krest'ian na chastnykh gornykh zavodakh i rudnikakh v Orenburgskom krae (nakanune osvobozhdeniia ot krepostnoi zavisimosti)," in *Arkhiv istorii truda v Rossii*, III (1922), 23–39.

29. V. K. Iatsunskii, "Rol' Peterburga v promyshlennom razvitii dorevoliutsionnoi Rossii," *Voprosy istorii*, No. 9 (1954), p. 96.

30. *Ibid.*, p. 98. For details on the new mechanized and partially mechanized textile plants founded between 1830 and the Crimean War, see *Ocherki istorii Leningrada*, I, 450–51; V. V. Pokshishevskii, "Territorial'noe formirovanie promyshlennogo kompleksa Peterburga v XVIII–XIX vekakh," *Voprosy geografii*, Coll. XX (1950), p. 126n.

31. *Ocherki istorii Leningrada*, I, 452; Pokshishevskii, p. 126n; A. F. Iakovlev, *Ekonomicheskie krizisy v Rossii* (Moscow, 1955), p. 62; E. Karnovich, *Sanktpeterburg v statisticheskom otnoshenii* (St. Petersburg, 1860), pp. 105–9.

32. *Ocherki istorii Leningrada*, I, 464.

33. A. I. Kopanev, *Naselenie Peterburga v pervoi polovine XIX veka* (Moscow and Leningrad, 1957), pp. 57–58; P. N. Stolpianskii, *Zhizn' i byt peterburgskoi fabriki za 210 let ee sushchestvovaniia* (Leningrad, 1925), pp. 113–14.

34. See Karnovich, pp. 44, 73, 135–37.

35. A thorough, if somewhat shallow, discussion of this topic may be found in Tugan-Baranovskii, *Russkaia fabrika . . .*, pp. 265–303.

36. Quoted in *ibid.*, p. 299.

37. For fuller details see *PSZ*, Series II, Vol. X, No. 8157; Tugan-Baranovskii, pp. 169–70; M. Balabanov, *Ocherki po istorii rabochego klassa v Rossii*, I (2nd ed. rev. and expanded: Kiev, 1924), 150–51.

38. See especially some of the issues of January and May 1860.

39. The best and most comprehensive example of this approach may be found in

F. G. Terner, *O rabochem klasse i merakh k obezpecheniiu ego blagosostoianiia* (St. Petersburg, 1860). Although Terner's views were criticized rather severely in the pages of *Sovremennik* (No. 12, 1861), it is evident that his approach was later to become an important strain in Populist ideology.

40. For a more detailed account of the Ministry's support for various legislative projects in the late 1850's and the 1860's, and for an explanation of their failure, see my unpublished doctoral dissertation: "Factory Labor and the Labor Question in Tsarist St. Petersburg: 1856–1871" (Stanford University, 1966), pp. 148–72.

41. "The Sunday School Movement in Russia, 1859–1862," *Journal of Modern History*, XXXVII, No. 2 (June 1965), pp. 151–70.

42. For detailed information in support of statements about statistical trends in St. Petersburg, see chapter IV of my dissertation, cited above.

43. For the views of the doctors, see the journal *Arkhiv sudebnoi meditsiny i obshchestvennoi gigieny*, beginning in 1865. The best source for the views of the specialists, technicians, etc., is the stenographic record of the first all-Russian industrial congress, held in St. Petersburg in 1870. The protocols were published in 1871 in a series of special supplements to the *Zapiski Imperatorskago Russkago Tekhnichskago Obshchestva*.

7. The Peasant in Nineteenth-Century Historiography

1. V. K. Iatsunskii, "Izuchenie ekonomicheskoi istorii," *Ocherki istorii istoricheskoi nauki v SSSR*, ed., M. N. Tikhomirov, M. A. Alpatov, and A. L. Sidorov (Moscow: Akademiia Nauk SSSR, Institut Istorii, 1955), I, 589.

2. V. I. Semevskii, "Ne pora-li napisat' istoriiu krest'ian v Rossii?" *Russkaia Mysl'* II (February 1881) Book 2, p. 237.

3. V. N. Berkh, *Puteshestvie v goroda Cherdyn' i Solikamsk dlia izyskaniia istoricheskikh drevnostei* (St. Petersburg, 1821), pp. 199–200; cited by Iatsunskii, p. 591.

4. For the significance of this development, see B. D. Grekov, *Krest'iane na Rusi s drevneishikh vremen do XVII veka* (Moscow and Leningrad, 1946), pp. 819–20.

5. Iatsunskii, p. 591.

6. V. I. Semevskii, *Krest'ianskii vopros v Rossii v XVIII i pervoi polovine XIX veka*, I (St. Petersburg, 1888), Vvedenie, xix.

7. Alexander Kornilov, *Modern Russian History* (New York, 1943), II, 11.

8. For a discussion not only of Pushkin's *Istoriia Pugachëva* but of Pushkin's general treatment of the history of peasant rebellions, see M. Mal'tsev, *Tema krest'ianskogo vosstaniia v tvorchestve A. S. Pushkina* (Cheboksary, 1960), especially chap. VI, "Istoriia Pugachëva," pp. 144–70.

9. O. Turchinovich, *Istoriia sel'skogo khoziaistva Rossii, ot vremen istoricheskikh do 1850 goda* (St. Petersburg, n.d.). The date is supplied by Iatsunskii, p. 589.

10. Turchinovich, p. i; cited by Iatsunskii, p. 589.

11. S. M. Khodetskii, *Obozrenie uspekhov sel'skogo khoziaistva v Rossii, s istoricheskim izlozheniem pravitel'stvennykh mer po uluchsheniiu khoziaistva* (Kiev, 1856).

12. A. K. Chugunov, *Istoricheskii obzor mer pravitel'stva k razvitiiu zemledeliia v Rossii* (Kazan', 1858).

13. Konstantin P. Pobedonostsev, "Zametki dlia istorii krepostnogo prava v Rossii," *Russkii Vestnik*, XV (June 1858), 209–48; 459–98.

14. Semevskii, p. 227.

15. Pobedonostsev, "Utverzhdenie krepostnogo prava v XVIII stoletii," *Russkii Vestnik,* XXXV (September 1861), 223–53.

16. V. I. Veshniakov, "Istoricheskii obzor proiskhozhdeniia raznykh nazvanii gosudarstvennykh krest'ian," *Zhurnal Ministerstva Gosudarstvennykh Imushchestv* (1857), Nos. 52, 53, 55. For a discussion of Veshniakov, see Semevskii, pp. 225–26.

17. A. V. Romanovich-Slavatinskii, *Dvorianstvo v Rossii ot nachala XVIII veka do otmeny krepostnogo prava* (St. Petersburg, 1870); M. I. Gorchakov, *O zemel'nykh vladeniiakh vserossiiskikh mitropolitov, patriarkhov i Sv. Sinoda, 988–1738 gg.* (St. Petersburg, 1871).

18. Konstantin Sergeevich Aksakov, *Polnoe sobranie sochinenii,* I (Moscow, 1861), 253–54.

19. Nikolai A. Dobroliubov, "O stepeni uchastiia narodnosti v razvitii russkoi literatury," *Polnoe sobranie sochinenii,* I (Leningrad, 1934), 211.

20. Dmitrii I. Pisarev, *Polnoe sobranie sochinenii,* III (Moscow, 1955–56), 171.

21. Cited by M. N. Pokrovskii, "A. P. Shchapov," *Istorik-Marksist,* III (1927), 9.

22. Nikolai I. Kostomarov, *Avtobiografiia N. I. Kostomarova,* ed., V. Kotel'nikov (Moscow, 1922), p. 148.

23. Kostomarov, "Ob otnoshenii russkoi istorii k geografii i etnografii," *Sobranie sochinenii,* I (St. Petersburg, 1903), 720.

24. Sergei M. Soloviëv, "Nabliudeniia nad istoricheskoiu zhizniiu narodov," *Sobranie sochinenii* (St. Petersburg: Obshchestvennaia Pol'za, n.d.), column 1123.

25. D. A. Korsakov, "Konstantin Dmitrievich Kavelin. Materialy dlia biografii. Iz semeinoi perepiski i vospominaniia," *Vestnik Evropy,* Bk. 10 (1886), 745–46.

26. *Ibid.*

27. Boris N. Chicherin, "Obzor istoricheskogo razvitiia sel'skoi obshchiny v Rossii," *Russkii Vestnik,* I (February, 1856), 373–96, 579–602; published later in his *Opyty po istorii russkogo prava* (Moscow, 1858), pp. 1–58.

28. Boris N. Chicherin, "Nesvobodnye sostoianiia v drevnei Rossii," *Russkii Vestnik,* III (1856), 185–257; republished under the title "Kholopy i krest'iane v Rossii do XVI v.," in his *Opyty po istorii russkogo prava,* pp. 143–231.

29. Ivan D. Beliaev, "Neskol'ko slov o zemledelii v drevnei Rossii," *Vremennik Obshchestva istorii i drevnostei rossiiskikh* XXII (1855), Section I, 37–50.

30. Ivan D. Beliaev, *Krest'iane na Rusi* (Moscow, 1860).

31. Vasilii O. Kliuchevskii, "Krepostnoi vopros nakanune zakonodatel'nogo ego vozbuzhdeniia," *Kriticheskoe obozrenie* (1879), No. 3, 1–14; reprinted in his *Otzyvy i otvety; tretii sbornik statei* (Moscow, 1914), 297–320; also in his *Sochineniia,* VII (Moscow, 1959), 106–25.

32. Kliuchevskii, "Pravo i fakt v istorii Krest'ianskogo voprosa," *Rus'* (1881), No. 28, 14–17; reprinted in his *Otzyby i otvety,* 365–76; also in his *Sochineniia,* VII, 153–62.

33. Kliuchevskii, "Proiskhozhdenie krepostnogo prava v Rossii," *Russkaia Mysl'* (1885), No. 8, 1–36; No. 10, 1–46; also in his *Opyty i izsledovaniia; pervyi sbornik statei* (Moscow, 1912), 212–310; also in his *Sochineniia, VII,* 237–317.

34. Kliuchevskii, "Podushnaia podat' i otmena Kholopstva v Rossii," *Russkaia Mysl'* (1886), No. 5, 106–27; No. 7, 1–19; No. 9, 72–87; and No. 10, 1–20; also in his *Opyty i isledovaniia,* 311–416; and in his *Sochineniia,* VII, 318–402.

35. V. I. Semevskii, "Krepostnye krest'iane pri Ekaterine II," *Russkaia Starina,* XVII (1876), 579–618, 653–90.

36. Semevskii, *Krest'iane v tsarstvovanie Imperatritsy Ekateriny II*, Vol. I (St. Petersburg, 1881).

37. For an account of this affair, see Part II of Semevskii's "Autobiograficheskie nabroski ...," *Golos Minuvshego*, V; Nos. 9–10 (1917), 7–49; also S. P. Mel'gunov, "Uchenyia mytarstva," *Golos Minuvshego*, IV, No. 10 (1916), xix–xxxiv.

38. Semevskii, "Rech' proiznesennaia v Moskovskom universitete pred disputom na stepen' magistra russkoi istorii 17–go fevralia 1882 g.," *Russkaia Starina*, XXXIV (1882), 565–78.

39. For a discussion of Semevskii's use of sources, see especially A. Kizevetter, "V. I. Semevskii v ego uchenykh trudakh," *Golos Minuvshego*, No. 1 (1917), 199–222.

40. Semevskii, *Krest'ianskii vopros v Rossii v XVIII i pervoi polovine XIX veka*, 2 vols. (St. Petersburg, 1888).

41. "Prisuzhdenie Imperatorskim Vol'nym Ekonomicheskim Obshchestvom ...," *Russkaia Starina*, LXIX (1891), 187.

42. Paul L. Horecky, ed., *Basic Russian Publications: An Annotated Bibliography on Russia and the Soviet Union* (Chicago, 1962), p. 80, item 375.

43. Vasilii O. Kliuchevskii, "Otzyv ob issledovanii V. I. Semevskogo 'Krest' ianskii vopros v Rossii v XVIII i pervoi polovine XIX v.'," in his *Sochineniia*, VII (Moscow, 1959), 426.

44. N. L. Rubinstein, *Russkaia istoriografiia* (Moscow, 1941), p. 408.

45. Lazar Volin, "The Russian Peasant and Serfdom," *Agricultural History*, XVII (1943), 59.

46. Jerome Blum, *Lord and Peasant in Russia from the Ninth to the Nineteenth Century* (Princeton, 1961). See especially chap. 27, "Some Conclusions and Generalizations," pp. 601–20.

47. N. Flerovskii [V. V. Bervi], *Polozhenie rabochego klassa v Rossii* (Moscow, 1869).

48. Mikhail I. Veniukov, *Istoricheskie ocherki Rossii so vremeni Krymskoi voiny do zakliucheniia Berlinskogo dogovora, 1855–1878* (Vol. I–II, Leipzig, 1878–1879; Vol. III–IV, Prague, 1879–1880).

49. Pavel A. Sokolovskii, *Ocherk istorii sel'skoi obshchiny na Severe Rossii* (St. Petersburg, 1877); *Ekonomicheskii byt zemledel'cheskogo naseleniia Rossii i kolonizatsiia iugo-vostochnykh stepei pred krepostnym pravom* (St. Petersburg, 1878).

50. Aleksandra Ia. Efimenko, *Issledovaniia narodnoi zhizni* (Moscow, 1884).

51. Aleksandr A. Kaufman, *Krest'ianskaia obshchina v Sibiri po mestnym issledovaniiam, 1886–1892* (St. Petersburg, 1897); *Russkaia obshchina v protsesse eë zarozhdeniia i rosta* (Moscow, 1908).

52. Ivan D. Beliaev, *Lektsii po istorii russkogo zakonodatel'stva* (Moscow, 1879).

53. Vasilii I. Sergeevich, *Russkie iuridicheskie drevnosti*, I (St. Petersburg, 1890).

54. Sergeevich, *Lektsii i issledovaniia po drevnei istorii russkogo prava* (St. Petersburg, 1883).

55. Mikhail F. Vladimirskii-Budanov, *Obzor istorii russkogo prava* (St. Petersburg and Kiev, 1888).

56. Mikhail A. D'iakonov, *Ocherki po istorii sel'skogo naseleniia v Moskovskom gosudarstve XVI–XVII vv.* (St. Petersburg, 1898); *Akty, otnosiashchikhsia k istorii tiaglogo naseleniia v Moskovskom gosudarstve.*

57. Stepan B. Veselovskii, *Soshnoe pis'mo. Issledovanie po istorii kadastra i pososhnogo oblozheniia Moskovskogo gosudarstva*, 2 vols. (Moscow, 1915–1916).

58. Nikolai P. Pavlov-Sil'vanskii, _Feodalizm v udelnoi Rusi_ (St. Petersburg, 1910); also in his _Sochineniia_, III (St. Petersburg, 1910).

59. Nikolai E. Fedoseev, _Stat'i i pis'ma_ (Moscow, 1958), 274–95.

60. Iu. Z. Polevoi, "Nachalo marksistskoi istoriografii v Rossii," _Ocherki istorii istoricheskoi nauki v SSSR_, ed., M. V. Nechkina et al., II (Moscow, 1960), 290.

61. Nikolai A. Rozhkov, _Sel'skoe khoziaistvo Moskovskoi Rusi v XVI v._ (Moscow, 1899).

62. Rubinstein, _Russkaia istoriografiia_, p. 570; see also the critical but complimentary review by V. O. Kliuchevskii, "Otzyv o issledovanii N. A. Rozhkova 'Sel'skoe khoziaistvo Moskovskoi Rusi v XVI v.,'" in his _Sochineniia_, VIII (Moscow, 1959), 368–89.

63. Pëtr B. Struve, _Krepostnoe khoziaistvo; issledovaniia po ekonomicheskoi istorii Rossii v XVIII i XIX vv._ (Moscow, 1913).

64. _Ibid._, p. 154.

65. _Ibid._, p. 156.

66. I. F. G. Evers, _Drevneishee russkoe pravo v istoricheskom ego raskrytii_ (St. Petersburg, 1835).

67. Cited by S. M. Dubrovskii, "Rossiiskaia obshchina v literature XIX i nachala XX v.," in _Voprosy istorii sel'skogo khoziaistva, krest'ianstva i revoliutsionnogo dvizheniia v Rossii_ (Moscow, 1961), p. 351.

68. Boris N. Chicherin, "Obzor istoricheskogo razvitiia sel'skoi obshchiny v Rossii," _Russkii Vestnik_, I (February 1856), 373–93, 579–602; published later in his _Opyty po istorii russkogo prava_ (Moscow, 1858), pp. 1–58.

69. Konstantin S. Aksakov, _Polnoe sobranie sochinenii, I_ (Moscow, 1889), 65.

70. Ivan D. Beliaev, "Obzor istoricheskogo razvitiia sel'skoi obshchiny v Rossii. Soch. B. Chicherina," _Russkaia Beseda_ (1856), No. 1, 101–46.

71. Elliot Benowitz, "B. N. Chicherin: Rationalism and Liberalism in Nineteenth-Century Russia," unpublished dissertation (University of Wisconsin, 1966), p. 38, f. 19.

72. Vasilii Nikolaevich Leshkov, _Obshchinyi byt drevnei Rossii_ (St. Petersburg: Academy of Sciences, 1858); _Russkii narod i gosudarstvo; istoriia russkogo obshchestvennogo prava do XVIII veka_ (Moscow, 1858).

73. Aleksandr A. Kiesewetter (Kizevetter), "Krest'ianstvo v russkoi nauchno-istoricheskoi literature," _Krest'ianskaia Rossiia_, V (1923), 25.

74. _Ibid._

75. V. V. [V. P. Vorontsov], "Ucheniia o proiskhozhdenii zemel'noi obshchiny v Rossii," _Vestnik Evropy_ (1910), No. 4, 256–57.

76. P. A. Sokolovskii, _Ocherk istorii sel'skoi obshchiny na Severe Rossii_ (St. Petersburg, 1877).

77. Vorontsov, p. 257; Kiesewetter, p. 26; A. M. Stanislavskaia, "Narodnicheskaia istoriografiia 70–90-kh godov," in _Ocherki istorii_, II, 197–98.

78. P. A. Sokolovskii, _Ekonomicheskii byt zemledel'cheskogo naseleniia Rossii i kolonizatsiia iugo-vostochnykh stepei pred krepostnym pravom_ (St. Petersburg, 1878).

79. Georg Ludwig von Maurer's works on this subject include his _Einleitung zur Geschichte der Mark-, Hof-, Dorf-, und Stadtverfassung und der öffentlichen Gewalt_ (Munich, 1854); _Geschichte der Markenverfassung in Deutschland_ (Erlangen, 1856); _Geschichte der Fronhöfe, der Bauerhöfe, und der Hofverfassung in Deutschland_ (Erlangen, 1862–63); and _Geschichte der Dorfverfassung in Deutschland_ (Erlangen,

1869–71). The first of these works was translated into Russian under the title *Vvedenie v istoriiu obshchinnogo podvorvnogo, sel'skogo i gorodskogo ustroistva i obshchestvennoi vlasti* (Moscow, 1880).

80. Vorontsov, pp. 258–59.

81. Vasilii I. Sergeevich, "Vremia vozniknoveniia germanskoi pozemel'noi obshchiny," *Zhurnal Ministerstva Narodnogo Prosveshcheniia* (1865), No. 1.

82. Aleksandra Ia. Efimenko, *Issledovaniia narodnoi zhizni* (Moscow, 1884).

83. Cited by Vorontsov, p. 260.

84. Kiesewetter, p. 27.

85. *Ibid.*, p. 28.

86. Vorontsov, pp. 267–68.

87. *Ibid.*, p. 279.

88. B. D. Grekov, *Krest'iane na Rusi s drevneishikh vremen do XVII veka*, pp. 62–63, 70–71.

89. *Ibid.*, pp. 71–72.

90. Rubinstein, *Russkaia istoriografiia*, pp. 528–29.

91. Aleksandr A. Kaufman, *Krest'ianskaia obshchina v Sibiri po metsnym issledovaniiam, 1886–1892* (St. Petersburg, 1897).

92. Vorontsov, pp. 271–72.

93. *Ibid.*, pp. 276–77.

94. A. E. Presniakov, "Sud'by krest'ianstva v russkoi istoriografii i zadachi ikh izucheniia," in *Arkhiv istorii truda v Rossii*, I (Petrograd, 1921), 45.

95. V. N. Tatishchev, *Sudebnik Gosudaria Tsaria i velikogo kniazia Ivana Vasil'evicha i nekotorye sego gosudaria i blizhnikh ego preemnikov ukazy sobrannye i primechaniiami iz"iasnenye ... (1768)*, p. 124. Cited by K. A. Pazhitnov, "Dvorianskaia istoriografiia o proiskhozhdenii krepostnogo prava v Rossii (v doreformennyi period)," in *Voprosy istorii narodnogo khoziaistva SSSR* (Moscow: Academy of Sciences, Institute of Economics, 1957), pp. 33–34.

96. Pazhitnov, pp. 33–34; Grekov, p. 808.

97. Pazhitnov, pp. 36–37.

98. See Note 95 above.

99. For a discussion of the views of I. N. Boltin and M. M. Shcherbatov on this question, see Pazhitnov, pp. 40–43.

100. *Ibid.*, pp. 44–45.

101. Nikolai Mikhailovich Karamzin, *Istoriia gosudarstva Rossiiskogo*, X (St. Petersburg, 1823), 120.

102. *Ibid.*, 352n.

103. N. G. Ustrialov, *Russkaia istoriia*, Part II (1839), pp. 94–95. Cited by Pazhitnov, pp. 51–52.

104. Rubinstein, *Russkaia istoriografiia*, p. 217.

105. Pazhitnov, pp. 50–51.

106. N. S. Artsybashev, *Povestvovanie o Rossii*, III (Moscow, 1843). See especially p. 342.

107. M. M. Speranskii, "Istoricheskoe obozrenie izminenii v prave pozemel'noi sobstvennosti i v sostoianii krest'ian," in *Arkhiv istoricheskikh i prakticheskikh svedenii otnosiashchikhsia do Rossii*, II (1859), 27–47.

108. *Ibid.*, p. 42.

109. Pazhitnov, "Dvorianskaia istoriografiia," pp. 52-53.

110. Boris N. Chicherin, "Nesvobodnye sostoianiia v drevnei Rossii," *Russkii Vestnik,* III (1856), 185-257; republished under the title "Kholopy i krest'iane v Rossii do XVI v.," in his *Opyty po istorii russkogo prava,* pp. 143-231.

111. Chicherin, *Opyty,* p. 191.

112. See, for example, A. D. Gradovskii, *Istoriia mestnogo upravleniia Rossii,* I (St. Petersburg, 1868), 5; and K. D. Kavelin, "Mysli i zametki o russkoi istorii," in his *Sochineniia,* I (St. Petersburg, 1897), 629. Both are discussed by V. E. Illeritskii, "Gosudarstvennaia shkola," in *Ocherki istorii istoricheskoi nauki v SSSR,* II, especially pp. 114 and 125.

113. Sergei M. Soloviëv, *Istoriia Rossii s drevneishikh vremen,* 2nd ed., II (St. Petersburg: Obshchestvennaia Pol'za, n.d.), 650.

114. Mikhail P. Pogodin, "Dolzhno li shchitat' Borisa Godunova osnovatelem krepostnogo prava?" *Russkaia Beseda,* Bk. 12 (1858), 117-60.

115. *Ibid.,* pp. 119-20.

116. Pazhitnov, pp. 69-70.

117. Konstantin S. Aksakov, "Popovodu 'Belevskoi vivliofiki' izdannoi N. A. Elaginym," *Russakaia Beseda,* III (1858), and in his *Polnoe sobranie sochinenii,* I (Moscow, 1861), 515-16.

118. Konstantin P. Pobedonostsev, "Zametki dlia istorii krepostnogo prava v Rossii," *Russkii Vestnik,* XI (1858), 211.

119. Nikolai I. Kostomarov, "Dolzhno li shchitat' Borisa Godunova osnovatelem krepostnogo prava?" *Arkhiv istoricheskikh i prakticheskikh svedenii otnosiashchikhsia do Rossii,* II, Part IV (1859), 1-28.

120. Beliaev, *Krestiane na Rusi* (Moscow, 1860), p. 97.

121. *Ibid.,* pp. 97-100.

122. See Note 33 above.

123. See Note 56 above.

124. Pavel N. Miliukov, "Istoriia krest'ian v Rossii do osvobozhdeniia (1861)," *Entsiklopedicheskii Slovar',* XVIa (St. Petersburg, 1893), 675-714; see especially 679-80.

125. S. A. Adrianov, "K voprosu o krest'ianskom prikreplenii," *Zhurnal Ministerstva Narodnogo Prosveshcheniia* (January 1895), 239-51.

126. D. M. Odinets, "K istorii prikrepleniia vladel'cheskikh krest'ian," *Zhurnal Ministerstva Iustitsii,* No. 1 (1908), cited by Sergei P. Platonov, "Der gegenwärtige Stand der Frage nach der Entstehung der Leibeigenschaft in Russland," *Zeitschrift für Osteuropäische Geschichte,* V (1931), 15.

127. D. Ia. Samokvasov, *Arkhivnyi material; novootkrytye dokumenty pomestnovotchinnykh uchrezhdenii Moskovskogo gosudarstva XV-XVII stoletii,* I (Moscow, 1905); II (Moscow, 1909).

128. E. Mikhailov, "K voprosu o proiskhozhdenii zemel'nogo starozhil'stva," *Zhurnal Ministerstva Narodnogo Prosveshcheniia,* XXVII (June 1910), 318-58; also "Obychnyi institut starozhil'stva v protsesse obrazovaniia krepostnogo prava," *ibid.,* XXXVII (January 1912), 75-120.

129. This formulation is taken from Platonov's article cited in Note 126 above, and is based on S. B. Veselovskii, "Iz istorii zakreposhcheniia krest'ian; otmena Iurieva dnia," *Uchenye Zapiski,* V (1929), 204-17.

8. The Peasant in Literature

1. A. N. Pypin, *Istoriia russkoi etnografii*, II (St. Petersburg, 1891), 357–58.
2. See I. Z. Serman's interesting article, "Problema krest'ianskogo romana v russkoi kritike serediny XIX veka," in B. I. Bursov and I. Z. Serman, eds., *Problemy realizma russkoi literatury XIX veka* (Moscow-Leningrad, 1961), pp. 162–82.
3. "Nashi belletristy-narodniki," in G. V. Plekhanov, *Literatura i estetika*, II (Moscow, 1958), 245–46.
4. P. V. Annenkov, "Romany i rasskazy iz prostonarodnogo byta v 1853 g.," in his *Vospominaniia i kriticheskie ocherki*, II (St. Petersburg, 1877), 50.
5. Quoted in V. I. Semevskii, *Krest'ianskii vopros v Rossii v XVIII i pervoi polovine XIX veka*, I (St. Petersburg, 1888), 197.
6. *Ibid.*, pp. 205, 208.
7. Quoted in N. P. Sidorov, "Krepostnye krest'iane v russkoi belletristike," in Istoricheskaia Kommissiia Uchebnogo Otdela O.R.T.Z., A. K. Dzhivelogov, S. P. Mel'gunov, and V. I. Pichet, eds., *Velikaia Reforma: Russkoe obshchestvo i krest'ianskii vopros v proshlom i nastoiashchem*, III (Moscow, 1911), 238.
8. *Ibid.*, p. 239. Examples from this literature are given on pp. 239–40.
9. *Ibid.*, p. 241. See the interesting account of what is apparently the only such work to slip by the censor in this period, the anonymously published *Puteshestvie kritiki*—which in many ways is a connecting link between Radishchev and Turgenev (pp. 242–45).
10. *Ibid.*, p. 248.
11. *Ibid.*, pp. 251–53.
12. D. N. Ovsianiko-Kulikovskii, ed., *Istoriia russkoi literatury XIX v.*, II (Moscow, 1911), 342.
13. *Ibid.*, p. 170.
14. Quoted in L. Grossman, "Rannie rasskazy Turgeneva," *Svitok*, No. 2 (Moscow, 1922), p. 102.
15. G. A. Bialy, *Turgenev i russkii realizm* (Moscow-Leningrad, 1962).
16. This point is developed at length by Boris Sokolov in his essay, "Muzhik v izobrazhenii Turgeneva," in I. N. Rozanov and Iu. M. Sokolov, eds., *Tvorchestvo Turgeneva, sbornik statei* (Moscow, 1920), pp. 194–233.
17. Sidorov, "Krepostnye krest'iane v russkoi belletristike," p. 263.
18. On Grigorovich's later novels see P. V. Annenkov, "Romany i rasskazy iz prostonarodnogo byta v 1853 g.," in his *Vospominaniia i kriticheskie ocherki*, II (St. Petersburg, 1877), 46–54; and T. Ganzhulevich, *Krest'ianstvo v russkoi literature XIX veka* (St. Petersburg, 1913), Chapter 5. On Zlatovratsky's *Ustoi, Istoriia odnoi derevni* see A. Skabichevskii, "Novy chelovek derevni," in his *Sochineniia*, II (St. Petersburg, 189), 541–60; P. N. Tkachev, "Muzhik v salonakh sovremennoi belletristiki," in his *Izbrannye sochineniia*, IV (Moscow, 1932), 180–310; and D. N. Ovsianiko-Kulikovskii, ed., *Istoriia russkoi literatury XIX v.*, IV (Moscow, 1911), 160–68.
19. "Vlast' zemli," in Gleb Uspenskii, *Polnoe sobranie sochinenii*, 6th edition, V (St. Petersburg, 1908), 108–13. According to the context, I have translated Uspensky's word *zemlia* at times as "land" and at other times as "earth." I have also on occasion eliminated the redundancies of the original—usually adjectival—without ellipses.

20. G. Krasnov, *Geroi i narod; O romane L'va Tolstogo "Voina i Mir"* (Moscow, 1964), p. 221. Krasnov's discussion of Karataev is highly interesting, particularly where he comments on the quarrels over the significance of Tolstoy's peasant (pp. 215ff).

21. N. S. Leskov, "O kufel'nom muzhike i proch," in his *Sobranie sochinenii v odinnadtsati tomakh,* XI (Moscow, 1958), 134–56.

22. *Ibid.,* pp. 142–45.

23. I. N. Ignatov in *Russkie Vedomosti,* 1897, No. 106, 19 April; quoted in A. P. Chekhov, *Muzhiki i drugie rasskazy* (Moscow-Leningrad, "Academia," 1934), p. 705.

24. The critic Fidel', writing in 1909; quoted in Chekhov, p. 723.

25. M. O. Men'shikov, in *Knizhki nedeli,* May 1897; quoted in Chekhov, p. 707.

26. S. T. Semenov, "O vstrechakh s A. P. Chekhovym," *Put',* 1913, No. 2; quoted in *Lev Tolstoi ob iskusstve i literature,* II (Moscow, 1958), 131.

27. Quoted in Chekhov, p. 726.

28. I. Gruzdev, "Korolenko i Gor'kii," *Oktiabr',* 1946, No. 6, p. 176.

29. *Ibid.*

30. V. N. Muromtseva-Bunina, "Besedy s pamiat'iu," *Novy Zhurnal,* No. 65 (1961), p. 236.

31. I. A. Bunin, *Sobranie sochinenii v deviati tomakh,* III (Moscow, 1965), 473.

32. Maksim Gor'kii, *O russkom krest'ianstve* (Berlin, 1922), pp. 23, 43.

Afterword: The Problem of the Peasant

1. N. Barsukov, *Zhizn i trudy M. P. Pogodina,* 22 vols. (St. Petersburg, 1888–1910); quoted from II, 17.

2. P. Lyashchenko, *History of the National Economy of Russia to the 1917 Revolution* (New York, 1949), p. 273. The latest calculation for 1897, which defines a place of 15,000 or more inhabitants as urban, puts only 9.8 per cent of Russian population in this rubric. Robert Lewis and J. William Leasure, "Regional Population Changes in Russia and the U.S.S.R. since 1851," *Slavic Review,* XXV, 4 (December 1966), 663–68, esp. 667.

3. A particularly striking and brilliant, although exaggerated and controversial, presentation of this cultural dichotomy can be found in N. Trubetskoi, "Verkhi i nizy russkoi kultury (Etnicheskaia osnova russkoi kultury)," *Iskhod k Vostoku* (Sofia, 1921), pp. 86–103.

4. See p. 40 above.

5. P. A. Zaionchkovskii, *Otmena krepostnogo prava v Rossii* (Moscow, 1954).

6. See p. 119 above.

7. See p. 180 above.

8. An able recent discussion of this "joint enterprise," emphasizing the impact of the peasants, has been provided in Michael Confino, *Domaines et seigneurs en Russie vers la fin du XVIIIe siècle: Etude de structures agraires et de mentalités économiques* (Paris, 1963). Professor Confino's findings apply in their bulk to the nineteenth century, at least until 1861.

9. See especially Theodore Schiemann, *Geschichte Russlands unter Kaiser Nikolaus I,* 4 vols. (Berlin, 1904–1919), III, 144–49. For a study of cholera epidemics in Russia in the first half of the nineteenth century, and of the reaction of the Russian

government, educated public, and the masses to cholera, see Roderick E. McGrew, *Russia and the Cholera, 1823–1832* (Madison and Milwaukee, 1965).

10. A. P. Chekhov, *Sochineniia* (St. Petersburg, n.d.), III, 5–9. "Malefactor" is not an entirely satisfactory translation of *zloumyshlennik,* because the Russian word indicates, most ironically in this case, criminal intent.

11. *Ibid.,* p. 7.

12. For the latest outstanding examples of the two explanations, see Professor Rieber's essay "The Politics of Emancipation," in Alfred J. Rieber, ed., *The Politics of Autocracy: Letters of Alexander II to Prince A. I. Bariatinskii, 1857–1864* (Paris-The Hague, 1966), pp. 15–58, which stresses the need of military reform, and Professor Gerschenkron's analysis in Alexander Gerschenkron, "Agrarian Policies and Industrialization, Russia 1861–1917," *Cambridge Economic History of Europe* (Cambridge, 1965), Vol. VI, Pt. 2, which stresses the government fear of the peasant threat to the established order.

13. I have treated Slavophilism in detail elsewhere, in particular in my book *Russia and the West in the Teaching of the Slavophiles: A Study of Romantic Ideology* (Cambridge, Mass., 1952), and in my article "Khomiakov on *Sobornost,*" in Ernest J. Simmons, ed., *Continuity and Change in Russian and Soviet Thought* (Cambridge, Mass., 1955), pp. 183–96.

14. Konstantin Aksakov, *Polnoe sobranie sochinenii,* 3 vols. (Moscow, 1861–1880), I, 291–92.

15. See my *Nicholas I and Official Nationality in Russia, 1825–1855* (Berkeley and Los Angeles, 1959).

16. *Sbornik Imperatorskogo Russkogo Istoricheskogo Obshchestva,* 148 vols. (St. Petersburg, 1867–1917), XCVIII, 114–15. Italics in the original.

17. Quoted from Barsukov, *Zhizn i trudy M. P. Pogodina,* IV, 38. Italics in the original.

18. Quoted from *ibid.,* IX, 305–8.

19. To buttress this statement and subsequent discussion, I would like to refer to my already mentioned book on the subject.

20. N. Grech, *Zapiski o moei zhizni* (Moscow-Leningrad, 1930), p. 499. Grech apparently belonged with those who believed that Russian peasants had no "true religion."

21. *Selected Passages from Correspondence with Friends* constitutes the bulk of the eighth volume of Gogol's *Works* (N. Gogol, *Sochineniia,* edited by V. Kallash, [St. Petersburg, n.d.]; quoted from VIII, 140–41).

22. *Ibid.,* p. 125.

23. See my "Pogodin and Sevyrëv in Russian Intellectual History," *Harvard Slavic Studies,* IV, 149–67.

24. Barsukov, II, 17. Pogodin was young when he wrote these words, but his thought continued along much the same lines.

25. See especially Herzen's writings in the early 1850's.

Index